The Jewish Preacher

Rabbi Emil G. Hirsch, Ph.D., LL.D.

Part One
Sermons and Addresses
Compiled and Edited
BY MYRON A. HIRSCH

Part Two
The Biography of
Rabbi Emil G. Hirsch
BY DAVID EINHORN HIRSCH

Collage Books Inc.
4244 Corporate Square
Naples, Florida 34104

Copyright © 2003 by Myron A. Hirsch

First published in the United States of America
in 2003 by Collage Books Inc., 4244 Corporate Square,
Naples, Florida 34104

ALL RIGHTS RESERVED

No part of this publication may be reproduced,
stored in a retrieval system, or transmitted in
any form or by any means, electronic, mechanical,
photocopying, recording, or otherwise, without prior
written permission of the publisher.

ISBN: 0-938728-11-3
Paperback

Library of Congress Control Number: 2002117130

Printed and bound in the United States of America

In Memory of
Edward Hirsch Levi
1911-2000
whose life of service included being
President of
The University of Chicago
and
Attorney General of The United States
exemplified the teachings of our grandfather

Acknowledgement

This work could not have been completed without the able assistance of Harriet Hirsch. Her optical scanning of fragile documents that are more than a hundred years old required the upmost skill and perseverance.

Her editorial abilities have enhanced this work and I'm most appreciative of my wife's efforts.

M.A.H.

Foreword

My grandfather, Dr. Emil G. Hirsch, was born May 22nd, 1851. I was born June 22nd, 1928. He died January 7th, 1923.

I only knew him through my father, David Einhorn Hirsch, and my grandmother, Matilda Einhorn Hirsch.

She entrusted me with personal papers of my grandfather, and also of her father, Dr. David Einhorn. She also opened my mind to the great theologian, her father-in-law, Dr. Samuel Hirsch.

The Jewish Preacher shares with you the meaning of life as expounded by these three great rabbis.

These sermons by my grandfather capture the essence of their teachings.

My grandfather spoke without notes and his sermons were recorded by stenographers in the audience. For clarity where the stenographer missed words, if possible, I have filled in the blanks; or omitted passages that appear to be an aside to the thrust of his thought.

Myron A. Hirsch, editor
January 7th, 2003

"We should remember that we have not broken with our past. We spin its thread out into the future. Judaism is not an external law, but an inward principal. It is a growth, not a command. To uphold the faith of the prophets and to live in accordance, therewith, is our duty."

Rabbi Emil G. Hirsch

Contents

Dedication	III
Acknowledgement	IV
Foreword	V
Contents	VII
Introduction	IX
Part One	
Sermons of Rabbi Emil G. Hirsch	
The Ethics of Marriage	1
Half An Hour With Genesis	21
He Who Knows Most Doubts Most	38
Yes	54
A Message From Plato's Apology Of Socrates	69
The Theology of The Jewish Reform Movement	90
New Ethics For New Economics A Sukkoth Sermon	111
The Education of Orphans	131
The Science OF Comparative Religion	
Part 1	152
Part 2	169
Was It Worth While? A Hanukah Message	189
Organization And Division Of Labor How Far are we the Chosen People	205
A Quarter of a Century after the death of David Einhorn	224
Wisdom	239
The Awe of Distance	255
The Privilege To Err	271

New Chicago Public Library
    Address by Rev. Dr. Emil G. Hirsch   285
Faithfulness   302
Will Rich Men Go To Heaven   319
One Hundredth Anniversary
    Birth of Samuel Hirsch Part 1   339
    Birth of Samuel Hirsch Part 2   355
Easter And Passover   371
The Crossing Of The Jordan
    Inaugural Sermon
    Chicago Sinai Congregation   388

Part Two
The Biography of Rabbi Emil G. Hirsch
    By David Einhorn Hirsch   409
Introduction   410
The Beginning   413
The Search For Truth   418
The Age Of Industrial Unrest   428
My Father's Public Activities   436
The Call To Temple Emanuel   445
The White House Conference   450
The Two-Hundred and Fiftieth
Anniversary Of Jews In America   461
The Concordance Of Judaism
And Americanism   464
The Jewish Chautauqua Society   481
The Last Years   508
Memorial Address
    by Dr. Stephen S. Wise   513

Introduction

THE RECORD-HERALD   NOVEMBER 3, 1912

What the Preacher is Like
Emil Gustav Hirsch

BY JAMES O'DONNELL BENNETT
EDITOR

When the minister of Sinai Congregation took up in his steady, reverent hands the story of Cain and Abel, and bent his sad, searching eyes upon it, the effect was of a savant who strips away the wrappings of a mummy. Fold upon fold he unwinds the trappings of ancient royalty, dispelling the dust of ages, coming at last upon something precious that tells him how this handful of dust was once a king who ruled and wept and builded cities and begat kings and departed when his work was done.

The husks have fallen away; the dust vanishes on the breeze that steals through the window of a curator's study. But something remains, and the world is richer by one more fact in human experience.

In his slow, velvety utterance, leaning heavily, almost languidly, against the pulpit of Sinai Temple, Dr. Hirsch began. "The story of Cain and

Abel," he said, "if taken as the record of individual deeds, lacks not pathos and dramatic power. The picture is a solemn one—the whole earth counting but four human beings, and among these the spirit of envy has taken lodgment. The craftier of two brothers slays the weaker."

With those brief strokes he brought out the enormous panoramic aspect in that fourth chapter of Genesis.

Then he touched upon the fabulist's naivete, slowly repeating the words of Cain—"And I shall be a fugitive and a vagabond in the earth; and it shall come to pass that every one that findeth me shall slay me," and then asking, as he straightened himself at the pulpit and put a quiet kind of definiteness into his voice, "Of whom could Cain have been afraid? There were no others on the earth save himself, his feeble father and his grief-bowed mother."

Summing up all that is naive and incredible in the narrative, such as the flight into the Land of Nod, which implied population outside of Eden, he remarked gravely, "To this we come if we pervert the footprints of humanity's development into notes of personal conversations. We could spend an hour in picking the record to pieces. That would be a popular proceeding, for he who tears down is always sure of the plaudits of the multitude. But much of this so called free-thinking is neither free nor thinking. It is only thoughtlessness."

With that he was through with his preliminaries, and suddenly he seemed to grip the listening people by the hand, and, steadying them so, he began to turn wave upon wave of light upon the ancient page.

It was exhilarating, and it was wonderful. The glow of his words and the spaciousness and splendor of the outlook he flung wide to the people made the mind leap to his point of view.

"But whatever," he said, "the pathos of the story, if taken as a chronicle of the far off days of the beginning, we know today that Cain and Abel are not personal names. They stand as the personified representatives of great cultural movements.

"This chapter of Genesis is a paragraph in the history of civilization.

"We have passed beyond the literal, I hope, and we know now that these biblical narratives were composite documents, unfolding, not the history of single families, but of great cultural movements."

The phrase, "cultural movements," was often on his lips, and, he uttered it with deliberation, as though he felt it were a phrase not to be lightly spoken, but with conscious gravity. Indeed, he seemed always a grave man.

Bringing the light to a focus, he drove it straight to the heart of the narrative when he said:

"Abel stands for pastoral institutions and habits; Cain typifies agriculture."

Musingly he repeated words from the second verse of the chapter: " 'And Abel was a keeper of sheep, but Cain was a tiller of the ground.'

"Here," he continued, "is the beginning of the unending conflict between one civilization and

XII THE JEWISH PREACHER: RABBI EMIL G. HIRSCH

another. The pastoral gives way to agriculture. The nomad loses his right to consideration and the sedentary farmer comes into his own. In these senses we have to read the stories of old if we would learn not merely how they rose but what they token. We see the identical struggle on all sides today. The lowest stage of human development is 'kill,' and of that stage the fourth chapter of Genesis is an epitome. Pastoral civilization had to pass away when man discovered that to clothe and feed himself he had other resources than his flocks, other resources less capricious. And when man began to see this, the shepherd was doomed, and a new phase of human progress sprang into view. This is the meaning of the murder Cain did. It is the victory of agriculture over the pastoral. It is victorious agriculture.

"It is the curse and the crown of man—that what met his sense of humanity yesterday will fall short today; but we cannot arrest the onward sweep of development, cruel though the processes of it are. But one thing we can do! We can remember—we ought to remember—that we are our brother's keeper. Pedagogic thought has long insisted that Cain became a murderer not when he slew his brother but when insolently he denied his responsibility to God for his brother."

That brought the preacher to his text—"And the Lord said unto Cain, Where is Abel, thy brother? And he said, I know not: Am I my brother's keeper?"—and to the bearing of that text upon the tendencies of modern life. Denial of the responsibilities of keepership, the preacher said, was not peculiar to antiquity. As recently as thirty years ago it had found tongue again in the phrase, "The public be damned." And the obligations of keepership today were infinitely more comprehensive because when one phase of civilization yields to another now, not one man but thousands lose their life.

"Philanthropy," he said, "would be the practical application of the law of keepership. Charity is not philanthropy, sympathetic charity—[and he spoke those two words with slow scorn]—sympathetic charity throwing crumbs from its overladen banquet tables simply because the sight of suffering is disagreeable.

"Do you know where that law of keepership is lived up to its very fullest? Don't open your reports of your Associated Charities to find out, but look into the homes of the dispossessed. They have little to give except themselves, but they do *give*. Children play at keeping store and they have imitation coins for the game. Much of our charity is storekeeping and imitation. This much lauded money, is it not the tribute laid in the lap of Cain, who has slaughtered his brother? Let us be candid. Money is only a necessary evil. Money is dead, and because it is dead it is deadening.

"Our advancing civilization is still a civilization of murder, unless we carry into effect the law of keepership. Where there is very pronounced success it means the ruin of some independent little business. You say you can't help it. [Remember that all this time the preacher was speaking to some of the most powerful commercial magnates

XIV THE JEWISH PREACHER: RABBI EMIL G. HIRSCH

in Chicago.] And say you can't help it. The age for that kind of competition was yesterday. It has resulted in combination. I am a socialist—enough of one, at least, to know that this development was predicted thirty years ago—that the Abel of competition would be slain by the Cain of monopoly. And now monopoly must be stewarded by all society. In Europe they have begun this. We shall get there, too."

But this packing together of widely separated passages of the doctor's discourse must stop if you are to have anything of the personality of the man.

Sallow, and heavy-lidded, he looks like a Turkish pasha, but when he warms to a great theme he speaks like a prophet of old. He delivered his sermon without a hint of memoranda and the flow was slow but steady. Sometimes he closed his eyes as he spoke, as though he were visualizing the even march of his sentences, and almost his only gesture was an abrupt thumping one on the pulpit, when he wished to command special attention to a special point. The sole trace of his Dutch origin, or of a Jewish accent—I don't know which it was—was a curious muffled note he gave to certain vowels; e, especially, which in the word "wishes was so uttered as to make that word sound like "wish-us," but not so marked as that spelling really makes it sound.

He is a man of somewhat chilling. dignity, and to an impertinent and ill-informed reporter he can be freezing—even brutal, I have heard some of the men say. Others of perhaps finer fiber say they like him much, and respect him more. In a casual meeting he is direct, and sometimes a little hard, but never pompous. That he is not ceremonious was indicated by the fact that he came into the pulpit in a black cutaway coat and that after he and the superb choir had exchanged a few passages from his father-in-law, "the sainted Einhorn's" Book of Prayers for Jewish Congregations, he remarked with entire serenity to the people, "Owing to lack of time we will omit the rest of the service, and I will read to you a biblical lesson, after which you will be entertained by an alto solo."

"Entertained" seemed a strange word to use in announcing a devotional song, and whether he intended the word as a satirical fling at what may have seemed to him the merely decorative part of the morning's worship, I don't know. He would be quite capable of it, for satire is a weapon he wields with awful impartiality in the pulpit and out. Once when he was called upon to respond to a toast at an annual banquet of the Jewelers' Association, he rose slowly from his chair and in the velvety tones that would disarm the most wary, he said: oh, so softly, "I come to these jewelers' banquets every year with much pleasure. not only because the first syllable of this name of your society makes me feel welcome, but also because so many members of my congregation belong to the Chicago Jewelers' Association, and this is the only time I can see them."

In the sermon he preached on Sunday a week ago—his people called it a "lecture"—he did not flay anybody alive, a task he can perform with

XVI THE JEWISH PREACHER: RABBI EMIL G. HIRSCH

surpassing skill and dispatch. But once in a sermon I heard him deliver many years ago he did it, lighting out on the congregation, or some of its members, for having got themselves married on rather a specious scale of floral and convivial splurge in the parlor of a boulevard hotel instead of in their own homes. "You, with your vulgar weddings at downtown hotels," he said, "turning one of the most sacred events in life into an excuse for a show. These are the things that make us a byword. Shame upon the indelicacy of such occasions, the indecorum, the disgusting publicity and the more disgusting seeking after publicity."

And all the time the velvety tone. The custom of hotel weddings did not survive.

The nearest he came to hanging, anybody out on the line in the Cain and Abel sermon was when he put reckless automobile drivers who run down children into his list of "these new Cains," and in the course of his denunciation he gave a capital imitation of two rich, fat women gossiping volubly in a silver-plated, silk-lined electric coupe and ending by running over a child playing in the street.

And yet the sermon ended on a note of tenderness and he said, "You see in how many directions this old legend has led us. and you see how the story, if correctly read, is full of strong and sweet accents."

And in his prayer of benediction, which evidently bore a reference to members of the congregation lately bowed in grief by the loss of a loved one, he said, "Teach them, O God, teach the weepers, that love outlasts life!"

He is a great, quiet, strong man, of the finest flower of Jewish scholarship, and there are no better scholars than Jews, because upon their scholarship, as upon their business, they concentrate; a stern man, who can put the fear of the Lord into the hearts of the purse-proud, the vulgar and the overbearing; a thorough cosmopolite, for Berlin, Leipzig, Philadelphia, Baltimore, Louisville and Chicago have been the seats of this Luxemburger's study and service at various periods of his life of sixty-one busy years; a worker always for the humanization of the ancient and austere faith of his people, yet, like his great father, who for nearly a quarter of a century was, by the King of Holland's appointment, chief rabbi in that country, a worker who seeks humanization without compromise or stultification.

Truly it is not without significance that he ministers today in the temple whose vast arches are graven deep with the interlaced triangles of Judaism and with the words, "Mine House Shall Be a House of Prayer for All Nations."

THE JEWISH PREACHER:
Rabbi Emil G. Hirsch, Ph.D., LL.D.

The Ethics of Marriage

Sunday, February 25, 1900

The common daily occurrences, the ordinary relations of life, have as deep an importance and hold as strong an appeal for reflection as do the rare, exceptional manifestations of power or the extraordinary temptations and trials of life. The blade of grass that is green unfolds the story of life, and the leaf that is seared and falls is momentous of the general law of decay.

Yet, how few of us pause to wonder about the miracle of the blade of grass, or to reflect on the monition of the seared leaf. We think the sunrise is majestic, the storm's rage is terrible, the tornado's sweep is tremendous, the Niagara's leap is miraculous—the same tremor and the same tremendousness is laid to our feet, and the same might and the same majesty are revealed to our eye, by the little globule of dew, the whispering leaves in the forest and the warbling of the birds in the bows.

Marriage is a familiar institution. It loses much of its solemnity by its familiarity. It is of daily occurrence. It is the ordinary destiny of most men and women, and therefore the fewest of us find themselves called upon to pause by the way and to ponder on its sacred meaning. That it is central to civilization, focal to all morality—that it is the cell, as it were, out of which the human organism is renewed, and of which it is composed, few of us bear in mind, accustomed as we are, to its ordinary frequency. And yet, the pillar upon which society rests is monogamous marriage.

That institution is the womb out of which appears and is born whatever is highly human and truly righteous. It matters not how man came to scale this altitude where monogamy is impressed by the sanctions of law and the sanctities of religion. It matters not that both biology and anthropology teach us that primitive man was not monogamous. It matters not that this last and this most solemn institution is the child of a long chain of evolutionary processes, the fruitage of a rich and varied harvest of experience. Who cares whether in the beginning man was given to polyandric sexual unions? Who needs care for the fact which is undoubted, that at one stage of man's development, marriage was polygamous? Who cares that even now on this circling globe, with the approval of religion and the conservative power of tradition and custom, the one husband and one wife union is still unknown, its place filled by the one husband but many wives sexual relation?

The fact remains unshaken because time developed finally this golden flower of conjugal love. This is proof abundant that monogamy is both the most natural and most human.

Polyandry disappeared. Polygamy is waning. Monogamy is recognized as the only dignified union of the most sacred and delicate relation of man to woman. Take it away and society crumbles. Destroy this focus of family life and humanity will cease to be.

The student of Judaism has every reason to feel proud of the truth that ideally, monogamy has always been central to the morality of its professors.

One who studies books like the Bible, must remember that in a literature of this kind monuments of various import are preserved. Often sociology lags behind ethics. The prophetic inspiration anticipates the birth of unborn hours. But it is this inspiration of the prophet that unrolls the picture of the true ambition of the prophet's people. Our own social institutions today are far from being morally perfect, and yet a later historian or judge would go far a field from justice were he to maintain that the better ambition had not yet found in this the last year of the nineteenth century its vocalized articulation. We know, and the prophets of our day have brought us this knowledge, that things are awry; that many of our social institutions stand in need of reformation, and the voice of these callers in the desert is testimony to the truth that the best and the noblest, and they are the expounders and the exponents of our true civilization, have recognized a higher law and are moved by a higher motive than that which has yet found incorporation and embodiment in our social institutions.

The same holds good of the Old Testament.

The tribal organization of old Israel has sanctioned polygamy. Wherever tribe is ultimate, there polygamy is to be found. The polygamy of the old Semitic tribal clan is not due to sensuous passion. It is not accursed by the taint of profligacy. He, who talks about polygamy in days of old and in the districts where the Islam holds the scepter, as due to brutal passion, has yet to learn the alphabet of sociological interpretation of social institutions.

The Arab chief has one solicitude. It is to have his tribe strong. The greater number of children the greater the strength of the clan. To have no child, to be without male issue, is of all calamities, to the thinking of the Semite of the desert, the direst. His peace on earth and his felicity after death are both endangered. To have a child, a son, is then the all overruling passion. To have many children, and many sons, is the sole gateway to honor in the clan, to influence among his fellows. That is the motif of the patriarchal story.

These old patriarchs are not types of perfect Jews, of model man, but they are carved figures of Semites living under Semitic notions, and in times when among the Hebrews (not the Jews) these Semitic ideas were the dominant and the determinative forces. Sociological institutions of this kind always embody themselves into laws. Change of law is the most difficult undertaking. Centuries must pass before laws creep up to the advanced position of a deeper morality. That is the sense of the well-known Latin maxim, *summum jus, summa injuria,* "the highest law is often the highest injury." We have laws in our times that are behind the further progressive and progressed morality; yet to change them is often a task beyond hope of fulfillment. The law preserved polygamy among the Jews long after the ethics of the Jew had denounced it and recognized it as inconsequential and insufficient.

Would you have a proof of this, my thesis? Remember the events I read to you this morning. The prophet describes the relation of Israel to his God in the symbol and simile of a marriage. "I betroth thee to me forever, by righteousness and love, by justice and faithfulness. Thou shalt no longer call me *Baali*, my possessor, (the Semitic patriarch with many wives); but thou shalt call me *Ishi*, my husband to whom she is to be betrothed, the one that is mate unto him, his helpmate, his equal." That marriage is indissoluble, it is permanent, it is monogamous.

Judaism, on the other hand, has never sanctified celibacy. It has always protested against casting a false light, as though it were of higher purity and saintliness, around a life that was of the single blessedness.

Celibacy has found two defenders. The one advocacy is trestled upon selfishness, the other upon sentiment, which is of spurious truth, and, according to the Jewish point of view, not worthy of commendation or of approval. According to Jewish thought a man who does not marry forfeits the best that there is in life. He is under suspicion of the lowest motives, and generally the man who does not marry is the rankest egotist the sun has ever shone on, and God's light should blush to give him illumination upon his lonely and often most lecherous path through life.

There are exceptions. Men often cannot marry because higher duties are theirs, and in that case they belong to the priesthood of ministers around God's altar. You know them and I do too, who had to forego the sweetest reward of human existence because fate, or God, as I would say, placed upon their shoulder the care of widowed mother, widowed sister, and her orphan children. In that case morality approves. But martyrdom is always exceptional. It comes to exceptional nations, and exceptions cannot be held to be other than evidences and proofs of the rule. In most cases egotism, and egotism of the most venomous character, suggests to him the loneliness of unmarried life.

Women often cannot marry. From the moral point of view that woman should go through life compelled by the egotism of man or by the imperfect organization of society, to remain without her mate, is the saddest indication of the imperfection of our civilization.

Economic conditions have, more than aught else conspired to bring this about. Defend the economics of our individualistic civilization as much as you dare—denounce those that preach of the necessity of lifting individualism to a higher potency through the magic of association; call upon bayonets to silence the voices of the protestants, and have recourse to bullets to put out of the way the disturbers of peaceful Israel. Reason that without the sting of individual ambition and the prospect into individual success, men will become slothful, stagnant and decay.

Your arguments and your measures lose what of pith and marrow they may hold, the moment the fact is put before you in its barren and bold importance, that under our individualistic economic civilization, many women are forced to forego their social function and are doomed to a life of disappointment and of bitter dependency; that thousands of women under our economic system are immolated at the altar of a frightful idol, which to mention is even not permitted let alone that a description of that Moloch should be attempted in a house like this and before a congregation like this.

At the root of that unmentionable evil, the curse of our civilization and the cause of million fold death and misery and wretchedness, lies our imperfect economic organization. But even under our social system, many lives might have found the compass whereby to steer their path to the port of marital happiness, had their eye not been blinded by selfishness, and their heart not been poisoned by cowardice, had the true notion, the moral aspect of marriage, been brought to their understanding and confirmed in their sentiment.

What is the basis of a monogamous union? In one word, it is love. Love, greatest of all sacred appellations—symbol and synonym of a deity. Sound substitute for the ineffable energy, might and power of the Creator—symbol emblematic of the noblest and the most illustrious devotion, spirit of sacrifice. But how many do understand love?

How many young people have been so guided as to realize the secret of love's implications. Cursed novels, yellow covered stories, most shameless theatrical plays and performances, have succeeded in casting around love a glamour of romantic unreality, or of weighting it with the sting of sensualist and the prospect of gratification of the passions. And a generation fed on the current literature such as comes from the pen of novelist, has but little chance to come to its own better self and to know what love means. The young maiden thinks that unless her heart flutters at the first sight of the young man, there can be no love between them. Others again look to the outlines of the face, the classic cast of countenance, the elastic frame of the body, the grace and perfect control of every movement, and are fascinated by this tempting and alluring exterior.

Others believe that love is manna of heaven; that the ordinary bread, the staff of life, cannot hold the elements out of which love draws its sustenance, and the consequence has been that many a foolish girl and many a man of equal lack of reasonableness, have missed listening to the voice that spoke, and having not heeded the call, have never again had the opportunity to hear those celestial monitions which they might have heard had they been guided aright.

In our novels a sort of atmosphere indescribable is cast upon this, the highest, the deepest phenomenon of our human nature. I tell you, that old Jew who informed his daughter that she was engaged to a certain young man, and who when the daughter objected that she did not love the young man, turned round to his wife and said: "Listen to the nonsense that Sarah prattles. Did you and I ever love one another, and did we not get along most beautifully with each other?"

That old Jew put a truth in a most striking form. The old Jews loved each other, though they called that feeling which they had one for the other, by a different name. Their love was not pinned on exterior—it was trestled on something deeper. A true love is not of the passions and of the senses. It is not of a sudden catastrophic character. It is not the flash in a night star. It is a steady sun that has its hour of dawn, its hours of the rise, of the ascent to the zenith and the mellow tones of the afternoon and the gradual eclipse in glory of his setting. It is not the fire of the volcano, but it is a lamp that shines in the darkness steadily and uncloudedly. It is mixed with confidence and assurance, faith and righteousness—the conviction that our life is but a half, and the life of the other is the half that completes our own into its fullness. It is, coupled to this conviction, the resolution to give more than is received, to complete the other life even though our own should be depleted. These are the elements of true love, and this love is indeed basic to monogamous marriage. Marriage contracted without this, or with designs other than these, has not the moral sanction.

In Europe, they have made marriage an arrangement, a bargain, a matter of parental adjustment. In France, in the higher strata of society, the young girl passes from the convent to the marriage altar. Youth is forged by links of iron to decrepit old age, under the temptation of pride of title, wealth, position the wife is sold to the husband, or rather the husband is purchased for the wife.

Thanks to the Lord, where Anglo-Saxon civilization has spread and where the true, sturdy morality of the Puritans has not yet altogether been wasted in a land like this, still fresh in the virgin possibilities of the opening hours of its day, marriage has not degenerated into a scheme for title or position, into an economic arrangement where the financial considerations are the determinants and the economic conditions are the prime prerequisites.

Woe to the young man who marries for money. It is possible to fall in love with a rich girl. Many young men make the most of this possibility. They have a good care of their heart to keep it under perfect control, and they will not give their heart the freedom until they have examined Dun's Agency reports concerning the fathers of marriageable daughters.

This is not the spirit which can consecrate and sanctify. Where marriage lacks the element of struggle for economic independence, where parental care or parental luck has placed before the young people a paradise which is without stimulating appeals; there the danger of drifting apart is a thousand times greater than it is under the stress of economic insecurity or industrial dependency.

In a household where youth even has the privilege of untold plenty, the communion of souls can only be that of the spending, not the gaining, and while it is true that even in the spending there may be bedded the elements of moral culture, still, ability to spend is generally fatal to resolution to spend in a righteous spirit.

I can fancy the household of young people blessed on either side by parental indulgence and parental fortune, to become the center of wise philanthropy. I can imagine that the young rich husband can become to the young rich wife, an inspiration and a guide to take upon their shoulders unitedly the responsibilities of their wealth; but how often do younger people under fortunate surroundings, attempt to rise to the height of this, their social responsibility? Their communion will be one of enjoyment, of pleasure to themselves, and with this possibility of an invasion by the germ of selfishness, their happiness is threatened.

Happier the young people who go out into their common life relying upon their own resources and faith in their ability to meet adversity without murmuring, and to receive fortune with a mellowed joy; the reward of their active endeavor and their unrelenting struggle. They that weep together are linked to each other much more firmly than they who merely laugh together. The alchemy of tears has the power to unite. The alembics of joy have the fatality often to divide. Wealth is not always a privilege. It is always a danger, and nowhere is that danger more to be feared and to be guarded against than in the young household where denial is not demanded, and sacrifice is an unknown appeal and energy.

For all this, it is true that love shall be under

the control of reason. Without reason it degenerates into erotic sensuality. Without reason love may become the stumbling block, the great source of misery and wretchedness. While those that would unite in marriage must really love each other, and love in the sense in which I have bunglingly attempted to define. It is true they must also know what is before them, and must have asked themselves whether they are strong enough or equipped well enough to meet what is in store for them.

They are not merely the arbiter of their own destiny. They hold in the palm of their hand, in the balance of their decision, the happiness or the wretchedness of unborn generations. No one has the right to marry who is not sound of body and sound of mind, and sound of soul. No one has the right to ask one to share with him his life who is not equipped with that moral strength and physical ability and intellectual resourcefulness which will enable him to provide a home, not of plenty, but a home that come what may, can stand, though the breaker may rush up to it, and the tornadoes may sweep by it. Ability, character, is of greater moment than competency provided by the father or great fortune in store when the father dies.

Were I a rich man, I should look to the young man's ability first and last, and though the gossips in the town might sneer and talk what kind of a match princess of millionaire's household made with this young lawyer, and this unknown physician, and this clerk; I should let them gossip to their heart's content. It is envy that makes them gossip always, and I would be rewarded for my indifference by the serenity that I had chosen well and advised well for my daughter.

Do you not know that parental fortune is wasted; do you not know the young man who has done nothing in his life except to live on the allowance paid by the indulgent father has never the surety that after father's death the allowance will not be wasted? Do you not know that then with the allowance cut off, the fortune changed, the trust company even having failed, the interest rates having declined, your daughter's fate is of the most terrible. Accustomed to luxury she has to confront want. But the young man who has character and ability will always be able to throw his arms around his wife and support her in days of trying misfortune, and to bewitch on her face the smile of contentment, the response of the happiness of her heart.

The law might perhaps, as it has been suggested, see to it that certain marriages shall not be contracted. We know that the stockbreeders have a great care in the selection of the parent animals. When we come to the fate of unborn humanity, we disregard every caution. Families tainted by hereditary idiosyncrasies are considered among the choicest, provided the gate is opened with a golden key; and families cankered by misfortune are also admitted to pour their blood into the veins of our grandchildren yet to come. The criminals, the paupers, the idiots, should be by law prevented from continuing their curse, and where the law cannot reach, the moral conscience should speak and protect. In this regard we have done but little, and one who, like myself, has so often to stand before young people, knows that more frequently than he is ready himself to avow, are unions that hold the elements not of physical health but of the very reverse; and many a life is sent into God's earth blighted because the parents had not the moral courage to allow their moral conscience to speak.

For these reasons parental obligation is deep, and marriages should not be encouraged except they have the approval of the parents. It is true the parents should well consider how far their advice shall work in opposition to the claims of son or of daughter. I read in one of my periodical excursions, where serious books are not to be studied, but the lighter moods require lighter food, an Italian novel, only last week. It depicts the life of a noble girl, prevented from allying herself in marriage to her beloved and loving choice, by parental stubbornness and bigotry.

The story is pathetic, and the last chapter, her father being dead—the father who had deprived her of her choice, she rushes on to become the nurse of a man who is dying, where she might have been the wife of his living days. This possibility of cursing a life, the parents should well consider.

But, on the other hand, is it not a shame that among us especially in America, this tide of disrespect and irreverence is sweeping even now over the barriers which the Jewish synagogue had always erected and the Jewish home always had protected—is it not a shame that a thousand and one young people in this land rush to the justice shop to marry, and then inform the parents. And our dear yellow journalists add a seasoning of flippancy, and we who take our kaffee klatsch from these yellow journalists, find much pleasure in being told how the mother, in her disappointment, received the interviewer, and what the father had to say about the elopement of his daughter.

And there are always more fools on earth than wise men. There are always foolish girls who think this is the thing. They rush off to Milwaukee or to Waukesha or to some other Gretna Green, and come back harnessed, to repent often in months that have no easement, for the folly and the triumph of a moment of insanity. And our dear clergymen, with very few exceptions, ask no questions. The license and the five-dollar fee are sufficient to ease their conscience.

Old rabbis even have spoken the words that made two young fools one, without stopping to ask why is father not present, why has mother not come? There are a few in the clerical profession that have some character left. They will not marry, no matter who they may be, without the presence or consent of the parents. Often such a clergyman, such a rabbi, is thereby exposed to indignities.

But better social animosities, at the risk of losing members even, be incurred than whose conscience of the man who has to speak the solemn words by the sanction of the law, and under the sanction of religion; should forever cry out: "You have spoken words which were the prelude to misery, and if you had withheld them, you might have saved fools who rushed on to their doom."

Young people, consider well what the parents might advise and do counsel. No union can be blessed if parental benediction is withheld. There shall be ethical, spiritual and moral harmony in a blessed home.

This brings up the question of mixed marriages. As a matter of theory, we believe that all men are equal, that one religion is as sacred as another; but the ethical and the spiritual unity of the home is always endangered where a different view of life is by education and environment fostered in one from that which has been inculcated into the other.

It is all self-deception to reason these differences away. And even if husband and wife have strength enough to neutralize these differences, their social connections, which they cannot break, will forever unconsciously and unintentionally activate and energize again these primary vital differences. And religion is about vital things. Religion is not merely a ribbon that may he pleated into the hair or not. It is not merely a mantel that may be thrown around or not. It is not merely a walking skirt or a long-trained skirt that may be changed with the tides of fashion. Men may have no religion and women may have none, and probably most of us have no religion in the sense that religion stands for vital things, but where religion is vital, it is of vital relations, of deeper themes.

Religion sets the rhythm of our life, and as little as two players can play together harmoniously each one in his own rhythm, even so little can two souls blend in accord with each other with rhythm different from the other. We Jews look upon life differently from what others look upon it. That is the result of our history. It is effective in our subconscious soul. It is not merely what we reason about, but how we reason. It is not merely what we feel about, but how we feel that is determinative. And a Jew reasons differently. He looks differently upon life than do those that were brought up under other conditions. And this is the fatal germ in unions where concordance of religious training is not present from the start.

Weigh well and ponder well. Experience has spoken. In exceptional cases the germ may be neutralized. Shall the home represent an economic unit? This is the question that becomes very insistent in our day. Advanced women you know, some very advanced, have been contending that the economic unit of the family shall be dissolved that man shall be his own economic exponent, and the woman shall be her own economic coefficient. Or, to speak more plainly, man shall earn and keep what he earns, and woman shall earn and keep what she earns. Mrs. Stetson, in her recent book, has theorized eloquently about the economic independence of wife from the husband.

There may be cases where such a plan may be feasible. There may be abnormal cases where the wife ought to be, and generally is the economic power and mind; but for most cases, and considering humanity's best interests, the marriage shall lead to an economic unit. There is equality under difference of function. The man is a man, and the woman is a woman, and you can reason about the equality of men and women, trim your hair long or short as you please, if you have any hair left, and it is supposed that young people have some hair left before they marry—you may trim your hair long or you may trim it short, you may wear bloomers or you may wear flowing garments; nature, God, has willed it that man shall be man and woman shall be woman, and man's work is not woman's work, and woman's work is not man's work.

I cannot go into details. Time is too short, and I have a distrust of the frivolity that characterizes some of the critics of a public speaker but this is the case, and the health of humanity depends upon the recognition of this difference under equality and thus the man is the provider, and the woman the preserver. Man is the executive. Woman is the inspirer. And where these two functions are harmoniously carried out, there comes economic happiness, as well as spiritual concordance.

No, I for one do not hold that the best; the moral interests of humanity are subserved by dissolving the economic unit into a loose financial partnership, or even financial independence.

But shall woman obey and man rule? Where love speaks there is neither rule nor obedience. There is gladsome respect, there is anticipation of wish and will. The wife that is a wife does not obey. The man who is a husband does not command. He is not the owner of his wife. She is not his property. He is constitutional monarch and she constitutional queen. Both have their sphere of volition, and both have their hours of leadership. Both guide and follow. Both give and receive.

Both bless and are blessed.

On an old ring which I picked up somewhere—I do not know where—in some museum in Europe, probably on an old wedding ring, I found this inscription: "Thee not thine. Take me to be thee, but not thine."

This is the tonic key of the scale of marital happiness. Where husband is the wife and the wife is the husband, in the spiritual sense, where one is the other, and not the other's, there is peace, there is happiness. Such a home becomes the center of the best that is humanity's glory and man's crown. Such a home realized what the first page in Genesis has so well illustrated that man really was created in the beginning man and woman. In such a home, both are helpmates, one and the other complement one the other. There is music. There is love. And such a home will stand.

The sun of that love will rise to the zenith, it will decline toward the evening, but the last hour, the hour preceding the eclipse by the night will be radiant with the purple and the gold recalling the glory and the glow of the morning hour after the dawn. And even when night has come, when one has gone and the other is left behind, when the night hath come, there will be stars to shine and speak of the sun that is set; there will be an after glow on the Alps where love has its home, on the Alps where the currents of life have their cradle—on those Alpine peaks where affection and duty, faithfulness and righteousness have their highest outlook and uplook, the night will sink, but for hours and hours will quiver on the crest and ridges of the chaste altitudes the gold of the day that is no more, the after glow of a love which lived and cannot die.

Amen.

THE JEWISH PREACHER:
Rabbi Emil G. Hirsch, Ph.D., LL.D.

Half An Hour With Genesis

Sunday, October 21, 1900

It is the voice of an old friend that spoke to us this morning. We are familiar with his message, for oft before have we listened to him. I daresay his words are in all probability the only ones that many of us carry in our memories of the many of similar import treasured in the old book, remnants of ancient Hebrew Literature.

Perhaps it was on my part a hazardous venture to ask this old friend to be our guest this morning. I ought to have remembered that we are of a generation which would have mind as well as eye feast forever on novelties. Familiar truths are disregarded. In our hunger for new things we forget that wine grows stronger as the years increase since the day of its vintage.

Holmes, the philosopher of the breakfast table, the genial autocrat, makes comment on this mania for the new things in disparagement of the better, older possessions. He remarks that a carpenter will use the same hammer, and none will object. He may ply the same plane, and none will say nay. But the writer, the thinker, will not be pardoned if he presses forward the same thought over and over again.

I have risked, in my desire this morning to have an old friend speak out old truths to us, this criticism "that for my high financial compensation I ought to have been able to compose something new for the pews and the few friends in the pews. That is my bargain with the congregation every week, to have a new bill of fare."

But I am incompetent, and especially incompetent to carry out this contract. My brain is not so gifted as to be able to find new truths, and as I survey what is offered as the latest finds in the domain of truth I come to the conclusion that some of the old verities have charms and power which many of the newer discoveries unfortunately sadly lack.

And so, let the old friend speak to us this morning. If we but pay due respect to his greeting, we shall be compensated; of this I am confident though the story he tells may have a familiar ring in our ears.

Genesis! Is there a high school boy or girl who will pause in the consciousness of one's deeper knowledge to tribute to the chapter that speaks of God's creation in the beginning, more than a sneer? Is not this opening gateway to Biblical literature the strongest proof that religion and science are hostile to each other, that science the bride of our younger love has completely and justly dethroned religion, the mother of our older affection? And, indeed, it must be said that for this hasty proclamation of the hostility between science and religion no one is in a higher measure responsible than the very priests who would throw the safeguards of authority, the bulwarks of positive dogmatism, around the altars of religion.

Genesis, according to the opinionated stubbornness of these would-be defenders of religious truth, speaks in the tones of a scientific disquisition. As it is described in this chapter, so the world leapt into form. Every stage in this world-creating process was actually as it is here intimated. In the beginning there was nothing. God's word sounded over vacancy, and vacancy ranged itself in keeping with God's omnipotent decree into beauty and order.

The light was first kindled, and then in volitioned succession trooped out the stars and rolled out the seas, rose the rocks and wreathed themselves with the garlands of ferns and flowers. Up came the multitude of breathing and moving things, as God called them into being, until at last, by a supreme manifestation of God's directive will, the King of all was led into his dominion. Man came, crowned with the diadem of divinely sanctified kingship. Thus, say the dogmatists, "it is written in the book" and to doubt that every word is teeming and quivering with truth were to lay the heavy hand of heresy upon the most delicate flowers of religious faith.

But science has disregarded this authoritative caution of the dogmatic churchman. She has gone out and asked the stars themselves for the story of their becoming. Science, softly knocking at the heart of the rocks and listening to the answer, as a physician who would auscultate and percuss the chest of a man, has heard the reply indicating that the condition of the life-giving organ is different than that assumed in this old story, and thus the conflict seems to be on. The issues seem to be locked. Here is religion on one hand, with Genesis for its support; there is science on the other, equally as strongly convinced that not as here described, but in quite different process, the earth assumed its present crust and the stars their now quivering luster.

There have been, you know, schools that painfully have felt the pang of this conflict—men equally devoted to religion and to science—lovers of religious truth and learners of scientific verities. They have endeavored to mediate between the conflicting hosts ranged in battle array. These men were of good intention but of bungling execution. It is to them, more than even to the stern dogmatists, that we are indebted for the cankering spreading disease of skepticism; for the irreverence with which the Biblical scroll is treated; for that arrent and arrogant attitude of ignorance, which claiming to have the sanctification of science, scorns to give audience to the humbler plea of strongly-moved and deeply-stirred religion.

These men who wish to compromise between religion and science put both science and religion on the procrastinator's bed. In order to fit the finds of science to the form of Genesis, they had to strain the meaning of the words and to wrench the momentum of scientific symbols.

Geology had taught us that the rocks are witnesses to the unshaken truth that the span of one terrestrial day is altogether too limited to

HALF AN HOUR WITH GENESIS

allow the possibility of their development. Down in the South, where the Mississippi waters sluggishly and hesitatingly wend their way to the Gulf of Mexico—underneath the folds spun of water by that mighty stream—the geologist has measured the alluvial deposits. And knowing at what rate the waters of the Mississippi lay down their burden of sand, which they carry from their distant home in the North, has computed that in order that this soil, this alluvial deposit shall have come to be how and what it is now, not merely six thousand years shall have run their unwearied circuit but perhaps six million years must have poured out their creative impulses.

Astronomers have computed the flight of light. We know what this philosophy is, how many miles its wings may sweep to nothing during the brief spell of one human breath. And knowing then this terrible flight of the heavenly wanderers, we can calculate at what distance yonder torches flame into space and measure what time must have elapsed between the birth of the ray and its welcome by our eye here on our quivering planet. And knowing all this, the astronomer has again given his deposition to the effect that if this book is taken literally, it does not afford room for the insertion into the scheme of creation of those mighty beacon torches in the empyrean above.

Thus, then, those that would reconcile religion to science came to the foolish conclusion that when Genesis speaks of a day it has in mind the lengths of a geological period, that it does not mean to imply that six times the sun rose and set and six times when the evening stars came out to sing their night-song, God said "Let there be light," but that six mighty geological periods rushed and rolled their appointed length, and that at the beginning of each such mighty majestic period God issued his decree, "Let there be." And, in order to carry out this thought which they held to mean the redeeming words in this conflict and contrast between science and religion, they strained the words.

Undoubtedly, many a congregation has been frightened into assent and fired into admiration by the use from the pulpit of the technical terms of Geology. I, too, might this morning send you home with a dizzy whirring brain, were I to recite by rote the table of geological periods and their subdivisions. I, too, might strike awe into your hearts at my wonderful erudition, by telling you of the Eocene, Miocene and Pliocene geological periods, by calling to witness in my behalf the Eozoic, Mesozoic and the Paleozoic geological revolutions. I might go into the formations of the rocks and entertain you with a few more crumbs gathered out of the dustpan of the geological banquet, but I must leave that to others.

I am not of the school, please, that by this road the final solution can be found. The rationalists, that is the name of this school, which endeavored by geological imagination to disarm science in its opposition to religion. The rationalists lay the hands of idiocy—even if of good intention—upon the treasures of religious literature. Admire, if you must, the rationalist who has found an answer to every problem. Give him credit for vastness of information, go into ecstasies when you read that, if you might thereby read what the Creator said or what Moses makes God say. Believe that this is the latest and the highest of liberal criticism and liberal philosophy.

Both the world of science and the world of religion have wearied of these childish puerilities, and the man who poses as a liberal because he still claims that these blocks are intended for the nursery, may perhaps attest merely that he has again become a child and is probably in his dotage.

Today we know that Genesis is a poem. The old Hebrews were as ignorant of the riddles and the resolutions of geology as are the little children playing with dolls or riding hobby horses in the paradise of infancy. Moses, if he wrote that chapter—and he did not write it—Moses or whoever wrote it knew not of the Eocene and the Pliocene and the Mesozoic periods. He knew nothing of the formation of the rocks and knew nothing of Devonian geology. He was ignorant of petrology and of mineralogy. I think I have used fine words and long enough words this morning to satisfy the most exorbitant.

Moses was absolutely ignorant of the scientific results of our modern master leaders in the domain of natural knowledge, but Moses wrote a poem, or Genesis opens with a poem, written out of the heart and sung out of the soul of the old Jewish faith and the old Jewish nation. It does not matter that it is an established fact that this book of Genesis, the opening chapters thereof, seemingly, are not original with the old Hebrew writers. We have found, as undoubtedly you remember, in the ruins of Nineveh, tablets of brick written over in curious signs, the so-called cuneiform inscriptions. We have deciphered those inscriptions, and we have read from them, and those tablets are now stored away in the British Museum in London, a complete creation story almost identical with this found in the Book of Genesis, the same rhythmic movement in the measure of six days, the same succession almost of the various children in Creation's household.

This creation-story of the Assyrians forms a part of the cycle of stories in the same manner as does Genesis form a segment in the circle of tribal or national tradition which comprises today the opening twelve chapters of Genesis. Now, this very find was thought to corroborate the accuracy of Genesis, and there are many among our students even today who are anxious to learn Assyrian from us at the university, simply because they think that these old Babylonian or Assyrian bricks will tell them something, which will stand in good stead for them in their anxiety to preserve the authenticity and to emphasize the accuracy of Genesis; but while there is similarity there is dissimilarity in the account, and these very dissimilarities tell us wherein consists the eternal undying value of that opening poem of Genesis.

There is not a nation on the face of the globe but has asked itself the question, "Whence the stars and whence the stones?" They are not men who pass through life without once looking up to heaven and wondering at the brilliant collection of diamonds clustered together in the Galaxy. They are but poor apologies for men who can walk through the forest and never are prompted to ask, "Oak, whence thou? Poplar, whence thou?" They are not men, who are never prompted to inquire, as their foot stumbles against a rock or their eye rests upon the silky, silvery back of the river, "Whence ye, whence ye?" The child even asks such questions, and while the child's questions cannot be answered always, it is their indications of an aroused curiosity, and this aroused curiosity tolls the birth hour, peals the birth hour of intelligence and consciousness. Go, ye, through life, and never ask "Whence?" You may succeed in your commercial enterprises, but before the tribunal of the human values little credit shall be registered on the page of the ledger graced, or as I should say, disgraced by your name. Go through life and never wonder and never ponder upon what the stars mean and upon what the planets tell, why the ocean roars and rages, and why the abyss yawns. You might be important in the circles in which you move, but your credentials shall not be accepted in the statelier halls where the true men congregate and the true women meet. It is a testimonium paupertatis, a testimonial of intellectual poverty, for one to say, "What to me what yonder stars token, what to me whence the flowers have their robes of gold and of beauty?"

So it is with a nation. Every nation, the moment it awakens to its own self-consciousness, has to put the query, "Whence?" And so in the literature of the world we find no people but had some account of how things came to be; their poets always put themselves at the disposal of the inquiring minds, the anxious souls, and brought reports as to how the heavens arched themselves above and the earth spread itself beneath; how the torches in heaven were lit and the sun was given its coat of fire; and how underneath the earth the deep caverns were flushed with water or were heated with flames anxious to burst forth through the mouth of lava spouting, quaking volcanoes.

So, our Genesis, like the tablets of the Assyrian, is but one in the series of world accounts of the world's creation. As a scientific description, it has no greater value than has any of them. The Bible is not a book of science. Bear that in mind. Cling to this in principle. Let it not be attenuated in your reflection. Religion is not bound up with the Bible, but religion is woven into the Bible, and that our religion is the very comparison of this poem of ours with the other poetry of the world devoted to the same theme and answering the same anxiety, will plentifully and beautifully show. Our poem, in comparison with the others, reveals it as saturated with the monotheistic idea. It is *one God* that creates, and *one God* alone!

Now, who of us will stop to think about the beauty and the strength and the vigor and the virtue of a monotheistic presentation of the creation? Well and good. We are not here to argue whether God is, or God is not.

What is implied in that monotheistic idea? Our book tells us it was a bold thought to think it out that from nothing God could make the world. "I know full well that" as one philosopher says, "ex nihilo nihil fit," out of nothing, nothing can come only. And here is that bold thought: Creation out of nothing.

Reject that theory? You are on good Jewish ground. Philosophers in the Middle Ages, Jewish philosophers such as Adonai Kreska, and such as Joseph Algo, they also said that it is not necessary to assume a creation out of nothing to be still a religious Jew. Say it is an impossibility! I do not quarrel with you. I have my own thoughts upon that subject. But behold, what beauty is woven into this thought. Creation out of nothing implies that whatever is has been made to conform with the intentions of the Creator. The world, as it is, therefore, is such as it is in keeping with the forethought of an Almighty and All-Wise and an All-Good God.

Now, translate these phrases into intelligible language. What do they convey? "And God saw, and he saw that whatever he had made was good." This monotheism is a proclamation of Optimism. The world is good. Now, assume that the world is good. It must react upon you. Then, your life is valuable, and then comes this thought, "Will not the heavens change you as they look down upon you and you look up to them?" The ocean you know changes its color in keeping with the sky above. When the sky is overcast the ocean has a lead-colored, inky hue. When the sun smiles above, the ocean is decked out with a caress which in its purple and in its blue blended coloring constitutes the despair and the envy of the lady of fashion. If she only knew where to find the secret of this pigment, wouldn't she dye her hair in keeping with it? And so the ocean has no color, but the sky above paints it with a brush steeped in gold or with a pencil blackened with soot. So it is that a line of thought reacts upon the color of your life.

Psychologists know this. Christian Science is founded on this. Hypnotism is a phenomenon in this cycle of psychological observation. Believe the world is good! Your life then is good, and life is worth living. That is the first note in this poem. Life is worth living. What is the use of believing that? Let the history of the Jews answer.

Was ever a group of people so maltreated as the Jew? Had ever humanity less to live for than the Jew? When they came to the Land of Promise, they had to turn the desert into gardens, they had to compel the rocks to give forth their scanty water, they had to struggle with Nature, bringing upon them their balmiest days of their national glory and national greatness.

But the world pained their soul. And when they had lost their nationality pessimism and despair found no lodgment in their imagination. The Bible would always be valuable as a book of cheer and of optimism. When I say, we lost our nationality, what had the world for us? Only curses and kicks. Never kisses and welcome. Fifteen centuries of this continued distress laid their terrible burden upon the Jew. In every group of men, Judaism groaned under a load. They carried the load, and retained—mark the fine long word—their resiliency. They never forfeited their elasticity. What gave them this power of resilient resistance? Their optimism. "God has made the world, and behold it was very good." Therefore, whatever comes is meant for good and for better. That is one of the flowers on the tree of Optimism, of Monotheism.

And the second. What is this? That, as God is the Creator and the creation comes in accordance with a divine wise proposition, man's life must be under that proposition. There has been much heated discussion as to Teleology. Teleology is, in philosophy, the term, which designates the theory of life, of the creation, as purposed, as planned. Even in the sciences we have teleological interpretation. Opposite to teleological is accidental.

Now, Monotheism is of the opinion that the world was planned. Therefore there is teleology. Of course, we can easily laugh at the teleological interpretation. Was God a carpenter? Did he fit one thing to another? And there is true teleology. The old notion that God gave the stag very thin legs so that he could run away, that is, for the purpose of making him a runner gave him a thin leg, inverts the finds of modern geology. Darwin has told us that the stag runs with thin legs because he ran, because he had to run, and he did not have them before he had to run; that a certain set of insects got the power of disguising themselves by neutral colors, just as our soldiers now are dressed in khaki, not because God had appointed them so in the beginning, but because in the struggle for existence they found out that if they changed their color they would be safest from the attacks of their insectivorous enemies. And so teleology has been discarded and self-volition substituted, the very thing which narrow-minded high school boys say it controverts. The teleology today is that one is forever nothing in the chain of life but what has its relation to what precedes and what follows after. And so, all this creation, says the Monotheist, precedes Man and it is related to him, as he must be related to somebody else.

So we have as the capping-stone of this creation, architecture, "And God said, 'Let us make Man in our image.'" Man is the creator? God is the Creator. That is the purpose of Man's life. That sets him in the relation of the Eternities, the powers that rule. That gives rhythm to his pilgrimage on earth. That gives consolation and courage to him. He is a king on this planet. To change it for human uses has God made the world for him. Carlyle, you know, says once, "Produce, produce." That is the outcry of the teleologist, "Man, produce, and produce!" Carlyle, in this ponderous outcry or sentence, merely puts the softer proclamation of the Hebrew poet, "And God made man in his image."

So, the second standpoint of the monotheistic view is, our life is related to whatever was before and has a purpose for whatever may come thereafter. Work is the equivalent of creation, and hence Genesis tells us that work is not a curse. Work is a blessing. Work is a benediction. Work is the resolving of all doubt and is the balm for all wounds, creative work. In one of my preceding sermons I have developed this theme more fully; therefore, I need not exhaust your patience in going over the ground again. We work for others, and we only work for ourselves when we work for others. We are made in the image of God.

Did God make the world that he might receive something? No, he gave not to receive; he blessed, not to be thanked in return. Can the individual work alone? There is no one that can. Can the individual man be master over the earth? There is no one that can. So, in this monotheistic idea we have the seed-germ of our modern notion, grand that it is, of the one created God-like humanity. But work shall not be the work of a slave, and so our poem winds up with the sanctification of the Sabbath Day.

Had the Jews given to the world naught but this, the Sabbath idea and the Sabbath Day, they would have given to humanity what is more precious than all the rest, than any other philosophy may have produced. It is true, Judaism did not give to the world a Parthenon; there are no ruins of a Jewish Acropolis; there are no traces of a Jewish Pantheon; there are no signs of a Jewish pyramid. In the arts, other nations have excelled us and in the annals of our glory there are no mention of such artists as Praxiteles, Phidias, Raphael, Correggio, Tintoretto or De Vinci. We have not given to the world even original music; the few musicians that we have given the world were, as has been well put, rather imitators than initiators. In the list of our contributions, we have not made pathfinders through the influence of our religion. We have given to the world only the Sabbath. But that Sabbath has been the bulwark of humanity. Take it away from man, what is there to his life? Take it away from him, what is there of his labor? The Sabbath preserves Man in his manhood; it gives him again a sense of dignity; it makes him again a full man, while his day-task dwarfs him into a part of a man. It enlarges his vision, broadens his sympathies. That is the gift of Judaism to the world, for man is not a slave when he works. He is God's image. Of course, it is ridiculous to say that the Sabbath is linked and chained to a certain twenty-four hour day. We must leave that to others. We must recognize that the Sabbath was made for Man and not Man for the Sabbath.

Let us then, if we have recognized this, make up our minds earnestly to at least have again a Sabbath. What we have so far is not a Sabbath. A Psalm service and a lecture make no Sabbath. There is no mention of those in the old book. But, if you please, Sabbath is a rest from toil, it is refreshment for the soul, it is study of life's deepest puzzles and is enjoyment of life's fullest pleasures. It brings Man again into intimacy with Man. It would make each one know and feel that his money is accidental, but his manhood is the essential.

So this Genesis poem has a ring like a vase in which are put the choicest flowers for our delectation and our inspiration, the most beautiful blossoms of thought and of inspiration. "God made the world" is the source of the optimistic outlook, and an optimistic outlook gives strength and courage. It may be a delusion, but even delusions have their values in humanity. "God made the world" gives to man his position in the world, and in God's image he is creator. He must live there with others, as he is for others, as he must live through others. And God created the world, and as the final grand diaphaneity of his entire creative symphony he struck that glad chord on the full orchestra, the last breath, as the Sabbath evening of creation, "the Sabbath was made for man," but only a Sabbath can make man.

So, let us go home, on our part let us believe that Genesis is after all not a bundle of exploded nonsense. Let us go home, let us occasionally, at home, on the Jewish day attempt to enjoy something of the flavor and of the fervor, fire and beauty of the old Sabbath-tide. We have that Sabbath-tide to bless us. We are the losers if, when she knocks for admission, we refuse to open the gates.

Genesis is not a dissertation on science. There is no possibility of harmonizing Genesis with geology. There is no necessity. Religion is indifferent as to when and how the world came, but religion is the proclamation that as the world came, it came under God's intention. As Man came, he came as God's image, and that, as such, his life is Creation's continuation, with the Sabbath as the eternal spring of divine strength and divine rehabilitation.

Amen.

THE JEWISH PREACHER:
Rabbi Emil G. Hirsch, Ph.D., LL.D.

He Who Knows Most Doubts Most
A Text from Browning

Sunday, November 17, 1901
Reading:Psalms 42

Browning was not the first who caught the thought that "he who knows most doubts most." His phrase in fact has a Socratic ring. That talkative philosopher who walked about the public streets of Athens putting puzzles to cobblers and making inquiries of old and young had—centuries before the English poet—called man to remember that knowledge, true knowledge, is always the gateway to realized ignorance. The primary condition of increasing knowledge is to know one's ignorance. The child in its blissful ignorance is spared the vexations of doubt.

Its world is complete. The child is an unconscious poet, and with poetic power construes a universe in which there are no problems to solve. The child knows itself from its instincts, consciousness of self, it reconstrues the world in terms of similitude to its own being.

All has life. The stars are persons, the flowers are acquaintances, the stones have feelings, and the running brooks have voices. The child's dictionary knows not the word impossible. Swift transitions from life to death, from man to animal, are not frightening for the child with gapping lacunae over which no bridge leads. For the child the world has no riddles. The child doubts nothing because in reality it knows nothing.

The same self-sufficiency is also found among persons of little knowledge. What little stock of information they may have laid aside is for them a fund inexhaustible. Having but little intimacy with the facts as they are, with the abundance of forces that sweep roundabout us, they do not feel prompted to examine whether the props that underlie their own opinions be stable and strong.

You come across such men at almost every turn of your life's road. Men who perhaps did not have the advantage of education, or men that had opportunities for amassing knowledge but wasted them, self-taught men for instance who browsed in one pasture and digested perhaps one blade of grass. They know everything and their opinions must never be doubted. What little light they have stands over their former density of ignorance with such full flood of beauty that they can never think that another man may have pushed beyond the very source from which their little lamp is fed.

Men of little knowledge never doubt, but men who know most doubt most. They doubt the sufficiency of their own information. They are not dogmatic, they are open-minded. The child is not open-minded, for the world of the child has nowhere puzzle or perplexity. The man of little knowledge is not open-minded, he clutches in his hand one grain or two, and in his conceit he does not feel that what he knows is after all but preliminary.

Hear him take part in debates concerning political issues, today as yesterday, he will rehearse his empty partisan phraseology. Men of little knowledge are generally found to be consistent. Inconsistency, as they call it, is generally the shadow of open-mindedness. Men that still have something to learn will always be ready to modify their opinions and to change their attitude in accordance with the later information.

Now, to leave this largely psychological field and to turn to what is perhaps more legitimate for me to treat, on to the field of religion and ethical conduct, again we find that they who know most doubt most. The child's religion is complete in the hour it is born. The race, too, once was composed of children; and what religion those children had, again before mine, seemed to bring the final solution of every inquiry, the final and ultimate reading of every riddle.

Dogmatic religion has the advantage of completeness. That advantage, a growing religion has to forego. Often today you hear among the Jews the plaint that things are indefinite, that no one really knows what the Jewish religion stands for. That compared with the Catholic Church, our condition is deplorable. That we should take steps to reduce the contents of our religious thought to a small but fired compass so that they who claim to be adherents might put the few paragraphs in the form of a newspaper clipping into their pocketbook. Ready at hand whenever the spirit should prompt them to consult the table of contents and the details of creed which go with Judaism.

Alas, they who plead for this fixity of form in the statement of faith have still to learn that knowledge, growing knowledge, will not brook these fast and forever fixed formula, these dogmas and credal paragraphs. It is true that a credal religion is a comfortable religion because it is fixed, it bars ingress to doubt and stops inquiry.

But so is the condition of the child comfortable. Shall we return to the mental condition of our infancy? We lived while in the nursery in a paradise, but that paradise had to be forfeited when we ate of the tree of knowledge, and so the human race had to leave paradise behind.

It is absolutely false to read into the story of paradise—as woven by Hebrew myth—the thought that this loss was a curse. Adam, eating from the tree of knowledge, woke from slumber the latent forces of civilization. His condition was not the higher, it was the lower. When paradise disappeared, the glory of humanity rose above the horizon.

When we leave the innocency or the ignorance of childhood, we place our foot on the first rung of the ladder reaching to higher outlooks and therefore to higher self-consciousness. In paradise there is not the joy of activity, there is not the triumph due to the doubt of the struggle, but out away from its blissful ignorance, away from its completeness, out beyond there is the field where honor may be gleaned, strength may be harvested, and truth may ultimately be found.

The conflict between science and religion is necessary to the growth of knowledge and of faith. We cannot go back to the older days, and they who misconstrue the philosophy of our movement as an appeal to go back to Moses, for instance, have still to learn the alphabet of our impulses. No, while one faction or another may have believed that the Reform Movement in Judaism was in a retrogressive direction, away from the Talmud for instance to the greater purity and profounder depth of Moses, the great men who were the pioneers, never for a moment had misgivings as to the direction forward towards which they must push in order to do what the spirit of their age and the fuller possession of their knowledge entailed upon them.

Science and religion, knowledge and faith, must war. You elicit the spark from the flint by striking it with the iron. You chasten iron by putting it under the rhythmic blows of the heavy hammer. From the compact and impact of two differently charged wires flashes forth the light which chases darkness.

Struggle between knowledge and faith is essential; it lies within all of human nature. Increased knowledge has indeed dethroned gods. We may deplore that these structures of beauty, these fancies of free imagination, which delighted the soul of Greece have forever departed.

That no Zeus presides over thunder, that no Neptune prances upon the stage when the ocean rises and falls, that no Vulcan is busy by his anvil whenever the mountains belch forth their fury; we may deplore that no Apollo pastures his sheep when the gentle wind drives the fleecy clouds toward the higher points of the horizon.

We may lament as we pass through the forest that we are not destined to meet fairies. That when the leaves rustle it is not the noise made by the flowing train of a beautiful goddess' garment. We may deplore that for us the running brook has lost speech and the shining snow has lost personality. But what has been given to us in return?

A world no longer poetic, indeed; a world however of law and order, in which caprice is no longer sceptered and whim does no longer wear the crown. A world which is under law unchangeable. A world in which most distant Sirius follows the same behest as does my hand when it is thrown out in obedience to a subconscious impulse which psychologically and physiologically directs the mechanism of my bodily frame. A world in which the plants come and go and the stars are lit and are quenched again according to the same law which rocks my cradle and puts my coffin into the grave. A world in which the tides run and the ebbs go out in obedience to the same law that calls tears from in my eyes, and wrings from my heart its sighs.

That world is indeed more easily lived in than was Olympus, though the gods have departed and beauty has retreated to its natal chamber, the imagination of man.

And again, my friends, we cannot with our increase of knowledge believe that we are living in a small world. And the larger the world in which our lot is cast the larger also is our own life.

How petty was the life before science had linked continent unto continent. Before the evening-star was made by man's will neighbor to the rising sun, what interest had they that drew breath in an age when the world was still contracted within the shallow range of each man's native heath?

Think ye back, ye who are older, did your life sing with as deep a melody when you were young as does the life of your own children today? What do men live by? By the range of their sympathies.

What is really the ripest fruit on the tree? Humanity! That interest and sympathy which we take in our fellow-man.

In ancient days, fellow-man was the one who belonged by accident of birth to your family, to your tribe, to your race, to your nation. Today, what tokens the family? A speck in a cosmos. Today, what is clan? But a drop in the ocean. Today, what is even nation? The world has become larger.

When we take our morning coffee, we listen to the gossip of Peking and to the street-cries of Paris. Today while we are preparing to leave our home to repair to our workshop on the way from the peaceful hearthstone to the war-disturbed counting room, we learn what emperors have decided who are enthroned over empires by thousands of leagues removed from our own life-place.

Today, what solitary thinkers have thought out in the solitude of their closet, what bold discoverers have wrenched from jealous nature, these things are ours. The world has become larger, and in this larger world a small religion cannot be a power and cannot bear fruit.

The dogmas of old were expressions of the petty religions, and were reflections of narrowed horizons. They are the children of days when knowledge was not abundant. Now with our abundance of knowledge could we believe that our God, the God of this larger world, the God who made the earth and who made also the distant solar systems removed from our earth by uncounted millions of miles, can we believe that God presided over the birth of the universe as would a carpenter direct the shaping of one of his creation?

Can we today coerce a timeless world-time almost into the term of six days? Can we hold that six thousand years are the measure of the heartthrobs of this larger universe. We feel that this enlarged universe.which science has shown us requires a larger God.

The very doubt that fullness of knowledge has brought about has established God's throne on much more secure foundation than it ever had when ignorant priest or prelate pointed out the nails with which God's temple had been held together in the desert.

The larger God is required by the larger knowledge to doubt, of course is not comfortable, and the call to doubt is duty, which demands like every other duty self-sacrifice. It is comfortable not to doubt, but they who never doubt have forfeited really that which is the most intensely human privilege.

Some of our acquaintances, both to the left and to the right of us, both because they pretend to be of our religion and also because they insist that the preliminary religion is the final one, will sneer at the duty to think out religious opinions.

Especially those that are of our religion are generally attributed with admiration on our own part, we think that their intelligence is of the keenest, that their knowledge is of the deepest. If they announce no religion, we bow before them, and we cannot understand that our admiration is not shared by others.

We feel offended certainly if from pulpit or in religious press the suggestion is made that these wonderful graduates of our colleges, our sons and daughters, have not after all attained ultimate wisdom. They do not doubt. What is their mind's attitude? Is it different from that of the child?

They are done with thinking. Is their condition variant from that of the monkey and the animal? This Philistinism, which has brought all this about, is the curse of our modern generation. Men that doubt are men that are intensely alive to the implications of truth. Men that have not doubted have never passed through the discipline of self examination.

Will you admire a man who makes a pretense at despising music? There are men who cannot enjoy music let alone that they will understand it, men and women alas too who feel much more pleasure in a tune ground out by an old street-organ than majestic symphony—the revelation of genius of Beethoven or of Brunz; but they are abnormal, they are not of the highest type.

None will say that men so disorganized as not to have responsive consciousness to music are

HE WHO KNOWS MOST DOUBTS MOST 47

the nobler representatives of our race. There are those that have no sense of culture; you can show them a painting by Raphael, a Murillo, a Van Dyke, they will merely ask "how much does it cost?"

And when they are told that some of these paintings cannot be bought they will shrug their shoulders and say that they can get for a thousand dollars a much newer painting in a much finer frame. And if you come home with them, in their palaces they will show you that their statement is true.

They are considered unfortunates, even if we are charitable enough not to call them vulgar, earthy, nasty. There are those that have no ear for rhyme and poetry. Read to them Homer's Iliad they fall asleep. Read to them an ode by never so great a man and they will become impatient, they have much greater pleasures than to listen to a succession of words. These men are not the highest, that is conceded on all hands. But when it comes to religion, there we are.

Now, what is the trouble with these men? They lack a certain sense, that sense has been allowed to be atrophied. By disuse it has died. The fish in the mammoth cave of Kentucky have no eyes. Why not? Because the sun has never reached them. Born in darkness, they spend their life in darkness.

Are these the highest of men? No. Their intelligence is by no means so keen as you think it is. They have never doubted, and therefore they lack consciousness that there is beyond the visible something which must be probed, that beyond the palpable there are forces that can be felt, and their life is the poorer, to them pleasure will stale and even success will lose its flavor.

Ultimately, man is what he thinks. We live our life in our thoughts. They who have never doubted have never thought, and they who have never doubted on the higher themes lack a source of power which can only come from inquiry into those momentous questions.

Why are we? Whence come we? Whither tend we? What means all this struggle? Why the sighs and the sorrows? Why the tears and the suffering? Why success and why failure? What am I to my next door neighbor? Why am I in this age, not in another?

These are fundamental problems, and in a measure we grasp them even if we do not finally answer them, our life becomes larger and our knowledge becomes deeper. They mistake religion's province who believe that it is a safe guide to the hereafter.

Religion is for this life, and our religious exercises have the purpose to make us understand our life with its labors and its luster, its lapses and its great achievements, all the more profoundly. We are the richer for coming here. They are the poorer who have no ears for those insistent questionings which awaken in the heart of him who knows most.

And finally, friends, the truth of this remark is also plainly indicated in the relations which man sustains to society, What is the trouble today? There are men in Germany that have said the people know too much, that they were happy and contented before they were admitted to the privilege of leaving behind their ignorance; they have reasoned it out, and seemingly correctly, that the cheapening of coal and oil, the introduction of electricity as the weapon wherewith to fight the night, have made it possible for men to read and that these men have become the agitators.

Yea, they have, and the statement is borne out by the facts. Today, the man who has nothing to sell but his hands may in the evening find the books, the book of Marx, the book of LaSalle, the book of Engles, books of sociology, books of political economy, he may pore over them until the midnight hour, for the oil that chases the midnight hour away and robs it of its terror has become cheap, and as long as the means of illuminating was small most workmen used a piece of wood stuck in the wall as the methods of illumination.

So long as this was the sole means of robbing night of its jealousy and of its ignorance no workman could dream or think of becoming the intimate friend of the greatest students of our social development. Today, they know their Marx, their Engle, and their LaSalle, much more deeply and thoroughly than our ordinary college graduates.

It is true the social condition is under examination. Is that to be deplored as little as was the fact to be lamented over that religion has through doubt examined its preliminary propositions?

Will you hold that our state, as it is, is perfect? I daresay none of you will have the shameless hardihood to insist that because he rides on the crest of the wave that wave must ever be regarded as God-willed and God-spun.

This very skepticism as to the justice of things as they are will be a wing for humanity to lift itself to higher regions. We must pass through this condition of doubt. It is the misfortune of men who are possessors that they do not increase in knowledge. It is to their own detriment that they with ready-made principles of social adjustment would in their transactions have their own working people proceed on the traditional plan.

Much of the bitterness of the strife would be obviated if we would take the trouble to become acquainted as thoroughly with the literature and the facts and the figures as are these men. They are one-sided. Are we less one-sided? But their one-sidedness is the one-sidedness of knowledge.

Ours is the one-sidedness of ignorance. Indeed, the successful businessman might learn a thing or two from the poor agitator in our ghetto and in the slums. Do not think that we are the better classes, that only among us is found any appreciation of the higher things of life.

The most touching incident that I have ever read is found in an article written a few weeks ago for the "Outlook" by Jacob Reese, a great friend of President Roosevelt and the man who more than any other contributed to the final defeat of that shameful organized corporation known as Tammany Hall in New York.

Speaking of what awaited the sweeping broom of men righteously indignant at the outrages committed in the name of party fealty and for party purposes, he remembers that the crusade for betterment was really initiated by the remark of a poor Russian Jewish boy between fifteen and seventeen years of age at a gathering addressed by Felix Adler. The professor of ethical culture had told these people that though their circumstances were circumscribed still even for them the higher life was a possibility.

Speaking as no one else can of the transcendent beauty of virtue as central in the universe, he had aroused the heart of every one of his poor hearers. The lecture ended. A young boy arose and said "You go home, you go home. Where is my home," and he proceeded to detail the horrors of a tenement lodging-house, horrors of physical filth and of moral foulness, he described against whom he would have to brush when he climbed up the slimy stairs to his garret-room, and from whom he had to snare even this room.

"You go home, the higher life for you is easy. What is it for us?" That speech struck the flame, the spark from which came the flame that has utterly consumed Tammany Hall. That speech taught Felix Adler that even beyond his theories there were other things to look after before the eternal, which is his God, might speak out in the full majesty of its sublimity.

And like that young boy there are thousands of other people in slums and ghettos who know, and therefore they doubt. We do not know, and therefore we do not doubt.

He who knows most doubts most. The child does not doubt. The ignorant man does not doubt. Half-taught man, the self-taught man who may have read Spencer before his mind was even able to digest Little Mother Goose, and now, like with every undigested food, is burdened with mental dyspepsia because he has eaten what he never has digested, he never doubts.

They do not doubt whose religion is childish, they do not doubt whose religion is preliminary, they do not doubt who do not know enough to understand what the social economy and the ethical import of religion be. But they who know doubt, and doubting have a larger religion, a larger God, and therefore lead a fuller life.

The businessman is required today to also have—and our universities are opening their doors for that purpose—a college training for businessmen on business subjects: insurance, finance, banking—for calculators of probabilities, the geographical conditions, the tariff legislations, and the principles and the economic arrangements of distant nations and neighboring peoples.

These things a man who wants to be a trained merchant and not merely a trader, must know, and knowing he must doubt, and doubting he will lead a deeper life. A man who wants today to be the man that he should be must know how society came to be. He must, knowing this, doubt that our present social condition is just, and doubting this he will have deeper sympathy with struggling humanity.

Duty is uncomfortable. It is much easier to deal in crystallized dogmas; be those dogmas of commerce, dogmas of political economy or dogmas of religion. It is difficult to find your way through the mazes of duty to an ultimate inherent and in itself complete conception of the world and construction of life.

Our weather prophets have discovered that as long as they merely take their observations at a comparatively low altitude their prognostications are vitiated frequently by unexpected currents. Knowing this, the great meteorologists have therefore devised the system of sounding the higher regions of the atmosphere. They have sent up in America thousands of kites carrying self-registering barometers, thermometers and hygrometers, the altitudes reaching sometimes to twelve and thirteen thousand feet above the level of the sea.

In France they have sent out what they call *ballons de sondeur*, which sound the depths of the oceans of air which surround our spinning globe, and hence the thinner the air the higher they go. Some of these *ballons de sondeur* have gone as high as forty-six thousand feet, and the thermometers have registered the degree of cold at the altitude of thirty-eight thousand feet.

We must do the same things. As long as our instruments are merely thermometers that are near the surface of the earth, their combined readings will give us not the surety of prognostication. Rise higher, away from your selfishness; send up your kites, your *ballons de sondeur* as it were into the higher altitudes; let the instruments there register and read what they say.

Then from the dew which lays the dust will be declared the eternally divine.

Amen.

THE JEWISH PREACHER:
Rabbi Emil G. Hirsch, Ph.D., LL.D.

Yes

Sunday, January 5th 1902
Lesson: I Kings 18

Little words, much wisdom. The unconscious architects of our linguistic cathedrals have placed great strength within the compass of mere monosyllables. Upon their correct use depends clearness of expression. Their introduction or omission gives wings to thought or freights it with dragging weight, but it is not merely in the exchange of thought where these little tokens play an important part. None of you, friends I daresay, but may recall that an utterance of a little word at the proper or improper moment has given twist and turn to his own fortune and fate. Had we spoken the right term at the critical moment we might have escaped disappointment. Had we foregone speaking one of those little words, we might perhaps have garnered the harvest which now fills the granary of another.

The importance, then, of these little terms is recognized both by the grammarian and by the common-sense of men. In the higher domain of moral action, in the region of intellectual conceptions, these little monosyllables have indeed a high dignity and a far-reaching function. It is for this reason that I venture to invite you to a series of discussions on these little words often neglected yet always so vital in their far-reaching consequences.

Yes is the term of assent, acquiescence and affirmation. In the whole company of verbal currency, I know none that outranks this in emphasis and in possibilities. And yet one who is acquainted with the thought drift of our age cannot but come to the conclusion that the disinclination to deal in strong and positive affirmations has grown within recent years. I, for my part, do not hesitate to say that the supreme need of our generation is to understand once more the necessity of cherishing and coining positive convictions.

Our religious life is suffering from the lack of positive, strong, well-determined and well-defined formulations of aims and of goals, of principles and of positions. Our public life, too, manifests the symptoms of the same wasting malady. Everywhere indefiniteness, where definiteness might perhaps work a marvelous change. In literature and in art the same tendency is discernible. Character, in other words, is lacking, for character is always positive, it is never indefinite or negative.

Now, it is easy to understand why we of this age are disinclined to formulate our thoughts positively, to state our views of life and world in resonant affirmations. Men, like water, follow the line of least resistance. Nature has fashioned man under a burden of indolence; inertia is not merely to be overcome in the planetary system, it is not merely a factor to be reckoned with in the formulae of economics. The engineer is not the only one that has to remember the all-pervading power of this negative force—if force it be—this condition which results in a disinclination to do, to move, which culminates in an attitude of listless abiding ease.

In our thoughts, in our ambitions as far as they extend to the domain of the intellectual and the moral, indolence and inertia also appear. It is much easier to analyze than to synthesize; to criticize seems an exercise of mental faculty, but at all events whatever place it may hold in the hierarchy of intellectual occupation it is less exacting in expenditure of intellectual force than is the effort to construe, to combine, to build up. And thus intellectually we of this generation have become mere critics.

In the religious field the same phenomenon appears. Religious liberalism has taken on, to the exclusion of every other wish and every other aim, the occupation of the critic. We analyze the concepts of the fathers; we examine the practices of our antecedents. We refuse to accept as final verity the statements that our ancestors left behind as expressive of the higher truths. We reject their notions concerning the origin of life and the destiny of all that draw breath. We refuse to recognize as valid their notions concerning revelation, bible, morality, the relations that man sustains to the source of all life, to the Deity.

Yea, and rightly so, we have put under the lens the highest concept that human mind ever formulated or human tongue ever stammered forth. We will not describe him in the exuberant vocabulary of our own forbears. God has become under that process, a shadowy indication of some mystery, some unsolvable quantity, rather than a real energy, a mind controlling the all and a heart aglow with a love for the largest and for the least.

We have criticized, and we continue to criticize; it is an easy pastime, which requires little outlay of force, but the consequence has been that liberalism has lost all pith It is reduced to impotency. Enthusiasm and passion are the prerequisites of constructive work.

In the whole domain of nature, new birth is conditioned upon preceding passion. Without its fire, chaos or consuming death would be scepter. It is only through this vitality of passion, fire glowing within, that worlds are renewed, plants are perpetuated, and the race is continued. Not merely within the range of physical procreation is this the law. No poet has ever sung except his soul was stirred under passion, no reformer has ever spoken unless fire volcanic, energy excessive of impatience, has taken possession of his soul. No artist has ever put chisel to marble or brush to canvas unless his mind, his whole being was set ablaze by a passion of thought, by a germinating idea.

Why is modern liberalism in religion absolutely so impotent? Contrast the work done by the liberal churches with the accomplishments of the most orthodox. The orthodox faith is positive; it may not be abreast of the discoveries of science, it may deal in antiquated notions concerning the world's creation and the origin of men's faith, it may be under the pall of fear, it may perhaps be stirred by apprehensions of what awaits man after death. Miracle may also perhaps be invoked to strengthen the demands of the orthodox faith.

But with all this, that faith is a power in the life of the faithful, it is an energy in the constitution of society. By that faith millions live and millions die. That faith sends out missionaries to brave dangers. It may be an illusion that lifts them up and carries them, as Muhammad was in the fables of Islam, on invisible angels' hands across oceans and deserts, mountains and jungles; but it carries them. It may be that error they offer in exchange for fallacies as easily recognized, but they affirm their position, they proselytize, they wish to change, they are anxious to influence the actions and attitudes of their fellow men.

Why this? The answer is ready. The orthodox faith is positive, and enthusiasm and passion can only leap forth at the positive pole of man's intellectuality and morality. Mere criticism is only preparatory, it tears down an old building but it cannot rear a new one. We cannot live in ruins; we cannot find shelter in houses the roofs of which have been taken off and the walls of which show dangerous cracks. This negative liberalism has taken off the roof, it has with its axe struck cracks in the walls, it has weakened the foundations. But beyond this it has done nothing, and hence it could not kindle a flame of passion, and therefore it cannot lead to a new creation.

Again, this obsession of negation is due to a false inference from a correct premise. We argue, and apparently with good justification that after all, our positive statements are only relatively absolute. Since Kant's days, and his thesis were merely reiterated by Herbert Spencer, we have come to recognize that all our knowledge is under the limitations of relativity. We can never know things as they are, we only know them as they appear to us, and we can never pierce through the source of all life and cognize God or the source of The All as he or it is in himself or in itself. We can only predicate of that source our own ignorance and such appearances of relations, as our mind may perhaps be able to grasp and to formulate.

This relativity of knowledge is also illustrated in a way, as to be easily understood by even such as have not studied technical metaphysics, in the recollection emphasized by daily experience that what yesterday was hailed as truth is today swept aside as error.

We know the time was when men believed that the earth was flat. Today, we maintain that the earth is round. Was then astronomy a guide unto truth when it operated with the notion of the earth being the center of the planetary family? And who guarantees to us that not tomorrow some new facts may wheel within the range of human understanding and observation which will set aside, as the Copernican system has the Ptolemaic, this our modern astronomy? We have weaponed our eyes with such potent instruments that when formerly physics and chemistry maintained that the number of the elements were limited, we today entertain serious doubts concerning this—the assurance but yesterday of the boldest physicists and the most competent chemists.

A few years ago they discovered a new element, argon, of which chemists before that day had been in absolute ignorance. We see that, turning from the domain of natural observations, the same law holds good in reference to problems lying within the plane of religious thought. Time was when People accepted the statements of the bible without further proof as authentic. Then came the period of rationalism. Rationalists still operated with the texts of the bible, they did not dream then that the text itself might perhaps be examined and found in itself to be, not a record of an actual occurrence but the precipitate of a poetic conception.

The rationalists did not doubt that Israel crossed the Red Sea. They did not doubt that Israel was fed in the desert on manna but they interpreted the record, which they never questioned according to their own way of thinking. "They crossed the Red Sea, but it was at a time when the winds had blown aside the dangerous tides of the ocean." "They were fed in the desert, certainly, but it was not manna from heaven that sustained them in those dire days, but some substance that oozed from a peculiar kind of tree, and Moses only a great Juggler he, a hypnotist of transcendent powers, made his people believe that his staff had control over the waves and that his prayer had opened the larder of the heavens and called down from thence the sustaining food." The rationalist was certain that his method was the exclusively correct one.

But lo and behold, today men are in the pulpits that will not acknowledge that the rationalist has discovered the key to the mystery. Men are in the pulpits today who have but little respect for the rationalist.

Men are in the pulpits today who, having learned of the new science of biblical literature, will not waste time upon the futile attempt to save the account. Never perhaps did Israel cross the Red Sea; never perhaps did Israel feast on manna in the desert. Ah, then, are these accounts bold inventions? No, they are the result of mythological historiography, their meaning lies in something else than the literalness of the account; their value is on another plane than is the recorded word.

Where now, then, is truth absolute? The physicist has no certainty that his theories will be triumphant over the mutations of time. The chemist cannot cherish the assurance that what he advances to lift the curtain from off the mystery of affinities and combination will have the same function twenty years after he hath vacated his post in the laboratory. The critical student of literature deals in hypotheses, which may perhaps tomorrow give way to another theory. Where then is absolute truth?

And thus our modern, pale, pithless, sapless liberalism, from this high and true premise, draws the inference that you must never have an affirmation because forsooth tomorrow what you affirmed yesterday will have to be modified. Did we refuse to burn anything else because even then the presumption was that candles would give way to gas jets? Did we sit in darkness because forsooth we knew that even gas as an illuminating medium was but temporary? Did we refuse to lay the rails in our streets, because we knew or hoped that sooner or later the horse would be replaced as the motive-power by some mechanical contrivance? Do we not still today, without grumbling, put up with a now antiquated method, the cable, when we know that sooner or later it is to be replaced by the trolley wire?

Certainly, it would be foolish for us to remain in our houses in darkness, because we may perhaps tomorrow find that the prevailing system of furnishing light has given way to a better mechanical appliance. It would be foolish for us to discontinue walking because an automobile perfected is perhaps the vehicle in which our grandchildren will scorn to ride, because it too will have been left behind by the onward discoveries of mechanical genius.

Yet in our mental homes, here we are, we liberals, we will not affirm lest forsooth tomorrow we shall have to modify. Modify we must, but we must for all this have a potent, strong Yes. We must affirm. It is time, liberalism, to get out of our silly inane, insane negations. Criticize you have for years. Have you not before your eyes the consequences of your mere negative attitude? Have you influenced those that are in nature destined to take your places?

The great key to this fact is within easy grasp.

Our mere negations could not kindle passion, they could not influence others, and they could not stir others. Better the rankest positive orthodoxy than this continual inane, pithless negative liberalism. Orthodoxy at least influences, it stirs; it fires. The negative liberalist neither stirs nor fires. He himself still believes that to be enthusiastic about anything is a sign of mental weakness. Mental weakness? The greatest men have been the most glowing enthusiasts. It was their enthusiasm that made them great. No man can be great unless that divine flame be glowing and burning within him.

Another reason why we are so loath to be positive is that the positive man naturally is the angular man; being positive, he cannot be elastic; being positive, he cannot easily adjust himself to his surroundings, desirous and competent to mould circumstance he will not readily yield to condition and environment, but he who wishes to be popular must never rise above the populous, he must be one of the mob, he must not affect to be himself. Positive men are themselves, they go through the crowd and their angularity naturally comes in contact and in collision with others, he cannot move about without giving a push here and a jolt there; wishing to move, he has to step, and if the crowd is too thick he cannot help stepping upon the pet corns of some one in his way, he cannot be popular, he is too angular for others. The cur moves through the crowd much more smoothly, he can turn much more readily. Angularity deprives you of this faculty and of this facility of wiggling your way through the crowd.

Hence, as we desire popularity we will not honor angularity. Positive character is an offense to the mob. The mob only loves the demagogue. The demagogue has the ability of saying nothing, of dealing in everything except an eternal, strong, sharply-defined Yes!

He has his ear to the ground, he receives his instruction from below not from above. Men of positive character cannot be demagogues. The demagogue must have versatility, he must in one breath call black white and white black, he must always be ready to call smooth rough and rough smooth, sweet sour and sour sweet. His positivity, if he had it, would be a hindrance and not a help, and hence we modern men who believe in majority and are misled by that most specious of all specious fallacies—*vox populi vox dei*—that what the mob shouts is the revelation of the divine truth, we would not be angular for then the majority, the mob would not approve of our attitude or of our action.

I have now given you the three reasons explanatory of the phenomena, our disinclination to positive statements of conviction and to positive defense of our principles.

What is Judaism? We believe in one God. That is a protest against polytheism. We believe in one God, that is a negation of trinitarianism. We believe not in the New Testament, we believe not in the Koran, we believe not in the Tripi-Karta of the Buddhist. We believe not in the Zend-Avesta.

"Thou shalt have no other Gods before me. Thou shalt not take the name of thy Lord in vain. Thou shalt not kill. Thou shalt not steal. Thou shalt not give false testimony. Thou shalt not covet." It is to the eternal *not* that the rhythm of the Jewish message is set, so we are told. And great men have led us to believe that this is truth absolute.

I grant you that Judaism is not positive in reference to the hidden things. Judaism has never authoritatively formulated its belief in the deity. Think of God in whatever terms you choose, no Jew has the right to tell you that you are outside of the pale of Judaism. Whether God be personal or impersonal, whether he be one or three or ten, assent to this or dissent from this, it does neither make nor unmake the Jew. Judaism again gives you margin in which to move about, without let or leave, concerning your opinions about biblical books and Talmudic documents. But for all this, and add the fact that Judaism has no positive statements concerning the life to-be, I say if you believe that Judaism is merely a negative quantity and therefore a negligible quantity, you are mistaken.

Your liberalism has still to learn the alphabet of Judaism. There is one positive statement that Judaism stands for; to weaken that would enfeeble the synagogue to such an extent that it could not stand, and for that positive statement we must still stand, be the historical witnesses of our enthusiastic prophets. What is it? Judaism does not pivot on theology, but it centers in anthropology. Not God, but man, is the solicitude of the Jew. And Judaism teaches in positive terms that man being more than brute or beast has other laws by which to shape his life than those that control the stars and the rocks and the rivers and the plants and the planets.

Whatever psychology on a physiological basis may advance, whatever ethical speculation may have us assume, whether the moral instinct be linked to our bodily frame and the thought-spark be but the flash coming from brain substance, or whether thought be something that working in brain substance is not the child of gray matter, or our moral conscience be a phenomenon undetermined by the elements of our dust, this is immaterial.

The positive Yes of Judaism is that no matter how thought came to man, and no matter what the pedigree of conscience be and the roots of morality, man is a thinking moral agent, he is under the law not of brute-power but of spiritual relations. That is the positive statement that Judaism has to advance. And by our history we have the right, the duty, the responsibility of being leaders in this the regenerated positive movement towards making men—the highest and the lowest among men—men, not beasts; men, not machines; men, not beasts of prey, but brothers, co-operators.

With no's and negatives we can accomplish nothing. The hour has come for liberalism, of whatever stripe or dialect, to leave the playroom of infancy. Little boys and little girls in the nursery may think they are doing wonders if they split the head of a doll and perform a surgical operation on the sawdust-stuffed belly of poor little harlequin. The little boy may take pleasure in breaking up a watch, he may want to see "the wheels go round", he may destroy every toy that he has received, and as a rule he does. The boy grows tired, too, of the drum; after making the neighborhood almost inhospitable by the noise he evokes through the magic of his drumsticks he finally wants to find out what is in the drum and he sticks the drumsticks through the drum and of course is then disappointed.

Our so-called liberalism has been almost exclusively of this order. We have made considerable noise with our drums. We have made people feel that it were time to move away, by our ten-cent whistles, by our little toy-trumpets. Ta-ra-ra-ra-ra! We are great! We are great! We are making a noise, we are playing in our nursery, we have drawn our wooden swords, put also a paper cap on the head of one and another, with a feather or an imitated bush in it, and put some epaulettes on another.

We have marched to war like little children, but the time has come for these nursery antics to be laid aside. The times are too serious for beating drums and playing on toy whistles and making life unbearable to neighbors by playing on toy trumpets. We must be out of work. We have been playing, and more serious men have gone out to work. It is time for us again to say Yes; to have a positive conviction, and as soon as we have that we may hope to influence others. Being aglow with our own enthusiasm, we may by its heat set ablaze the hearts of others and illuminate the minds of others.

Little words. Much wisdom. The Master's style shows this. Daily experience verifies his observation.

But in the domain of morals, in the region of religious aspiration, these little words also have their far-reaching energy, and especially that one little word. Yes. We must become positive. About the problems of life we must have a positive answer. Negative prepares, but is not final. Negative cannot strengthen and cannot impel, but the positive even if it has to be verified is a source of power. You may change your belting in the machine; you may arrange the wheels differently so as to save energy, light and fuel. You may contrive appliances whereby the steam once employed may once more be harnessed to the driving wheel, but after all you must have fuel.

Fuel is enthusiasm, and the mind out of which that fuel comes is a positive, definite, a strong conviction, a conception in plus terms of world and life, not merely in minus signs and syllables. Let me wish to you, on this first Sunday of the New Year, a greater zeal for a positive religious conviction, a conviction which will also engender a greater enthusiasm for a positive work in the redemption, the rehumanizing of the world at large.

Amen.

THE JEWISH PREACHER:
Rabbi Emil G. Hirsch, Ph.D., LL.D.

A Lesson From Plato's Apology Of Socrates

Sunday, May 6, 1906
Reading: The general subject of Truth, comprising passages from Jewish literature and from other writings.

The righteous shall shine like the stars in the firmament, with an effulgence of glory that shall know no setting. If to anyone this paraphrase of the sentiment, which is the final chord of the biblical Book of Daniel applies, it does to Socrates. He, the Greek, fellowships with the prophets of all nations; he keeps company with Buddha of India, Zoroaster of Persia, Isaiah of Babylon, with Confucius of the furthest East.

We cannot think of the greatest without including his name in our offering of gratitude. His day, however, failed to recognize his worth; he shared the fate of the best of our race, which must work out their heart in futile effort, only to be condemned to death by the very ones for whose elevation they shed their life's blood and spent the richest their genius contained.

As that of a martyr to convictions, of a victim to the prejudice and myopia of his contemporaries, his name symbols such service as is always asked of the truest of men. Centuries gap between his day and our own, we have not risen measurably above his neighbors that refused to listen to his appeal or tower above his opponents that sentenced him to death.

His most illustrious pupil, eager to do honor to the character of the man, has left behind what he calls an apologia, a defense of the master. He privileges us to be present at the final trial when Socrates confronts his judges. We are bidden listen to the speech addressed by the accused to the court.

Plato, a master of style without many peers, has perhaps written nothing that ranks in perfection of good taste and flow of easy speech with this plea of defense put by him into the mouth of his beloved teacher. Every sentence of the address is ringing, not with resentment at the indignity offered, but with the consciousness of the speaker's worth; every word uttered by Socrates is vital with the energy of truth. Pity, not contempt, much deep love, not withering scorn, inspire every paragraph, and lend pathos to every statement and exposition.

It would lead me too far afield to give a complete analysis of the argument put forth by Socrates in rebuttal of his accusers' arraignment. At the very threshold we must tarry, leaving an inspection of the interior, as it were, to some other visit. In the very exordium of the oration we meet an observation that cannot but be fruitful to us—provided we understand it perfectly.

Why was Socrates pilloried? Why was he accused? Why were motives imputed to him that he and his friends knew were not his? Why was he credited with intentions of which he was deeply conscious to be innocent? His experience is but typical of what men that feel the call to speak when truth flames and burns within them have always had to encounter.

Socrates had been charged with atheism. They had accused him of dethroning the gods, misleading the young men into disrespect for the ancient divinities. The word atheism has had a wonderfully instructive history. This term always has found lips ready to syllable it when the world was about to move onward. It is always heard in the streets when a great man has appeared who urges an indolent generation to effort. The best of the race have been branded as atheists, for an atheist is always deemed he who refuses to bend his knee before the fetish, be they made of stone or of thought, at the altar of which thoughtless or selfish men prostrate and prostitute themselves.

The so-called atheist dared voice the conviction that the gods, worshiped by the masses and the mob, are but counterfeit deities. He who destroys the idols will always be stigmatized atheist by them who have an interest—egotistical, narrow—maintaining in splendor the sanctuaries of old, but wretchedly inadequate, representations of what is beyond all form; what to express the human mind has no power and the human tongue no eloquence.

In these our modern days, of course, we have abandoned the terminology of theology. Even when we wish to affix to an opponent the stigma of dangerous intention, we do not consult the dictionary formerly gleaned by the religious fanatic. We do not libel men atheists today for our conceit considers vocal atheism a mark of progress upward and onward. We hail him who denies what is invisible as one consecrated by a deeper consciousness of truth. But we resort in the same narrow spirit to other phraseology. Our jargon does not lack expressions whereby to label as dangerous one of our society. Formerly, in the day of Socrates, in the day of Abraham, the greatest men, the pioneers, were decried as atheists. Today we denounce the men that call for the advance, as our vocabulary is different, socialists and anarchists. Our method and motive have remained unchanged.

Men do not like to be disturbed. In every age there have been men to whom profit and position accrued from the world's immobility. In the days of Socrates the priests, those that had comfortable berths at the oracles and the temples; the sophists that made it their business to dress up in plausible argument, old exploded theories; the sophists that by their skill effaced the lines between truth and falsehood—these, and many more, had a deep concern that no one should be led to probe to the foundations of belief, that no one should be stirred to recognize that which had so long passed for truth was, after all, but preliminary, a faltering step toward more complete truth.

Socrates had dared inquire. He had tested and examined. They, therefore, called him atheist; they contrived to bring him before the court as a corrupter of the young.

In a memorable meeting with the old prophet Elijah, King Ahab says "Art thou the disturber of

Israel?" The prophet replies: "Not I, but thou." The men that sound the advance are not the disturbers of Israel, though petty monarchs on the throne may dislike their proclamation, and sluggards may deplore their insistent urging. They do undoubtedly strike terror into the petty minds of men who, cankered by selfishness, cannot understand that what shall be of benefit to one, must also be of use to all. That only through the common wealth of all can individual possession be sanctified and rendered legitimate. Let them that will, call these Elijah's the disturbers of Israel.

In a theological age such disturbers were branded atheists, but these atheists prophesied of a profounder knowledge of God. In industrial civilization they would make "socialist" a byword of reproach. Yet true socialism has been the inspiration of the noblest lovers of our kind just as the despised atheists have always been the pioneers of progress.

Think what would have been the result if there had been no Abraham to smash the idols; if there had been no Moses to teach Pharaoh that a new God had spoken to him out of the burning bush. If there had been no Isaiah and no Jeremiah to bring home to the mighty on earth that not sacrifice and not prayer, but righteousness was the fulfillment of God's law.

They killed Socrates, did they not? He drank the cup of hemlock, but who gave Greece immortal life? The conservative judges that pronounced the sentence against him? No. The teacher whose mouth they wished to close forever still speaks to us across the centuries. His word, as heard throughout the world, is still ringing with prophetic accent. It still is competent to awaken in human hearts spontaneous enthusiasm for the genuinely true, good and beautiful.

Socrates was mainly charged with atheism because he believed and taught that the standard of truth was to be found within man, not without him. He brought down ethics from heaven; he showed mortality to be rooted in the very nature of man. What the prophets of Israel contend he, too, had realized; his god was the god within. He felt in addition to his material corporeality, he had a spiritual and mental entity. This personality when activated, he called his divine demon.

So in every man there was body, but in the body there lived mind and spirit, and society was intended to bring forth the concordance of all spirits, the harmony of all striving souls. That was his crime.

If there never had been a Johanan ben Lakkai to bring home to his generation that even if the temple was fallen and the altars thrown anon, there was in mercy and in benevolence an ample compensation for sacerdotal ritual. And in righteousness and in the search for truth Israel held the secret of rejuvenation, making it strong to outlast the destruction of state and to survive even the passing away of the sanctuary.

What if there never had been a reformer in Israel to call the Jewish congregations to the recognition that legalism, if mechanized, was fatal to the development of character? What if there never had been heard voices telling us that not in prayer and not in official observance of days set aside by others as sacred, but in righteous conduct and in love were to be found the consummation of Israel's religious intentions? What would have been the course of human history?

And yet, every one of the men whose names I have mentioned, every one of the band that caught the spirit of the new day before its birth, when the world around them was still wrapped in the thickest of night, was branded an atheist—simply because he had heard God speak in a new voice and had read the law of god in a new alphabet.

Alas today, having outgrown old theological preoccupation, because the sweep of our life has taken on the rhythm of industrial and commercial activities, we change indeed our vocabulary, but the old intention abides. Everyone looked for his throne there, therefore he was an atheist. But the temple of the gods that he was said to have overthrown have fallen into ruins.

Socrates' creed, if creed it was, his confidence in the spirituality of man, has become the common property of all thinkers, and today we pilgrim to his grave—if grave of his there were—today we lay tribute before his memory, knowing that though he died a criminal in the eyes of his day's law, he was the prophet of generations unborn, the teacher of truth ever more and more brilliantly unfolding, and ever more and more brilliantly enlightening the minds of all.

What were the tactics of his opponents? In the speech which Plato puts on the lips of his master before the tribunal Socrates complains that they attributed to him the conceit to be able to turn good into evil, to make the higher the lower; that he aspired to the possession of obscure art and denied that such possession had come to any other mortal.

In other words, they attempted to make him ridiculous at first. They wanted to make him out what we would call today, an eccentric crank; they wanted the people to distrust his sanity; they called him a fantastic fool, claiming to possess powers not ordinarily given to man.

Today, when men point out that the great technical advances have not resulted in alleviating the lot of the masses, that they have accrued, as a rule, merely to the advantage of the few at the expense of the many. These men, too, are called first cranks when their name is mentioned; significant gestures are made to indicate that we must have patience with them because they ought to be patients in an insane asylum.

And especially is that the case when young people brought up under circumstances where the advantages of the social system accrued to them, step out and openly declare that they, even, have recognized the great wrong done to the masses under the prevailing system. Then certainly there is no doubt but these are cranky; they are insane; they go off, as the vulgar phrase has it, "half cocked," and their whole mental organization is out of the ordinary, and therefore is abnormal. Is this not true?

Is that not the criticism passed upon every one of the young men who of recent years have taken up the burden of the prophetic proclamation?

Far from believing that these increasing protests come from the well-to-do against the continuation of the present system—far from assuming that these phenomena are symptomatic of increasing insanity, they are the most hopeful signs of the time—when they who are the beneficiaries of our system have begun to feel that the system itself is susceptible of change and of correction. And that they speak out proves to any one who knows what has happened before, that a new day is about to dawn. That the poor should cry out, that indeed may perhaps be passed as normal and natural; that the rich shall cry out, like in the case of Socrates so in theirs, it is a sign that they are somewhat cracked-brained.

But it has always been for the cracked-brained men that the world has been moved onward and upward. The cracked-brained Socrates lifted up Athens to potency in the intellectual world that without his insanity, the world would never have grasped after or would have had the faintest presentiment. The cracked-brained martyrs to fate, cracked-brained patriots to country, they always have been fire-brands indeed that devoured the old, but that made room for the new. And many of these have been the builders of the new, the founders of the better things and the better institutions. They have been the teachers of the better words and of the better convictions.

In fact, every creative man or mind passes always for abnormal, for every one that knows how to do something, which others do not know is looked upon by them who know not, as an accusation against themselves. They cannot allow that they are not as perfect as he, but as he is distinct from them, they must blur the line of distancing by calling his distinction eccentricity.

Yes, the eccentric men, those that were out of the ordinary, like Socrates and Isaiah, like Huss and Luther, like the great prophets of modern times—the great so-called socialists and anarchists—they have always been the pathfinders.

And the path that they found and that they blazoned has by later generations been trodden, enlarged. That path has become in turn the ordinary, and after awhile again it became necessary that the eccentric person should arise and in eccentric speech call for the advance, and point in his own life the advance, and pay for his venture often by his own lifeblood.

And why did this Socrates incur the bitter hostility later of the men that first called him a crank and a fool? He also tells us why. According to Plato, Socrates had been told by the Delphic oracle that he was the wisest of all men in Greece. In his modesty he could not understand the meaning of this oracular declaration, and he set forth to refute it. He went forth to consult those that were in repute of being the wisest among the Greeks. Meeting them he discovered that if they were the wisest, he certainly was entitled to be called the wiser.

He went to the poets, the writers of drama; he thought they certainly would impress him as being wiser than he, and thus give the lie to this oracular declaration; but he found that outside of the passion, as he puts it, the romantic passion which they possessed, which depersonalized them, these men were not wiser than he. Then he thought to consult the artisans, the men of technical skill that had a vocation and a trade in which they excelled, and he found that they would do tricks which he would not do, not having enjoyed technical education, they were unwise to a degree simply appalling. And this, contrary to his own desire, the oracular declaration, that he was the wisest of the Greeks, had grown upon him.

Plato probably injects into this presentation something of his inclination to utilize mythological elements. Socrates probably did not believe that the Delphic oracle had spoken true, but that which roused hostility to Socrates was his insistence that wisdom was more than what was current under that name among the Greeks, and that they who claimed to be the wisest were after all not the wisest.

That is the case today. Men are expected to bow most humbly before the self-valuation of others. If one believes that he is the wisest, it is safest not to disturb that belief. You may deny today God, you may call into question veracity of history, but do not, if you value your comfort, cast the least doubt on the self-valuation of the men among whom you live, with whom perhaps you have to work. Everything will be forgiven save this. That is the unpardonable crime.

Socrates could not bring his conscience to be reconciled with connivance even with the self-valuation of the conceited and arrogant of his time. Here were the sophists, they declared to be in possession of all knowledge, they peddled out wisdom at so much per hour, they instructed the young people in the art of being wise. In their skill of argumentation they could change white into black, they could turn right into wrong. And they who were most skilled in doing this were hailed the wisest.

And here came Socrates walking about the market place, insisting that words shall have a definite meaning that what was right had to be right , and what was wrong was wrong; that you could not turn wrong into right and right into wrong. And in this, his insistence upon truth he brushed against the conceit of the professional sophists.

This crank had become exceedingly dangerous. Insane at first, he was now turned into a perilous fool, and hence, away with him; he does not recognize our superior wisdom.

What he says of the technical workers applies perhaps to our own day in a certain sense. This is the age when experts are required in every domain of human activity. In consequence of this we are specialized as never before. Even in commerce, even in the professions, specialization has progressed to such a pass that no one can claim today to be an expert in all the departments even of his profession, even of his business. Specialization alone seems to be able to save him who perfects himself in specialized specialization from being swept away into the great depersonalized current of dependency.

Organization on the one hand on a scale that has never before been attempted, and as a counteraction toward and against this organization, specialization. In an age where specialization is so intense because it is the ultimate anchor of safety, men. without any specialized specialty are looked upon as absolutely useless.

You can also state that in terms of profit. We always ask, what good does it do to us? Everything must do some good; some tangible effect must come to us; some palpable result that can be formulated in terms of the market or in terms of pleasure. What does not directly seem to be expressible in these terms we do not value.

So Socrates brushed against them, the technical workers They had skill which he did not have, but nevertheless he did declare he was the wiser of the two; that their wisdom was limited, and his apparently useless wisdom, was without limitations. Theirs was accidental; his was essential. And so he incurred the opposition of the men proud of their technical skill, who in their day anticipated the conceit of our own generation that the man who knows how to do a certain thing, to do it well and do it definitely, is superior to the man who does not know how to do a definite thing. But who speaks of the general principles, who points to broader outlooks, who insists upon deeper relations between man and man than those that are involved in the problem of doing this and doing that, and finally in the problem of *how to do* the doer of this or of that.

This applies especially to religion in these our days. Why do we need religion? We have outgrown the belief that we shall he punished or that we shall be rewarded in measure as our religiosity is intense or is pale and blurred. No one of us here, I at least, do not believe that for my coming here or your coming here we shall get a title to a reserved seat in heaven.

I am not afraid that if I do not come here or you do not, something terrible will befall me. I do not pretend to know what is in store for those who leave us. I do not know anything about the streets of heavenly Jerusalem. I know that some of my colleagues seem to know it. They seem every time that I hear them speak at a funeral to be so terribly certain in which street and which house in the heavenly Jerusalem the one that has left us is now residing. I cannot aspire to that knowledge. My Judaism is of a kind that does not pretend to give me information on that point. Nor is my religion of a kind that assures you.that if you practice it you will not have the earache and not the toothache, and not the toe-ache.

Why is this craze for Christian Science on the increase. Religion must be useful, religion must do something, than if you have Christian Science then you won't be sick. You can, at least, imagine that you are not sick. It may help those that have imagined themselves to be sick. By the putting of one "thought" in the place of another "thought", the original "thought" is crowded out, and certainly the "thought" that you believe you are not sick is more comfortable than the "thought" by which you believe you are sick.

I daresay many a woman has been the cross of the physicians. She has come to them with this ache and that ache and the third ache , and all three aches together. Every physician knew she was blasé and he had to do something for her, and occasionally he gave her what in common parlance would be merely sugar and water, and she believed that would help her. And as long as she believed that that would help her it did. But she now discovers the deception and it does not help her and she goes to a healer, and the healer puts into her mind something that makes her feel that she is well, and then she is well. That is a perfectly natural process.

As we have outgrown the belief that religion is a sort of a life insurance company for the hereafter and that the Rabbi has the power to sign a bill of lading which is recognized in heaven, an invoice on which you can often collect in advance, which you can get discounted at some bank or other.

Now what is the use of religion? Where does it come in? What does it do? What do you do? How often have I been asked what do you do the whole week?' How do you spend your time? What is the use of having you? Yes, we want to support you out of pity. Such cranks like you must be supported. They cannot make their living outside of that. But what do you do? What is the usefulness of it?

So was Socrates asked, according to Plato, by the men who had a special vocation, where is your wisdom? And Socrates had to bring home to them that his indefinite wisdom, as they thought it was, was of greater vitality then their definite skill. What is religion? What is philosophy? Philosophers have no specialty in the ordinary sense of the word. They are not physiologists as such; they are not historians as such; they are not physicists as such; but they take what the psychologist and the physiologist has discovered; they take what the historian has brought to light; they take the discoveries of the physicists and astronomers, and upon these as the bases they build up the vision of a world that is not in parts, but is a totality.

They show the inter-relation of the separate functions in this all-life, and out of this separation they bring into flower the consciousness that when the lightning flares out, or the ocean arises, or thought, even, flashes into our brain, there is an inter-relation between each phenomenon to a central purpose. The vitalizing of all this is beyond the grasp, as it lies outside the sphere of the specialized science. What Goethe calls the "geistige gewandt", the thread that binds it all together, that is what the philosopher is searching for. And in measure as he has discovered it, his philosophy becomes what the compass is to the mariner it points the needle to the North Pole in order that we may find track in the waste, the pathless waste of the ocean over which we sail.

And that is what modern theology ought to be, what Jewish theology is in fact. It is busy with the results furnished by other sciences. The modern theologian has to be a sociologist he has to be a student of ethics, and as ethics is expressed in literature and in institution, he has to be at home in the literature of ever so many nations and in the institutions of ever so many civilizations. He has to be at home in the psychology of the individual as well as of society. He has also to know what the great works are that are brought to completion in the laboratories where the chemists handle tests and physicists with delicate apparatus measure the flight of the sun or the length of an electric spark.

In all these things he cannot be an expert, but he must by no means be a stranger. And why all this? In order to bring together out of this disjecta membra, to use a Latin term, out of these disjointed limbs, a whole organism, a totality; to read purpose into what seems to be purposeless, and to show relation in what seems to be unrelated, and that especially with a view to the particular practical effect upon life.

It is characteristic of our day that we have not a comprehensive conception of life or of the interrelation of man to man. We are drifting without compass, and it is religion's duty today, whether you call religion ethical culture, or call it by whatever other name is indifferent. It is religion's duty and vocation today to give to this generation of ours again a consciousness of the inter-relation of the parts of life.

Each one of us is a part. The whole week we are this, we are that, we are the other thing. We are a merchant, we are a physician, we are a lawyer, we are a teacher, we are a preacher. We all have our prejudices, which means our narrow, contracted angles. We must get out of our part, up to the heights where we see again the totality, where the vision enlarges , in order that we may come to our senses.

That is what religion purposes to do for us, and that is the special function of the teacher of religion, always to search for the total things out of the mass of disjointed things. Ah, of course, the preacher is not an expert in literature, No, you who can read Gerhard Hauptmann, certainly you may. But if the preacher has had the proper training, when he reads Gerhard Hauptmann he does not look for beauty, it is not the artistic instinct that brings him there, but he asks, why does Gerhard Hauptmann speak as he does?

And that question he is competent to answer by connecting Gerhard Hauptmann and the forces of the age in which he was cradled to the growing needs of the deepening conscience which Gerhard Hauptmann perhaps among others has first heard speaking the command "Thou shalt no longer abide by what is, but thou shalt proclaim that which is not , and yet which must be, and shall be in the future."

And so perhaps the political economy of the preacher may be defective in so far that he may not at his fingers' ends have the latest tabulated results of the movement of trade; he may err in claiming that so and so many bushels of wheat were disposed of here in Chicago, and so and so many yards of flannel were shipped here in Chicago. If it is absolutely necessary that he should know the amount he can turn to the tables well as the specialized merchant and credit man. He may perhaps not have these things at his fingers tips, but as Socrates found with the workman at the shoe bench, he knew better how to make a shoe, Socrates, than the shoemaker, for he had the ideal of the shoe and the shoemaker did not have it.

In the political economy and in the sociology which the preacher must be familiar with if he is to be a preacher, he must recognize the ideal relations, find them, and utilize them and bring them home unto his people.

Socrates ran counter to the prejudice of the conceited shoemaker, among others. "What he could make a shoe better than I could? What if he knows more about business than we do?" Yes, Socrates knew more about business than the shoemaker did. He knew the business of humanity, and the shoe was only an incident in that humanity. The shoemaker accused him, as Plato tells us, and Socrates was forced to drink the cup of hemlock. But do we know the shoemaker's name today? Socrates has never died; and Socrates is named among the benefactors of the race.

All honor to the shoemaker; all honor to the expert; all honor to the specialist; all honor to the merchant; to the physician; to the lawyer; to the engineer; and what not. They have their intense usefulness. They have their divine legitimacy in the evolution of the social facts and factors, in control of the social forces.

But all their specialized efforts will event in nothing except strife and chaos. They need the supplementary direction making for inter-relation, making for the concept of the totalities and the real values which the modern religion—call it ethics if you so choose, call it by whatever name you desire—which modern religion and the competent teacher of modern religion can only point out, enforce, illustrate, clarify.

Through the zeal with which the modern preacher does this, his task can make a force, vital force, potent force in the actualities of individual striving, of social inter—dependence.

That is the lesson that I would bring to you from the reading again after many years of Plato's Apology of Socrates, Socrates the atheist simply because he was the herald of a new day, the prophet of a new thought, the proclaimer of a nobler God than the gods that selfish men and petty minds worshiped. Socrates, first an abnormal fool.

So are all the men that speak a new language fools in the eyes of them that are too indolent or too incompetent to learn the new vocabulary. Socrates, the presumptuous fool, denying all wisdom. Ah, many a man upon whom the prophetic touch has been laid has stood exposed to the conceit of men of narrow range of vision, not in selfish arrogance, but in devotion to his duty. The widest, the deepest, the noblest wisdom is that which lifts the specialty and the specializing out of the narrow groove and sets him and his skill into the relation vital and beneficial, with the totalities, with the humanities with the divinities.

This we might learn from Socrates' life. And if ever again temptation should come to us to brand one of the leaders of the unborn moral an atheist, a crank, an idiot, let us think that such titles were always given by the real fools to the prophets of the new day; that every pioneer and pathfinder, Socrates, Buddha, Isaiah, whatever their name, was, at one time or another pitied for insanity, denounced for perilous stupidity, hated for selfish presumptuousness, perhaps sacrificed to the prejudice of the masses, killed by decree of court. Yet for these fools, these atheists, the world has become better and nobler, the graves of the fools are the shrines to which the growing humanity pilgrims with the sense of a debt that posterity would like to cancel, but finds it impossible to make good.

Socrates, they called thee atheist! If ever there was God-intoxicated soul, it was thine. They called thee fool; thy folly was prophetic enthusiasm. They believed thee to be selfish, and yet thou gave thy life for truths' sake. Thy name be blessed among the blessed. Thou shinest today with the glory of the stars in heaven, with the effulgence of the morning's dawn; and thou wilt shine on in this splendor as long as there will be one eye on earth to delight in what is true, one soul to feel the uplifting power of what is eternally righteous, one heart to beat in response with that which is perennially youthful. Prophet of the good, the beautiful and the true Socrates, thou did destroy the gods that God might be recognized all the more truly in the majesty of beauty, in the holiness of character, in the obligation of truth.

Amen.

THE JEWISH PREACHER:
Rabbi Emil G. Hirsch, Ph.D., LL.D.

The Theology of The Jewish Reform Movement

1897, Month & Day Unknown
Reading: Job 12

Might, Majesty and Mystery are written across the face of the universe. Power, pathos and perplexity are the rhythm of all lives wrought into the universe. The stars tell the story of power. They unfold the picture of beauty. They spell the great riddle of mystery.

Strength is proclaimed by the rocks. The rivers sing of sublimity and the all tells man to be modest, because no matter how far his knowledge may reach, it is after all but an island on either side of which beats an ocean wrapped in secrecy. The curtain is not lifted by never so bold an eye from off the face of the true, the eternal things of creation, of history, of individual experience.

He that studies the religions of the world with an open mind, cannot but come to the conclusion that one or the other of these three accents—Might, Majesty or Mystery, has been the lite motif of one or the other concrete religions.

Most of those denoted, for the want of a better name, as pagan, have worked out the symphonic measures of the theme of power. The heavens to the pagan declare a strength greater than that which is come to man. He feels his own littleness because he stands face to face with that large life which may make and mar him whirl and whelm him, according to its cruel whims and its despotic decrees. He bows, conscious of his own impotency before the symbols of strength stupendous.

The Greek religion again, and in another way the religions of India, have set to rhyme the flowing movements of majesty, of beauty, of sublimity.

To the Greek mind, strength is not the keynote to the all, but cosmos, beauty, is the refrain to the one grand hymn which is sung by the rising sun and repeated by the dying day star, which is entoned by the little flowers and rehearsed by the foliage of the forests, the one hymn of joy and beauty which runs from the dust to the divine, from the stones to the stars.

The Indian religions do not particularize. They conceive of the universe as one, grand whole. As such it speaks to them of the sublime. Man face to face with the majesty of life feels that to him has come a measure of existence seemingly over and against that vaster ocean so full and so teeming, so stirred and so troubled, without any quantitative and qualitative value.

And thus oppressed by the sublimity of all and by the lack of worth of his own little self in this mighty ether of being, he contents himself in meditation to feel after the divine in contemplation to drink in the delights of the completeness which the heavens shadow and the earth seems to symbolize. Here—you know it already—we are brought to the threshold of a third movement in the grand symphony of adoration paid by the orchestra to which human hearts have been the instruments, and of which human minds and human longings have been the different single measures.

The third accent or movement—mystery. If India leads from the region of the beautiful through the gateway of contemplative sublimity to the obscure shrine of the mysterious, Christianity in its fundamental tones is the religion of mystery.

Sin and salvation are mysterious. Man and God stand in a mystic relation. They taught it in the books that indeed man and God once at one—that the peace and harmony which ran from heaven to earth and rebounded from earth to heaven was once incorruptible, but in the fullness of grace in their mysterious instrumentality, God re-established the relations between the heights and the depths. He gave to man the impotent instruments of once more stringing the harp of his heart with unbroken strings, and of once more waking from those strings the mystic melody of celestial harmony, answered by the refrain of earthlike ecstasy.

Of this mystic and mysterious element in Christianity, we have a fair and otherwise incomprehensible instance, in the revivalist's power over millions and masses, mobs and multitudes.

His words coldly printed spell in no sense to the mind that analysis. Remembering the background of the mystery, recalling the ecstasy of sinking self in the weaving so strange and weird of the chords that sound mysterious elements, these words so full of passion and pathos, of appeal and of admonition, receive a glow which the skeptic cannot deny to them, which even the doubting mind must admiringly concede to be most marvelous and most important in the constitution and the conduct of even modern man, so inclined to weigh so much, always on the alert to measure and to ponder.

God then has power, is the proclamation of Paganism. God has majesty and beauty is the confirmation of Greek minds and of Indian dreamers. God as the mystery in whom all streams of life meet and from the heart of whom all mainspring of conduct and motives flow out, is the one, the eternal song of hope of Christianity, of all religions whose fundamental tone is salvation—soteriological dreams, soteriological aspirations.

What is the God of Judaism, and how does that Judaism which claims to be more of Judaism than any other form of Judaism, conceive of God? This is not denied or questioned: The days are past when dogmatism of church and synagogue could be met by dogmatism of arrogance and atheism. It is true forty years ago there was provocation for meeting the challenge of church by the insolence of vacant atheism. Then indeed perhaps he who was positive in his declarations that all the ages before him had been under the influence of a delusion in positing God somewhere in power or in pathos or in perplexity, had justification, but today there is no such justification. Science and philosophy have advanced beyond the dreary outpost in the desert of despair marked dogmatic atheism.

The young man who dreams of his greatness and wishes to emphasize his intellectual prowess, who believes, to quote Job, that he is the people, and when he dies all wisdom will come to an end—this young man, if today he repeats nothing better and nothing fresher than the broken beads of a rosary of atheism, writes himself down not as a leader of modern thought, but as the camp follower of a devoted army, despised both in the church and in the academic details of clear and consistent thinking.

The greatest men today refuse to avow themselves atheists. Undogmatic as they are, they have fully understood that atheism is as much of a dogma unprovable and unproved as is that peculiar form of theism, which has found incorporation in our academies and is taught with a nauseating weariness from our pulpits and repeated as the very staff of life of religion by the faithful. When a suggestion of a better life and a deeper love might open even their hearts and minds to the realization that the stars are eclipsed when the sun's glow and glory is uncurtained with the breaking day.

The modern scientists are modest. These men of science refuse to dogmatize. They call themselves agnostic, which means one who knows nothing.

Huxley certainly knew much more than many of our leaders of great commercial establishments ever will know if they live to be one hundred years of age. But out of the fullness of his knowledge Mr. Huxley wrote himself down an agnostic.

Not that he denied the mystery of existence,

but because he felt that retorts and scalpels, anatomical dissections and physiological researches, the astronomer's excursions into the starry Africa's and the biologist's investigations into the beginning of things, do not suffice to tell us what life is—what nature is—what lies beyond—what lay before our quivering, our uncertain knowledge.

So even from this platform, which must be addressed always with the advancing tide of your wisdom—even we from this platform may today hear without a blush at the possibility of being considered behind the philosophical development of the age, the great question of how Judaism, our Judaism, views God.

Power, Majesty and Mystery are the three fundamental accents, combined or separately emphasized by all other forms of religion Power, Majesty and Mystery—strength, sublimity and secret might, pathos and perplexity—they have not been able to bring man near unto God, or God near unto man.

Judaism has taken another channel to bring as a potency in life, as a principle of conduct, to man the ken of his God. Judaism does not spell God as equivalent to power—it does not spell God as the exchangeable term with beauty—it does not call God the mysterious unknowable underground and undercurrent of all things that be were or shall become; but leaving, the heavens alone and abandoning the outside world for the moment to its own fate, the prophets of Judaism descend to the depths of the human heart, and from thence outward they throw the light of their find there upon the heavens and upon the depths of life and of being.

Certainly the theology of the reform synagogue does this and does it most positively and most insistently. That perhaps may astonish some of you who have perhaps paid some attention to the catechisms written by one or the other of the great men who have done so much for the establishment of Reform Judaism on a rocky foundation of scholarly thoughts and the results of scholarly investigation.

But mind you, these great men had all their limitations. Each one of them had his special field in which he did great things. In another field his contributions were less original, and therefore less valuable. Take those men, the names of whom I recalled to your memory last Sunday. There was Zunz, the great literary critic. From a literary critic you cannot expect a philosophical analysis of the theological concepts. Zunz was not a philosopher.

Take Geiger. Geiger is the historical critic—a man of wonderful gifts, recalling in his composure of analysis the great masters of Greece. A man who had the intuition to see the jointure between age and age, period and period when thousands of others had passed over the same ground and could not detect the footprints of the generations that passed from one period into the other and thus bridged the seeming gap which opened between them. But Geiger was not a philosopher. Historical criticism lies in one domain and philosophical analysis in another. Geiger never presumed to be a philosopher.

All these great men understood their limitations. They spurn the men who knew all, and out of the fullness of their wisdom said: "We are the people, and when we die, when our congregation ceases to be, or when we refuse to listen to you, then all wisdom is at an end".

Take David Einhorn, though he wrote a book with a philosophical tendency and with a philosophical purpose, yet not in that sphere lies his importance. The catechism which he left behind is in those chapters where he treats on God, not better than the thousand and one other chapters written by other men on the same points. And those that were instructed by him by that catechism were naturally led sooner or later to doubt what he had taught them, and thus many of his own pupils—I could mention names of young physicians here in this town—have, though confirmed by Dr. Einhorn, become the most ardent adherents of a Godless religion, as they think it to be.

No, Einhorn's great importance was in the first place, in his rugged independence. He cared not for majorities in his congregation. He called out the president—think of it—the president of a congregation and told him, unless this and that be done tomorrow, your Dr. Einhorn will not preach. He did that in Philadelphia. Think of another rabbi today even, daring to tell his president, unless this and that be done! Why he will have the constitution thrown at his head and he will get his walking papers one way or another sooner or later. But Einhorn called out his president, and said, unless the second day of

Rosh Hashana worship be stopped, you will have no Einhorn on the first day of Rosh Hashana.

And so then as at all times, he told the administrative boards of his congregation, "You mind the finances. Let me take care of the pulpit: I have studied for that pulpit. I have prepared myself for it. I am able to read the Talmud as far as I know, you are not. I am able to speak German, and some of you are not." So he told his administrative board, "Let the provinces be established. You attend to the pew sales and the hiring and those things, and I shall take care of the theology."

That was his great merit in American Judaism, for the men were few then, as they are rare today, who at the risk of losing bread and butter, will stand before congregations and refuse to bow to the fetish of congregational arrogance and congregational conceit. Einhorn spoke what he thought, and he thought when he spoke.

His second merit was to be a man like Isaiah of old—of a fiery temperament. Yes, he too got angry. He would not allow the synagogue to be turned into a circus for the display of individual or congregational conceit, and mutual self admiration. He would not allow that what was holy to him should be made merely the frame for gossip and for social conversation. He spoke sharply when the occasion called for it. But this man, with this fiery temperament had the gift of eloquence as it comes to the fewest of mortals. When he spoke even the skeptics felt there was an honest soul giving the best he had.

He was a patriot. In Baltimore, a southern city,

at the risk of his life, Einhorn preached day in and day out against the iniquity of slavery, and when his congregation objected, he told them the pulpit may be yours, but I am not yours. If you want slaves get someone else. Einhorn is not a slave, and he will not tolerate slavery or even ignore this great crime against humanity and religion, though your business may go to pieces and your accounts in the South may in consequence become uncollectible. Here is the great service rendered by Einhorn to Reform Judaism.

But a philosopher he was not. His theology in his catechism is not worth more than the theology of a thousand and one catechisms written by other men and learned by heart by you. Did you ever study the book? It is called The Eternal Lamp. Its pages are of wonderful value and instruction, especially when he turns to the ethics of one thought, the sanctification of individual life running through it with a majesty unequaled in any other book, and a severity of appeal unequaled anywhere under God's heaven.

But his theology is the old theology. It posits a concept of the mind, then gives to that concept the attributes without which self the concept would not be self sustained. Of course if you posit God, you must give him omnipotence. If you posit God, you must give him omniscience. If you posit God, you must make him the creator out of nothing. Without this, your conception of God will not be self sustained. But this is not proof and this theology a priori theology, is not worthy of the modern philosophical exposition.

So, even though it sounds something like an

attempt to crown with laurel wreaths one who was the dearest to me that I ever possessed, and to whom I am more beholden for direction of thought and even absolute knowledge then to any other of my many teachers, still the truth must be said: in that company of great minds and great men, there was one who was a philosopher.

As a student of Arabic, Geiger certainly eclipsed him. As a Noah of bibliographical titles—title pages, of old musty Hebrew books, there is a man in this city, a rabbi who perhaps is much more important than was he. Each one had his specialty, and each one of us today has his specialty—some of your admired rabbis have the specialty of pleasing their congregation at all hazards—others have a specialty of displeasing their congregation on all occasions. Each one has his specialty. So it was in those days.

But it is recognized by great philosophers, professors of German universities, not philosophers in the pews of our congregations perhaps—not men who think that "we are the people and when we die all wisdom comes to an end", but men who occupy chairs in German universities—that Samuel Hirsch, of all modern rabbis, was the only one perhaps, who had a philosophical mind, and who developed an original system of philosophy.

His chapters in his catechism on theology are altogether different from those written by anyone else, and the teachings of this pulpit for the last seventeen years have been only the echo of the chapters in my father's great writings.

In his Humanitas Religion, and in his theology, he refused to look outwards, but he looks inward.

He was the first rabbi who openly declared it—to the present day he and I perhaps are the only ones that have in Judaism come to the proper appreciation of the limitations of theology, who have openly declared that the so-called demonstrations of God's existence do demonstrate absolutely nothing, and if we depended for our belief in God on the so-called evidences of God's existence, agnosticism and atheism even, would have their strong pillars whereon to rest their life structure, so that even it, how illy timbered it may be, might stand unmoved and unshaken.

The so-called demonstration of God's existence may be summed up under three heads. There may perhaps be more, but three will suffice.

There is first the ontological demonstration. Now ontological is derived from the Greek word which means being. In this demonstration the general argument runs about as follows: Every movement must have its cause. Every change must have been caused. In human experience, change is produced by a change in power—a power, which effects the change, and so in this wise motion changed growth is always the result of an antecedent motion an antecedent impulse, an antecedent cause. The human mind must be driven, following along this chain, to put somewhere a beginning to that change, and thus the first cause and prime mover, an original condition, which has produced all other conditions.

This is a great argument, and it is repeated even in Jewish pulpits, especially by the younger men who have come from the seminary at Cincinnati, and all, without exception, the first year of their life, deem it essential to prove that God exists.

I have not met one of those young graduates yet but he, in the second or third days of his preaching, would tell his congregation the demonstrations of God's existence, and the fourth he will go into the immortality of the soul. But this demonstration from cause to effect is absolutely, to a philosophical mind, untenable. It posits that which it has to prove. Change, as far as human experience goes, is the result of antecedent cause. That is true enough; but Hume has shown that our reasoning from our own experience is absolutely not cogent.

You probably will think me a crank if I tell you that we have absolutely no certainty that tomorrow morning the sun will rise. Because the sun has risen ever since we have a record thereof, is only a probability that tomorrow the same phenomenon will take place, but it is no proof.

The fact that through some electric arrangement this beautiful lamp throws its radiance over me and is reflected again from here over you, and has happened every Sunday morning, is not a philosophical proof that will happen next Sunday. This lamp may be next Sunday eclipsed. There is absolutely no proof, from a philosophical point of view, what was will always be. That applies to the ontological demonstration of God's existence.

The second objection is that cause and effect are after all only two terms of one judgment in the philosophical acceptation of the word, not in the legal commercial meaning of the terms of one judgment.

While for purposes of analysis we differentiate between the cause and the effect, the effect is the cause, or rather in the effect is the cause. The power, which produces change, is in the change produced, not outside of it. Therefore, this positing an original cause for whatever follows philosophically speaking, merely says whatever follows is identical with the original cause.

That every tyro in philosophical reasoning will at once grasp. I may perhaps not succeed in making it plain to you, but think a little on it, and you will find that the proposition is even clear to you, though you have to deal with other judgments than we have in our logical and philosophical schools. The ontological demonstration is philosophically absolutely irrelevant to the question of God.

The second is called—now do not become astonished at the big word—is called the physico-teleological, which is to say, it posits a purpose in nature, and because here is this wonderful world of ours, and everything fits into that world so well a purpose and plan seem to be demonstrated all over. Hence they posit a mind as having purposed and planned the world.

In the first place so many things are in the world, which seem to be absolutely purposeless do not fit into the plan. Take that vermifuge appendix of ours. If it have any purpose in man, it is to show how great advances modern surgery has made; but outside of that there seems to be no purpose unless it be a way Providence has of multiplying the graves in the cemeteries.

And there are a thousand other things, which a naturalist will tell you are not perfectly planned. The human eye, as a rule, is quoted as one of the great things that prove the complete purpose and plan of the arch architect. But an ophthalmologist will tell you that the spectrum constructed by Helmholz is mathematically much more perfect and better adapted to its purposes than is the human eye.

They tell you that God made the fishes in the mammoth cave in Kentucky without eyes because the fishes in the dark there had no need of seeing. So God put those fishes sightless into the mammoth cave, adapting them to their surroundings. Modern biology says and proves it too, that the fish in the mammoth cave have no eyes because their surroundings prevented, accidentally or otherwise, the development of the optic instruments.

And so, the deer is not swift footed for the purpose of escaping from the hounds, but because the deer was hounded; by dint of exercise he developed his nimbleness of foot. And the rabbi's lungs and reasoning and resonier powers are not purposed, but they are developed. If he has a congregation that deserves resonier, that resoniering power will be developed; and if he has one that deserves reasoning, his reasoning powers will also be developed. So modern biology has absolutely dashed to pieces all this argumentation from physical purpose and plan.

At best that would prove a blind force, a force which could develop it into something would not prove a God, for God would mean much more than a power that can do certain things and adapt certain things to certain ends.

The last one is the doctrine from Descartes, and before him from Anselm, the church father. It is this: that being and thinking correspond always. As you think a God, God must be. And this world is the best possible world, therefore presupposes a best possible creator, for unless the best possible world were, the least good world might be the best possible world, and because this is in thought self-contradictory, therefore to the best possible world must correspond a best possible God.

But the identify of being and thinking is absolutely unprovable. Descartes, with his famous dictum "I think, therefore I am" did assume what he started out to prove.

So these demonstrations of God's existence must be thrown overboard. But my father's Judaism, searching through the ages and literatures of Judaism has found one key to the riddle of deity and human life. He says the question is not "what is God in himself"—that question no one can answer—therefore my father was an agnostic.

In 1854, that is twenty years before Huxley ever framed the word or uttered the thought. Consult my father's Humanitatus. The question is not, what is God in himself. That none of us knows; but what is God for us—what was God for the old prophets?

You perhaps have the prejudice that Judaism has always taught God—that monotheism makes or unmakes Judaism—that Judaism in ancient days believed in one God, spiritual, bodiless, father omnipotent, and omniscient, and it is believed so today.

That is taught in pulpits; it is repeated in Sunday schools, and will be written in wonderful essays before the woman's council tomorrow or the day thereafter. But for all that, that is not true.

Look at your old biblical literature. Why, the old prophets believed in a God who was localized, who was in Jerusalem—there he reigned and nowhere else. Joshua escaped from that God, or tried to escape by getting out of the country. God was not in Parshish, he was only in Palestine. The old prophets believed in a God with a mouth, a hand, a foot, a nose, stands to reason. Read their words. They believed that God was a body, and not a spirit. It was only the later prophets that made God universal—it was in the later works that God became universal.

There is a Hebrew book which describes God's proportions—gives a graphic description of the length of his arm, of the length of his nose, of the length of his ears ; all the parts of his body are described. And when Maimonides began to protest against this belief, a great rabbi in Israel protested against Maimonides, and said "Greater men and better men than thou art, have believed in God's body—not that he is a spirit."

The metaphysicians of the middle ages have a theology, which is again absolutely different from the theology of Bible or Talmud, so that the identity of theological teaching is not to be posited as a fact and a force in Judaism. Every age made its own God, had its own conception of God, but to

THEOLOGY OF JEWISH REFORM

all those conceptions, one thing is in common.

The God of Israel spells for us the moral purpose of human life and of history. Thus not Might, not Majesty, not Mystery, but Morality is the accent of Jewish theology.

Now, you say, whence do you know that man has to be a moral being? Why, we feel it—we know it. That morality grows does not disprove, for the moment man is, there is the nucleus of a moral life, the germ of morality—that is what makes his humanity.

The man is a moral being from the beginning when he is man. The anthropoid is not—the simian is not, but anthropos is an exchangeable term for a social being—a social being means a moral being. There is the relation between man and man.

But is this relation merely human? History shows, if treated on a large measure, that there runs a moral purpose, and our own experience shows that only by a moral purpose can our life receive that which it has not without it—harmony and happiness.

These elements then prove that there is in man, and if man has found it in himself, in time and in all space, a tendency toward the more comprehensive morality. And that the moral purposes are independent of the individual man, for we may refuse to be moral, but morality will be wrought out, the moral purpose of the ages will be effected. That is all there is to our theology. That is found in the pages of my father's catechism. Otherwise he and I are agnostics.

I do not fancy I know what God is in himself,

but my God for me spells that law eternal which rings out from the past and o'er the waters of the unborn future—man thou shalt, and because thou shalt thou canst.

It spells the universal reign of responsibility—it posits as the aim and end of all things that are as far as I can see the purpose to serve moral ends. It gives to my life harmony and position, duty and obligation. It binds man unto man, and therefore links zone unto zone under the great ambition to live for a universal reign of justice and of righteousness.

This is the Jewish God. Whatever else there may be to that idea, this is the fundamental essence, this is the kernel around which the husk has grown. The husk changes, but throughout the ages, ever since prophet spoke, the diadem of our God had the jewels of righteousness and of justice.

That is the theology of reform synagogue. Has Felix Adler anything else to offer? Is there reason, because we pray and posit God, to leave the synagogue? Before Felix Adler wrote, my father had written. What is true in Adler's position was accentuated and proven to be Jewish in the documents left by my father. I believe I was fortunate in having him for both my father and my teacher.

If I stayed within the synagogue, it is simply due to the training he gave me, to the thought that he implanted. That Jewish teaching was agnosticism, but for this, out of the human experience, the harmonies of human heart, it draws the conviction and a certainty of a moral purpose, in whose service man is a minister, and with whose purposes man can round out his life into a completeness, which gives happiness and harmony to self and to society.

Thus then the theology which I learned, and which I confess and profess, is not atheism—it is not simply agnosticism. But it is what I would call ethical mono-pantheism, which posits personality as the highest we know in us, and therefore presumes to symbolize the still higher life in the formula of a greater personality.

What personality means, and how far we may pray, and what other things we have as to the religion which believes in a God, I must leave for a discussion next week.

But let us take hence today: Reform Judaism more than any other kind of Judaism emphasizes not majesty and not might, and not mystery, but morality, as the garment in which is clothed he whom we in our human language call God.

The theology of Reform Judaism proves once more that the motive of Reform Judaism was not to have less of Judaism, but to have more of it. That the result has been not to lead men out of it but rather to lead minds into it.

Will we understand this at last? I hope we shall. Then we shall not say "We are the people, and all wisdom will die with us", but rather in the words of Job, accepting the seemingly inexplicable differences and inequalities in outward possession and pomp, between the successful sinner and the unsuccessful saint, still maintain that innocence and morality give life success—their absence, notwithstanding gold and power, pomp and pageant failure.

God rules in the hearts of men, and these hearts sing; the eternal jubilant affirmation—there is a God who speaks to man, not in the tones of the thunder which proclaims his might, nor in the charms of the starry dome which tell of his beauty—nor in the meditations and contemplations of that which is hidden from human eye, the undercurrent and the underground secret of God's existence in himself, but in the moral strivings, and in the moral compensations of human life, there is God; that is his revelation through time and space, through history in one life or in all lives this God I profess.

Need I worship Him? How can I worship Him? What more do I know of Him—what more need I know of Him? These questions I shall attempt to answer when next we meet for common study and common inspiration in this house.

This house, which shall forever be the home of deeper thoughts than those, which come to us from the bustle and whirl of outward strife and outward struggle. For that success which profiteth not and against those failures which cannot inflict the thinking man with the load of a bitterness that knoweth no sweetness.

God is not in power and not in pathos, nor is he perplexity; but he is in the eternal proclamation of "man thou shalt, therefore man thou canst."

Amen.

THE JEWISH PREACHER:
Rabbi Emil G. Hirsch, Ph.D., LL.D.

A Sukkoth Sermon
New Ethics For New Economics

>Sunday, October 19th, 1902
>Reading: Deuteronomy 16, verse 11
>Isaiah 56, verses 10-12

This day, these symbols, this Sukkoth booth, take us back to distant ages and recall to our memory a form of social organization that has passed entirely away. If but modestly gifted with imagination we can paint to our mental vision the scenes that were yearly enacted on the soil of Palestine, The harvest was gathered; the owner of the field and his helpers had worked faithfully together, and now that the fruitage of their common labor was safely stored away in the wine cellar or granary; all of them that had a share in coaxing from the soil its wealth were bidden to the feast. There was the patriarch of the family and his sons and daughters touching elbows with the bondsman and the man servant. Yea, even such as had no share in bringing the golden grain to the threshing floor, or in carrying the bursting wine crates to the waiting wine presses, were invited to come. Gladness sounded from every heart, and joy was reflected from every eye. They had worked honestly, and therefore they could rejoice deeply in what their work, their common work, had brought to all of them.

This scene is taken from the agricultural life with society organized on the patriarchal basis. From that form of social inter-action to our present day of social distraction is a far cry indeed. And yet we cannot understand the motives of our day. We cannot hope for insight into the vexatious perplexities incidental to our modern social maladjustments unless we keep before our eyes the whole course of social evolution. From primitive gregariousness through the intervening stages of the nomadic clan scheme, and later the agricultural patriarchal type, then the despotism of a social structure resting as it did partially in antiquity with the exception of Palestine, upon the foundation of human slavery. From this, on again through the feudal plan with its classes organized into guilds, and then to the modern day with its passion for social disentanglement, its enthusiasm for personal liberty, its blind belief in the equality of all men.

The latter period is about running to its close. Yea, it has done so to all practical intents and purposes. The Eastern clouds are painted red. Some read in that tint the omen of destruction; others standing on the higher peak of the outlook hold that the blushes in the Eastern sky are the promise of a better and a brighter day for humanity.

We have outgrown in successive efforts nomadic clan organization, the patriarchal agricultural form recalled by this booth, by this lulav, this Sukkoth day.

We have, thank God, learned that human society shall not be anchored to the shame and the pain of human slavery. We have also left behind the feudal type, its restrictions, but also, alas, its responsibilities. For over one hundred years we have reveled and boasted in the high flood of individualism, the gift to the human kind by the French Revolution, fathered by the French thinkers of the Eighteenth century. And now as the Twentieth century is stepping out boldly towards its ascent up the heights, we are slowly but painfully learning that liberty is not the last word, and equality is not the deepest accent. That again, from the individualism which intoxicated us when it burst out its passionate creed in protest to the lack of freedom in the social scheme of feudalism—that liberty and individualism—I say, must give way in turn now to the deeper socialized interdependence of activities, and of factors and forces in the social, economic industrial upworking and outworking of the human destiny.

I, of course, shall not weary you with a detailed account of nomadic clan social organization. I take it for granted you are familiar with its peculiar traits. Nor shall I dwell upon the agricultural patriarchalism, which is the type of social life that the bible in its institutions pictures before our eyes. I shall not go into details either as to the slave system of ancient Greece and Rome, philosophized about by Plato and Aristotle. I shall not waste time either in lecturing to you about the feudal system, or guilds, and what they did, and wherein their weaknesses lay. But I must—though it is a tale often told here—I must dwell upon certain features of the French Revolution and its creed. For that creed is prelude to our own attempts to lift humanity to a higher plane, and to meet problems that have arisen out of the dogmatism of French philosophy applied to economics and to industry. I have mentioned the sacramental words of the French Revolution—*Liberty and Equality.* They could so passionately insist upon liberty of the individual man because in their day liberty had been denied to man. They had been starved, and in their paroxysm of impending death they saw liberty, an aureole in glory, so that in their thinking no other word could hold its own. But the liberty which they proclaimed was the liberty of protest, and liberty as such is always protest. Hartman, the German philosopher, has never written a truer note than when he insists—in his treatise on ethics—upon that one great and grave consideration, that liberty is never absolute. Liberty from what, is the great and grave point, salient and emphatic. And so the French people that shouted *Liberty* meant liberty from the artificial restrictions of the social system and the political scheme in the mediaeval times.

In their philosophy, the French thinkers turned to make man a God because the church and the state, before their day, had conspired to make of man a slave. The individual unhistorical man was central to the speculations of Diderot, and that unhistorical—therefore, also unnatural man—that nowhere lived and nowhere breathed—the universal man that nowhere had his home—this generalization and abstraction came to be the pivotal conception of the English economics.

Let man act in his own individual capacity, free from any other consideration except that which burns within him, and that is the desire to preserve himself, the desire to maintain himself, the passion to gain and to have. Let him act upon this, said Adam Smith and his followers, and out of this struggle with selfishness will leap social harmony. And thus they acted upon competition; they built commerce and industry upon individualized forces. They compelled a man to be a mechanical man—that is to say—a creature without nerves other than those of greed and the desire to maintain himself in order that through this independent but strenuous insistence upon his own humanity, might be lifted to the altitude of social peace and social well-being.

Adam Smith lived, of course, before the days of invention and the application of the steam power. That invention of which we rhapsodized when we were young, the glorious results of which constitute the main thesis of every high school composition we ever wrote—that steam power showed, if nothing else did, the inadequacy of Adam Smith's economics based on absolute and abstract individualism, or man ceased to be an individual under the draconic rule of steam. He was no longer a man; he became a hand; he became one of a mass, and was lost in that mass. Steam forced the gathering together of men into factories, and steam compelled the decentralization of labor to such an extent that the individual laborer ceased to be a whole man, and never did a whole thing. He became a little cog in the machine.

He became an inconsequential quantity. He had to keep up the pace with the man that worked before him, and see to it that he was quick enough so that the man behind him was not delayed. His soul was withered out of him. Adam Smith reasoned that man was an individual and that demon, steam, whose demoniac power we learned to chain, laughed to scorn the theories of Adam Smith. Not an individual, but a hand; not a man, but a mere tool; not a producer in the larger sense of the word, but merely a menial doing a little bit of a thing in monotonous reiteration without knowing why and without capacity of reasoning out where his work proved its social utility.

The invention of steam then, was the first power that laid breach into the dogmatism of the English school of reasoning that individualism and liberty were the final potency of the truest social form of life.

And another thing also sounded the death knell of Adam Smith's individualism. The struggle for existence became more intense. There was another assumption in Adam Smith's theories, which if it had been true might have legitimatized whatever conclusion was drawn therefrom. That was the other word, the other sacramental word of the French Revolution—*Equality*. Peasant the equal of Prince; Count no higher than clown; all are equal. A word of protest, legitimate in the vocabulary of the Revolution, but shorn of potency when the task had to be confronted to build-up society with the assumption that men are equal.

The economics of the English schools assumed that men were equal; and thus they spoke of the freedom of contract. Between equals the equation can easily be found in dealings that they have with each other; but are we equal? Is a capitalist, when he makes a contract with a laborer, the equal of the laborer, or the laborer his equal? Are they on one level. Does the future mean for the one the same alternative as for the other?

However small your capital may be it is sufficient to keep hunger away from your modest home at least for a certain length of time; but he who has merely his hands to sell is always, if he is alone and unsupported, met by the alternative to accept terms or to face starvation. That Adam Smith's economics did not consider. But as steam forced men out of their individualism into the factories the men began to bethink themselves of the false basis of the system under which they worked, and they attempted to counteract the pernicious results of a false philosophy by combining, by sacrificing their absolute liberty at the shrine of unionized efforts. What have the unions done? They have created the possibility of putting labor on a footing of equality with capital. They give to the individual laborer a feeling of security. He is no longer confronted with the alternative: Accept even the dry pittance or else you must resolve to meet the pangs of starvation.

The unions have, in the second place, accomplished that market conditions shall be equalized throughout the world. You know, men of commerce as you are, what I mean by conditions of the market. You try to buy where it is cheapest and sell where it is dearest. And it is your policy to create conditions for buying cheaper, and for selling higher. Sound commercial philosophy. Yea, but the individual laborer cannot provide for the cheapest purchasing market nor for the dearest selling conditions, but the union may, and the unions have done this. Read any treatise on the effects of trade unionism, of England, of America or of Germany, and that is the point most strongly brought out. The economics of Smith would not tolerate trade unionism; but as steam had shown that Smith's system was not final, but preliminary, unionism urged the laborers to act upon the newly created conception and try to make at least real the second principal of Adam Smith, the equality of the contracting parties under the social arrangement. Then came a stop. Capital itself learned that Adam Smith's competitive ideal was a colossus standing on clay feet. In ancient Greece they tell the story of a God consuming his own offspring. Competition consumes its own offspring.

And thus we have entered into the stage of even capitalistic organization and combination. Capital has learned that the orthodox economics of England did not provide for contingencies arising today in consequence of the wonderfully enlarged control that man has over nature. Had no steam been invented, individualism might perhaps have redeemed the faith of those that believed in it; had not electricity slaughtered time and annihilated distance, individualism might perhaps not been found a flirt, smiling but unable or unwilling to turn the smile into love.

But here we are. Even our country is too small for us. Our country is too limited though within its borders we have the Arctic winter and the Tropic summer, and we have a variety of mineral and other productions of the ages stored away in the mountains. We have a multiplicity of soil that laughs at climate and robs famine of its terrors and the drought of its torture. And when one who ships wheat from this central gathering point would consult the horoscope of his commercial prospects, today he has to figure not merely upon what natural impediments may arise from the conditions of this country and the ocean's humor and caprice, but he has to cast his eye towards the Argentine Republic—a distant name, a mere sound a few decades ago, but within the next five years he has to calculate the speed of trains and the amount of cars at the disposal of the Trans-Siberian Railroad. The whole world has come into competition, one with the other, because distance is no more, and climate is no more.

We are cosmopolitan in everything, and in consequence of this, a condition which Adam Smith never could dream of, a condition that those great economists that discuss strong matters when assembled for their lunch, because these conditions have arisen, capital itself has felt that individualism is inadequate to meet the new circumstances of a new age. Declaim against trusts as much as you may; they have come not through the malice of one Master genius of finance. They have come as things always come,

I say as a theologian, by the decree of divinity—or, if you will not allow this, they have come in obedience to the necessity inherent in the evolution of the human race. Capital itself has ceased to be individualistic; it is under cooperation and it is under combination.

Those forces that I have merely sketched to you I could detain you for hours with detailed proof. Those forces which I have merely indicated have resulted in splitting the industrial world into two camps, and the third camp between the two, bearing the blow from one and suffering under the blindness of the other: Capital organized in combinations stupendous; labor organized too on an enlarging plan, and between the upper and nether millstone—society, humanity.

At this stage of the evolutionary process we have arrived. We are passing through a period of transition. Every period of transition is dangerous. And why? Because on the one hand we have not outgrown the theories of an antecedent day; and on the other hand we have not fully grasped the import of theories to fit the conditions that are even now upon us. Here we are, all operating still with the fetishism of individualistic economics.

We speak of the right of a man to sell his labor at whatever price he chooses. We say—and one of the ministers that went to New York, and would not allow himself to be fooled into staying in Chicago—Dr. Hillis said at a banquet of imbeciles from Chicago—"If millions of bayonets shall be marshalled to protect one man in his right to sell his labor as he chooses, the nation must order the levy or write its own epitaph as dead or dying." That is one theory—the echo of an individualism which practically has ceased to be in operation in factory, in foundry, in counting room and behind the cashier's desk in the bank. If we were still in an individual condition, if we could be—if steam had not been found, if electricity had not been discovered, if wireless telegraphy had not laughed at the jealousy of the ocean—we might still operate with this ideal, the ideal of individualism and then say Yea, man shall be an individual; he shall be free to do. But we are not, and the new economics have adjusted themselves to the new conditions.

On the other hand, labor is still operating with the old notion of equality and hence they insist that one man shall be considered as valuable as another man. They insist that the better organized brain shall not receive higher social reward or wage than that brain which is dull. They restrict him who is creative to take the snail pace of one who is merely not only not creative but is absolutely incompetent. Why this? Because they, on their part, still believe in the equality, which never was and which cannot be maintained in the new social organization.

Here then are the sins of the capitalist on the one hand and of the union laborer on the other. The capitalist has outgrown individualism in his own organization, but he still would deal with individual men and he still invokes the power of the state to make the individual man accept what terms they assume the individual laborer would elect. The laboring men, on the other hand, rejecting the doctrine of labor of the individual, insist that individuals are nevertheless equal, forgetting that they are not. That in the social fabric there are distinctions and differences that must be considered, which cannot with impunity be ignored.

The immediate result of this want of logic and consistency, of the partial abandonment of the former creed, is a state of war. We shall only come out of this state of war when we learn a few simple principles of ethics. Ethics in business, Sunday School and bargain sale. Such a thought can only germinate in the cranky brain of a cranky rabbi. Indeed! Yea, that may be the comfortable assurance of the commercial travelling community, especially loudly and vulgarly emphasized when their palate is tickled by a few glasses of champaign, and their boiler is well fueled by a partridge or a prairie chicken. And between making a hole on the links and talking nonsense to the nonsensical girl, they may also comfort themselves that ethics and economics lie on different planes. The greatest thinkers of the day for the last fifty years have come to the conclusion that economics is ethics. And ethics is not merely that negative twaddle about goodness. If it be, I am sorry I am ethical.

Then you must buy your ethics at another stand. There you may get that inane, insipid, disgusting concoction of sweetness and of light that seems to be the whole story of life in the appeal to "be good, and be true, and be kind, and be noble."

That is not ethics. It is related to ethics as is the gibberish of a child just learning to speak to the style of Shakespeare. You might as well believe that your wonderful baby—and whose baby is not wonderful when he or she begins to say "Ba-ba-ba"—is talking the deepest philosophy, as to think that this twaddle about "goodness, and sweetness, and light and love" is ethics. The trouble is we have deceived the world; the trouble is we have sold this soda water, insipid, disgusting beverage, for the wine of truth in all of our churches and in all of our Sunday Schools.

Ethics teaches life; and if ethics has no voice for the living, if religion is merely for the dead then the world is doomed to death, and men are cursed to perdition. Yea, the deepest thinkers of the day have recognized that ethics and economics shall not be divorced, and where they are, there is trouble and there is mischief, Before coming away from home this morning I picked up, to look up one point, a treatise written in German by a Professor of a German University. It is called "The Handbook of Economics" and as I turned the pages I just happened to strike upon that one paragraph relating to the attitude of the successful man towards the men who tell him that morality and not money is involved in the social struggle. So Professor Gustave Cohn as early as 1881, was of this opinion. American writers too, might be quoted to prove to you, my critics, that this is no cranky notion of mine. But I shall not detain you with those proofs, Take any modern treatise on economics—unless it be on the old exploded theory of Adam Smith—and you will find that against the distribution of production, of selling men and buying men, are treated as paragraphs in the bible of ethics and religion.

Now, a few simple, plain ethical principles we most remember if from this present state of war and of distress shall come the higher type of social organization, no longer individualistic but cooperative under the plan of combination and mutual helpfulness. The first plain principle is that human life is more valuable than property. You yourselves are agreed to that. When, in the coal region, they beat a man to death you all shout for the militia. You speak of violence, brutality and murder. When they dynamite a railroad you exclaim, "Help, Cassias! Help, Cassias, Ceasar is sinking." "President of the United States, send one hundred thousand soldiers." This railroad dynamiting endangers life. The man murdered has lost his life. Railroads are sometimes dynamited on Wall street, and no one ever shouts for the militia to come. They are dynamited as effectually as when dynamite is put under the arch of a bridge. We lose property then, and we know property is not as sacred as human life. We must apply that to our economic adjustments. What does that mean? That the standard of life must be high and must be maintained. It is not true that men can be sold as goods are; it is not true that demand and supply alone arrange the price of life, human life. The standard of life must be maintained. You have also agreed to that, my friends. You have—at least our nation has—for thirty years now without interruption acted upon the theory that cheap labor is not conducive to national welfare. It is the only excuse for our barbaric tariff. Cheap labor does not comport and is not compatible with American citizenship. You have excluded the Chinese. Why? With what right in the world have you done so? They cheapen labor! Adam Smith rise to protest. In your system, cheap labor is the very acme of financial and economic prosperity. But the American nation says "No." Not the cheapest labor is basic to national prosperity.

No, you say the nation has also agreed that life is more valuable than property, and that the cheapest labor is not compatible with the highest dignity of American civilization. The standard of life must be maintained, and therefore no man has the right any longer to sell his labor at a price which lowers the standard of life. We must be socialized. As yet we have a brutal system of driving that home to us; as yet the bayonet and club—brutal and nasty ways—but as we apply ethics, brutality will give way to conviction, and men will see that they are not in morals permitted to sell themselves; that they must have an eye to the conditions of their class—their social class. They must socialize themselves, for human life is more valuable than property.

And the third point: Property must be differentiated into various classes. Property is sacred. Misunderstand me not. God grant that for once I may be understood truthfully. Let the slanderer be struck dumb when he leaves this house if he says I have uttered word or syllable against the sanctity of property. Property is the tribute that nature pays to man as its king.

This kind of property, especially when the whole nation is dependent upon its use, is not private property in the sense in which my beautiful sermons are my private property. This kind of property belongs to all, and hence must be under a different plan of administration than what is the conventional, natural private property. Abuse of this property must not be tolerated, and non-use equally an infraction of the law. We shall get there. Have you watched the trend of public opinion the last few months? Newspapers that were capitalistic to the core—Adam Smith's worshippers—as never in England or in Europe, have turned completely, and not because they were afraid of the masses.

I know some men who breathe their thoughts and confidences into the ears of the American nation who are not cowards. They would not care for the masses or the asses. They are not moved by pelf or self. They have come to the conclusion that certain classes of property are not private property, and they have been advocating even violent measures to bring to society what is her own—the privilege to use what nature has produced and to pay him who applies the machinery a fair equivalent for his genius, for the risk he has taken and for the capital he has invested. We shall get there twenty years from now; a plain ethical principle.

A fourth one, and with that I shall be done. You say that capital has responsibility; there is something on which society through court can fasten to compel compliance with the law, but you say that labor has no responsibilities. They have the same measure of responsibility.

How shall we arrange that? The State shall be

the guardian and insist that as capitalistic combinations shall be incorporated so combination of labor shall be incorporated. That will give a guaranty of good faith. It will give something to hold on to; it will take away the subterfuge that you can make contracts with irresponsible parties.

Another thing, our labor leaders must learn the ethical value of responsibility. They must recognize that no longer can they insist upon the equality of men unless they also concede the liberty of men, which equality and liberty go hand in hand together in the French Creed, and if they abandon one they must abandon the other. The union shall guard the weakest without doing injustice to the strongest. And then when we have come that far we shall have social peace.

You say "compulsory arbitration;" a contradiction in terms. No friends, it is not at all. There is a procedure of compulsory arbitration. If you believe I owe you a dollar and I deny the debt; you hire a lawyer, who will charge you more than the dollar; he will take your case to the court, and the court sits in judgment. That is arbitration, compulsory arbitration, and I have to submit to the decision. If the court says I owe you a dollar, the court will see to it that you get the dollar. Once upon a time these transactions were individual, private privileges. Even murder was at one time an affair which the State did not concern itself about. Men could compound felonies; they could compound murders. In Europe every transaction is under the eye of the state. It was as much of a revolution, when people were forced to arbitrate their debt accounts compulsorily, as it is today to arbitrate the difficulties between capital and labor under compulsory arbitration. We shall get there.

Now we have found a way that is almost legalized, thanks to that glorious man who is in the presidential chair of America. We have found an ethical way to arbitrate difficulties. That precedent will become gradually legalized, and we shall come out of the territory state. The torch before us is ethics. Neither union or trust is the ultimate, but marshalled conscience is. We have lost personality; we must bring it back.

I see another plan of organization. Hitherto our unions have been horizontal; we must get them vertical. They are now horizontal because only their own class is in the union. They should be vertical, and the employers would be in the union as well as the employees. That is the democratic plan of social organization, not my hallucination.

The Pennsylvania Railroad Company has applied that even now, and, if they would apply that in the coal district, we would not have strikes. If they would learn that human life is more valuable than property, we might have peace. If they would not try to have cheapest labor control the American system, we would have concord.

The transition period is upon us. Manchester economics have suffered bankruptcy. We are in the age of socialized activity. We shall proceed along those paths until at the final Sukkoth Day, again, thou and thy son and thy daughter, thy man servant and thy maid servant, the stranger within thy gates and the Levite, the widow and the orphan shall be brought together in a union not on the one hand of labor and on the other of capital, but a union of labor and capital, and all men allowed the right of their humanity; the responsibilities of their manhood will have what we have lost, the joy of life.

When that Sukkoth day comes, which is not distant, the sword will be turned into the plowshare, and the lance will be turned into a pruning hook, and every man will sit under his own fig tree. Ah, says Isaiah, "The watchmen are blind; where they, like the watchdog, should bark, they are asleep." Each man today runs his own race, wanting more, more and more; and others say, "Come, let us drink , let us have a good time. As it is today, so it will be tomorrow."

But it will not be so tomorrow, unless the watchmen can bark and give the signal of danger, and their cry be heeded. Go on, ye Manchester idolaters. Go on in your stupendous blindness, for nothing will save you. Then tomorrow, good God offended! The heavens will be red, and the earth will be red, and as out of the struggle of the French Revolution, after a night of terrors came a purged, new generation. We shall have to pass through the valley of decision and drink from the bitter cup of Divine wrath in order to get what we might get of our own accord; the baptism of peace and the instruction of a social conscience telling us that no man lives for himself alone, and that no man can use life or property to the injury of his fellow men. Tomorrow will not be as it is today; it will be a night of horrors, and it will not be a dawn of peace. Come then, peace to all; be thou the Sukkoth of plenty and of joy for all men on earth. Teach us through the smallness of thy fruit of Esrog that not the large things are valuable but that by the small things men are judged and society is built. Come, Peace! Tarry not. Bless us; bless this land especially.

Amen.

THE JEWISH PREACHER:
Rabbi Emil G. Hirsch, Ph.D., LL.D.

The Education of Orphans

1891, Month & Day Unknown

There is no Jewish community of any pretension whatsoever but has recognized this obligation. The old historic congregations in Europe may point with pride to rich endowments, the intention of which is to rear to perfect manhood, orphans, the children who had to battle with life without the protection of those who had called them into existence. And young as our American Judaism is, for its history does not extend beyond fifty years, one might say, in almost every city of the union we find associations banded together for the purpose of giving training, home, and education to the orphans.

The duty thus, to appeal in behalf of orphans, is upon the man who occupies the pulpit; that all of us recognize. It is our obligation to provide for the fatherless. In this we are all agreed. There is none within the hearing of my voice, I am positive there is none in this Jewish community of Chicago but willingly accedes to the proposition that we have no more sacred obligation than this, to come to the rescue of the children; to help those that cannot help themselves, being left to battle with life when yet they are not strong enough to bear the brunt of the conflict.

But this is a duty; to read aright this universal sentiment. Impulsive benevolence often defeats its own desires. The impulsive man may claim the credit for his good intentions, but he needs guidance. And whence shall that guidance come? It can only come from the light of experience. The thought of those who have paid attention to this subject shall be carefully weighed.

One system and another must be conscientiously compared. We must not act upon the first thought. The second sober thought is always the safer, and whatever is planned shall only be executed after a careful study of the advantages and disadvantages that go with one system or another. Which educators and philanthropists suggest as the most potent and the most likely to attain, at the least outlay of material resources and the richest return of moral fruitage, the coveted aim.

Do not misunderstand me, friends. Had there been in this city an institution for the care of orphans on the old system, the asylum plan, I should have deemed it my duty, at least to keep silence. It has been my policy never to injure what had been created, and I believe I may claim for myself this, at least, that at all times, to the full extent of my restricted ability, I have been willing to cooperate, whether I approved of the system or not, and I say it here, and say it most emphatically, we have an asylum which is our own.

It is true, that institution is not within the

municipal borders of our city. It is true it is not situated even in our own state. I need not name that asylum to you. You know it, it has won for itself an envious fame among the many model institutions of which the Jews in this country and any other land may boast. I can say it without fear of possible contradiction, as an asylum it is a model institution. None is more glorious; none has been more carefully managed; none has reached greater result, than the Cleveland home for our orphans.

Thus, it is not my intention, and I beg of you, do not misunderstand me, to take issue with the existing asylum. Were this the only question, I should raise my voice to stir you, as far as possible, to greater efforts in behalf of that philanthropic undertaking. It needs our help today. We cannot shirk the responsibility of a partnership, which now covers almost twenty-five years. It is treason to say we shall leave Cleveland now and establish our own institution. If there is not resource large enough to support both, the old and something new, in the name of justice and in the name of true benevolence I must say forego the planning and the planting of the new and give your support to the old in the richest possible measure.

But here is the situation. The cry has gone forth in the midst of us: We need an orphan institution of some kind or other. The Cleveland Orphan Asylum does not take all of our orphans. The proposition is laid down as self-evident that it cannot take them all. That proposition, I doubt. I know that Cleveland Orphan Asylum will take all worthy cases. There may be certain orphans among us that will not be admitted to the Cleveland home; but they should not be admitted to any other home, for even benevolence has its foundation in eternal justice. The duty to provide for the sick does not set aside the duty for self-protection.

Take as an illustration our own hospital. It is primarily intended for the sick and the sufferers in this city. It cannot be claimed that it is the duty of the trustees of that hospital to admit to its privileges the sick from all the country round about here, so that all that is necessary for them to do is to send their patients here and we are bound to take care of them. The same applies to our other benevolent institutions. We cannot provide for orphans that are imported. The children that are orphaned in Europe should be provided for there. To import them here and then to claim that they are orphans and on that plea ask for admission to our institutions, is an injustice done to us.

It is not as a matter of right, a proposition that can be entertained. Yea, if our resources were without measure; if the Jewish community of these United States were able to carry the load of the whole European eastern world; then, certainly none of us would say no, to whatever appeal is made. But facts are hard and unpleasant factors. There is a limit to our resources; and being limited we must first provide for those that are nearest to us. And as a matter of protection for them, it is just that the trustees of the Orphan Asylum in Cleveland have made the rule that none shall be admitted that was an orphan before he or she crossed the ocean.

That is self-protection, and no matter what sentimentalism may say, and no matter what many a misguided woman may urge, it is right that this rule be observed. We cannot allow ourselves to be flooded by the misery of the whole world. We cannot bear the load of misery of the whole hemisphere. We have to provide for our own, and if there is something left after that, then certainly will we take charge of new burdens and make openings for newcomers. Thus the cases that are always pointed out as proving the proposition that the Cleveland Orphan Asylum does not do its duty must be discredited.

An asylum on the Cleveland plan does this for us. None have been more loyal; none have been broader than they; and to urge this now as an evidence that we must sever our relations, which for twenty-five years have been of the most pleasant and intimate order, is something to my mind irrational and unjust. We have not neglected our duty by our orphans; we have discharged it. Cleveland Orphan Asylum is as much our institution as is any institution located within the limits of our municipality.

But now suppose my argument does not hold and the necessity is upon us of providing also in addition to what we do and what is done in Cleveland in the same institution of the same kind for the care of those that are not admitted there. What, then, is our duty? Is it fair and just that we shall blindly rush on and say: We have had an asylum we must again have an asylum.

Are there no other lines along which we can work? This duty, to my mind, has not been discharged by those who have opened the crusade in this our city.

I claim to be an expert, if in anything, in the charity work. I do not claim that because my experience has been abundant, but because I have given thought and time to just these subjects. I have once before said it and at the risk of being misunderstood, once more I say it: The leaders in charity are not misfit rabbis, are not broken down teachers, are not social workers out of a job, are not women that are carried away by their sentiment, are not men that follow their impulses; but those that have given thought and time to the systems practiced elsewhere.

As such an expert as I claim to be, let me this morning present the advantages and the disadvantages of both the old system and the one that, if we must adopt here in this city; something I would urge you to follow. For I claim for it under our situation, the greatest advantages and the most direct benefits to the community and to the orphans themselves.

It cannot be denied that nature makes no mistake; that evolution has reached certain conclusions, which we cannot undo, and which are for the benefit of all parties concerned. How did humanity begin?

It began as a herd. Natural science teaches us when time begins humanity was organized, as are the lower animals, in groups, in herds. The children were nobody's children. They belonged to the tribe; just as the monkeys today move about in large groups. No monkey knows exactly to whom he belongs. So the men of old moved about the earth in groups and herds. But this herd plan of necessity in gradual evolution departed and reached finally the stage of family life. Thus nature and evolution demonstrate that the family is the foundation of the higher type and that the child is to be reared in the family, under normal conditions.

Therefore those at once in favor of the family plan are being more natural. If it were not so, humanity would forever have remained at the notch of the herd plan. This, then, being granted, is there not sometime the necessity of departing from the family basis?

It is claimed by the advocates of asylums that in case the family has by death been dissolved, it is necessary to leave the family type. That there are certain advantages in the asylum plan none can deny. The discipline that there prevails cannot but react beneficially upon the physical and to a certain extent upon the moral constitution of the wards. The military drill in the barracks of the German army, for instance, leaves its impression upon body and mind of the German soldier; and none will deny this, that the course of training had in the military camp has to a certain extent, an advantage to him who receives it. But for all that, will any of us say, that military discipline is absolutely indispensable?

It is true they receive good training, they are amenable to commands, they know that a certain thing is to be done at a certain time, and cannot be done as well at another time. These advantages I will not dispute. But there are exceptions to every rule. Even in the best regulated families accidents will happen. It is true that sometimes both parents are unable to cope with the vicious tendencies of the child. For such children as these, certainly the more rigid discipline of a military establishment will be beneficial.

But it requires but little reflection to prove that the cases of this kind are not normal. We send our children, to boarding school only when we are too indolent, or absolutely incapable of training them at home. And a boarding school of all schools is the worst that can be devised. Ask any educator and he will tell you the great danger that lurks in the herding of children. One rotten apple will spoil a whole basket full. One vicious child is enough to infest forever all children that come in contact with it.

Now, I know that our superintendents of orphan asylums take exceedingly great care to guard against these dangers; and I register my testimony here that in the Orphan Asylum at Cleveland this danger has been minimized, thanks to the men who are at the head of this institution. But if they have been fortunate enough to secure these children against this danger, we are not so certain that we would be so fortunate in the selection of our force; that under other conditions these dangers would not he so successfully met. It is the experience of all educators; and ask them, if you doubt my word—that the bringing of children together in one large institution, where they eat and where they sleep, notwithstanding military discipline, is disadvantageous. These dangers I need not particularize. Every father is aware of them; every teacher is on the lookout for them; and it is sometimes exceedingly difficult to stamp them out when once they have taken a root in the soul of the child. This danger cannot be disputed.

And another thing cannot be disputed; that individuality is scarce possible under rigid military discipline. I know the superintendents are all men full of sympathy for those that are entrusted to their care, I know they do all that can be done to let the child keep its individuality. But can they? We have in this city established a Home for Aged Jews. It has at present, say a dozen inmates; it will perhaps speedily have more. But being a home, an institution, these dozen must be amenable to discipline. Even in this society individual men and women cannot be recognized.

You cannot run the institution on the individualistic plan. The lights must be out at a certain time. They must all eat at a certain time. Their walks must be taken so as not to conflict with the economy of the house. Rule and regulation are necessary, even in the conduct of a small institution. Now, take an asylum of five hundred, or as they have in New York, a thousand children. Can there be scope given to individual children? Now and then perhaps the superintendent may make an exception; but in order to conduct the school successfully, the children must play at a certain hour, and play in company, whether they feel like playing or not. They must be studied separately.

For instance, I have five children, and each day I find that each of those five is a mystery in itself that I have to study. Each child of my five requires individual attention. I must probe my child's own character. I must find out whether this child is amenable to kindness or severity. I know all children differ, even though children of the same parents. The one has a sanguine temperament and the other has a timid disposition; the one takes things seriously, and the other takes matters lightly. The one is playful, the other is anxious to read or work.

The parent must study the disposition of the children, and must correct them if they need to be corrected, and the most in the work of education. Now, with the highest regard for the men that we have placed in our orphan asylums—and I have taught since I was fifteen years of age, making twenty-five years of teaching; though I have found myself confronted with small classes and large classes; by young children as well as grown up students—I cannot conceive of one man finding out the disposition of each child, and conducting the institution so as to fit the disposition of each.

It is an impossibility. The individuality of the child cannot be considered. Military discipline must be preserved. These are some of the disadvantages. Let me repeat again: I know that in some of our Jewish orphan asylums this danger is less urgent than elsewhere, for our Jewish institutions are under the influence of that which the world calls clannishness; the tribal sentiment; paternal relations between parent and child.

But notwithstanding this, the system that allows individual development, is the better; and if we have to begin, why not begin on the better plan. Why blindly rush on, and say: Because the Cleveland Orphan Asylum is a model institution, we must have an institution like it in this city? Why not study the other plan? In the family the child is placed by birth; in the family the child should be reared in normal circumstances. And I claim that the orphan child too, can be so reared, if the effort is made earnestly and seriously.

What are the economic advantages of this plan? We need no institution costing $300,000 invested in the building. The interest on this sum would be $18000. We know that no institution could be built here that would be large enough to meet the necessities of the hour for less than that and we certainly would not build with the necessity of undoing at some future time what we might do. There would be $18000 wasted in the institution and the salaries of superintendents and assistants, which might be saved. Then add the cost of maintaining the building, light, heat, etc., all must be reckoned as dead investments before the child receives the benefit. That is the economic side of the question.

But where will you find the families for these children. Most of these children have one or the other parent left. "Ah!" say you, "the mother is not fit to rear the child." If that is the argument, then we come too late if we wait till death forces the duty upon us. Then we should, if we are convinced of this, before even the father has died, take measures to take the child away from the parent. But the proposition is so ridiculous, that none of us will maintain it. None of us will go back to the Spartan plan, of taking the child away from the parents on the plea that the parents are unfit to educate. It therefore is the duty of the state.

The voice of nature has always a true ring and no matter how ignorant a mother is, and how weak she may be; it is always safest to leave the child with her who brought it into life with throes and pain. The most ignorant mother is better for the child than the most educated stranger, who may or may not have sympathy or love for the child. But is the family plan so deficient as not to provide rectification for the defects of the mother?

Does the mother become all at once an autocrat as to how to bring up the children? Under the family plan every child has a guardian. The guardian is the friend of the mother. He has to visit the mother, consult the mother, and aid the mother in the rearing of the child. And in Philadelphia, my sainted father, twenty-seven years ago, and up to the time of his death, and now by his memory, practically carried out this plan. No child that has had a guardian but that the guardian did not come to be the friend of the mother; come to be the friend of the child. And I have spoken lately with certain guardians who told me that if the society were to disband, they loved that child so much they would defray the expenses, rather than have the child taken from them.

So strong was the affection, that whatever the mother's faults the guardian will remedy them. But, say you, if the mother dies, who will take the child? Generally there will be one in the family that will take the child. Will you tell me that Jewish women will refuse to take the child of a dead sister. That a cousin will refuse to open the doors to an orphaned child of a relative? I will not believe that. I have moved too long in life, and have had too much experience in that line to believe it. Our Hebrew relief societies find asylums for these children. There are none so ill-disposed toward them but will take them.

Let a Hebrew come to this society over on the west side; there are friends that have taken them in and have given them a welcome. This cannot be denied. And with this disposition of helpfulness, will you tell me that they will not take the child of sister or cousin that has been left without the necessities of life.

Why don't they do it? Because their financial resources are not large enough. Here the society steps in and pays. The cousin is helped, the poor families are helped, and the child is helped at the same time. And what is more, the child never needs to know that he is a recipient of public charity. The child in Philadelphia does not know that the guardian comes there and brings money to the mother. They look upon the guardian as the friend of the family. They call him uncle; they call her aunt. They think he is some distant relative.

Can you avoid that in our public institutions? Why, you say, the children are happy. Out of one hundred, ninety-nine are happy. But if there is one that feels the abnormality of his situation, you have clouded the life of that one child forever.

Say I am drawing upon my imagination; I am not. I have seen children in our orphan asylums that were cheerful, bright, joyful; but I will never forget that I have seen some timid, shy, broken down children. And it was because their poor hearts were broken down; they while only children had lost their gift—their parents. That is not a trifling thing.

Under the family plan the child does not know that he is the recipient of public benevolence. The mother knows it; the guardian knows it. And there is another advantage of the family point of view. The children. are not paraded as orphans and dependents. I am now touching upon a tender spot. Believe me, I am not personal in my remarks; but it has always made my blood boil to see the children put on exhibition for the benefit of the patrons. Why, good God it is an outrage, from my point of view, to do anything like it; to have these people pointed out as their benefactors. Who are these benefactors? Men who perhaps have paid five dollars a year are presented as benefactors. That is an outrage and all these institutions commit this outrage. And friends, who have done this, let me ask you in this holy spot, to discontinue it.

When the children leave this institution, they are looked upon as graduates of an orphan asylum. Some do not mind it; but I have met with men who cannot bear to hear the word orphan asylum, because those who come from there are pointed at as something beyond the usual order. This will be obviated if the family plan is adopted.

But suppose there is neither sister or relative of the mother, who will take the children? There are always hard-working families, childless couples, which will be glad to receive these children, if they are paid for it, because their economic system is not disturbed by it. But you say, "they do it for money." Don't I preach for money? Don't you in your business work for money? Are you less faithful because you are working for money? Do not our superintendents of orphan asylums work for money? Do not their assistants receive salaries? That is no argument. No woman, if she is a woman, at all, will merely look for the stipend she receives.

Why, it is natural that the little child will grow into the affections of the mother, the adopted mother, the foster mother. Yea, among non-Jews it will grow. Is not the guardian there to see that no cruelty is committed?

Here comes another argument against it. These people all come from the quarters of the city that are squalid. Will you leave the children in that part of the city? The orphan plan will perhaps be the means of taking some child out of the filth; for if the mother refuses to go, then the child will be taken away.

In Philadelphia I have had such an experience. Another disadvantage to these poor is that they are reared in the houses of poverty. That is no shame. The advantages of our beautifully appointed orphan asylums are so out of contrast with the surroundings in which the children will have to live again when they come from the orphan asylums that I for one hold that a serious objection to the orphan asylum plan; for the children reared in comparative luxury will find themselves discontented when after the thirteenth or fourteenth year they go back to the home of the parent.

The family plan will not take them away from the home. The home may be poor; that is no reason why they have to be moved. I am the son of a poor man, a man who from his thirteenth year on had to struggle with poverty; and who died not the least famous among men in the horizon of modern Judaism. That is a fact which history attests.

And as here in America we have so many examples of this kind, we may leave these children in the homes that are poor, and need not fear that thereby they may grow up bootblacks or mere peddlers on the streets. And in this city is there any doubt of trying this plan?

Our maual training school is now working as a missionary in that quarter of the city. We would have the cooperation of that school, and they would be trained in that school to love work, and the danger that they would grow up as bootblacks is almost zero. In the family plan once in a while the child will grow up bad. But in our orphan asylums there is the same danger.

Yea, a gentleman who controverted my position the other day told me that he had adopted a child from the Philadelphia Orphan Asylum, and that he had to be sent back; that he was a liar. So that is a possibility that happens in an orphan asylum, as well as under the family plan.

But the crowning glory of all I have not touched upon; it is the influence upon ourselves. We give money. We pride ourselves on that; but few give themselves. The directors give their time, their person; the president of the Cleveland

Orphan Asylum devotes his whole time to the work, but he is one of the few that give themselves. Others think they have done enough with giving their money. Where is the advantage of giving ourselves? What is the bane of modern time? Our children are reared in seclusion. The children that live on the avenues and boulevards are separated from other children. We are afraid of their being contaminated. Let our children come in contact with the poor children, they will be benefited, but our children will be benefited more.

In Philadelphia the guardian takes the child into his own family and the children of the guardian learn to play with Joe. And they become friends for life. The barriers are broken down, and forever thereafter the children of the guardian receive an impression that never can be blotted out from the memory, or neutralized. Say it is for the guardian an impossible task. Say in this city you cannot find families. Will you tell me that we have not two hundred ladies who will each one take care of an orphan child?

Why I believe much better of my own friends than to take this pessimistic view. It may be difficult to find the homes. It may be difficult to find the guardians, but the difficulty is not proof that the easier plan is the better. Every guardian will become better for his charge; as the directors of the Orphan Asylum in Cleveland find their soul-life broadened and deepened.

So in this plan, without marking the child off as something distinct from all other children, two hundred men and women may become richer by coming in contact with them. It has been said that a woman that has no children does not know the sweetness of life. So it is with every new responsibility; every new burden gives life an increased sweetness, and it is for your own sake as Jews, and for the sake of the children that I would plead for the family plan, in this city. It is the cheaper plan. We need no large building; we need not waste a single cent on salaries; we need not waste a cent on office expenses; it is morally safer, and it is a benefit to the guardian, as well as those that keep the child.

I have spoken. I do not expect that my views will carry; but at least it is the fate of us in the pulpit seldom to be heeded until it is too late. We are looked upon by the largest class of people as the paid prayer reader and whenever we have views of our own we are made a target for abuse and some of us are howled down.

But I for one decline to voice sentiments which are not my own; to be merely a trumpet voicing the views of others. Unfortunately I am not rich enough, notwithstanding your great generosity to me and my family, to undertake a work of this kind. But I say this, if we have to do something for the orphan; why then this blind, impulsive, imitative way? Why not try the system that has the endorsement of the deepest thinkers on public charity? At the convention held last summer in Denver, and when a Jew, an orthodox Jew of Philadelphia—who certainly did not love my father any too well—rose up and told them of the work of the orphan asylum there, the assembly rose to their feet applauding the system as the most perfect, the most benevolent, the most advantageous to all.

Now that assembly was not composed of cranks. There may be a few professional philanthropists among them, who think that their views should be carried, and if not carried they will withdraw. They pose as benevolent men.

But there are serious thinking men that endorse the plan. And in this city, Mr. Gage and others, have organized a society for the training of waifs. The Jewish papers may say about me that I am talking "through my hat", but they will not talk about Mr. Gage that way. He knows what he is talking about. There is a school at [Glenwood] Glenville conducted on this plan. They build a few cottages; for the plan is to make a few children grow up in the right way; and then after they have had them at the highest for a year, they place them in families. Not an institution with iron bars; but individual development in the home. That is the plan of a man who never talks "through his hat", as the Jewish papers say I do.

That is the correctness of my position. We need no orphan asylum. We have an orphan asylum; and I doubt whether in this city you will ever succeed in duplicating that institution at Cleveland. It is our duty to support it. They are better off in Cleveland than we would be here. They have larger grounds than we could possibly afford. To remove the child from the mother altogether is claimed to be a disadvantage. But the cruelty of having the mother visit the child every week is greater than removing the child for six years from the mother's gaze. Every visit of the mother to the child hurts; and it is better that the distance be great.

That orphan asylum at Cleveland is a model institution. If we must have an institution—to use a phrase somewhat vulgar—"it fills the bill" as no other does, and the superintendent of that asylum has earned our gratitude. We need no orphan asylum here. If there were cases that do not fall under the protection of the orphan asylum there, some of these cases would not fall under one here.

Some people take care of everything with sympathy, till it comes to hard dollars. I see in this agitation for an asylum, names of people have cropped out that were never heard of before in our charity work; and if I applied to the individual the excuse was given that they, were too poor; and if I wanted money they could not give; but they can give money to carry out their design, which is absolutely unnecessary.

Their are those whose honesty of purpose I do not doubt, but they are misguided. They know not the situation. We cannot afford an institution of this kind here. Our hospital is indebted; our Home for the Aged is in difficulties, and no one knows what the outcome will be. We must go slowly. In the meantime let us adopt the cheaper plan.

The Frank fund has done what I have attempted to describe; though perhaps not as fully. If it must be improved, let it be improved. Why then this waste of material energy? I register my protest against this in the name of the community. Let those that begin this campaign think twice and three times, And notwithstanding all the endorsements of those that have come here, of strangers that have come here, I say that I know the Jewish institution too well; it will injure the Cleveland institution, and it will help no one. It will be a burden under which we will all be crushed.

If the time has come to do something here; after we have placed Cleveland Orphan Asylum in a position no longer to need us, then let us come and study the plan.

I for one will cast my vote for the family plan as the most economic, the most natural, and that promises the greater returns to the orphan and the friends of the orphan.

Amen.

THE JEWISH PREACHER:
Rabbi Emil G. Hirsch, Ph.D., LL.D.

The Science Of Comparative Religion
Part One

Sunday, December 5, 1897
Reading: Genesis 24

From the little piece of coal in the scuttle in the kitchen to the gorgeously splendid majestic and mighty forests of mammoth days, seems to be a far cry; and yet even high school boys in these days of general knowledge and culture, such as it is, know full well that the little bit of black diamond by whose breath we are warmed in the chill days, by whose power our mighty engines are set into motion, is not merely the descendant, but the actual person, so to speak, which once, in days removed from ours by stretches which baffle imagination to compute them, were forests long before there was man on earth to assert his supremacy over all things created.

Who would think that the cry of the fetishist, the fears of the ghost worshipper, are of the same family as the refined chant filling with music a temple like this? And yet, as the geologist knows that the coal today was once the foliage and vegetation of a luxurious growth, and a unimagined wealth, so the student of comparative religion

THE SCIENCE OF COMPARATIVE RELIGION
PART ONE

knows that the crude cry of the fetish worshipper and the fear of the ghost revered, are identical with refined thought of a worshipper in this, the most glorious and most liberal and most advanced and most cultured of all religious congregations in the world.

The science of comparative religion is of recent birth. It counts scarce more as a distinct science than fifty years, and if we include the preparations for its work, we cannot enumerate more than ten decades measuring its glory.

Generally the world at large knows nothing of the stupendous finds made by the student of comparative religion. Naturally, his discoveries have no bearing on the one supreme and always intense ambition to make money. Perhaps his thoughts run along the groove where the suspicion ripens into conviction that money is the least of the vital things in humanity, and that the possessor of the b*iggest* pocket book, if it were merely this, is but a cipher in the greater cooperative and spiritual tendency of the true mankind.

And for this reason, the books on this science are companions of a small band of devoted students alone. The churches themselves have been disinclined to admit to their councils the teachers of this new science. Naturally, the Orthodox Church found itself free of the necessity to encourage these studies. Why, has not orthodoxy truth and all truth? What is then the profit in following the errors as they develop among those that were not dignified with the reception of divine revelation?

A science which presumes to place on one level

Christianity and Mohammedanism, or Judaism or Fetishism, is on its very face presumptuous, not to say blasphemous. And so the church has for once allied its influence with that of the money seeker and money maker, who is the lord of this creation, to rob this science of a hearing and to stop its finds from being more generally known; and yet it must be said that among the glories of this nineteenth century, there is none that will eclipse this belonging to the domain of researches in this department.

It is true we admire the chemist, and we listen intently to the report of the physicist. We are lifted to the sublime heights of admiration when the astronomer tells us what he has read from the alphabet of the nightly sky, and when the geologist assures us that there are coal seams and coal measures that promise not to be exhausted for thousands of solar cycles. Our eye glistens with satisfaction for all these things have their bearing on our daily life, and on our daily comfort. Chemistry enters our very kitchen, and the science of physics has bearing on our physical well-being. Astronomy teaches the mariner how to thread his way in a trackless waste of water midst storms and midst wrath of waves lashed to fury, but the science of religion seems, in the first place, intent upon rotting the religious heart of its confidence, and certainly has no charms for him who has no religion and boasts of this his mutilation as a wonderful accomplishment.

But for all this—I repeat it—in the crown of glory which modern man may wear, which this century will bequeath to its successor, there is

THE SCIENCE OF COMPARATIVE RELIGION
PART ONE

none that in radiancy, in brilliant jewels, can compare with the wreath that the science of comparative religion has prepared for man's, modern man's brow.

Perhaps you are a little curious to know what that science is doing, for it seems that science and religion cannot be yoked together. You have heard it, and perhaps thirty years ago, most of you, and if there be a few younger men here who were not able to hear thirty years ago of it ,they have learned it yesterday from Mr. Ingersoll, and such men as he, that science excludes religion—that where knowledge appears, faith takes its flight. That there is absolutely no possibility of reconciling one with the other; that where they have been yoked together, science suffered and religion did not profit—and here we are speaking of the science of comparative religion.

What is a science? A science is knowledge, in the first place, organized. It is facts collected and grouped under certain views, so that from the facts, certain conclusions may be drawn. And the scientific spirit, furthermore, is not satisfied with gathering more facts as they are and grouping them under certain heads, but he is constantly craving for more facts. He is never satisfied with what he has, with what he has found and what he has worked. He would find new things—more of old things, in order to be sure on the one hand of his conclusions, or on the other to correct than if, in the light of the facts, they appear to be incorrect.

Scientific knowledge, for that reason, is altogether different from that which among non-scientific and non-scholarly men passes as knowledge. A man may have ever so much of scrapbook learning; he may be able for instance, to tell you in a moment when the compass was invented, and at what time of day William the Conqueror set his foot on the English shore, or how many people were killed in a riot twenty-five years ago, and how they came by their death; or he may chatter along interminably about the stars and the flowers, and even convey correct information.

He may know his Chumesh and his Rashi to perfection without even making a break in one quotation, or he may even know Schiller and Goethe and God knows who else, of German literature. Unless all this knowledge be organized, be arrayed under certain heads, his knowledge is not scientific; and unless from his knowledge he has learned to draw correct conclusions, even after it be arranged, and systematized, his scientific education has been sadly neglected. Many a waiter in Europe talks six languages, and perhaps seven if he talks through his nose, in addition to the six he talks with his mouth, but for all that he is not a linguistic scholar. But in our university or in any university there may be a teacher who speaks only one language and that English, and he teaches French, though he cannot talk French; and he teaches even Spanish, though he cannot understand a word of Spanish when it is spoken to him. He may have a scientific knowledge of languages, for while he has merely a reading knowledge thereof, while he understands it with his eyes and not with his ears, and has never twisted his tongue sufficiently to bring out the foreign sounds, and to detect the foreign words and connote the ideas, he understands the growth of that language, its relation to other languages, its position in the family of languages; he understands the life of that language, of that group of languages. For that reason his knowledge is scientific. The waiter's knowledge, the mere speaker of language's knowledge is not scientific, even if it be correct. The waiter who never in Germany spoke English as we sometimes hear it here even under that condition his knowledge of English is not scientific.

If this be the characteristic of science, you can understand full well that there can be a science of religion; for, as I said last week, religion is a fact, and religious history is full of facts, and where there is a fact and where there are facts, there is the invitation for systematic study of these facts and for systematic organizations of these facts.

The science of anatomy studies the human form without any regard to the utilitarian application of the knowledge inculcated and the anatomist does not care, as an anatomist, whether through his knowledge the science of therapeutics be enlarged or not—he treats the dead body as an object, no matter whether that object in its stilled and chilled silence have broken the heart of a mother that weeps for the child on the dissecting table. Or whether it be that of a tramp who had nowhere to lay his head, and leaves behind no one to remember him and no grave will now claim him. The anatomist treats the dead body of the child as an object without sentimental relations, and dissects the body of the tramp with as great an attitude of concern as he displays when his scalpel severs the ligaments or opens the thorax of the poor baby's dead mortality.

The scientific theory excludes pathological affection—it is free from sympathies; it confronts a fact as an object and that object has to be studied for all that there is in it and for all that through it is connected with it in the greater organism of life and of thought, of universe and of the world in its fullness.

So, if religion has facts it invites scientific study. But that scientific study is free from the assertion of the truth of the facts of religion or their errors. The student of religious science is as much interested in the superstition, as we call it, of the spirit worshipper as he is in the religious convictions of so liberal a congregation as I have the undeserved fortune to address this morning.

For the student of the religion of science the crudest error and the most shocking rite of the savage tribe is as attractive as the most refined religious aspiration, and the most cultured religious symbolism of 19th Century liberal religion.

The student of this science has neither to prove the error nor to demonstrate the truth of any religious conceit or the necessity and legitimacy of any religious action, symbol sign—of any religious hope or any religious delusion. And in this spirit the masters of the science of religion have proceeded. Whence do they get their facts? To gather facts about living religions would seem to be a matter of considerable ease, and certainly the living religions they studied as they were presented to them in their living formations; but what about the dead religions, or the religions that are practiced in those forgotten and God forsaken corners of this world? How did they there gather the facts and from what sources aid they assemble their material?

Without the auxiliary science of comparative philology and the newest science of comparative literature, religion could never have been examined correctly, as it should have been under the demands of science and scientific spirit.

Philology opened to the student of the science of religion a vast arsenal of facts. One hundred and a few years or more ago, the world was stirred by the report that somewhere in India, a language was spoken which seemed in its construction to remind the traveler of Latin or Greek, and that that language had a wonderful literature in the keeping of priests and pundits, still poring over the long forgotten leaves and commentating incessantly the old documents. That language was the Sanskrit, and with the discovery of this Sanskrit language the modern philology began to unfold its wings.

I shall not weary you with the account of the successive victories accomplished by this science, but that science has given to the student of comparative religion the key to the religious documents and religious documents are by no means few. Our Bible is as far as bulk goes, the least significant one in this collection.

The world has had many Bibles—seven of them having in their respective religions exercised identical influences—The New Testament; the Old; the Tripitaka, The Kings, the Zend Avesta, perhaps even the Edda and the Vedic Hymns and Homer—all these are bibles, and all these had to be read, and all these had to be interpreted. Had these students of language not preceded the scholar in search of light on the facts of religion, the latter would have failed and failed ignominiously—failed disastrously.

But there are religions that are not dependent upon written records, and there were religions that were not dependent upon religious records—at least, they have left none for us to study.

Here another science stepped in and extended her hand to the student of religion. It was ethnology—one of the greatest and most gifted powers in the temple and the study of anthropology—the science of man. This science of ethnology gathered all the curious customs and preserved all peculiar practices. It visited the savage tribes of Australia and the pygmy hordes of darkest Africa—and studied their life and followed with rabid curiosity their religious exercises. Here it picked up a tooth—the tooth of an elephant, and there it gathered a broken javelin; yonder it stumbled upon arrows curiously shaped and there again upon idols most horridly carved; there it exhumed a totem pole or bargained for its purchase from a willing and mercenary tribe; yonder it brought home the description of a dance or it actually reproduced the intonation of a war cry; and again at another time some traveler reported that in some mountain fastness of the Himalayas or in some thick jungle of the plain, or in the thickest forest of Africa, he found the same words almost and the same motions at the same occasions, here in Asia on the heights, on the plains, or yonder in Africa along the river's courses or in the God forsaken forest and ramparted wastes of the darkest of the darkest continent.

All these things and many more the ethnologist brought home, and the ethnologist studied and arranged, and the student of religion peeped over the shoulders of the ethnologist—he went to the Field Museums and the other storehouses, of the curiosities and helped the ethnologist to arrange these things, and he explained them to him. This elephant tooth was not merely an elephant tooth—so much ivory but that was a tribal fetish. With that elephant tooth wonders had been wrought. That elephant tooth had in times of danger strengthened a tribe to resistance, or yonder song that the ethnologist took at first for the ditty senseless, the trained ear of the religionist discovered to be a sacrificial chant welcoming the rise of the sun or wailing for the death of springtime.

And so the ethnologist and the student of religion worked side by side. The one told the story of civilization and the other told the story of the development of the highest in civilization—the religion of the human race.

And still another science had to teach before the science of religion could assume to come to correct conclusions. Religion, was after all, something that man had, and whatever man has is rooted in what, for the want of a better name, we call man's soul. Now, I know enough, I assure you, my great critics—I know enough not to use that word *soul,* and I ask you, do not go home and say I used it in this sense—the word soul in the sense of an entity that is pumped into us at some stage of our prenatal life, and is pumped out of us again at some stage when we go to sleep in death—in that sense I do not use the word soul. Nor do I use it in the sense that there are separate faculties that are bundled together somehow or other and act independently. We have a faculty of memory, for instance and a faculty of emotions—a faculty of this and that, and that all these faculties together are some kind of an expression, an index of a life that is not dependent upon the body or is dependent upon the body and still is separate from it; and that this bundle of faculties gets into the human body at a certain period of gestation before birth, and gets out of the human body when we are called hence, as we are called hence, as we say, to the better life.

I have also, though an ignorant poor rabbi, learned something of psychological philosophy, or physiological psychology—fine language words—my lecture is fine today, you say—I have learned enough of physiological psychology to know that there can be no talk of separate faculties, that all this soul is functional life, functionally dependent upon neurotic (that means nerve if I do not talk fine language)—nerve conditions—neurotic conditions, and that that the neurotic apparatus influences the soul life. All this I have learned, and all the scientific students of religion had learned and are learning now—but with all this they know that there is a certain function in the human organism, which produces certain effects, and that these effects are what we call religion. Therefore, in order to understand religion as an effect of this human organism, we must first understand that human organism.

The science of psychology was thus the third in the noble group of allies that opened the temple of religion. And now psychology of the individual is not finally simple, because the individual is not final. No individual living today has begun anew the history of the world. It is true there are men with whom history begins a new page, and it is true undoubtedly that I have the honor of addressing one or the other of this kind with whose coming the world received a new impetus and was spinning along in space with a new philosophy and a more intense alacrity; but even these great men had antecedents, and their antecedents had antecedents, and their soul then, to use that old term with the limitations I have asked you to remember—their soul then at birth was not autochthonous, self made, springing from nothing into the greatest possibilities—was not free from prenatal historical influence for better or for worse, but had at the very first moment of its conscious assertion the ear marks of the history, the family, the race, the nation, the civilizations behind it.

No individual is in himself more than an epitome of all time that stretches behind him. The individuality, which he can exert simply in this: in utilizing what time behind him has given him for the purposes of the time before him. But he cannot begin time anew. Furthermore, no man is the whole thing in himself.

This twaddle about individualism is of all inanities and asininities the most unbearable. There is no individual. No man can say I have made myself, and I am making myself alone. We depend one upon the other, and your soul life depends upon the contact and impact with, and of, others.

You speak a language—is it your own? Sometimes it is; for in the wonderful way in which English is sometimes spoken, it is not the language of Shakespeare and of Milton; but unless language is so originally maltreated as it is, and thus has the stamp of your originality upon it, it is not your language. The language of all others you have received. You think that your mental genius is your own. You get it from others. If you come to analyze the component elements of your genius, you will find that but a very, very infinitesimal grain of productiveness of yours is in it, while all the rest is merely reproductive of what others have thought and what others have taught, and what others have willed.

We are dependent one upon the other. This has produced in Germany a new science called the science of folk psychology. That science tried to study the soul life not of an individual but of a nation. And nations have souls. The nation's soul comes to light through the nation's language, through the nation's literature, through the nation's art, through the nation's government, through the nation's ambition.

The Frenchman is a Frenchman by virtue of being a Frenchman, he thinks differently on all subjects from an American, for even for him twice two makes four, rings out with a tune, which is altogether different from the air in which it strikes the mind of the English or the American or the German or the Russian.

And so we Jews are by virtue of our history, associations distinct and differentiated from all others. There are things which must be rebuked in Jewish congregations which need not be in all others, and there are on the other side, things that call for praise in Jewish congregations, which are absent in all others. And, turn yourselves whichever way you wish—get baptized or become avowed ethical culturists with ethical culture left out, or become merely club Jews, thinking that those playhouses are the glory of modern Israel—or be Lodge Jews—talk of the race, and the glory of the race—you are Jews, whichever way you turn—your whole habitus of mind marks you as such, and it will mark your children and their children for many, many circling cycles to come.

That is what the Germans mean by the soul of a nation of a race—and this to study is the ambition of the Voelkerpsychologie, and this Voelkerpsychologie, called the science of religion, and said, "Listen to me. This religion of this class of tribes is different from the religion of that class of tribes, and would you know why? It is not simply due to climate, it is not simply due to the fact that the one is a mountain tribe and the other has its tents in the desert—but it is due to something which was produced by those factors and other factors—it is due to the national soul—the tribal soul of this tribe whose religion you would now study. And the science of religion listened intently and attentively, and has learned at the feet of the masters in this new investigation of a national soul.

And another one came—that was folklore, which is distinct from folk psychology as the photograph is distinct from solar chemistry. Of course photography depends on solar chemistry; but photography has its own accomplishments, which are as far as they assert themselves, independent of the wider domain of solar chemistry—for there is such a thing as solar chemistry, though we cannot put the sun into our chemical retorts, there is such a thing, and it is taught in the Yerkes observatory, as solar chemistry.

Now, folklore is a department of ethnology but it has its own methods and it is looking for its own finds; this folklore is busy with little ditties, with peculiar customs; it registers how often a child will cross itself because it is afraid something will happen, and it also records the fact that a thousand and one enlightened Jewish women will not sit down when there are thirteen at a table, and it also tells us that the most liberal of Sinai Congregation's members is often tempted when there is a death in the family, to hang some kind of a cloth, cheese cloth, whatever it is, in front of the looking glass. And folklore will also tell of the thousand and one plays in which children today engage, and in which savage men and women once engaged. And folklore explains the origin of the expression unbeschrien and unberufen, or why certain days are considered unlucky and why others are believed to bring good fortune; and it will also explain why the gambler, for instance (I am not becoming personal, I beg of you) will change his seat in order to got a new "streak of luck", or why he is afraid when the cat comes in the room, or why he cannot bear that someone shall look over his left shoulder, while perhaps he is very anxious that he should look over his right shoulder. All these things folklore tells us and registers, and then the science of religion comes and peeps into the books of the folklorist, and extracts from his material new pointers for his own investigation.

That is the method and these are the preliminary studies of the science of religion, so after all, to be a theologian today is not so easy. The science of religion is so very important in the range of studies which the modern student of religion, and the minister should be a student of religion, has to pursue.

This science of religion has now brought to the surface certain results. What they are I shall attempt to tell you when next I shall meet you. For today, go home with this one thought: that science and religion are by no means antipodal, as you might have believed, and that the student of religion is as scientific if he is a student, as is he who lays his ear on the bosom of the heavens and tries to hear the heartbeat of the world's great aorta.

To be a teacher of religion many things have to be studied, and are studied, of which the people at large take no notice, and of which they know nothing. The modern religion is like a mighty cathedral—the scaffold, which supports the worker, has disappeared. The spire alone points out how difficult it was to raise the quarried material to these heights—the completed work, a work of beauty and enchantment to the heart of the beholder; but that it might do this, in the silence of their study the architects had thought, and in the bustle of their drawing rooms, the architects had drawn, and what they had confided to paper, they then translated into stone, and in order to do this, the scaffold had to be raised.

Of all this, he who worships in the cathedral feels nothing and remembers nothing; yet without this, the cathedral would not invite him to bow in reverence before the mystery and the might and the majesty of that life of which his own life is but an echo, and his own thought; but a glimmer. Yea, the science of religion has earned its right to be one of the chamberlains in the courtroom of modern mind's majestic monarchy. What that science has done for our views of religion, let us try and learn when next we come together.

Amen

THE JEWISH PREACHER:
Rabbi Emil G. Hirsch, Ph.D., LL.D.

The Science Of Comparative Religion
Part Two

Sunday, December 12, 1897
Reading: Jeremiah 33

If one would get the right appreciation of the work done by the science of comparative religion he should recall the views as to the character of religion which held sway in the minds of most men before this science began to proclaim its finds. Thirty years ago two parties, if we leave out of consideration the minor differences, occupied the stage, each one dogmatic to the extreme, each one claiming to be the messenger of truth absolute.

On the one hand was the church, the believers, the faithful, they were insistent that religion was the result of revelation. Man himself had not developed the views and outlooks, the doctrines and the duties, which together made up the teachings of the church. Has God not in his grace, descended to light the torch whereby to dispel the darkness of despair and ignorance, man would have continued to grovel in the dust, his unopened eyes could never have taken in the splendor of the stars above.

When the adherent of this view was confronted

with the facts that a strange similarity often protruded itself upon the attention of students, between the religions so called revealed and the religions so styled natural, the church had a ready answer. It would not yield that religion was one of the productions of man's history and rooted in man's nature and his necessities, but the faithful would hold that in the beginning of time there took place an original, primeval revelation, the recipient of which was Adam in Paradise; that as he fell the faculty of remembering what God had revealed failed proportionately, and that the strange similarities, which could not be denied, are due to these reminiscences, scattered all over the earth, of this primeval revelation.

Or, another school, mighty in the church, resorted to this explanation: The devil is competitor most alert and most insistent, of God Almighty. He imitates the methods of the divinity, and thus, seeing that God proclaimed truth, the devil opened the ears of others to listen to his message, and tricky, crafty as his Satanic Majesty is, he tricked out and trapped out his counterfeit proclamation in the same colors misleading, as did God array his own revelation. If, therefore, in the church and in the pagoda, we come across two accents that at first blush seem to be identical, the one that issues forth from the pagoda is struck by the devil, the other which runs out from the aisle and nave of the church is intoned by the celestial choir under the baton of God Himself. Thus the church contended that religion held no organic relation to human nature.

On the other hand were the rationalists. They

were divided into two schools, both agreeing that religion is an invention. That man in his natural condition and man in his fully attained maturity and stature is without religion. Religion, saith the one school, which may be called the malevolent rationalists, is an imposition. Some crafty men, some intriguers, some shrewd exploiters of the people, knowing how easy it is to gain influence when one knows how to awaken the fears of the ignorant, speculating on the ignorance and the credulity of their race, palmed off what they called religion coming from God, which, however, was their own invention, upon their deluded followers.

The priests, intent upon enriching themselves, invented the body of doctrines and the system of practices which compose religion, and their successors, the spiritual heirs of these original inventors and intriguers, have well preserved the trickery of their predecessors, for they find their host in speculating upon the ignorance and the craven superstition of the multitude.

Were it not said these malevolent rationalists, were it not for priests that could not earn their bread in any other way, were it not for preachers who find it much easier to be loafers and loiterers the whole week, and in exchange for large money play to the tune most agreeable to their congregation but once a week, religion would disappear from the catalogue of men's solicitudes, and speedily none there would be to pay it even scantiest reverence. Were it not for the grave and the death chamber, for the tolling bell lamenting the demise of one of human kind; were it not for the ignorance of the masses kept under bondage to ignorance by crafty priests and shrewd preachers, and ignorance which will not lift the curtain from off death and will not allow light to pierce the darkness of the grave, were it not for the delusions and illusions of the hereafter to which the priests and the popes claim to have the key, and from which they can bar all those that do not swear by their words, temples would not be, congregations would dissolve, priests would have to go to work, and preachers would have to earn their bread and butter, which we in our charity do provide and in our ignorance continue to provide for them. Kill, therefore the priests! Expose the craftiness of the preachers and humanity will be saved from a yoke more galling than which no despot ever superimposed.

That was the cry of the malevolent, malicious rationalists thirty years ago. It is the cry of Mr. Ingersoll today. As for making money, I think Mr. Ingersoll succeeds much better in that art than even the pontiff situated on the throne of Rome, and if one of the preachers should ever lose his job and have to work for his bread and butter, if at all gifted with tongue and mind, he could double the largest salary that any Jewish or Christian congregation pays, by imitating Mr. Ingersoll and repeating the stalest and the most untrue attacks against religion. He could rake in ducats which would make even a prince of commerce green and livid with jealousy and rage. It is today not the priest or the preacher that may be charged justly with mercenary motives. It is the malevolent, malicious rationalist who knows how to make his nonsense fill his pocketbook.

Thirty years ago there were also benevolent rationalists who agreed with their more malicious colleagues that religion was an invention, but they conceded that this invention had some good qualities. Moses, for instance, knowing the character of his Jews, and knowing that they would not receive however noble a thought if it was his, pretended that his instruction had come from behind the cloud curtain of smoking Sinai, and thus, though he knew that he lied, he, for the purpose of benefiting his people, palmed off his own thought as of divine origin. They granted that religion has its influences for good; they contended that truth, naked truth, full truth, could not be digested by the people at large. Of course they, the rationalists, they the Chumesh and Rashi, the trained great minds and men, they could do without religion; they possessed all truth, full truth; they, the giants of intellectuality could absorb whatever came from heaven or rose up from the ocean beneath. But the people at large, who were not as enlightened and as intellectual as they were, they needed to be guided, and for the purpose of guiding them aright, a Moses and an Isaiah and a Jeremiah, a Jesus and a St. Paul, Buddha and Confucius, all of them palmed off their human thoughts as coming from God, for the purpose of bettering the morals of the masses. The weak persons must have religion, not the strong, was the second contention of the benevolent rationalists thirty years ago.

Religion is good for the children, and it is good for women—it may have its uses for men who are womanish, not for men who are manly. The ignorant, yea, they must be enlightened, but not the well instructed, and hence—and we have not outgrown this habit of mind today—appearance at a Temple, according to these benevolent rationalists, was in itself an admission of weakness, and per contra, absence from Temple was regarded as a certificate of conscious strength. Those that came to religion, as religion was merely for the weak or the womanish, avowed that they were not strong, and those that stayed away, thereby challenged the world to admire their great strength and the depth of their intellectuality.

That was the attitude thirty years ago. The church on the one hand and the two kinds of rationalists on the other, both agreeing and both arguing that religion was not organically related to the human mind, and had no essential function in the economy of human life.

Today, one who would earn the title to distinction as having progressed with the age, and as understanding the spiritual tide of his time, can neither repeat the dogma of the church nor the dogma of either malevolent or benevolent rationalism.

The science of comparative religion has shown beyond the possibility of doubt that religion is not an invention, and not an intrigue and not an imposition from without, whether that without be located in the heavens or be thought to reside in the scheming mind of a crafty priest. Religion springs from within man, and it is the essential mark of humanity.

Many distinctions have been sought to keep man distinct from the beast. Some have thought that language drew the line of demarcation. Thus that man was the speaking animal, the animal that had the gift to communicate his ideas and volitions to a fellow animal by means of articulate sounds. It is true, on the whole, language is the distinguishing function of humanity, but even this is not essentially distinctive as is religion; for the animals, especially the animals who live in herds, the animals who lead a social life, the gregarious animals therefore, to use the technical term, have means of inter-communication, which are virtually language. They lack, of course, articulated sound, but if you have ever watched a tribe of birds migrating from place to place, you will have taken home with you the confidence that those birds know how to communicate their intentions one to the other.

And so a pack of wolves have certain signs and sounds through which they render intelligible their designs one to the other. Language in this broader sense, is not the peculiar property of man; but religion is. On the one hand all our researches in the domain of animal life have not enabled us to find a single herd or horde of animals in the possession or in the practice of anything that resembles even faintly that which we call religion or religious institutionalism, but on the other hand, we find nowhere a human society, whatever the crudity of its state, or the refinement of its development, that was without religion and religious institutionalism. The latest scholars are emphatic in making this declaration. Some of you will remember I have no doubt, that Sir. John Lubbock and Spencer after him, deny the general and unexceptional rule of religion in human society. Spencer and Sir John Lubbock have contended that in the very earliest stages of savagery religion is not found even as a rudiment, but the more careful ethnologist—and Spencer is not a careful ethnologist—the more careful observers, the better trained travelers that have made a special study of the life of the Bushmen in Australia, the Hottenentots in Africa, the Zulus and the stammering Peskirawas of Patagonia; all of these have come back with the assurance and demonstration that even in these human families, there is always a most emphatic and most insistent religion and religious life. Today no scholar will repeat the contention of Spencer and Sir John Lubbock. Today all scholars are agreed that where man is there religion is, and that religion therefore is the distinctive, essential quality of humanity.

If this were so, religion is not the invention of priests, prelates, prophets or pretenders. Religion, if this were so, is not revelation from God above, but is revelation from the mind of man within. If this is so, religion is not artificial, but it is always essential in man, and today without religion or aught that resembles religion amounts to self mutilation, or atrophy.

Not every man, of course, is normal. Everyone of us has his eccentricities. There is in every specimen of humanity some eccentricity—some departure from the normal type. Some of these abnormalities are more pronounced than others. There is such as are color blind. They cannot distinguish between red and black. These are abnormal. There are others that are tone deaf. I know some people, of course the fashion requires that they should be enthusiasts as to music, and they witness every performance of the grand opera, and are present at every concert, and still they could not tell a symphony from a Strauss waltz if they attempted ever so hard to find out the distinction. They are simply tone deaf, and a brass band in the distance, when they cannot see the wind instruments, sounds to their ears as though it were a reed band or a string orchestra. They are abnormal, and any medical man who has made these abnormalities his special study will corroborate my statement that there is this abnormality, this eccentricity, which renders individual incapable of distinguishing one movement in music from another, or one tone, and the quality of a tone from a distinct and different tone sounded at some other time.

And there are those that are religionless. These are either abnormalities due to atrophy, or they are eccentricities due to mutilation at early time, or they are due to a latent condition of the mind which has not yet been awakened into life by the wand of better thought training, and self effort; but all in all, though these eccentricities prevail, no man can claim to be the full man, nor is man a full man without religion.

This is shown universally by the fact that human nature does not tolerate a vacuum, Extirpate religion from your heart and always something will crowd in to take the place of the extirpated element.

Why is it that in these days of vulgar atheism,

for every atheism is vulgar, a refined nature is never atheistic—it may be agnostic but not atheistic? Why is it in these days of vulgar atheism, in these days of triumphant science, we have so much of spiritism and so much of Christian Science and faith cure? These aberrations of the human mind, so multitudinous today, are proof to the discovery which the science of comparative religion has made, that religion is organic, not artificial in human society.

We are not, generally speaking, in the books, and many are led to speak so through their instruction in the Sunday Schools, about false and true religions. The church especially is very emphatic in declaring that certain religions are true and other religions are false. In the science of comparative religion, and by the lights of its discoveries, there are no false religions.

All religions are true, true for the age and true for the people that evolved their religion. The distinction made in our catechism, this distinction made between false religion and true religion, is scientifically untenable.

The religion of the spirit worshippers is as true and as legitimate for the social environments of the spirit worshippers as is your religion, the religion of this cultured congregation. The religion of the Buddhists, as foolish as it may appear to be to us, is as correct and as wise for the Buddhist and his social economy, as is the religion of Israel today here or in any other synagogue, temple, or what not.

There are no false religions. All religions are true. For what is religion? You open your catechism, and you find on the first page probably this statement—and that statement is repeated at confirmation exercises with a great deal of pomp and éclat, to the great joy of the congregation and their presiding officers, at the great show and parade, that they have succeeded in evolving from the depths of their inner consciousness. You find it there, and it is repeated with as great regularity as the Chinese prayer wheel turns round: Religion is the knowledge of God and his law, and the obedience of God's law.

That is not religion. God is a secondary consideration in religion. There are religions without God or gods, and there may be much of verbal belief in God and very, very little of religion.

I, for one, doubt whether this catechism and this parrot like recitation at confirmation exercises, in which the congregations take so much pride, is at all religious. It is a vulgar concession, as a rule, to the pride of parents and to the delight of congregations, to make Parade of themselves. As a rule—and my confirmations are not an exception—they leave no influence behind. They might as well be abolished, and I shall use my influence to abolish these things at whatever cost to myself. In these things religion is misrepresented, and that is the reason—on account of these definitions, thousand and one of the best and the noblest are not led to find the religion which lives in them, which cannot be mutilated, and which should not be atrophied in their spiritual and moral organism.

In other books, you find that religion is the sense of dependence. Great men have sponsored this view, Schleiermacher, among others—and certainly, pygmy as I am, I would not dare, uncorroborated by the researches of other great men, question the finality of a definition come from that giant brain, the great poetic defender, the platonic thinker of modern days in the domain of religion; but religion is much more than the mere sense and sentiment of dependence on someone else.

Religion is again by others defined to be the natural craving for harmony—for man cannot abide in fragments and among fragments. All knowledge is fragmentary. Man, therefore, builds for himself a universe that is complete, and he complements those parts of the universe which knowledge has not revealed, by faith. That definition is not correct, for it does not cover all cases of religious life. There are religions that do not care for universe and universal outlook. They are very little interested in complementing their fragmentary knowledge of the world.

Others, and this is perhaps the latest school, have contended that religion is the child of the inherent desire and necessity of man to connect cause and effect—that every happening on earth is supposed to have had a cause, and that finally, the final causes are no longer sufficient to carry this chain, and therefore we must go beyond the secondary or finite causes, until we come to the ultimate, the final cause of all.

But this, while it agrees with rationalistic religion, or the religion of the rationalist—this metaphysical blood thin pale and sickly something, which has taken the place of the pulsing blood and the rushing impulse of a strong religious temperament is entirely out of rhyme with the facts produced by the investigating curiosity of the student of religion. There are thousands of religions, and they are all true for their time and true for their environment, which care not this much for cause and effect, and whose devotees are never interested in establishing the chain of cause and effect.

What then, is religion? Religion is the attempt to link your own self-consciousness with the hypothecated positive self-consciousness of the universe.

Man is the cradle of religion. He knows himself to be a self, and he finds that his life is under the control of volition, and thus he fancies that the universe round about him; or whatever is round about him, is also under the control of self determinate conscious volition. And this is present in every religion: first man self conscious of himself, of his weakness, or of his strength, of his desires or of his failures, and beyond that man a world which he believes *is* determined by the same qualities and limited by the same limitations as he is himself. This is the definition of religion.

Or to put it in plainer words: Religion is the self-conscious floss of man linked to universal ends and purposes. In this way, religion is anthropologic. Feuerbacher, who first said this, spoke truth. He meant of course, as a rationalist of his day did always mean, by thus describing religion as anthropology, to rob it of its value; but if religion is anthropology, that is the science of man and of human life, it ceases to be dependent on any other factor but the factor that underlies it—man himself. And the first religious duty then and the first religious enlightenment then, is *Man, know thyself,* and if thou knowest thyself, thou findest that which is called religion, and from that find develops what we call religious culture.

I said there are no religions that are false, and there are none that are not true. One more problem, and I shall be through for this morning.

And, therefore, are all religions of equal value? The rationalists of a hundred years ago thought so. If they are all inventions with a good purpose, what is the difference which religion one does profess, and today much of this vapid sentimental, bloodless but self-admiring liberalism, which have found too strong a hold even on congregations like this—this liberalism still believes that it makes no difference which religion a man professes, and that a man can profess a religion at will, or reject it at will.

Even Lessing's fable of the three rings is symbolic of this view that all religions ultimately are frauds—frauds with a good intention, and that it makes no difference which religion one professes. "What makes thee a Christian, makes for thee me a Christian, and makes thee for me a Jew," and these quotations from Nathan der Weise are bandied about as though they spelled gospel absolute and truth ultimate.

No, today no one who has learned anything of the results of scientific comparison among the religions can, with unblushing face, maintain the thesis that one religion is as good as another, though one religion is true as another.

Conditions are the mothers of religion, and these conditions are actual or they are pre-natal. And some religions have the power to grow out of certain conditions into new conditions, and upon their power depends their eternality, if I may so say—their triumph over the rodent tooth of time.

Religion and language may be well compared. Every language is true—the stammered language of the Hottentot who cannot count more than four, not merely figuratively speaking, but actually speaking—who cannot count more than four—when he gets to five, he has to say many—a great multitude—that language is true, but will you say that this Hottentot stammering language of few words and few sounds is as good as the idiom which I attempt to speak, the ideal of a Shakespeare, of a Browning, of a Longfellow and of a Tennyson? On its very surface the proposition is detected as ridiculous. The Hottentot cannot, as long as he is under Hottentot conditions, evolve a language which goes farther than the halting flow of thought and sound which he receives at birth from his mother; but English, for instance, the living language, has in its composite character, combined streams that have come from different watersheds, that have come from different heights, certainly from different sources and has guided on that stream to ever new potencies and to ever new powers and triumphs.

And so it is with religions. Certain religions cannot outgrow their conditions. Others do outgrow conditions. Certain religions cannot assimilate—others do assimilate, and among the religions, which have this rare gift, pre-eminent stands

Judaism. Judaism is a life—an historic life, which has developed out of certain very rudimentary elements, but it has had from the very beginning the power to grow out of conditions into new conditions, and having this power, it is in religion what the English language is among the languages—destined to become the world medium of the thought of man's self-consciousness in his relations to the universe—to establish the final solution of the question: how can man preserve himself as man under the greater laws and the deeper necessities of universal life.

Or, in another figure—study your nightly sky tonight. What do you find there? You find above you a number of bodies whirling about in space, who have all of them certain similarities to all others, and who are all under the same law. But as you inspect these bodies more closely, you will find that some of them have no atmosphere around them, and others have an atmosphere, and you go and consult your teachers, or such as know more of these things than we do, and they will tell you that the atmosphere around some heavenly bodies is still luminous—is full of gases, incandescent; that in other heavenly spheres the atmosphere has almost totally disappeared—the gases having been liquefied, have spread the deep seas with which the planets are covered; that for instance in planet Mars, there is the absence again of this liquid element to such an extent that only at the poles there is a rim or cap of ice, showing that at one time Mars had an atmosphere; but in the process of development of that atmosphere the gases were turned to liquids, and the liquids were absorbed to such an extent that only at the poles now there is something that resembles water, and may perhaps irrigate the planet.

Coming to our earth, we find that these incandescent gases that have been around the sun have all disappeared, and that on earth they have liquefied, and that still a mantle of gases is around us, but gas in such a form as no longer to be self-incandescent. And going to our companion traveler, going to the moon, we find there that all atmosphere has disappeared; that the moon is a dead body, having neither water nor gas, neither the liquid form nor the attenuated form, and no longer the incandescent form or cap around it. So it is with the religions—some are still in that highly ignitive state—the rude nebulous mass of confused tendencies—all however under the common law of self-consciousness—Others have progressed far enough to have life in them, and their atmosphere, so to speak is translucent, while no longer incandescent. And other religions, like other languages, are like the moon—they are dead bodies, and shine not by their own light, but merely by the reflected rays.

And our earth has still another advantage, which seemingly none of the planets enjoy. Our earth draws its life through its atmosphere, which is kept from cooling into space at too rapid a rate through its borrowing process—draws light and life from the sun. Were the sun tomorrow to be quenched, our earth would speedily give out into space the heat of its atmosphere, and our planet would spin in space thereafter, another moon without light and without life. So it is with religions. Our religion, Judaism, is like the earth— It has the mantle of a translucent atmosphere, and above it stands the sun, from which it draws light—that light of one thought which it alone has, and which I shall dwell on at length next time—the characteristic thought of Judaism that the self-conscious man can put himself into relations with the supposedly self-conscious universe only through one method, the method of righteousness and of justice.

There are many methods, as there are many planets. Some claim that by sacrifice, others by prayer, others by spell words, others by magic incantation, others by belief, others by the avowal of sin, the self-conscious man can preserve himself in and over against the universe. Our religion, as I shall attempt to show when next we meet, stands on the one essential thought that the self-conscious man in his desire to preserve himself over against and in the universe, will succeed only if he adopts the solar light beyond the atmosphere, If he adopts the thought that righteousness and justice are the fundamental foci of the universe and hold the power of life for man, self-conscious man, desirous of self-preservation.

Yea, the science of comparative religion has taken the infallible metre from off the head of the church, but it has forever silenced the presumption of the rationalist. Religion is not an invention; it is not an intrigue. Priests have not fashioned it, but it has fashioned priests. Books have not made it, but it has made books. Religion is co-extensive with man. No man is without religion unless he be an abnormal man, and no human society is without it. Some religions grow, others decay; some religions have fuller life and deeper light, and others have scantier light and have limited life; some religions are dead and others are living, progressive; all religions are true, none of them is false for the time. It is only when it is out of time that it becomes false, and when the time is for the religion, the religion is born for the time; all religions are temporal, all are revealed and all are natural: this our science has taught us, and having taught this, this science is an ally of that Judaism which I have attempted to teach these last seventeen years in your midst—attempted to teach God knows not with success, far from it, but God knows also with fidelity that needs not blush, and a fidelity which will stand by what it sees to be right, come what may, come death or life, peace or war, dissolution or cooperation—with that conscience within us, we, the teachers of that Judaism know that though we may fail, the future will see the seeds sprout up, for our teachings are consonant with the latest science and the deepest thought, and to have learned that latest science and to have familiarized ourselves with this latest thought, none of us have had the time to dance attendance at the boudoir of some fashionable lady and none of us had patience to be satisfied with his equipment when he had mastered Chumesh and Rashi. We all have been students and devoted students, and for that reason we say, your orthodoxy is at fault, your rationalism is behind the age. The new religious thought of the age is ours; we have the light of science and the love of science, and through it we work for man, and therefore for religion. Religion is anthropology. It is the science of man. Higher science than anatomy or physiology, than psychology and ethnology. The science of all sciences, the scientiarum, the leader of all thought and the molder of all opinion.

Amen.

THE JEWISH PREACHER:
Rabbi Emil G. Hirsch, Ph.D., LL.D.

Was It Worth While?
A Hanukah Message

Sunday, December 16, 1906
Reading: Isaiah 60

Was it worth while to resist the despotism of the Syrian King? Was it worth while to call the few brave and honest and self respecting Jews then found in Palestine to arms? Was it worth while to win the victory? Was it worth while to cleanse the sanctuary of its defilement?

Many a now living Jew will say it was not. Then Judaism was saved. Had Nebaithias not inspired his sons to resistance; had the Maccabean armies met defeat instead of triumph on the hotly contested battlefields, Judaism would have disappeared and the Jew would have been saved the martyred career; his pilgrimage over stones and thorns and briars, through water and fire, across oceans and deserts of martyr agony, of suffering and of persecution. And we today then would not be Jews. We too would be spared having to face a world not altogether benevolently inclined to us.

Would that be the proper tack to take? There are many that take it, but again I ask, would that be the proper way? Is this selfish and this cowardly view characteristic of deep thought, or is it but the frothing of shallow brainless conceit?

It is the latter. The Jew certainly was then saved for suffering. It is true had the Maccabeans failed we should have not had to walk through life laden with distrust, pointed at by the mob, pelted at by infuriated crowds incited against us. But what would the world have lost? That is the profounder problem.

Oh, the world would have lost Christianity; the world would have lost Judaism; for only because Judaism was saved from annihilation, Christianity could be born. Had the Maccabeans not crowned their brows in modesty but in selfishness, with the laurel wreath of their remarkable achievement, no Christ would have been heralded or hailed, no new religion would have been proclaimed, for the hilltops of Palestine would have been silenced of song and would have been raft of prophecy and of protest. Would that have been a gain to the world?

There are these pseudo philosophers who would maintain, and do insist that the loss of Christianity and the death of Judaism as precedent to the loss of Christianity would have been a gain to the world. Have not dungeons been masoned by the hand of priest? Have not prelates given the order to erect funeral pyres? Has not Galileo pressed his thinker's brow against the bars of his cell, muttering that the world does move, and suffering there because he would not refrain from heralding his new law of universal motion?

Have not priests confined in dark caverns the

best of men, men of light and of leading? Are not the Jews themselves historic proof of the fanaticism fostered by religion and applied by the Christian Ecclesiastics? The world would have lost tears had Christianity never been cradled, say they, and the Jew would have been saved tears, and worse than tears had he not obstinately clung to the law which the Syrian King with deeper philosophy, say they, intended should be abrogated.

Shallow judgment this, and equally shallow is that which insists because some dogmas of church and some poetry of Judaism are in discord to the teachings of modern science, therefore Christianity's undoing was a step forward, and the forgetting of Judaism marks the progressive mind.

Yea, science has found truths of which the writers of the Bible were in utter ignorance; Yea, the geology of Genesis is not scientifically defensible. Yea, the belief in spirits, in demons, in miraculous powers are contained in the writings of both church and synagogue, but would a world without Christianity—and she a daughter of Judaism—have not lost more than what science could ever have given, or giveth, and art ever can supply or ever has supplied?

The pivotal issue in that contest in Palestine was the right of the weaker to his humanity, was the right of man to his personality. Pagan religion, as Pagan culture, knows but one decision, that is the decision of strength, brutal strength. The weak are forsaken of the Gods. They are given over to the hands of the mighty. The weak have no purpose in themselves, no worth in themselves.

What purpose is theirs is that given to them by the mightier ones, conceded to them by the richer ones. They are dependent upon the graciousness, the generosity, the forbearance of the strong; the limit of indulgence is set by the quantity of strength at disposal.

Rome is the typical state and civilization grounded in the notion that strength confers rights and weakness will be suffered to exist if it forego its claim to worth and personality, if it consents to do the bidding of the more potent and the more affluent. And the Syrian Empire was at that time but an exaggerated form of Rome, an imitation, and as every imitation is worse than the original, where imitation is of weakness, so the Syrian caricature and travesty of Roman life and Roman culture of those days was infinitely worse and infinitely more depraved and infinitely more corrupting than ever was Rome.

The Maccabeans fought there for the rights of men to be men independent of accident of circumstance. Civilization is not measured by the strong, it is gauged by the weakest. That is the fundamental note in Jewish proclamation. That was also the note in Greek culture. I mean to say, of course, the note that dominates in Rome and Syria sounds also through Greek culture, especially the Greek culture that prevailed then, which was not the Greek culture at its best.

Greece had outlived its vitality; it has fulfilled the mission to which it was assigned in the economy of the world. It had enriched the world with types of beauty most perfect and most marvelous; but having attained this its predestined goal, having given to the world all it had to give, it naturally and necessarily fell into decay; and it was decaying Greek culture that found imitators in Syria and apes in Palestine.

Greek culture when still in the making, when still striving upward, Greek culture even at its zenith certainly is messenger of humanities, but not of a humanity that has recognized the ethical implications of human life and of social relations, but a humanity that would in its own physical and mental equipoise represent in human guise the perfection and the equipoise of cosmos, the world bathed in beauty and the world a symphony of celestial harmonies.

Form, not force; compliance and consonance, not individual conduct under righteous consecration; the largest men, the due proportion, that was the fundamental ambition of Greek solicitude through the climactic accomplishment of Greek culture and of the Greek nation.

But that Greek culture which prevailed in Antioch and in Jerusalem then was caricature. Greece had been attacked. The microbes were at work and when the Jew and the Syrian assumed the Greek vestment and exchanged his ruder speech for the more fluent syllables of Athens, it was not Plato, it was not Praxitelles, it was not Aristotle, it was not Demosthenes, it was not Escalus that appealed to him; but it was the speech of the athlete, it was the vocalization of the outcast woman; it was the jargon of the flowing goblet of wine and of free indulgence that crowded out of his mouth the gutturals of ancestral specific speech, and out of his heart the consecrations and the sanctities of ancestral stern and unbending religiosity. The religiosity that insisted upon righteousness and upon right, not upon beauty of form and concordance proportionate of conduct and compliance with canons universally recognized.

Imitation is always dangerous. Imitation is fatal when the imitator has lost power of assimilation, namely that force which taking what is not indigenous transforms it to force and blood in his own being and in his own mentality. Thus Greek culture came upon the Jews as do the germs of a disease. They decayed; they were cankered under the sweep of Greek low vulgarity. But even Greece at its highest had no consecration of the ethical life, and it was this that had to be saved, and it was this that was then saved, and saved by the Jews, saved by the Jews for the world, though upon the Jews their victory laid a burden of centuried martyrdom.

The modern scientific spirit is no different from that of Rome. If I believed in nothing but what the sciences now teach me I should indeed become a Roman in the sense that I would only know myself; no higher law but my will, no limitation but the limitation of my strength.

Under that law society will be dissolved into competing and combating atoms, each one for himself, and the devil take the hindmost. If science is the last word, and her proclamation is the ultimate truth, then why should I refrain from stealing and robbing as long as another thief or robber is stronger than I, as long as there is no society that will repress my predatory instincts? And modern vice is placed upon a scientific basis in its deification of selfishness. Could society have endured? It could not have.

The Christian world at least in theory proclaimed the right of the weaker, proclaimed the divinity of the weakest, proclaimed that there were standards by which to judge men other than those that prevailed in the market.

Judaism proclaiming the identical thought, located the struggle of the weaker against the mightier and the justification of the weaker against the powerful in this world. It spoke to the powerful in tones of thunder, not as did Christianity asking him to resign his power; it did not say to the young man "Sell all that thou hast and follow me"; it did not call to the rich to become poor and to the potent to become impotent; it thundered into the ears of the powerful, power abused calls for God's judgment, and God will judge. Power is given in order to make others stronger, not to crush others into greater weakness. Was it worth while then to save Judaism, that out of its loins Christianity might spring forth? It was.

What are we proud of? What have we a right to be proud of? When we look back upon the pages recording the doings and the dealings of men, can we be proud that our cities were devastated by soldiers sent forward under the insanity of popular greed, or of tyrannical avarice? Certainly not. Can we be proud that pyramids were built? The pyramids are monuments of man's slavery to the despotism of the few and the depraved, of the many. No. Can we be proud of our Generals, of the engines of destruction placed at their disposal? No. Can we be proud that the ocean is furrowed by swimming fortresses out of whose mouths of iron and steel can belch forth destruction to reach in devastation for more that fifteen nautical miles? No.

What can we be proud of? Man had a loving heart; that he bethought himself of the weakness of others; that he remained humble withal. And pray again, who were the benefactors of the race? Was there ever aught done that helped the race that could be paid for in the currency of the market? Has Beethoven been paid? Has Schiller been compensated? Could you pay a Beethoven and a Schiller? You could not.

Millions will disappear like drops in the bucket before the sum is weighed out that is the due of Beethoven, that is the due of those unknown men of searching and of hoping who have discovered the agencies that nature fashioned in order to minimize human suffering and to maximize human life.

The best things are not exchangeable in terms of currency, in terms of the market. Iron, steel, wheat, cloth, leather, what are those? Mind, art, thought, they are all. No, not what the mill handles, and not what the mine produces, and not what the rivers bring, nor what the fields produce are the expressions of the humanities, but that which man puts into those things.

And what is that? It is the use man makes of those things if the brain is energized. And what is that? Righteousness; and the men of brain and the men of righteousness, known or unknown, outweigh billionaires and millionaires, outweigh mine owners and railroad speculators. They outweigh because they stand for that which is the differentiating element of humanity over and against brutality. And it is this that was saved when Jerusalem was cleansed; and it was this that even in dogmatic form, and in other worldly terms, Christianity brought to the waiting and despairing world.

Was it worth while to save Judaism? Yea, it was worth while. And if it was worth while, then it must be worth our while to preserve it today.

Traitors are we to humanity, if it was worth while to save it, then to allow it now to die the slow death through indifference, through arrogance, through worship of the false idols of gold and silver and what not. In the Rabbinical implication of the scene with which the lesson begins that is read this week in all synagogues, we find the following suggestive and most powerful parable: Said these Rabbis, "When God was about to give truth into the keeping of Israel he asked for sureties.

Said they, we offer heaven and earth. God replied, they will pass away. Offered they the patriarchs. Said God, they themselves, require vouching for. Offered they their prophets. Know ye not, answered God, that like the fox in the vineyard, so with thy prophets, Oh Israel. Wilt thou, master of all, accept as surety our children? Yea, said he, I shall; but beware; let default be made by the debtor and I shall be a cruel creditor on these your sureties. If you forget my truth, quoting the phrase from Hosea, 'I shall forget your children, Oh Israel'."

Here we have it; our children must be our surety. Unless we transmit to them the patrimony which is ours, they will rise to curse us; in their spiritual poverty which we create for them they will have cause to abuse us. We are robbing them of that which alone makes life, human life livable. We are making of them puppets, or what is worse, walking incarnations of crime, selfishness and of vice. We rob them of all the contents of life, of all the sweetness of life. Where is parent that knows what parenthood means that can be self satisfied with conditions like those? We do not save them from what is the law under which Judaism sanctities are not fostered within their hearts and are not shining through and glowing in their very soul being. We are making them poorer and poorer; you have no idea of the struggle which is theirs from which they cannot escape. For even when they would make themselves ridiculous and more exposed to the same attacks as did those before them who rushed into the broad spaces of unnoticed indifferenciation they cannot escape. We do not equip them with thought and with resolution and with understanding why they must suffer and for what they must struggle.

Oh, I am unjust, am I not? Are we not extremely charitable? Where are aggregates of men so liberal as we are? Have we not institutions, hospitals, benevolent associations galore? Are not the very men that spurn religion the ones that are more active in those lines and more successful in raising revenue? Ah, we are, we are. Let me bow before you; we are. But again I say, such charity as this which merely consists in money is charity that the world is tired of, and the world rejects. Even in these charities thought should lead, not money, and righteousness should be the pole star, and not a financial equation. What has been the curse of our state has to live; but we make the burden all the more galling to them because we have deprived them of that which is the antidote to the poison that the world has for us. Why should they be Jews? We have not told them, we have allowed them to believe that the Jew means nothing. But the world has not let them go; the curse is upon them, and they know not why. And this very ignorance adds bitterness to the cup which the prejudice of the world will always insist that they shall drink.

They are not admitted, notwithstanding their culture. There be some among them that have culture; but it is the culture that is lifeless, because it lacks the religious spirit, it lacks ethical consecration. Many a man that knows nothing of Browning and of French novels, and of Hauptmann, and of Sudermann, and of D'Annuncio, and goodness knows who else, many a man that is ignorant of the logarithmic table, is giant in the philosophy of life. And is millionaire, not merely millionaire, but millionaire in the recognition of life's compensating sweetness, whose righteousness has the power and force of influencing every thought and directing every ambition, when these our walking encyclopedias of knowledge are dead and poor and miserable and wretched because the flame of religion and the fervor of ethical charities is lacking. You will perhaps grant that while I am too ignorant to know anything about charity, having been appointed by the Governor as a member of the State Board of Charities, and not being altogether idiotic, I have had some insight into the workings of charity. Of course I am too ignorant to have anything to do with Jewish charities. The Rabbi, what does he know? He should be an echo, and he should take his cue and ought to be kindly ready at any time to trumpet for charity. He ought to know his station, and be happy that some great contributor to the charities occasionally speaks to him and asks him to say something for the charities, even if it is one who never comes to the synagogue. There might be others there whom I might be able to influence for the charities, and the Rabbi should always listen to appeals from him who never comes to this temple, or any other temple, asking him to address the members of the empty pews they do not occupy, I suppose, in the cause of charity.

What is the curse of our so called public charities? Economy, not politics, the idea that men must be housed and fed at the cheapest possible minimum of outlay. And why this? Because forsooth the rich people's taxes will be increased, and as the rich people have means not to pay their taxes of course the burden rests always on the poorer; that is the reason why this state has merely custodial institutions, institutions that never make the attempt to help those that ought to have been helped. Thank God now—and it is not false pride

WAS IT WORTH WHILE? A HANUKAH MESSAGE 201

on my part to say I had a part in this—thank God, now that through the cooperation of the Governor, who is an honest, energetic and intelligent man, and through the combined physiological wisdom of a great physician, your Rabbi, and a woman of considerable experience in those things, and through the appointment of two men at least in the larger institutions of this state, that are progressive men of science, this state is now about to abandon the policy of economy.

Charity that is merely a matter of money is a curse to the recipient and a curse to the donor. Greater are the men that give thought than men who give money, greater are the men who give consecration than the men that give however large. a contribution.

Had we this consecration your charities would not be imitations, they would be patterns. In one respect you received this week your compliment; the Tribune acknowledged that the Jews had solved the problem of raising revenue without the vulgarity of a Street in Paris and the frivolities of a fair; but it took ten years before that thought germinated here, and though it is forgotten, I have documentary evidence to prove it, when no one thought of this I wrote about it, and thank God that is on record. I say, your pulpit it was, your Rabbi who first protested and suggested the plan; ten years before anyone else had lifted a finger I called in my own paper for the establishment of what I then called a clearinghouse, what is now The Associated Jewish Charities. In that respect we were pathfinders and I was not in the rear ranks, even if it sounds conceited on my part to say that. So in all other respects we might and should be pathfinders. We should not have a single institution; the institution is not needed.

Ah, the institutional plan is the more economical plan. I have no doubt it is the easier plan. It is very easy for the children to put them in the institution. Am I the only crank that protests against this? Last week we had here a Truant's Conference, a conference on truancy, and one who not being a Rabbi, but a judge has some influence with you, participated, and at that conference another man who was neither judge nor Rabbi, spoke to that assembly of men that are experts, saying, "Your institutions curse the inmates for the length of their lives; until they die they have lost their independence and individuality." I have preached that, and what has been the result?

I have protested against this feature of institutional life especially with all my might and main, that of making the inmate means of maudlin sentimentalism, taking them on a platform and exhibiting them. Yet in my own Temple this week children were taken from an institution and exhibited here, by well meaning women, and there was no one here to protest, and none here to protect me against this insult, that in my own Temple where I have taught my principles to my members, principles that must appeal to every woman of thought, my child could not be exhibited, no parent will make of his child a manikin, to be placed on a platform, even if that child blows the bugle and beats the drum. Why then should children that have no parents, no homes, be so exhibited, at a fair at that? I ask that question. Oh, I make enemies, I know it. But sometimes it is an honor to have enemies, sometimes it is a disgrace to have friends.

But I speak for your sake and for humanity's sake. If we boast of our charities then we provoke the testing of our charities, not by our good intentions, but by the standards of the new science; and there are some among us that have made that science their specialty, who have pursued that science in addition to their other studies, as experts.

And I know a Rabbi, and he is not a thousand miles away from here, whose words on certain subjects of charities or philanthropies are quoted by the professors in the classroom. I know him, and you know him.

Is that all we shall have to transmit to our children, these charities? Don't you see that without their religion, even of these charities they become indifferent. Who are the largest givers, the readiest givers? Men and women that have had religious surroundings. The exception proves the rule. Now let that continue and in ten years from now you will have your difficulties, you will have difficulty to maintain your congregations.

But, say we, what of truth there is in the New Testament was ours; we have not been Parasites, but we have been producers. Then we would kindle the Hanukah lights again. If it was worthwhile to save it, it is worthwhile to defend it, it is worthwhile to propagate it, it is worthwhile to transmit it to our children. And upon no congregation rests this so rightfully as upon a liberal congregation.

If it was worthwhile to save Judaism, and it was, then it is worthwhile to transmit it to our children in rich measure. Oh, might this spirit come to us. Even before the gentleman from Russia had spoken last night I had planned to use the Rabbinical story which he told you, for I know some of those Rabbinical stories as well as he does.

He said when God had commanded Moses to build the sanctuary and to collect for the maintenance of the sanctuary from each Jew half a shekel. God showed Moses a shekel made of fire and said "Like that shekel must be the contribution to the Temple." A shekel made of fire nonsense, is it not? But what did the Rabbis mean? Gold, silver, glittering gold does not build sanctuaries, but the shekel of fire, the spirit of enthusiasm alone builds sanctuaries and congregations. And it was that spirit that saved Judaism on the battlefield.

That was the spirit that saved it, when men had to die for it and women had to die for it and children were burned for it. That spirit we must again have would we build our sanctuary and rededicate it as was dedicated the Temple on this historic day. Oh, spirit come at last, come fire and claim our hearts; come light and lighten our eyes; come, blaze forth, Oh, thou Israel, thou, Oh Congregation arise and shine, thy light may come, must come. Arise, arise and shine.

Amen.

THE JEWISH PREACHER:
Rabbi Emil G. Hirsch, Ph.D., LL.D.

Organization And Division Of Labor

How Far are we the Chosen People?

Sunday, February 5, 1899
Reading: Exodus 19

The old interpreters of the Bible, especially the Rabbinical schools, were of the opinion that the arrangement of the succession of the stories in our Pentateuch were by no means accidental. They knew that no attempt had been made at preserving chronological sequence.

There is no temporal exactness in the arrangement of the different sections—this was one of their often quoted principles. But on the other hand, they were convinced that if one occurrence preceded another, the recital of one happening before that of another must have been for a deeper reason than haphazard combination. And often, upon closer analysis, a modern scholar is surprised to find that in this Midrashic fancy, as it is so often styled and divided, is imbedded a deep truth.

This is certainly the case, in the architecture of the section part of which we read a few minutes ago. The chapter that precedes the passage tells us of the visit paid Moses by his father-in-law and the advice that Jethro proffered to his illustrious son. Jethro suggested a plan of thorough organization. He noticed that under the prevailing anarchy, Moses was wasting away his limited strength to no purpose, and having observed this he laid before him a scheme to overcome these difficulties with the least expense of moral and vital energy, so Moses could still discharge his high duty as a leader of the whole people.

The counsel of Jethro is worthwhile laying to heart. Many of our institutions suffer because the principle announced is ignored. Very frequently one hears the story that if a certain president were to die a whole institution would certainly come to grief, and again the counter comment on this plea that the president of this institution devotes so much time to the welfare of his pet child, so much time as no one else could spare.

Whenever a president of an institution organizes his administration so foolishly as to necessitate on his part undue sacrifice of vital energy and more than reasonable tribute of time, he ought to open his Bible and learn the lesson which Jethro impressed upon his own illustrious son in law. Every businessman today knows that half the secret of success lies in right organization. You must have faith in human kind if you would gain advantages even in your commercial ventures. They cannot keep touch of every button that is sold and of every spool of cotton that comes in. They must have confidence in their clerks; they must organize the army of their employees in a perfect line of ascending hierarchy—they at the top have personal knowledge of important occurrences and responsibility for vital and fateful decisions.

What applies to business holds good also in the administration of our philanthropies.

Whenever an institution is so managed that the president must be informed of every orange that comes into the kitchen and every bit of parsley that is put into the soup, something is wrong or rotten. Like in the case of Moses, in this modern instance Jethro may protest that the candle is burning at both ends—that it is high time for a radical change.

However, it is not my intention to enlarge upon this aspect of this morning's biblical lesson. I only wish to observe that the first half of the Pentateuch section, read yesterday in all the synagogues, is laying down the principle of sufficient organization and division of labor. But immediately after, we come across sentences so familiar and lines so deeply true, apparently however out of all connection with the economic and sociological advice which precedes: "Ye have seen what I did to Egypt and how I carried you, as it were, on eagle's wings and brought you unto me, and now if you will harken unto my voice and really obey my covenant, ye shall be unto me a peculiar property—but mind, mine is the whole world—but ye shall be unto me a kingdom of priests and a holy people."

This passage has perplexed many an honest Jew and has furnished weapons for attack to many a dishonest hater of Judaism. The claim *the chosen people* has often been hurled into our teeth. "You consider yourselves to be better than all other children of humanity. You set yourselves up an aristocracy more exclusive than any other that ever cursed earth. Your doors are barred against all. You complain of being unjustly treated by the world—your heart is filled with the spirit of hatred, *odium generes humani,* of all mankind. You hold yourselves to be the elect of God and look down with ill-concealed contempt upon all others that share with you the tenure of God's footstool, this spinning earth of ours." In many and multiform variations runs this very popular accusation against the Jews.

A little reflection, following out the method of Midrashic interpretation, will lift the doubt and expose in its nudity, the fallacy of the accusation of the Jew hater. Jethro teaches the principle of division of labor. That principle applies in the great workshop where the master is God and the employees are men, individual men or men in groups, in races, in nations.

Consider history from whatever point of view you may. Agree with me that history is the great and unending revelation of God's purposes; that as events happen on earth, the great "Divine Comedy," not in common sense of the term, but in that used by Dante, is worked out in larger measures and movements with deeper poetry than ever poet could conceive of, or believe, if you so will, would be superior philosophy.

That history is but a succession of unplanned and unpurposed happenings; you cannot—be ye stupidly religious, as I am, or grandly philosophical—you cannot be blind to the fact that certain adaptabilities and corresponding opportunities are given to certain races, to certain nations, which have not come to other nations and to other races; and that there is no race, no group of men, no nation but has in charge some one or other thought principle or possibility vital to the life and to the light of all humanity.

This assignment and alignment of humanity according to certain gifts and for the purpose of making certain contributions, none who reads history critically, can dispute.

Thus the principle of division of labor is verified in the actualities of unfolding time, and according to this principle every nation is a chosen one, every people has a peculiar mission. The Greeks were chosen to be the priests of beauty—the Romans were elected to be the missionaries of law and order—the Anglo-Saxon is dowered and therefore dutied unto the task to be the representative and the missionary among men of individual liberty, reconciled to cooperation under common law—and our dearly beloved America is also chosen for a purpose, a destiny.

Our America is chosen to be a democratic priesthood, a missionary in these modern days of ours. That is our mission, and for that mission, America is a peculiar people unto God to whom all the earth belongs.

A sensible Jew—they may be few or they may be many, it does not matter and the Jews in the pulpit sometimes are sensible and sometimes are the only sensible ones that are to be found—a sensible Jew, especially in the pulpit, has never maintained that the election of Israel implied higher prerogatives.

From the very first day the prophet announced the doctrine to this the latest hour when I repeat it and reaffirm it—the ground note—the key tone to this doctrine was higher duties and responsibilities, never exclusive prerogatives, never exclusive advantages. The Jew believes himself to be chosen for a purpose vital to humanity, which came to him in no other manner than came the mission to the Greek and to the Roman.

In the organization of the humanities, it was necessary that the principle announced to Moses by Jethro should be applied—division of labor and assignment of duty. Thus came to the Roman, law, to the Greek, beauty, to the Jew, righteousness and justice. For that end the Jew was chosen—chosen not miraculously, not because any inherent merit was in him, not because he had the right to this high position, but simply because in the economy of mankind, it was necessary that there be a historically developing organism to discharge this function so important to the health and the prosperity and the morality and the humanity of all that drew breath on God's spinning globe.

There is no mystery about the election of Israel—there is no mysticism involved in it—it is a plain fact. It is in accordance with the law as clearly operative in history as are the laws according to which the planets revolve in space, traceable across the maps of the heavens and observable in the observatory and repeatable in the laboratory of every physicist and astronomer. No mystery and no mysticism, but in obedience to a universal law that regulates and governs all history, the law of division of labor, of assignment and alignment according to certain tasks left in charge of certain people for the advantage of all humanity.

Why are now certain people chosen for certain tasks? Why is Greece chosen to be the priestess of beauty and Rome to be the exponent of law? Why is Israel chosen to be the priest people of justice and of righteousness? These whys are pointless. There can be no answer to them except the answer that cometh from faith. Faith tells us though it is not corroborated by a priori fact, that men are chosen by the grace of God, as the theological phrase runs, for certain tasks and certain duties. And if we reject this, there is only one other possible explanation. In the great men of the nations comes always to light and life the possibilities of all the other people. Not every Greek was a Homer or a Hesiod, an Eschylus or a Euripides, a Thucydides or a Themistocles. Not every Roman was an Aeneas, a Virgil, a Horace, a Sallust or a Caesar. Not every Jew is a Moses or an Isaiah or a David, or a Joachim ben Sacohi or a Maimonides or an Einhorn—but still every Greek had the possibility of responsiveness to Mahomet and Ilesiod, to Euripides and to Sophocles, to Plato and Aristotle. The tune struck by these great men awoke to vibration a corresponding note in the mind and in the heart of their people.

Thus to great men comes creative energy, to the masses responsive echo, and wherever this relation is established, there the doctrine of that relation tending to verify the fact of election for a purpose, is corroborated. And so it was among the ancient Hebrews—because they were the parents of a Moses—they were chosen to be the echo to Moses' words. Moses made Israel the people of priesthood unto righteousness.

Every great man makes an organization the factor it is. Take away the one that gives value to the ciphers behind, and nothing remains but zeros, and with the one the zeros are lifted into significance. That is the law of history. Moses made us the chosen people for Mosaic ideas and our own history gave to us the echo power to the appeal of Moses' truthful doctrine. That is the reason why we were chosen. There is no other. In being chosen, came to us no higher privilege, and our election is not a violation of the covenant of humanity, but is rather a corroboration of that compact which binds Israel unto the world. "Mine is the whole earth" is said in the same chapter where we are told that we must be a kingdom of priests and a holy nation.

There is no violence done to our scientific conscience. We all can maintain the doctrine as ever it was maintained in Israel and still be admitted without any equivocation into the temple of liberalism, and retain our standing at the altar of learning, even of Darwinian evolutionism. Evolution, if anything, proves the soundness of the principle invoked by Jethro—the principle verified in the history of humanity as the guiding plan of historical development—division of labor and assignment according to certain possibilities and according to certain responsibilities.

It may be granted that up to a certain time in

history there was room and call for the mission of Israel—there was necessity then of preserving the missionary agent, the historical people in its historical organization. But in this connection many a thinking Jew now questions the need for further preservation of this missionary agency, for as little as Greece is needed to give us suggestions of art, as little as Greece as a historical nation is required to awaken our mind to the beauties of what is true and beautiful and good, even so little is Israel needed to awaken the eyes of the world to the truths that once came to Israel through Moses and the prophets, truths now the common property of the whole world.

If the latter were the case—if the truths in our keeping are simply because these truths were our own finding and now were the property of the whole civilized world, there would be no answer to the argument—there would be no need for an Israel on historical basis idea identical with its own self and the past for the realization of its promised future. But perhaps this assumption is untrue. It is true Christianity maintains that our mission was fulfilled on the glad morning when the light of Bethlehem rose like the sun in the East and chased away the mists of lingering night.

Now again, if our truth were merely the belief—mark the word, the belief in one God, I say there would be no need for preserving our historical organization, for the world has become monotheistic. It is certainly a presumption on the part of this Jew and that Jew to claim that if he were not in the world, men like Whittier and Longfellow, men like the great pathfinders of humanity in our day, would not know the truth about God. It is certainly true if there were not a single Jew living today, the thought that God. is one could never be blotted out from the minds of thinking men. Why, philosophers that never came in contact with Jews—philosophers that never had means to know of Judaism and its literature, discovered the unity of God. Plato was a monotheist if ever there lived one, and Aristotle was a close second to Plato in his insistence that the divine principle of world and of matter is but one. And in India, we find men and minds impregnated, saturated vitalized, rendered fervent in their enthusiasm by the magic, the alchemy of monotheism. For mere belief, formulation of the doctrine that God is one, Israel would not be needed.

The great Isaiah believed that God and Jerusalem were bound together by ties that would never be sundered. Jeremiah is perhaps the first prophet, if it was not Micah, who dared to think out the thought that temple and Jerusalem and God were not held together in an inseparable relation. He was the first who said the altar of Yahweh, the ark of Yahweh, the temple of Yahweh—that temple will fall—God is not in the temple alone.

But Isaiah—if ever there lived a missionary of Jewish truth it is he—still believed that God could never leave Jerusalem, and that therefore Jerusalem was safe for all time to come. So all these so called distinctive elements of our belief fail. It is not for the purpose of belief that we are needed today as a missionary people.

Our belief is not so much in God as *in a* God, whatever He may be in Himself, a God of righteousness and justice—a God who hateth iniquity and loveth righteousness; a God who is with the downtrodden, who resides with the contrite; a God not of the majorities, but of the minorities; a God who defies the survival of the strongest and replaces that brutal law by the triumph of the morally fit. That is our peculiar discovery. That is basic to all our prophetic elements; that runs through all Judaism—Talmudic Judaism as well as Reform Judaism. Our radical Judaism was radical by going back to these roots of our doctrine, of our mission and message to the world. We must be the pattern people for righteousness and for justice.

Will you maintain that righteousness is done in this world? Will you maintain that justice is triumphant or supreme? Do you wish to say that care of a brother is the actuating motive of your life? Our commercialism is tainted to the core by the poison of selfishness. Make money is the one appeal that runs from morning to night, and if thousands of men are robbed of their humanity and tens of thousands of men are rendered slaves, two or three that can combine to accomplish this result for the purpose of filling their pocket, have no scruples to do so, and there is no law in the land that will stay their wicked hand, ready to grasp by the throat poor humanity, starving humanity, suffering humanity.

Why, the Jew's history itself today is corroborative of the fact that justice is not done in this earth. If justice were done would the Russian Jew have to suffer what he does? Would there be so much hatred against the Jew? Why is the Jew hated? Because he is the evil conscience of the world. He proclaims by his very presence that there are other principles than strength or power or brutality. By his very presence today, every Jew, rich or poor, Jew by heart or Jew by descent alone, confounds and confronts the doctrine of materialism. That has preserved the Jews. Not their stronger vitality, but their vital morality, their faith, their belief in righteousness and in justice, their belief, let me state it, in their God who lives and dwells with those that are. contrite of heart.

Will you say that today there is no need for the pattern people? There is need for the pattern people also because the modern world has gone daft on nationalism. Everywhere here in America, in Europe, in Asia, the cry goes out—the Nation! The nation is the last in the chain of human development. America for the Americans, and the destiny of America to be one of the land grabbers of the distant East—destiny of America for the purpose of expanding its commerce. That is the new doctrine of this day in our America—the fruit of the war undertaken for humanity's vindication.

And so it is in Germany, the young emperor is constantly clanking his spurs, has his hand on that hilt of his sword, and tells the world Beware! Beware! Germany for the Germans and the world shall feel the furor the Teuton's fury, if he is thwarted in his purpose or crossed in his ambition.

And France, the most miserable spectacle of what length of insanity this modern nationalism will go—France dissecting her own self and suspecting her purest children simply because the insanity of nationalism has taken hold of her and blinded her eyes to the demands of justice and of self respect.

Nationalism is supreme. And over and against this nationalism we need an organization based on history, which transcends the limitations of nation. The Jew is a cosmopolitan, and as a cosmopolitan he is needed today. Our cosmopolitanism does not deny duty to nation. We are loyal to our flag. The Jew in Germany is loyal to Germany. Our Judaism tells him "Be a loyal citizen." But Judaism knows beyond the nation and nations are necessary according to the principle of division of labor—stands humanity—and the Jew in Constantinople, in Chicago, in Berlin and in Bombay, in London or in Liverpool or Leghorn, the Jew the world all over, is the exponent of historically asserted principle of the oneness of humanity.

We need the Jew today, and there is call for his message today if ever there were call. Of course if the Jew merely speaks of his mission, then the world becomes impatient of his prating, his prattling, his presumption and his pride; but if the Jews were to live their message, soon the clouds would lift. The Jew must be the pattern; hence in his organized life he must create institutions that are pattern institutions.

In this regard the rule seems to be inverted today; I speak hesitatingly, but I feel that I must speak—all our charities, as we have them, are still organized on the obsolete principle of institutionalism. The new world has recognized that institutions do not solve all of our difficulties; that for certain natures, institutions are not a blessing but a bane, and that the blessing they give is bought at an outlay which is economically foolish where the moral principle comes into play: thou shallt not waste either moral energy or material resources. Instead of being the leaders today we are the followers in our Charities.

I do not deny that institutions do good; but they do good at a price in moral energy and in material outlay which is altogether too great, and the world has learned that the basis of all character is individual, and that society can only be built up upon individual men, and that the first molecule of social organism is a home and not a military barracks, and not a boarding house, and not a hotel, but the home is the basis of social organization.

Modern science has declared against these large institutions, and where institutions are needed, they are needed simply as temporary shelters until homes can be found—until individual opportunity can be offered those dependent children that are bereft of father and mother.

Nor are we the leaders, as we might be, along the paths of bringing righteousness and justice into our workshops and into our counting houses. It is all very well to talk about justice, but justice is here and now. It is all very well to talk about humanity, but humanity is the humanity of your clerk, is the humanity of your laboring man; and if we continue as we have begun, the day of social revolution cannot be staved off much longer.

What capital does, labor will imitate, and we finally shall stand in two camps—the few capitalists and the millions that are hungry. Do you think that hungry men will spare the millionaires? They will to the booty. The French revolution was child's play in comparison with the horrors that the day will bring when the masses will rise and ask the right which they ought to have, for they were born without their consent and they will not die without their consent. They will to the contest, and woe to the civilization that makes no preparation to arrest this tendency.

Here is the opportunity for the Jews—here is their social mission. Their mission to make true their belief in humanity, and if they do not, who will be the first who will find the heavy hand upon him? All revolutions give the answer. In 1848 who was the first who got the blow? The Jew. In 1830 who was the first who felt the hand? The Jew. The first to feel the blow when a new social age is being born amid the painful throes of the birth and the agony of the death of an old civilization. Let the Jew take heed. The blow will fall on him unless he comes to discharge his mission.

What if the Jew would be the pattern people? If not merely in their homes, but in their public institutions, they would be the pathfinders, not only in public institutions, but also in their relations with each other they would illustrate that there is a possibility of life on this earth without robbing fellowman of humanity or of the opportunity to make a living; that the right to work is a sacred right—a right as sacred as is the law "thou shallt not steal."

If I cannot live by my work because work is denied me, then I say I have the right in God's own sight to steal, for God's law, "Thou shallt not steal," is conditioned upon his law "Thou shallt work and none shall take away from thee the coveted opportunity to work, for a mother bore thee without asking thee, and having received life without thy consent, society must give thee the opportunity to work honestly and sufficiently to make thy living."

Our mine millionaires violate that law. I hope there is none in this congregation that has any stock in any mine, and if there is, let me assure him I do not mean him personally, or else there will be again a resignation, and God knows that is the law our mine millionaires violate. They force these miners to work only three days so that there will be no overproduction of coal, all for the purpose of making money. Let the humanity of the poor miners go to grass or go to ruin. And as there, so in a thousand other instances the law, 'Thou shall not steal but thou shallt work," is violated.

Let the Jews be the first to organize their business on the basis of the broader humanities. You say that is impossible. It is not. Many an industrial establishment in Europe and in America has begun this great task. Every industrial establishment can do its share towards bringing about the social peace.

Glorious has been our past. They do not know what glory is who complain that they are made Jews. Why, there is no page in history so splendid as is the history, which tells of our fathers. They were not rich. The rich Jew is not mentioned in the annals of time; but they were righteous, and for righteousness' sake they suffered, and to have had ancestors that suffered is the greatest luster that can come to man.

Who are they that are remembered in life? The sufferers. Who is the messiah? A sufferer. And the Jew having suffered is granted his messianic splendor and crowned with messianic dignity. Coward he—despicable cur is he who refuses such glory. But that glory must lead to duty and to action. Here is the call for the modern Jew, and this is the opportunity for modern Judaism.

Judaism is not a mere religion. It has a mission, and all self-intoxication of prayer, all fasting, all Lord knows what else, is at best but religious and as such not a fulfillment of Judaism. All these agencies, prayer, song, ceremony, Sabbath festival—have only the one purpose of awakening within heart and in mind the thought, and in the hand, the will to do, not to believe, but to do righteousness and justice on earth.

Will we at last awaken to our opportunity? Will we? May God grant that we might. The Midrash says very significantly, "God offered his law to all nations." None would accept it. But Israel accepted it of its own free will. Then God said, having accepted the law you are responsible for it. I am like a king who owns a garden. That garden God offered to many a person for the purpose of having him tend the garden, but none would take it until one man came, and hearing the proposal, accepted. Now that man neglected the garden.

Upon whom is the wrath of the king kindled? Not upon those who refused to take the garden, but upon the tenant who accepted the obligation and then failed to discharge it.

By virtue of our history we have accepted the trust. If we neglect it, God is not angry at the world that has refused that trust—he is angry at Israel, and God's anger is always executed against Israel. The baptized Jew is a Jew still; the Latinized Jew is a Jew still, and the ethical culture Jew is a Jew still. We cannot run away. It is manly then to stand our ground. It is divine to do our duty. Gardeners we are, and Sinai Congregation too, and what God has said to Israel I say to you.

It was your own free will that chose the garden. No one compelled you. You have a garden. If you leave that garden to go to thorns and briars, the contempt is upon you. You are not an ordinary congregation that can be satisfied with ordinary doing. A Sinai congregation, a Sunday congregation, cannot be satisfied even with a cheap Sunday talk; that you can have a Sabbath on a Sunday, that God is not interested in days. That is as stale as the ages, and every rational mind can say it, and there is no courage in saying it. The courage is in denying it today. Much more courage is required not to be a Sunday sabbatarian than to be one.

But if we have this garden, that garden must grow the fruit of life, which must be on a small scale. And Israel is on the large scale, the missionary heralding the message of justice and righteousness out into the world. Judah and

Israel, chosen not for privileges, but for performances, and the doctrine of election of Israel is in keeping with the principle laid down by Jethro, the principle of organization and division of labor.

God assigned to the Jew the trusteeship, the stewardship of the tree of life. That tree the fruit of which are justice and righteousness, fraternity and liberty, love binding man to fellow man—not by might and not by power—but by this spirit is the echo of that people's history who were the kingdom of priests, and a people consecrated unto the service of these vital, these fundamental ideas and ideals of true, as yet unrealized, humanity.

Amen.

THE JEWISH PREACHER:
Rabbi Emil G. Hirsch, Ph.D., LL.D.

A Quarter of a Century after the death of David Einhorn

Sunday, November 6th, 1904

There is nowhere on earth, there was not even in Jerusalem, a Westminster Abbey of Jewish consecration. No monuments in marble tongue or bronze eloquence tell of the great men that cradled in the household of Israel gave their lives to the sacred cause left behind thoughts, and then passed away to their higher reward. Moses' grave was never found, and the disciples of Moses share perhaps with the greatest master this fate that scarce any know where the place is in which the marble dust joined again the maternal dust whence they were formed.

But in good old Israel the custom prevailed in those days that recalled the parting hour of one great and loyal; to devote a hour or two to the study of the leader's words, and in obedience to that custom I have ventured to dedicate this hour to the memory of one who perhaps has passed out of the memory of the present generation—perhaps was never known by them who now are standing at the threshold of maturity.

But who is perchance not all together forgotten by a few of us, a man who did more to lend dignity and character to the synagogue in America than

QUARTER OF A CENTURY AFTER DAVID EINHORN 225

any other.

Today, with your indulgence—though the task transcends my limited ability—I will try and do justice to both the man and his ambitions, and his intentions. For, alas, I cannot speak of his accomplishments. In sober, cruel truth, he might as well not have lived for all the results that are shown today in the American Synagogue.

The sad, pathetic fate of his may reconcile others to the same destiny of bitter disappointment, and if the others have their moods of despair they may take courage to persist by the illustrious example set by him, to whose memory I would dedicate the ensuing hour.

Why do I choose this theme today? It is because twenty-five years have run their course since at the summons of God his soul rose to the higher academy and joined the congregation of immortals. Twenty-five years! They have wrought much; but they have also been faithless in much. Perhaps—though I do not believe it—pondering again on the illustrious example set by that man, and reflecting again on his principles, may work a needful change among us. But I do not believe it, for even if a God were to come from Heaven today he could not move a generation steeped in materialism and fettered by conceit such as never before forged shackles for any set of Israel's children.

Were he to come, whose words I have read, the Unknown Prophet of the Captivity, the unmatched orator, the man with the soul of flame for truth, and a tongue enabled to vocalize truth so sweetly and yet so strongly, he too would find deaf ears and cold hearts. And still, it may perhaps be profitable to dwell upon that other great man's life whose death hour I remember today, after twenty-five years. Those of you who have approached Gibraltar coming from the west will carry in their memory never to be obliterated, the impression made by the sudden rise before their eyes of that rock, symbol of purity and significant of unwavering fidelity. Like that rock, so stood up the man whose memory I Would enwreathe again with flowers plucked in the garden of gratitude and admiration.

A man he was, a man such as in the legend Moses is described to have been. Like Moses, he too had received a call to go and free his people. Like Moses he too experienced the bitter lot that they to whom he brought liberty were the last to appreciate his service, or even to bring him the tribute of respectful attention. He was a man like Moses who would not quiver nor quake before kings, and would not tremble before the most despotic of all autocrats, the senseless thoughtless, feelingless mob. Like Moses, he too had to hear the murmuring voices questioning his integrity and complaining of his leadership.

But he cared not for censure or for praise. His pole star was "Duty". He steered by the compass of truth. He would, above all, be true to himself, and true to himself he was. Small wonder then that he despised more bitterly than any others the men that flattered the mob. Small wonder then that his sharp arrows of condemnation, of burning irony were sent directed at those among his so-called colleagues who listened intently always to the wishes of the mob, the vulgar mob, the ignorant mob, who deemed approval by the many proof of their success, and valued the applause of the crowd more highly that the approval of their own—alas, too often—dormant conscience. Read some of the sermons he preached. Listen again to his scathing rebuke administered to the men of the white neckerchief, men who pleased the women, and who never had a word of opposition to the mighty in their congregations. It was this giant, David Einhorn, who coined that strong phrase, "the barons and aristocrats by the grace almighty of the Dollar". And he hurled that into the teeth of the most potent and richest congregation on this our continent.

They, the barons by dollars, had the impudence to pass resolutions bidding their minister refrain from speaking on resolutions adopted in Rabbinical conference. They, had the arrogance to prescribe what should be said and what must not be said. They, though scarce one of them could write correctly, sat in judgment on the utterances of men who were known to be masters of philosophy and leaders along the highroads of thought. And against this he hurled that protest in the flaming denunciatory, yet true description.

He craved not for popularity; he craved for the approval of his conscience. I said he reminds one of the rock that rises out of the Mediterranean, there where the Mediterranean meets in conjugal embrace the larger Atlantic. He was true to himself; he never changed. Do not misunderstand me. A man has a right to change; a man without mind will never change his views. Men with mentality will change.

Einhorn changed too. In Budapest he had Sunday service. In America he hesitated to engage in the experiment again. Perhaps he knew why. He saw the deeper things, therefore he hesitated. He was honest when in Budapest he preached on Sunday; he was honest when in New York he cautioned and advised against it. He was a rock with all this. He wanted to be true to himself above all, and true to the implications of his teacher's position in his work. He was a positive man, not one of those soft natures that can be easily impressed.

Einhorn was not of these soft natures. He was strong, like that rock that rises out of the Mediterranean. Strong! He was the leader, and the others were to be led. That gave him the right to insist the leadership was his! His knowledge, his erudition, his studies. It was not the presumption of the clerical; it was not the idea that he by virtue of his office had prerogatives that were denied to any other Jew. Einhorn had said that Jews do not recognize the distinction between clergymen and laity. Every Jew is a priest by virtue of his birth, and that priesthood cannot be denied to anyone. "But" said he, and his words are true today, as they were true then—"Judaism has at all times drawn a deep distinction between the *Talmudian*, the learned men, and the ignoramus."

Ignorance even with money behind is ignorance, and learning even in rags is learning. And because he was a learned man he would brook no interference with those things, the decision of which demanded learning—interference on the part of moneyed ignorance. He was a leader by virtue of his erudition; therefore he would not be led by those that had not the credentials required by an aspirant in the temple of the chosen guides. He was a man of light and leading, and knowing this he insisted upon the prerogatives of his appointment.

Not for self aggrandizement oh no, but for the cause. Ignorance cannot lead, and where ignorance leads disaster is inevitable. It is the leadership of ignorance that to a certain extent would throw upon us the dominancy of indifference. I blame none for refusing to listen when ignorance speaks and prates. I am as exacting as anybody may be in my demands upon the pulpit. I know that the college graduate has a right to refuse to listen when high school boys presume to guide them and lead them. And I say, and Einhorn felt it, that where the pulpit is equipped as it should be, it has a message to deliver, which it alone can deliver, a message of vital importance to them who wish to understand what life is, and who are grasping for knowledge in the highest of all sciences which we call religion, the science of the truly human life, and of the organization of society on the basis of a true humanity.

Einhorn was a man who did not believe that piety consisted in making sour faces or that prayer was specially effective when spoken with closed eyes and in curved posture. He was a witty man. That again is a characteristic of the sanity of his mind and the soundness of his spirit.

That is reflection of his Jewishness. The wit that he had was winged by Jewish appreciation of the joy of life and the beauty of life.

Einhorn laughed. I read only this week a book by a great Greek scholar, in which the contention was advanced that the Hebrew genius was void of humor that it was due to its exclusive ethical preoccupation. The Greek genius of course, was touched to laughter. As the rippling current that ran down from the acropolis ran in rills and sounded in trills, so did the Greek soul in its course through life strike the note of laughter and of joy and gladness.

That great master of Greek language and literature is misled by the natural confusion between Judaism and Puritanism. Puritanism is not Judaism, and Jewish literature is not Pentatuchial exclusively. Wit and humor are the Jew's dower; and the great Jews all had it. And Einhorn was a man of wit; he was a man of smiles; he was a man that knew that soundness and sanity of life are close to sanctity of life and of conduct.

So much for the man. Now what of his ambitions and his intended achievements. That he was a leader of the Reform movement we know. What does that mean? An answer to that inquiry is especially timely now when we have begun to forget the ultimate intention of the Reform movement.

From the East has gone forth in this country the proclamation that Reform was simply cradled by the desire to lay down a burden; that Reform was sponsored by the cowardly intention of escaping responsibility and minimizing holy obligations, Reform is the religion of convenience.

I excuse the men that of late years have sounded this accusation. They are not blind. They have eyes that see and ears that hear; and looking at things as they are they could not but to come to the conclusion that if this is the fruitage of the Reform movement it must have been cradled in ignoble intentions.

By the fruit, they argue, you can judge of the tree. And what has been the fruit? According to them, indifference, vulgarity. The self-assertion of ignorance over erudition and knowledge; the money high in authority the final decision resting with them that have the millions, and the masses dead to all that is high and noble. The young, strangers to every synagogue; and especially the descendents of the rich men in their frivolous attitude, not even ready to concede that the synagogue has for others some message, and Judaism has some meanings. Of course, these men argue that the same conditions prevailed even in countries where Reform Judaism is not known by name.

I walked last summer through the ghetto of Rome. There was no necessity for them not to observe their Sabbaths. I walked through the ghetto on Saturday morning, and to the right and to the left of me I noticed little shops that were open; I noticed cobblers at their benches, and tailors busy with their needles, I asked one of the tailors whose countenance seemed to indicate that he was a Jew, and he was. An Orthodox Jew at that, a proud Italian Jew who thought himself way beyond in aristocracy any German or Polish or Russian Jews, and I asked him why he worked. He laughed. Why shouldn't he work? He had never heard of Reform Judaism. So the conditions are identical everywhere. The only conclusion that can be drawn from this identity of sad conditions is that Reform is as important to stem the tide as is Orthodoxy.

But I hold that the indifference that has grown among the Reform auspices is due again to the arrogance of ignorance. I have not taken you in mind when I say that. Not you, my friends, but the thousands in and outside of our congregation, who are so perfect that they need no message, who never have any doubt as to what is right and wrong, never any desire to learn what the great men have thought what they have advised. These men, perfect in their knowledge and perfect in their character, they have never taken the trouble to study what really was the underlying motive of the Reform movement as conceived of and conducted by men like David Einhorn and my own sainted father, Samuel Hirsch.

Was it to lighten the burden? That would not have moved them, for their whole lives showed they were keenly alert to do their duty. The sacrament that they preached was "Duty" and "Obligation."

Had they been cowards their lives would have been more comfortable. Einhorn would not have had to leave Pest, where his Temple was closed by the Austrian Government. He would not have had to run for his life in Baltimore when the rabble and mob stormed his house, looking for him, because he had dared for years to protest against slavery.

He was not a coward; he would not shirk responsibility. Why then should he have escaped from responsibility by the motive of the Reform movement; why should he deny in his very character, and belying his conduct in life? Why should he there give tether to the cowardly, the mean spirit of desertion and of rebellion against the moral law, the sacred law of obligation and responsibility?

These leaders of the Reform movement believed that there was a special task assigned to the Jew in the economy of the world. It is not for me just now to discuss this, their belief. They honestly believed that to Israel as an historical organism had been assigned a certain part in the development of humanity. And they found that Orthodox Judaism contravened the implications of this responsibility in the larger life and broader fellowship of man.

They found that Orthodox Judaism maintained that Judaism was a law miraculously revealed somewhere and somehow, a national law which the Jew was bound as a member of the nation to observe. They also found that the Orthodox Jewish conscience declared that the Jew was a stranger here in the West; that his home was there in the East; that his compulsory abiding in the West was in the nature of a punishment for his sinning, for in the West he could not keep that law.

Therefore the Orthodox Jew prayed "Take me back to the East, to Jerusalem, that I may again offer my sacrifices as the law prescribed." Seeing this, Judaism was reduced to a law, and a national law at that, seeing that by the philosophy of orthodoxy, Judaism was declared to be a stranger in the occidental world.

These men coming to their task from the either true or false assumption—I again leave that question open—that in the providence of God, or in the evolution of time in the economy of humanity a peculiar task had come to Israel, found in the orthodox view the very denial of the possibility to fulfill that task on the part of the modern Jew. And therefore they said, "Open the gates. Tear down the walls. Judaism is not a law; it is not a nation."

We are appointed to exemplify humanity not as an accident, but as an essential force in the world. That is our duty, and that is our mission.

Much discussion has been had on that fundamental concept, the mission of the Jews. Both within and without our own memory they have laughed at that. Some have said, "Here is the old Jewish arrogance. The creed of the chosen race is an anachronism, in these, our days." And others have said, "What mission? The Jew has no mission, except to be a Jew, and he can only be a Jew if he is in Palestine".

The mission of Israel of course, becomes a mere arrogance when it is only a verbal declaration. The mission of Israel is an insult to the world at large, unless we Jews make real the mission that we assume to be ours.

I declare that I too believe in the mission of Israel, and. you who have often heard me, know on what grounds I maintain that in the development of humanity to it a certain work has come. But if that work has come to us, as I believe, we cannot claim to be true to that work by merely phospherating about it.

The mission of Israel, in the sense of Einhorn stands for something grand, if only we would live up to it. The Jew has no right to say that he has a mission unless he lives it, unless he sacrifices for it. The mission of the Jew is to be the leader of the true humanities. Are we those leaders? Are we the leaders in any movement making for the better or the broader life? A few of us are; but on the whole, we are not; and in view of this sad fact again I have a hesitancy, for one, to lay a little emphasis on this, Einhorn's central idea, the mission of Israel.

The missionary Judaism would be this: The Jew as Jew could be first, the most eager to live up to humanity everywhere. In his relations to his employees he would make for justice and righteousness. He would not be satisfied that his social duties are done by subscribing a few dollars to the Jewish charities, out of all proportion to his income; he would not feel that he was entitled to special credit for building a hospital here or an Orphan Asylum there. The others do this, and do it on a much larger scale. And as far as the Orphan Asylums go the others have learned that they are anachronisms, that institutionalism has had its day, and is declared to be impotent and ineffective by the experience of applied philanthropy.

But he would make in his social relations Justice the star. He would ask for self little, and give to others most. As a citizen of his country he would first ask what is right and what is true, and then vote for it. He would not be a leader of any movement to land in Congress a man who has no qualifications. The Jew who knows what his Judaism implies will have nothing to do with this. As a citizen he would set right above party loyalty, and decency above all promises of party politics and party support.

The Jew would resent the slurs cast upon his President, unless they were proven. He would resent to the last minute such a slur, for the President's honor is the honor of the country, just as a Rabbi's is the honor of the congregation; either he is worthy or he is not.

But it reflects upon a nation, upon the man at the helm, who is charged with being worse than one who steals in the street, and the Jew that feels would resent that slur, would speak out against that slur even if he be charged with talking politics in the pulpit.

If he talks politics in the pulpit, he knows what his mission is. Einhorn talked politics in the pulpit. They told him in Baltimore, "Stop talking on slavery. You are hired to preach, not to talk politics." He said "Religion, not politics?" "Would to God you had less politics in your religion, and more religion in your politics."

"But as for me, take your pulpit, do with it what you choose. When I am in the pulpit I shall talk against slavery." He did. And the congregation offered him a life contract if he would only cease talking against slavery. He tore that contract into shreds and threw it not figuratively, but really into the face of his Majesty the President that had the impudence to bring him that contract with that condition.

He talked politics in the pulpit as long as humanity decreed that it should be talked. The Jew who knows his mission will be the leader in every movement making for the better, nobler, deeper life. He will be the last to bend his knee before the moneybag.

That was the intention of the Reform synagogue, and the Reform movement was there to be positive and not negative. The Reform movement is to bring to the Jews the understanding of their duty, not to themselves, but to the world at large.

My time is exhausted. To do Justice to Einhorn one would have to write volumes. That grand man and that sacred intention of his was a flame too broad and too deep to be encompassed within the limit of one hour's talk. He is no more. Few are they who remember him. His own nearest congregation even has forgotten him. He breathed his soul into his own prayer book, and that prayer book has been shelved by them who claim that they sat at his feet and knew what he taught. Forgotten! Forgotten! His work apparently a failure, and a man such like he but rarely found, and never understood, in the Jewish pulpits.

Sycophants and flatterers, idiots and ninnies are now the leaders of American Reform Judaism. Indifference like a pall and a pallor, that brings conceit all over—a conceit of the pocketbook, or the conceit of culture, because where some have learned to sell shoes, others have learned to sell doctor's knowledge and legal tricks whereby to defeat death or the Sheriff's constables. Culture, the conceit of one, or money, the conceit of the other, a grave—the synagogue, in Europe, and here, and all over.

Has he lived for naught? I believe not. The day will come—unless all truth is false and the word *Justice* is a mere illusion. The day will come when the world will feel that he lived, will pilgrim to his grave, grateful for what he was, what he taught. And as for me, he has risen to those heights where they shine with a luster of the stars who have taught many and brought many to righteousness. We need his inspiration, the few of us who have their moments of despair. We need to remember what he suffered, how he struggled, not like the cowards who run away.

We need him. He does not need us, His fame is secure, and his immortality is beyond all doubt. Twenty-five years have gone since we bedded him by the River Hudson. A marble slab in Hebrew words tells the visitors to that home of peace who he was, where he lived, and what he aspired to be and do. That marble slab in Hebrew words becomes eloquent when we, the few who have read of him and listened to his voice, or who have studied his words ponder over his example and in the spirit pilgrim to his grave. And I have asked you to be with me. You, the few of this congregation who are true and loyal, must feel, all the better for having paid that visit. And thus will you rise in honor of him who was great and good, and say with me, as his children said in his home, [Kaddish].

Amen.

THE JEWISH PREACHER:
Rabbi Emil G. Hirsch, Ph.D., LL.D.

Wisdom

Sunday, February 14, 1904
Reading: Proverbs 11

Wisdom is a gem that most men desire to own and most men foolishly desire to display. In a certain portion of biblical literature wisdom plays a dominant part, and many are its distinctions, though the biblical writers full well understood that the seat of wisdom is hard to locate; that it is easier to bring to the surface of the earth, from the depths of mines, gold and silver than to put into the hand of man the rare jewel of wisdom. Still today the chapter tells us that *he who winneth souls is wise.*

Were I to address a class of technical students on this phrase, I should probably take occasion to point out to them that the Hebrew text in this place requires emendation, for the Greek version presents an altogether different reading, and one that commends itself as the better to the scholar, because it carries out the scheme of the whole chapter in which the first part of such statement *is* counterbalanced by an antithesis in the second part.

But neither you nor I have come hither today

for the purpose of technical instruction in the intricacies of Hebrew manuscript tradition. Our interest is more vital, we do not study manuscript; we would learn to understand life, our own heart, and our own mind. We would come to knowledge of what really constitutes wisdom that should guide us to the end, which we are aiming to attain, and for that reason I prefer to base my discussion on the subject of the translation of the Hebrew words that *he who winneth souls is a wise man.*

The term winning souls has an under note for us not altogether pleasant. We remember that the church has been busy for many centuries winning souls; we recall from our own history to what intensity of fanaticism this emotion to win souls has led men not naturally of cruel temperament.

To win souls ecclesiastes have castigated bodies, dignitaries of the church have outraged the instincts of humanity. To win souls men have been burned on the funeral pyre; have been garroted at the stake. To win souls Israel has been persecuted. To win souls tears have been pressed from the eyes of innocence, and sighs have been wrung from the hearts of the purest of human kind. To win souls, methods have been resorted to—yea, are still resorted to in our times, in church and chapel that strike us as grotesque, not to use the stronger term designating them as absurd.

The proselytizing zeal has been abroad on earth disturbing the peace of family and disrupting at times whole communities. No wonder then that the Jew sometime is inclined to be skeptical that the highest wisdom should be ascribed to the one who makes the attempt to win souls.

But, my friends, perhaps the phrase, winning souls implies an altogether variant message. Perhaps in the spirit of him who thus defined wisdom the winning of souls means something radically different from what the church and other agencies of religion have therewith associated. Yea, I have no hesitancy to say it, if we penetrate more deeply into the double meaning of the words, light will come to us and we shall be forced to agree that he who phrased this definition was indeed of deepest thinkers one of the deepest.

Do we know our own soul? Let that be the first question to which we shall endeavor to find an answer. Do we know the soul of our fellow man? Let that be the second query that we approach with deep earnestness this morning. Do we know our own selves? Who of us will presume to answer in the affirmative? Mystery is indeed spread deep o'er cloud and clod, o'er star and stone. The rustling leaves of the tree are sighing under the burden of a mystery, and the roaring oceans are echoing the plaint that mystery unfathomed is their symbolism; but however thick the mystery of heaven, of spinning planets, of growing plants; however deep the unlifted curtain which enfolds within what man standing from without would fain know and can never unravel, what is mystery of sky, of star, of stone and of planet compared to the unanswerable unanswered mystery of our own inner life, of our own destiny and duty?

It is merely because we have become blind to

the mystery, which is within us that we at times fail to realize that if there is miracle in the Milky Way, there is greater miracle in the emotions, the impulses, the monitions, the memories that combined constitute our inner life, our soul.

Or is it not so? We think: What is this but mystery? Is there not a gap between matter and mind? You know that impact comes from without, that irritation that ensues at the end of a nerve or other; that this impulse from without travels along the wire, as it were, strung by nature along the supporting factors of your body; but how from that impact aid impulse, and irritation from without, can leap into light and into the solemn thought that your chemistry has not answered, your philosophy has not established. There is mystery then in every thought of yours.

And what about that small still voice, which will speak whether we ask it to, whether we listen to it, or refuse to heed it; that still small voice that thunders at times with the majesty of a law imperial and eternally regnant, and at times sighs in tear laden syllables and brings to our consciousness the sense of degradation and to our conscience the burden or remorse?

What about this still small voice, and whence its solemnity, and whence its might, whence its persistency, whence its authority—for it has authority however we may rebel against it. We may at times fancy ourselves free from it, we nay dare the world and it to condemn us, but the moment strikes when all of our insolence is wafted away, and in the nakedness of our shame we may be forced to give answer to that authoritative query, Where art thou? What art thou now? Is this not mystery? And to know that law, to wonder at the marvel of thought power, does that not constitute the highest wisdom?

He who wins a soul, his own soul, is indeed the wise man. Or am I mistaken? Is this not the broken echo of belief's whisper that we, freer children of a better day of knowledge, have every right to disown? Is it knowledge of self, the recognition of the solemnity of thought voiced within you, bowing humbly before the majesty of that law, which will speak and does speak its eternal "Thou shalt" and "Thou shalt not"—is this not antiquated concession to the old superstition?

Let us see whether it be or be not. You search for other things to fill your lives. The one reaches out for gold and heaps ducat upon ducat; he feels he is a power in the land, for as his wealth increases the number of his slaves and parasites is always augmented. He believes that he has found the secret of life.

Has he? Is he the wise man? He thinks himself master of his own destiny. He has calculated most exactly and accurately all contingencies that might happen. From the eternal hostility which the elements bear to man, their temporary master, leaps in revengeful spirit to satanic destructive activity, a little spark, and that which he prides as the son of the wisest philosophy, that on which he relied, from which he drew his patent of authority, that which made him master over slaves, is consumed. Warehouse after warehouse totters; palace after palace is laid low; the treasures of India are consumed by the ravenous appetite of the greedy flames. What about the wisdom to call these things, which fire can destroy, which flood can sweep aside, the principal content of human life.

You boast of your physical strength. Perhaps you are a Greek, a Greek living in these later days, and that your life is meant as an opportunity for development of bodily frame and corporeal form and you have succeeded; a breath of air approaching you in cowardly insidious treachery makes you helpless. Your body wastes. Were you the wise man? Had you found the secret of life when you reasoned that beauty of form was the appointed fulfillment of life's opportunity?

Or a better mold than either of the two mentioned so far and of finer ambition than they and their company, you sought the content of the fleeting days and therefore contentment for yourself in the accumulation of knowledge. Yea, your fame was carried from zone to zone as a mastermind, and in your home circle, if your name was not known beyond, you were regarded as the paragon of all science and knowledge. They loved to listen to your voice; whenever you opened your lips others hung upon them breathlessly expecting to see drop from your mouth pearls of wisdom. One fatal moment a slight blow, perhaps on your skull—a shock not very intense either—and your mind became a blank and the lips that once gave forth a torrent of eloquence now trickle with driveling or insane gibberish. The wisest then, according to your definition, has clutched to his bosom what is not of permanency and on which no one may rely in the security that never will totter, or the pillars upon which his palace is reared shall be laid low.

But if you gain your soul, if you strive for conformity with the eternal law that sounds within you, you are the wise man. Come what may, your life is complete. Ideals different to them which conform to this eternal law leave you forever in the condition of a torso.

The richest man dies without being rich enough, and his riches do not endure; it has to be divided, apportioned. The wisest man has something beyond that line if he is mentally wise. The greatest explorer has not lifted off the mystery from all that is. The men of valor that have led millions to the slaughter-house, that are acclaimed as greatest of all ages by blood-intoxicated races, they leave some field unconquered, some port unentered, some fortress unreduced.

Every other ideal of life, save that which harmonizes with the eternal law that is within you, leaves you at the end incomplete. Your life is a torso. There is something lacking; there is always the element of deficiency therein. But the man who conforms his life to that law, which is within, is at no moment incomplete. Let him be cut off now, snatched away by the powers of death at this very moment, he is complete.

As correctly attuned instruments at any time a true note may be evoked, so the man who has found his soul, at any moment rings out the story of a harmony that has not to be supplemented by something subsequent. You are complete at any time, in any condition, if you have found in that sense your own soul, So it would seem to me that the writer who wrote thus knew what he was speaking on; and that winning of souls, if it is only your own soul, is indeed the gateway to possession of the highest and deepest wisdom.

Do we know the souls of others? We may attempt to win the souls of others. And does the winning of souls of others constitute part of wisdom? To my mind comes a saying, variously attributed to the French or to the Turks, which read: *He possesses as many souls as he speaks languages.* The more languages one speaks, the more souls one has.

What is the meaning of this? What is language? It is the expression in certain form of the inner life of the people. Hence the more expressions of the inner life of a people you control, the more souls are given unto you; for language is not merely mechanical. Every nation, or every race has produced a language, looks at life from a different angle, and what it sees from that angle it cloaks into sound, making the sound the vehicle for its enormous convictions and its deepest anticipations. Therefore it is utterly impossible to translate fully without loosing something from one language into another. It may seem as though the translation were adequate, but the best, the most thorough, loses something which the original contains and conveys to them fully, that which the original has cloaked into syllable, the pushing thought, not fully expressed In the weaker translation. Therefore it is true the more languages one speaks, the more souls one has; and the wider the range of one's vision, the deeper the insight into the secret, the solemnity, the sanctity of human life.

There is language not conditioned by syllable. There is language unuttered. Every man has a language, which he speaks and no one else speaks. That is the mystery of human life, that no matter how often life is reproduced into human form, each human life has something which is distinctively its own and which none other has. There is something to you, my friends, that is your own; there is something to me that is mine. Hence every man has his own prejudices too. Yea, his own prejudices. He views life from his own angle of vision. He sees life, as no one else sees it. You see yours. It is not true that you see what I see. Because you are you, you see; because I am I, I see. But what we see is different, is not altogether identical.

Each one has something, which is his, and that something enters into his conceptions, into his convictions, into his judgments. That something constitutes possibility of power, but also potency of prejudice. Every man has his own prejudices. Modern psychology has led us to know that, that subtle something, which we call the soul, is also power in groups of men. Races have souls, nations have souls, religious communities have souls, and yea, little cliques and circles of societies have souls that are their own.

The members of a race think differently than the members of another race. As the individual has something that is his so the race has something that belongs to it. The nations too have their souls, and hence they are national idiosyncrasies —idiosyncrasies which are possibilities of power, but also potencies of prejudice. There is no man without prejudice; there is no nation without prejudice; there is no race without prejudice; there is no religion without prejudice.

Now the wise man tries to win souls, that is to say, knowing by the constitution of human life, he as an individual has his limitations, he does not survey the whole scope or sweep of life, and even if he did, he would translate what he sees according to his own individual aptitude and capability; knowing also that as a member of a race, a nation, a religion or a clique or of a profession, he has his limitations; the wise man, I say, therefore makes the effort to win for himself souls, to complement his deficiency by what he learns from another.

This winning of souls in the sense in which I have tried to put it, leads not merely to the completion of your own stock and store of force, but to the understanding of your fellow man's limitations, and therefore it engenders a spirit which is ready to understand the limitation of the neighbor and to overcome that limitation.

Because men have not remembered this, instead of clasping hands, they have raised fists one to the other. Because men have forgotten that they viewed things from their point of view, and the neighbor could not view things from the same point of view, they have become estranged. Because religions have been oblivious of this law which limits the soul of each, and demands completion of the soul of each by the contribution drawn from the soul of all others, religions, instead of having been ministers of peace and concord, have been the minions of discord and hatred among men.

The wise man winning souls understands his limitations and the limitations of others. Therefore he is charitable; he is not dogmatic either, for dogmatism is the tendency, the attitude that forgets the law of limitation and the law of individuation. Dogmatism holds that truth, complete truth, all truth, has come to one, therefore he is to be the final authority, and his statement must be accepted.

No, they who win souls are wise, because they understand the operations of their own life and the operation of the lives of others, and thus become charitable, are glad to learn, are eager to modify, are anxious to complete what their limited vision has brought to them in incomplete state and in always preliminary form.

If nations would remember this, if races would remember this, there would be peace on earth; and if men remembered it there would be concord and brotherly love among men that now walk the same path of life and still are strangers one to the other, if not enemies and bitter opponents with hate where they should help.

What constitutes the great fortune of America? Some have invoked the prairies, these oceans without water that spread out their immensities; that pierce the barriers following the flight of the westward shining sun. Some have invoked the oceans, and attribute to their influences all these characteristic constituents in the mental possession of America, saying that these oceans were briny bastions that kept this western continent free from the narrowness and the obsessions of the ancient world.

But it was not the sky that arched over our land, nor the topography that marks it, which gave us what we have a right to say is ours. The fact that here from the very first men of different racial origin, of different religious training, of different national traditions, came together, is the secret of America's peculiar broadmindedness. For men learned here to supplement and complement each other, and the national soul of America was indeed made of many souls.

America won souls by being the most hospitable land under God's shining sun. Or take Israel's example: you have in a different way a repetition of what I claim are the providential benefits of which America has been and still is the beneficiary.

We have not been in possession of a land favored in its topography, in its climate or such advantages as are generally ascribed to the American continent. We have had no land, and have no land now; and some of us believe that we shall never have a land of our own again. But we have been forced to brush against every civilization. We have come in contact with every phase of thought that leapt from the human brain, with every desire, aptitude, passion, anxiety and aspiration that flamed forth from the human heart.

We have been in touch with all movements of thought, and hence the symphony of Jewish history is a many-movement poem, a tone poem, richer in variety, and therefore in content, than the 9th of Beethoven or even the masterworks of the newer schools, which, fretting at rhythm and the rigidity of musical form, assert their independence and demand the largest freedom for expression through light motif, and merely cast out suggestion.

Our history is significant because it made Israel a winner of souls—not in the church sense of the word, God knows not. We never proselytized, we never persecuted for Religion's sake, except our own. We never attempted to convert the world; but we were converted by the world in the sense that the world became complementary to us; hence as Jews we have had our own limitations, but the future of having a providential guidance to our career, which gave us that which no other historical group is endowed—such variety of view, such abundance of wealth of soul possibilities.

So you have in the American experience, in the testimony of Israel's history, the proof of the soundness of my insistence that he who wins souls is the wise man, for the more souls he has in the sense in which I put the phrase, the richer, the deeper, the stronger his humanity.

But before I close, a suggestion—the extract of my thinking on this exceedingly interesting theme: If each one has limitation, if each is under the law of complementing what he owns by what another has, is it not then necessary that conscious effort be made toward complementing, and therefore to induce another to complement what he possesses by what I may bring to him? It is my duty to bring to him what I own. There is miserliness and avarice of mental possession as there is miserly greed and avarice of material goods. The miser will gratify himself by looking at his growing hoard, but what use to the world the fruitage of his labor, the excess of his economies?

The businessmen need not be reminded of the fact that their property must be socialized in order to be effective. Hence you put your money into the bank where it becomes potentially three-folded, though in the ledger its value is only booked as one. Every dollar put into a bank becomes in power three dollars. If you keep your dollar for yourself, you can take it out of your pocket any minute and look at it and be gratified by the fact that you have a dollar.

But money is dead unless it is activated through the channel of industry, through the magic and alchemy of finance. So must your moral, your mental goods be potentialized. You must not merely have; you must give; and every true process of giving does not entail a loss to the giver. Quite to the contrary, do we lose by putting our money in the bank? We gain and every one of us gains. Not merely the banker.

That is the policy of our socialistic friends, our Bryanite shouters, that up to the present time have never understood that the banking system entails a loss on none, gives undue profit to none. In every, true gift you lose nothing; you get, you gain, and your brother gains and gets. You must potentialize your mental gifts, your moral possessions as well. Hence it is duty for the man who has a vision to display it before his brothers. Hence it is an obligation most sacred for those that have sought for truth and have found some of it to let others know of their discovery.

Draw the lesson from yourself, and it becomes your duty by example to lead others to find what you have found, that man is constituted as to be most affected by example. Many a man thinks, "I need no instruction. What to me the public service? What to me the words of a preacher?"

I daresay there are many men who are superior to preacher, who have all the wisdom that the so-called minister of God may perhaps claim as his own. But even so, theirs it is to potentialize what they have.

And as example influences men more than argument, it is their duty to set an example. Most men are so constituted that they cannot say they have all they need, even in mental culture and in moral power, never have all they need; they increase their store and decrease their deficiency by cooperating with others, by letting others influence them and by making the attempt to influence others.

That is the meaning of public service like ours, of meeting hours appointed for discussion in the manner, which we pursue. Each one is taught to look at life from a different angle by finding himself together with others. It is the preacher's task not merely to express his own view, but by dint of study and searching, to vocalize so that others can understand the views of others—especially the wisdom of the ages incorporated in the literature of the Jews, which is the literature of a wandering people. The Jews have absorbed the best that the world owned, and transformed it into potency for the world's improvement and the world's uplifting.

Hence they were an influence, and we must become an influence again, an example; Reform Judaism totters unless its conscience is kept alive; our history is meant for nothing else, the exponent of the totalities of life, because under God's guidance, the Jewish mind was taken out of its own limitations and put into the broad world, coming into contact with all sorts of influences, potentializing them all and focalizing them all.

Thus, my friends, perhaps you will agree that the old Hebrew proverbial philosopher knew what he phrased when he said, *He who winneth souls is a wise man.*

Win your own soul first, and win the souls of others, and after you have won your own and won that of others, make what you have a source of power. You will gain, never lose; and your gain will be the gain of others.

And as Jews remember again, gain your Jewish soul and understand the souls of others; and what from your own knowledge of self and the knowledge of others you glean, make your capital not a dead capital, but a potentialized capital for the moral uplifting of the world. Then you are true to the mission of Israel and your life will prove that indeed the Jew is chosen to a task for which God has given him opportunity and power, but for which God and history holds the Jew accountable.

Yea, let us go hence and deeply inscribe on the tablets of our memory the phrase *He who winneth souls is the wise man.*

Amen.

THE JEWISH PREACHER:
Rabbi Emil G. Hirsch, Ph.D., LL.D.

"The Awe of Distance"

Sunday, May 3 1903
Reading: Obadiah

The awe of distance is one of those phrases for which the philosophy of Nietzsche is entitled to our grateful acknowledgement. In this expression, the German thinker casts his patient protest against the assumption, popular indeed but not profound, that all men are equal.

This dogma of the equality of men carries of course some truth, but its real intention is lost if it is lifted to be an absolute truth. As a burning appeal to undo artificial and unnatural inequalities, the doctrine of the equality of man acted beneficently in the destiny of nations. When the streets of Paris rang with the furies of the sacramental words of the French Revolution the term "equality" thundered the doom of many unbearable distinctions, which in the atmosphere of court life had flourished.

There is no absolute truth. Liberty, equality and even fraternity, are words coined for the moment, but not commissioned to symbol verities for all eternity. But our age has mistaken the intention of these revolutionary terms, and it is to the credit of Nietzsche that he was the most strenuous in raising his voice in protest against the fetishism of equality.

Men are not equal. Some are called to higher service than others. Some are gifted by the hand of nature, or, as I would put it, some are intended in the economy of God to more laborious duties, and therefore endowed with greater capacities than are others. Mentally, morally and even physically, one man is not the copy nor the counterpart of any other man.

As physically those men are differentiated and individualized, so mentally and morally men are distinguished one from the other. Practically, the world has never acknowledged the theory of the absolute equality of men. As in the domain of theology, so in that of practical attitude of one to the other, conduct and conceit have belied doctrine and dogma.

In theology men have denied God; they have read in the universe merely the expressions of a blind power. But the very men that are loudest in their protestations in belief in power, blind force, purposeless matter, were the first to turn to spiritualism.

The ages that were steeped apparently according to their professions, most deeply in the turbid waters of Atheism, were those that were most intensely superstitious. While they were shouting anthems to force and matter, to eternal mindless law, men were consulting mediums, were discoursing on the mysteries and the possibilities of the fourth dimension, heard spirits knocking and received revelations from the supernatural world.

The very age that has tried and tested with the biting acids of skepticism the foundations of Church and of Synagogue, talks glibly about Christian Science, and maintains that mental attitude can conquer physical discomfort and even neutralize the action destructive and corroding of microbes or other germs.

Another phenomenon in the same direction and to the same purport suggests itself readily to the student of religion. Buddhism set out with the clear intention to be godless; yet scarce had Buddha, the great teacher, passed from earth when his disciples turned him into a God.

Similarly is traceable the development of our idolatry of equality. The nineteenth century proclaimed the democratic age. From house tops the gospel was preached "men are equal." Yet that very nineteenth century spawned the French Revolution, which beheaded aristocracy with patents dating back over the centuries. That revolution tried to smother in blood the distinctions historical and hereditary that former days respected.

This nineteenth century tottered to the grave with the whole world on its knees to men perhaps without patent of nobility consecrated by ages, to men perhaps without distinguishing capacities of mind and of soul, to men in control of the resources vitalized by the labor of all, the capitalist, the men of money—a millionaire or multi-millionaire.

The true distinctions are ignored; the artificial lines of differentiation are heightened. As in the domain of theology, God ignored, some new kind of pagan spiritualism reappears. So with the true distinction obliterated and forgotten, artificial demarcations are emphasized and accentuated.

In such a time and under such obsession, the man who dared to recall to the memory of men that there are distinctions, which cannot be ignored, is entitled to grateful recognition. There is much to object to in the philosophy of Nietzsche; but his appeal to remember the awe of distance is certainly one that commends itself to the approval of every thinking man, of every thought-filled man.

Men are not equal, they cannot be equal. For unless humanity constitutes itself on the level of the weakest, the lowest, the dullest, and unless injustice be done to the best, the strongest, the noblest, the most capable, the wisest, this doctrine of equality cannot be carried out. Life ignores it; and as life ignores it, it behooves a thinker to examine what the purpose or intention of life be, that life which makes men unequal, and where the philosophical solution be for these inequalities.

Absolute equality and a doctrine based on it are certainly not verified either by observation or by philosophical speculation. Men are made in the workshop of Nature to be distinct one from the other. Look but into the schoolroom. Why is it that this young lad leaps over all difficulties with a light foot, while yonder lad, of equal age, falls and stumbles over? Why is it that this boy at once responds to the invitation of the book, while yonder boy of equal age is disinclined to listen to the voice that speaks from the primer or the speller?

Why is it that the boy who has apparently no

inclination toward letters wakens at once and becomes stirred and thrilled with impulse when the anvil sings out its gladsome song, when iron shouts for him to come and beat it into pre-purposed shape and use? Why is it that the involved propositions of mathematics are as clear to the eye of one boy as is the sky. without fleck of cloud and without curtain of mist, while to the other boy the simplest theorem in geometry remains a cuneiform document to which he has no key, and for which he has no understanding?

Yea, to leave this domain of intellectuality, look at the field of the moralities. One goes through life; he is tempted, but he knows not that he is. The smiles of sirens and their songs do not stir as much as one fibre in his being to quickened vibration. He is even tempered. Anger is unknown to him. He does his part, moving through life with evenly measured pace. Whether the road be steep or be easy, whether it means ascent or descent, nothing disturbs his equanimity.

The other is moved by the least breath that wafts across the field. He has eyes that see seduction in flowers that do not as much as intrude in the faintest degree upon the vision of his fellow man walking the same path and apparently brought up under identical influences. You would certainly suppose the character of twins were one the exact counterpart of the other; and yet we know it, pedagogues know it, psychologists know it, and common observation will confirm it, that one of a pair of twins will develop ruggedness of moral power and the other may be as weak as the reed that bends before every wind and sways with every whim.

So men are not equal in the sense in which equality of man has so often been boldly and enthusiastically accentuated. What is the consequence then? Nietzsche pleads for the awe of distance, in other words, for the recognition of these inequalities and the corresponding attitude of one to the other.

Before Nietzsche spoke that a certain awe should possess us in the presence of the distinctions and the inequalities of distances that gapped between man and man, it was Goethe, unless I am mistaken, who spoke of the peculiar German idiom, very difficult of translation into English; the rudeness which characterized the conduct one toward the other under the presumption that one is just as good as the other.

From the moral observatory it becomes plain that this is the curse of our day, and that unless we come again to a sense of the distance between men and again become permeated with the awe of distance, we shall have to pass through many bitter experiences, and perhaps may regret the day when thoughtlessly we allowed ourselves to be trapped by the snare of this artfully constructed doctrine that men are absolutely equal.

The loss of awe of distance is even pernicious in the field that many thoughtless people would hold to the outside of its influence, the field of industry. What has that to do, many a one asks, with a proposition in philosophy or in morals? Factories are not churches and commercial houses are not Sunday Schools; business is business. So, how can the recognition of the equality of men or the recognition of distinctions between men affect industrial relations or commercial operations?

But it does. The attitude of the trades unions on a certain point always in controversy reflects how far the loss of awe of distance has had practical results and has determined certain demands constantly iterated and with passion insisted on.

They believe—and they act upon that belief— that there is no distinction between men, and they draw the radical conclusion: If there is no distinction then none shall receive higher wage than another. Men that work at one occupation shall all be remunerated alike; their wants are the same and their capacities are the same. The skill that one has cannot exceed the skill that the other has. Therefore the wage must be identical.

Practically speaking their theory fails. They know too that men in the same occupation will display different degrees of capacity and of dexterity; but their theory is so dear to them that they will not permit actuality to interfere, and thus they take the other horn of the dilemma and insist that no one shall display greater dexterity and no one shall allow his native capacity to appear, lest their demand shall not be granted of an equal wage for all.

Here is the demonstration of the fatality of the doctrine in a field that apparently lies entirely out of the region of influence of dogma or of doctrine. And as in this domain we shall have to learn that men are not equal in capacity, in dexterity, in moral will, in sense of responsibility, as men are not equal even in their wants, in their desires, in their passions, in their appetites, so throughout our whole life — and that is the work of the twentieth century — we shall learn the lesson that the awe of distance is essential to the fabric of humanity, that with it eliminated the thread becomes weak and may snap.

With it reintroduced in proper proportion and with proper understanding, there is hope that the development of the race shall proceed peacefully and progress to its ultimate harmony end concord among men that are distinct and distinguished from one another, but who nevertheless, each according to the measure that is his, will cooperate for the welfare of all.

We need the sense of the awe of distance right in our families again. "Honor thy father and thy mother" is the old formula for that which Nietzsche calls "the awe of distance." Is it true or is it not true that our family life has suffered from the philosophy of absolute equality? Why should parents be honored? The materialist will not recognize that even the sacrifice that father or mother brings in behalf of son or daughter entitled father or mother to special honor.

Father or mother is responsible for the life of the son or the daughter; therefore it is not more than the daughter's right or the son's right if father or mother gives care to the child. The son and the daughter did not ask to live; they live because father or mother desire the son shall live; therefore it is the son's clear right to be taken care of by father or mother during the period that he is not able to lookout for himself.

Honor father and mother for what, asks the

materialist. Why should father and mother be honored? Because there is a distinction between father and son, between mother and daughter. There is, in the first place, the distinction of age, the distance in years. Life is a school; and the longer we are in that school the greater our wisdom; we absorb wisdom unconsciously. The stripling of ten years cannot have the wisdom of the veteran of forty.

There is this element in the first place, the distance of years. Then is the distance of affection. Father and mother have given more than son or daughter can ever repay. Never is the quantity of love by son and daughter equal to the quantity of love come from father or mother. There is a distance between the two. Hence, the awe of distance; therefore honor due to him who gives more than he receives or ever can receive in return.

Then there is the distance in selfishness, or rather in unselfishness. The true father and mother never do for child with the expectation of getting back. The son and the daughter expect. The father and mother expect nothing. There is this distance in unselfishness; and hence its equivalent should be at least honor and respect.

From the materialistic point of view there is no reason why father and mother should be honored; from the point of view of the equality of man, with the presumption in favor of the younger to the disadvantage of the older, father and mother should not be honored.

But what is involved in the word "distance" rings out why father and mother should be honored. The family life is, after all, but in small measure the reflection of public life. What is lacking in our public life is again this awe of distance.

If we are all equal, then each one is competent to judge what the other one does. If we are all equally competent, then each one is entitled to set up his standard as the highest to which the other should conform. Whosoever departs from this equality naturally departs from it downward, not upward. That is the presumption that runs through our public life. Each one can criticize every other one, and under this publicity, this fury of criticism, distance is obliterated.

The President of the United States is placed on one level with the lowest of politicians. That there is a dignity which goes with office, a dignity which creates distance, we forget. There is a symbolism of office which is justified on the theory of distance, which is entirely unjustified on the theory of equality. What does the President's office token? The majesty and the might of the whole nation. He represents the nation in the eyes of the world.

That symbolism of his office includes the doctrine or the presumption of a certain distance between him and the undistinguished mass; yet that awe of distance is entirely forgotten in our passion of criticism, and the result is that reverence is lost to us. We have no reverence, which is but another word for awe of distance.

"Familiarity breeds contempt." That is a true observation. They who would save respect must set up hedges against too great a degree of familiarity. However much we may talk about equalities, practically we ignore them; we ignore them by the invoking of standards that are not the highest but the lowest measurements of distinctions and distances.

We recognize the inequalities of wealth, don't we? There is a certain degree of presumption which the wealthy man is entitled to, if he was the creator of his own wealth. I can understand why a man who rises by dint of energy, by sagacity, by sacrifice, from the depths of poverty to the pinnacle of wealth, should feel his worth and should occasionally, yes, perhaps always, emphasize his consciousness of power, his self knowledge of worth and of value. There is in his money something of his personality; his millions stand for work and services, for shrewdness, for capacity which others perhaps did not possess.

But what about the presumption of those that have not made their money, the presumption of the heirs of the second generation? Good God! Is there any reason why they should presume? And presume to what? Did they make the wealth which for them is the patent of their distinction? In the chapter that I read, if you paid attention to it, the prophet with cutting irony asks Edom whether thieves have come upon him. There you have it. That which thieves can take away cannot be the standard of distinction. If thieves can overleap the distances, then that distance is not entitled to respect or to awe.

A modern writer has said: "We have made a stealable standard of distinction; things that plead with us for recognition of distance may be stolen." Hence they are exterior to men, they are not permanent, they are not noble. A thief, a sneak thief, or whatever thief he be, of all thieves the forger is of all men the most despicable, and what the most despicable can take away we would exalt as tracing lines of distance.

I repeat, the creator of wealth has shown capacity. I am also willing to acknowledge that he who is the heir to a large fortune which he has not made does not forfeit the right to be regarded as standing at a distance from others if he has grown into the responsibilities of his exceptional position.

If he, instead of becoming a drone, is an active worker for the principle that power stands for *responsibility*. If he is a factor in the social life of the community, and utilizes the means that he has not created, which have come to him through the channels of heredity, for the enlargement of all the movements making for the deeper and the nobler human life, then I grant that the original justification of distance which the father had is in some measure also his.

But, Good Lord, why should the fops and the silly girls who parade diamonds and silks that money they made could not buy, why should the young men who are merely good businessmen because their fathers have built their business, presume to be better than men that work and women that work, and accentuate their presumption on every occasion? I know of what I am speaking; I know the temper of the people. The masses have not exception against the man who worked himself up. Quite the contrary.

With the fewer exceptions the men that have risen from the ranks have had ears for their complaints; they had sympathy with them in their troubles. They were ready to listen to pleadings for justice. They met their men half way. But these masses are impatient of recognized divine rights for which there is no equivalent in human work and in human sympathy.

Says the prophet to Edom: "Even if thou should rise as high as the eagle and build thy nest of gold in crags of rocks to which the foot of human wanderer could never approach, even thence I shall hurl thee down." Rise to crags of mountains, build your fortresses of gold that is not yours! Thence you will be hurled, and the day of reckoning is not far. A spurious distance will not be respected; a stealable standard will not be acknowledged.

What the thieves can take away, that is not warrant for distinction, and it is not the line of demarcation by which distances shall be measured. By what is man entitled to the respect, which comes from distance? By the things that he does, by the sentiments that he cherishes, by the capacities which are his and which he develops— develops for the benefit of all and not for the advancement alone of self. Wisdom, knowledge, and science are higher than gold.

Your commercial establishments would be invaded by thieves; your safety deposit vaults would be exploded with dynamite; your streets would run with blood tomorrow were it not for the work of the men for whom you have so little recognition—the men that work at stipends even less than the wage paid to the successful advertising agent. These men in schools and on the platforms, from pulpits and by the pen, extoll the nobler things of life. They are the builders of the humanities; they are the prophets of principles, principles which go into the haunts of poverty and bring there the knowledge that life, after all, human life, means other things than to eat and to drink and to be merry or to enslave fellow-men, to utilize men for our own selfish purposes and advancements.

These principles are the only checks now. It is the awe of distance that is the salvation even now of our society. Stifle the voices of these men, refuse to listen to them, and let the masses become unlearned in the principles that these men have found and teach, and the deluge will be trifle compared with that torrent of devastation which then will sweep aside whatever is.

Before the Revolution broke out in Paris, the aristocrats, the wealthy refused to hear. Why should they have care for the mob, the trash, the dirt? The young count was busy studying the pleatings of his frills. He was adept in all the various perfumes; and he knew what kind of perfume to use in the morning and with what kind of aroma he had to be scented when he made his bow at 12 o'clock at night before the reigning belle of the season. What did they care for the masses? Those masses rose in fury and in anger, and the scented heads of the heirs of aristocracy, filled the basket at the bases of the guillotine.

"Even if thou should raise to the heights where eagles nest, even thence will I hurl thee down." That is the call of history. We were all happy and contented in this country when we were a nation of workers. Today we are all disturbed because we have ceased to be a brotherhood of producers. We have established or are establishing a new aristocracy here—the aristocracy of wealth. It cannot be, and it shall not be.

There are inequalities which are divine, inequalities of mind, inequalities of heart. But they are utilized always in the service of all; the greater the distinction, the greater the sense of duty. A great painter does not paint for money. Money is incidental and accidental. He paints for the none to purchase; and he is glad when his picture is seen by millions and millions, though it bring him not a single cent of a million. And the poet sings because he has to sing, not for hire; but he is glad if his song brings joy to joyless houses and to sorrow-filled hearts. The physician, if he be a true physician, speaks not of his business. He gives what he has to give; and comes rightfully in the pay of a rich man, but he places what he has at the disposal without asking of the poorest as well.

And so in all these higher distinctions the money standard does not enter. There are other compensations; the compensation of service, the consciousness of being something to others and helping others, through the distinction which is ours, to rise and to live. These distinctions are recognized. They have their warrant, and for them we must have the awe of distance, as Goethe puts it, the awe of distance is predicative of good.

In family, in nation, in society, in all the ramifications of humanity that awe of distance is the source of life. It spells the counterpart and the recognition of duty founded on distinction.

The Jew is the historical exponent of the principle. That is the Jew's historical mission, to preach the awe of distance; and until the world has learned that principle the Jew's past is not ended.

May we all carry this away with us today that responsibility confers nobility. If we are young; let us learn to have the awe of distance in the presence of our elders; if we are unlearned let us learn to respect distance in the counsel of the learned; if we have done service at the altar of love, charity, philanthropy, let us believe that we have received a patent of nobility, and let those of us who have profited by the devotion of others bear in mind that they have devoted themselves in our behalf.

As Jews let us have the sense that there is something noble about the Jew, and then from that "Noblesse Oblege" whatever the relation we may be placed and whatever our situation in life may be, by keeping our distance we shall become distinguished and thus be urged and stimulated and inspired for greater service, not for self, but for all.

May that God we call distant, but who is still so near, give to this His blessing, His wisdom and His insight.

Amen.

THE JEWISH PREACHER:
Rabbi Emil G. Hirsch, Ph.D., LL.D.

The Privilege To Err
A Line From Goethe

Sunday, April 29, 1906
Reading: Prologue Faust

Dem Fertigen kann man's nie recht machen; ein Werdender wird mir dankbar sein, They who believe to have attained complete stature, will never be satisfied with work of others, but one who still wishes to grow and is anxious to develop will always be filled with gratitude.

These lines, freely translated above, in the original quoted to you, are taken as you know from the prologue to Goethe's *Faust*, and here, as so often, this great poet thinker strikes the note of truth.

The book of the human soul in all of its chapters is familiar to him, the inscriptions therein he read with a wonderful versatility and a marvelous thoroughness. The description of the attitude of men that believe to have attained complete stature is perhaps one of the most striking that we owe to his wonderful genius, and at no time have men of observation so ample an opportunity to become impressed with the correctness of Goethe's delineation, as in our own day.

The men who believe that they have nothing more to learn are in the majority. Life seems to be a subject so easily mastered. What is there to life that we do not know, especially if we are successful or if somebody else has allowed us to be the beneficiary of his success. Where is there riddle in life that we have not read? Is this not the argument, either spoken or tacitly urged by most of those with whom we come in contact in our daily pursuit of our daily tasks?

If old men come to the conclusion that life has no longer any mystery for them; if men that have for years and years stood in the forefront of battle and borne its brunt have, out of the wealth of their experience, extracted the gold whose luster they believe cannot be heightened, then perhaps we must concede that there is, if not justification, at least explanation for this, their attitude.

But sad it is when you find young men and women that are still on the morning side of life's ascending hill, cherish the conceit that they have fathomed the depths of life. Sad it is indeed when young men and young women by their indifference to all that stands for search of life emphasize their arrogant claim that life has nothing more of puzzle for them. That their philosophy needs no further correction, that it fits every problem and solves every riddle, and that is practically the attitude of most young people these days, the exceptions proving the rule.

Their indifference to religion marks this their conceit as perhaps nothing else. They are indifferent to religion because they believe that they have a philosophy all comprehensive, or perhaps the other diagnosis suggests itself, that by long disuse of the searching faculty the very faculty has atrophied as in the Mammoth Cave in Kentucky where the fish have no eyes, simply because they have been living in unlit darkness. So many of the children of our day, having never come under religious inspiration, have lost even the power to feel that there is something wanting in their life, that they are *fertig* in another sense of the word than in which Goethe uses this adjective. *Fertig,* in German also means "spent, exhausted."

Young people ought never to be *fertig*; they ought to face life with insistent curiosity. The fact that they have been successful in their business ventures is not a sign that they have attained completeness of intellect and growing power of soul. "They who are free from the conceit will always be grateful" even when their own mistakes are pointed out, even when the incompleteness of their information, the restrictions in their horizon are called to their attention.

They would grow and they know that limitation is fatal to growth; error if turned into truth, throttles what should be vital, asphyxiates that which should be of the essence of life. If gratitude, then, marks the growing mind, error as well, an error recognized, is symptomatic of adolescent intellectual faculty of developing strength of soul. And in that same prologue in which we find the introductory couplet, we read the following: "Man will commit error as long as he is ambitious to rise, is solicitous to grow."

I have often heard the following argument:

What is the use of bothering about things that are in their very nature unsettled. Why should I sit at the feet of a teacher who himself has to acknowledge that what he proclaims is preliminary, never ultimate? How many conflicting views of religion, of ethics, have found utterance and credence and are today urged upon us by men of serious intention and of consecrated scholarship. Not two pulpits in this city will on Sunday agree, no matter what the proposition be which is under discussion. Is it then not better for me to save my time and nervous energy if they who claim to be masters are not agreed?

If the teachers have doubts why should I not wait until they come to a concordant conclusion and are ready to announce definite results?

This argument tickles the vanity of him who advances it, but this argument has overlooked the privilege to err, and is ignorant of the impelling power which lies in recognized error.

Had it not been for this faculty to err, man would never have emerged from brutalism. It is characteristic of the beast to be saved from every doubt, to escape every uncertainty. Instinct guides the lion and any other of the family of non-speaking animals. There is neither temptation to the animal, nor is there failure to the animal; as long as its material functions operate without interruption through pathological process.

The animal is always sure of its footing, never makes a mistake. Would that be the enviable condition for man to find himself in? Is it not expressive of man's distinction that when Nature fashioned him she placed upon him the obligation of the doubt, the possibility of error, as an instigation by his own efforts to grow, by his own failures to learn.

Had humanity been "complete;" had there been no vision as yet uncurtained before its eyes; had there been no peak to scale, no phenomena of Nature to search, no power of Nature to tame, man never would have become more than what is the ape today, than what is the lion today.

And they who never read a book, never ask a serious question of themselves, never probe life to its depths, who pass through life untouched by the sunshine and unmoved by the clouds, who measure life merely in terms of material success; and when they have attained it do not know what this material success may mean, how it shall he energized and utilized.

They practically lead the life of the beast. Their reason is contracted into a contrivance to win in the game of chance. Their intellect is dwarfed into a mere provider for the instruments wherewith to fight the battle with another, a competitor and a rival, and. that which we call soul is altogether withered by this hot blast of self-sufficient, self-admiring, self-complacent completion which they predicate of themselves.

That is the sad, sad concomitant of the sight of young people who know only themselves and no one else. Who know themselves so imperfectly as to have no question to ask nor admit that there is a problem. Religion, if it means anything, is just the incentive to ask the deeper questions, and the religious mind is not a mind that is *complete*, but is a mind that is hungry.

As the proverb puts it: "Where prophetic vision is not had, there the people are apt to lapse into misery." It is vision that religion wants to place before us and the religious mind is not the believing mind, it is the searching mind; the religious mind is not the satiated mind, it is the hungry, the open, the growing mind. And because religion is this, under true religious consecration the privilege to err is always emphasized. Dogmatic religion is a *completed* religion. It seems to be easy to reduce to formula the contents of religion.

In the same book, *Faust*, Goethe says, what you have in black and white that you can consolably, confidently, easily carry home with you; but what you can carry home and lock away because it is reduced to black and white ceases to be vital. And that has been the fatality of dogmatic religion, that all its vitality was lost. You could carry it away, lock it away in a cupboard; you could have it in books, but never had it in life. It is the glory of our religion that it never was a *completed* religion.

They cry out:"Tell me what Judaism is?" From the pews and even from the pulpits has come this appeal, tell us what Judaism is. And then we are told again by them who have no appreciation of the genius of Judaism, every congregation has its own Judaism, every teacher has his own construction, it is confusion; lead us out of this chaos, tell us, ye men what Judaism is. And some of our leaders have come under the infection. We have heard it in all sorts of keys of the gamut: we must come together, organize a synod, we must declare to the outer world what Judaism stands for; we must have a standard of faith whereby to regulate our religious life, whereby to decide who still belongs to us and who does not. It will be a fatal day for Judaism when these intentions shall be carried into effect.

But the truly Jewish congregations and the teachers who have appreciated the genius of Judaism as a growing and never as an ungrowing religion, they will as before insist that our religion, even if we err, even if confusion results—to err and to be in confusion is infinitely more profitable, is infinitely more abundantly vital than is dogmatic fixation of principles.

Lessing said, were a good God to offer him in one hand truth and in the other the search for truth, he would humbly address God as follows: "Withhold from me truth; grant unto me the search for truth." Never was a deeper verity more happily formulated than in this most profound observation of the great German critic. Lessing was the first among modern thinkers who developed a theory of history as a divine process of education. He was the first one to anticipate the hypothesis of evolution. If history is a process of education it is necessarily a succession of developments from the lower unto the higher. And this has made Lessing, though he lived during the latter half of the eighteenth century, an essentially modern mind.

We cannot pilgrim with as great a confidence to the works of other thinkers of the eighteenth century. Most of the eighteenth century philosophers belong to what is called the philosophy of illumination or enlightenment. While when compared with the dogmatism of church their insistence must be hailed as the outrider of a new dawn. Still we cannot get over this one fact, that all of this philosophy is as dogmatic as ever was church or as ever was the mosque.

They operate with a *completed* man; their ideal of man is static, not dynamic; they have the view that natural man can never err, that conscience, for instance, is infallible and that if we only heed the voice of conscience we never can go wrong. We must admire their moral enthusiasm, but their moralism became exceedingly shallow. They did not understand that to be vital even morality must be growth, and that if conscience is to speak and to speak the words that shall inspire, conscience as well must be under the impulse to refine itself, to grow, to deepen, to enlarge, to broaden out. Lessing was an essentially modern man; he regarded the history of humanity as an ascent, a process of education.

Now what is true education? They are not educators who believe that the transmission of knowledge constitutes the educational process. You can be an educated man even if you lack knowledge. It is impossible today for any one to know everything. There are no encyclopedic brains in ordinary existence. Occasionally a phenomenally gigantic, powerful man will arise who will have in absolute comprehension all the knowledge that up to his day had been placed on the banquet table before minds that were hungry and souls that were thirsty. Such a man was Alexander von Humboldt, for instance, and in a certain sense such a man was Wolfgang von Goethe; such a man was Bacon in his day.

But it is extremely doubtful whether, today, one could arise that would know everything. Education is not transmission of knowledge, but it is awakening of power. It is the rousing of the sense of hunger for knowledge and for knowledge to be applied to self-development and to the growth of the society in which we are placed. Knowledge is but a means to an end in the process of education. They are not educated that come from school with that self-sufficient arrogance that now they know all, that now they need learn nothing more.

That school has failed, which sends its pupils out into life self-satisfied, perhaps surfeited with knowledge. The school that sends men out with a knowing consciousness of incompleteness, that school has fulfilled its task; it has blessed those that pass through it with something more and something better than wealth of knowledge, a competency even to perform certain tricks. And the school that is dedicated to this task, which is under this holy consecration, will not save the people from committing errors.

The philosophy of error will be applied, the students will be allowed to go astray, they will have the privilege to commit errors, and from their errors they will learn how to avoid them. As long as they are growing and developing minds they must not be guarded against falling into mistakes. Moral education, as well as intellectual education should also remember this vital truth. If the moral life is to be a life of growth it must not be walled off against the possibility of mistake.

We Judge character too often by action, not by

intention. There are thousands of men that never have committed sin, that have never deviated by one inch from the narrow and straight path. In their pharisaical self-righteousness, they are impatient of others that may have lost their footing, that may have wandered off, that may have committed sin, even transgressed the law. And it is true, nevertheless, there has been more moral life in men and women that have lapsed than there is to be found in these straight-laced Pharisees that have never been tempted and that have never fallen from grace.

It is not a Jewish prayer, "lead us not into temptation." We must be led into temptation if our strength is to develop; as we must exercise our muscle in order to have strong arms, so our moral dower of strength must be put to the test. Better it is that occasionally we fail than that we should never be searched. Yea, I repeat, and I have no fear of being contradicted, it is best that we should occasionally commit errors and they who have committed them, not out of wickedness but out of blindness, generally come out of the dark night purified, improved, strengthened and uplifted.

You must have asked yourselves why it is that sinners are so often placed before us on those boards that token the world. Is it merely out of a beastly, depraved appetite for that which is filthy, for that which is slimy? The little gods may perhaps, knowing the perverse appetite of our *completed* generation, speculate on the love for what is mean and nasty and with a view to the flowing current of gold, write with filthy pen of the filth that still clings to mar humanity.

But they who have scaled the heights of Parnassus, they who have been kissed by the Muses, have never yet felt impelled to pander to lust and to speculate on depravity. They are of a higher mission, they hold a nobler commission. And yet if they put on the stage these that cannot assume the perfectly white robe of unfailing form, what may be their high purpose? To teach a pharisaical generation the deeper truth. That, even in the morals, often they who have erred have been of nobler texture than the straight-laced, self-sufficient, *complete* men, who never have felt the heat of passion and therefore never have had the sweetness of compassion.

You must have been under trial and stress would you understand the terror which assailed the fellow man, the sister woman whose hands are not clean but may be cleansed if to them is brought the news of helpful understanding.

Madame de Stael said, "When you comprehend you must pardon." The spirit that will not pardon is the spirit of ignorance. The spirit that forgives remembers that to vital life and striving life—in God's life—in God's wisdom was opened the possibility to fall and to fail, to err and to go astray.

Now, finally, it is not necessary that we should hold to the same views always. Clinging to identity of opinion marks not the growing man, it is symptomatic of mental and of moral decay. They who never change their views have never had views worth the changing or worth the holding.

Often you meet men that tell you, why should

I listen to you; you are not consistent. I remember ten years ago you advanced this theory and now you, perhaps, voice almost the opposite contention. The privilege to change is involved in the privilege to commit error.

They who are self-sufficient of course never commit errors. Their opinions being *complete* they never study, never search again, never probe again, and hence they never amend, for what is perfection needs not be amended. But the growing mind is conscious of the preliminary character of every statement. The growing mind reserves the privilege of amending, reconstructing, recasting, casting aside entirely and beginning anew. Where there is openness of mind, there is mutability, there is anxiety to change, to grow.

There is, of course, a difference between change and change. Some men vacillate. As the prophet says, they are limping on both feet, one day Baal, the other day Jehovah. Zigzag is not the curve that life, the fuller life, the growing life, will trace. But the curve with its heights and its depressions marking the growing mind shows nevertheless some continuity, if it be only the continuity of purpose, the unifying quality of intention. A weak mind vacillates, it drifts with every tide, with every current. It follows the impulse of the popular passion. It cannot resist.

For this kind of mutability I am not pleading. That is pathetic; it is not powerful. But I am pleading for the right to change, to grow; for the right to change under continuity of purpose. The desire to rise upwards must precede the faculty and the privilege to commit error.

I leave to you, my friends, the application of the thought. Happy we if we disabuse ourselves of the conceit that we have nothing more to learn. That we have studied life's volumes from the first page to the last; that there is no inscription thereon still baffling our searching eyes. No puzzle still waiting for our solution.

Some of those that are indifferent to us in the professions, as well as in business, presume to represent the intellectual elite. Something with pity in their mind that they meet us, something with patronizing condescension that they suffer us; they have nothing more to learn from preacher or from pulpit, from platform or from the lecture bureaus, agents and ministers. No, they know it all.

They believe that they are the intellectual elite. They are not. They are the *fertigen* of whom Goethe speaks; but I myself believe that Goethe meant when he used that word, to apply it in both senses, *complete* and *spent, exhausted, dead.*

Their intellect is not vital. He who can pass through life and is never moved to ask a question, what does it mean; who faces triumph and trial and is never impelled to ponder. He who has success and is never urged to ask himself, why am I successful and why not another. And he who has failures and is never touched to inquire why he has failed and what failure may mean to him, may believe himself a giant; he is a dwarf.

Let us not be *completed.* Then we shall always be grateful for the incentive, grateful for the impulse. We shall err but err because we are striving. Then our errors may be pardoned. The error of self-sufficiency is not pardonable; the error of growing intellect, of enlarging morality is pardonable.

It is a pathway to fuller knowledge, to deeper, holier intention. Happy are we if, out of our anxiety and ambition to grow, we commit error. They have to be pitied who never err, because they never think, who never go astray because they never doubt. Be they young or be they old, they must be pitied; their arrogance is laughable and pathetic.

We wish to grow; we therefore are grateful for the impulse to grow. We ask for nobler light, for clearer light because we would rise higher and higher, where sunshine has its purest, its longest day. Where the stars are nearest and on the pure breath of the zephyrs comes to us the sweetness of a peace which is not without struggle, the peace of good intention.

Amen.

THE JEWISH PREACHER:
Rabbi Emil G. Hirsch, Ph.D., LL.D.

New Chicago Public Library
Address by Rev. Dr. Emil G. Hirsch

Library opened
Monday, October 11, 1897

Mr. Hatch, in introducing Dr. Hirsch, said: I have the pleasure of presenting to you a citizen, a scholar and an orator who has often done honor to the city of Chicago and whom the people of Chicago always delight to honor. For nine years, covering the entire period of the construction of this building, his talents and learning, his justice in administration and his wisdom in council, gave dignity to our deliberations and added luster to the name of this institution. This library has no truer friend, no wiser counselor, than the Rev. Dr. Emil G. Hirsch, who will now address you.

****

Mr. President, Ladies and Gentlemen: If I deserve only half the description which my successor in office as President of this institution has given of me, it is certainly due to the inspiration which this work has given to us all, and to the consciousness that a city like Chicago is looking toward us to do for it the best we could. For I daresay that in this million-hearted city there is no home, whatever the dialect in which the ditty is sung over the cradle it rocks, or whatever the language may be in which the protection of God is invoked, whether the home be humble in its furnishings or luxurious in its draperies, but rejoices with us tonight that the library has at last crossed the Jordan and entered the land of promise on a career of fuller and still more valuable service to humanity.

The thousands that have passed through this spacious palace and admired its classic proportions and full equipment and have been surprised by the artistic finish of its decorations were not drawn hither by idle curiosity. Their presence under this roof, as yours is tonight, was a testimony that the library had won its way into the hearts of the people and had filled a place in economic and private life throughout this grand city. A public library has a sphere of its own. And this we may say here tonight, that those who successively have been charged with the administration of this great trust have also kept in view, steadily and without swerving, both the peculiar opportunities and the peculiar obligations resting upon an institution like this.

Carlyle it was who complained that every village in his surroundings had a jail for the accommodation of the criminals, but none had a public library. His antithesis suggests the old thought that education is the mighty enemy of inclinations to vice and to crime. It is, alas, too true that in our country the population of our penal institutions is exceedingly large.

On the other hand, it cannot be said that our

people have been deaf to the appeal, which the Sage of Chelsea clothed, in such plaintive fashion. New England is certainly dotted with public libraries, and the young giant states of the Northwest, are largely peopled with the children of those states with their traditions to link them to Plymouth Rock and the Mayflower. These states were colonized by the flower and the best that Europe had. These giant states of the Northwest were early alive to the duty of emulating New England and the original states along the Atlantic border in providing at public expense institutions where the young people could find the sources of knowledge and be induced to drink great draughts of the limpid stream of refinement.

Chicago certainly understood the suggestion of that generous gift which, in the days of her darkest trials, came across the ocean, and the first Board of Directors mapped out, with a wonderful catholicity and an exceedingly marvelous grasp of the possibilities of a public library, the policy of this institution which in the main has been adhered to, to the present day, not to the detriment of the library, nor to anything but the advantage of the whole city and it millions.

The Public Library is not organized to compete with the scholarly collections of original manuscripts and old tomes and volumes hoary and dusty with age. No, it constitutes one of my prides that I am able to say that in the alcoves of our library many a scholar has found the tools for his arduous labor, and many a learned man in the pursuit of original knowledge has been surprised to find in our collection what all the other libraries in this city or elsewhere perhaps, would like to have placed at his disposal but were unable to do it. Many departments of our collection are so complete as to rival even the great places of pilgrimage to which scholars repair, the British Museum, the National Library of Paris, the Royal Library of Berlin and the Vatican, or the other collections for which Europe is so famous.

But while service to the scholar may be rendered here, this is but accidental and incidental. The main purpose and the main province of a public library is to become the people's college and the people's university. (Applause.) And under no form of government is the establishment of a people's university, free to all regardless of condition, sex, color, erudition or, the want thereof, so essential as it is in a land which founds its system of government on the suffrage of its free citizens. For in this country every question of public interest, whatever its nature, whether political, financial, economic or social, is submitted to the arbitrament of the ballot; and it is indeed essential that those who deposit their vote to shape the future of their land shall have within easy reach the sources of information whereby to confirm or to confound the statements made to them on the hustings, and even in the Public prints.

Far be it from me to deny that our press is doing a grand work in the cause of enlightening the voters. I do not belong to those who detract from the influence of the press or love to fling criticisms at the literary style of the busy men who perform their duty with a zeal, an energy and a devotion that challenges my admiration as they lay on our breakfast tables the news of whatever happens throughout the world—the thoughts of rulers, the whispered rumors in secret of cabinets, discoveries made in the starry dome above or the wealth found in the deepest mines under the earth. I do not belong to those who question even the literary value of most of the daily productions of the press, for though there exist much higher than newspaper English, I say that on the whole the English which our newspapers give us is pure and strong and vigorous, and is a valuable contribution to the architecture of the noble language in which Shakespeare wrote and Lowell sung.

I say also that Dr. Rush was wrong when he charged the newspapers with being panderers to popular habits of disjointed thinking. Their thinking is not disjointed. If it is faulty it must not be forgotten that it is done in a hurry; there is no time to verify their facts. It is work that must be supplemented, often corrected, even neutralized, by the influence of the public library. The public library is of the greatest service to the men in editorial rooms and in the reportorial quarters, for often they must repair to these halls in order that they may be enabled to do justice to the duty that is upon them.

Again, this Public Library serves as the repository of their own productions. Here are kept together for the future races and for the enlightenment of unborn generations the papers that come from the press every day which otherwise would be lost. The files in yonder newspaper room constitute not the least valuable possession of this grand library. A study of these files is exceedingly interesting, if for no other reason than to show that even editors are human and therefore fallible, that even editors learn something in the course of their career and may modify tomorrow the apodictic statement of yesterday.

Therefore the newspapers having their duty, still the library also has its distinct province for their sake and for the sake of bringing the information to the whole community, especially in days when great issues tremble in the balance and the American people has to decide at the ballot box its future, and with its future perhaps the future of the whole human race.

A people's university has been this library, as every public library should be. Ignorance and passions arc the rocks on which republics have been wrecked. Ignorance and passions lead to prejudice. Ignorance and passions are the opportunities of the demagogue, and there is no greater master of shams and no greater detective of the counterfeit than the books in the public library. (Applause.) The people's university is the palladium of the people's liberty. This has been the work of our library. This it shall be for ages to come. (Applause.)

A university is consecrated to two distinct aims. The first is the cultivation of the humanities, and the second the inculcation of the strongest patriotism.

We wish to bring home to every reader, to every child, man or woman the consciousness of his or her humanity. A man that is not at home in this world in which he has to live, a man who looks up to the stars above and cannot decipher the human inscriptions there, a man who can pass by the flora and be not one to curiosity and inquiry, a man who does not know why the seasons follow each other and by what laws the whole of the world spins in space, such a man may have all the physical attributes of humanity, but he is not a full man.

At the threshold of the humanities stands a knowledge of the nature a part of which we are and under the law of which we also have to spin out our lives. Therefore in a public library a prominent place must be assigned for the books which deal with discoveries of the laws of natural sciences, and this library at a very early time recognized this incumbent obligation. Long before the time when to its solitary luster were added the three other stars in the constellation of our library firmament, each one with the understanding that all the others should chase each its own orbit and pledged to follow it and it alone to that the equipoise and the balance of the library firmament be not disturbed, the men who organized the work of selecting the books had a clear understanding of the peculiar province to which this institution was confined and in which it had to exercise its energies.

These books were not brought together by haphazard chance. A well-devised plan presided over the choice or decided the exclusion. And if books on natural science were introduced, the men who purchased them understood full well that a man who was a stranger in the world, part of which he is and which he is called upon to control, is indeed not fully initiated into the potentialities of his own humanity. It is not true that these books on natural science were chosen with a sole eye to give one inventive genius perhaps the means to carry out his native instinct.

Not because our age or our country is bent on technological pursuits did we purchase so many books busied with the laws of electricity, with the swift flight of the lightning, with the roar of the ocean with the rise and flow of the tides. No; as a means to culture and refinement primarily, as the instrumentalities for disseminating a knowledge of this wonderful world, did these books come to our shelves, and there they stand, torch-bearers and light-bringers for the millions, in order that they may become better men and better citizens.

Across the sky is written in large and golden letters the words Coordination and Subordination; Cooperation, and not Competition; and the citizens who have learned this lesson from stars or stones, from rocks or rivers, from plants or planets, will repair to the ballot box knowing that the highest triumph of a self-governing people is to allow those to govern whom the majority has entrusted with this high task.

Thus as a means to the humanities, and patriotism even, our books dealing with natural sciences were chosen. These natural sciences are but at the threshold. The mighty chamber of knowledge is stocked with other treasures. The Delphic oracle told us in thundering tones thousands of years ago *Man know thyself,* and the knowledge of men and of man constitutes the burden of the literature that we have brought together.

Anthropology, the science of man, embraces every department of knowledge; the physical nature of man; the physiological functions which go on in his frame; the workings of his soul and of his mind; the experience of the race; how the human family grew and has developed from small beginnings to the present grand consummation. What the people thought, what they felt, what they dreamt and what they believed—all these things and many more belong to the department of anthropology. And I dare say that no library, public or private, scholarly or at the most merely intended to act as a center of information, has a richer collection in this grand and most important department than has the Chicago Public Library.

In this connection I may answer one criticism, which perhaps has risen to the lips of one or the other and has occasionally found place and voice in the writings of our daily press. The figures of our circulation show that a large percentage of the books taken for home reading belong to the class called fiction, And there be those who claim that it is not the province of a free people's public library to provide books for idle amusement, as they say, or books to stimulate the imaginative faculty and to create an unreal atmosphere around the reader. Indeed, those that claim this do not understand the province and the possibilities even of works of fiction. Certainly in these days of degeneracy, in these days of depraved taste, the number of novels that are worthless and vicious is legion. But they have been excluded from our stack rooms.

But novels of even mediocre workmanship have their right to be admitted into a collection like ours; for no matter whether the thought be pure or shallow, whether the outline of character be faulty or perfect, no matter whether a great problem be treated by the author of the novel or merely some old and familiar scheme be the center of his development, one thing is certain: every novel, even of mediocre workmanship, brings to the front human types, introduces to us men and women under the lash of certain passions or under the load of certain burdens. And thus every novel, no matter what its workmanship may be, may arouse in one or the other sympathy for the eternally human, and thus lead to the refinement of soul and the building up of character.

Besides, the highest novels are those that ought to have their place next to the Bible. Is there any doubt that the men who thought and pondered over eternal problems and the deep temptations of our humanity, and in the guise of creations that have been famous for their poetic fancy, have tried to strengthen the mind of man in his struggles or have been eager to broaden out his horizon and bring forth new ideas, have had the prophetic gift, and as such sought to be made welcome in every story where the human heart aspires after inspiration and the human mind craves fuller information?

Moreover, novels do not stand outside the atmosphere of the age, which creates them. No novel is written but has the stamp of the generation for which it is intended, and thus through novels may come a knowledge of the age, its difficulties and its duties; and I could name many works of fiction which have brought about this.

Again, novels show the national disposition. They are therefore instrumentalities for inculcating patriotism, Our American novels are always a mine of American individualism. The men that the American novel deals with, whether located in a hovel, in a mine or on the prairie, are men who represent the principle incarnate in the American, that "a man's a man for all that;" that conditions and circumstances are secondary, while character and energy and independence are the primary factors of true humanity, (Applause).

Would you exclude these novels from a collection like this? What if occasionally chaff is mixed with the wheat? The winds of discrimination will carry it off. And if we attract one thither by our novel department and hold him for a certain time, it is but natural that he will become more refined, and after he sees the many volumes on our shelves will be attracted to read better books than novels whose only purpose is to illustrate whether at the end of the plot the minister is called in or the undertaker has found a job. (Laughter.)

That for children stories of imagination and adventure are proper, it seems to me no one will deny. The human race illustrates this fact. Every literature written during the time when men were children partakes of the element of imagination and the marvelous, the stupendous, and the heroic. Homer and Genesis, the Edda and the

Veda, written at a time when the race and the nations were still infants, mere children in their nursery, were no doubt the precursors of the modern fairy tale and story of adventure. I know to what I am witnessing, and I say it with a full understanding of the bearing of my words, that in this collection of books which we have housed in this palace, so rich in many a gem, there is none that is more precious and more serviceable than the department consecrated to literature for the young, Our Juvenile books challenge the admiration and call for the approval of every true lover of young boys and young girls. These books going forth from this house will bring cheer to many a lonely heart and will contribute to arousing a sense of manliness and a determination to be heroic in the minds of the young boys and the young girls, the future citizens of America.

And this brings me to my second point, that a library like this must be the great prophet of patriotism. Let us not forget that America, the youngest child of the world, exemplifies in its history the whole history of the race. Let us not forget that economical and social questions and questions of finance are in the foreground of public discussion and call for adjustment through legislation or through the ballot of the free citizens.

We have brought together here an immense collection of books in every language, on social problems, on problems of finance and currency, on problems dealing with the constitution and development of human society. In other lands they are aghast at our audacity in submitting these problems of finance and currency to decision at the ballot box. Our public library makes it possible that this experiment can be carried on without risk and without danger.

The last Presidential campaign was fought out in the reading room and the reference room of the Chicago Public Library much more intensely than it was on the hustings or on the stump, or even in the Chicago or other daily newspapers.

Why, it was wonderful how the workingmen, the men of moderate means, the clerks, those who were slaving in sweat shops and those who were free men in their own counting rooms, came and sought information either to confirm or to confound the statements that had been brought to them from the platform or the public prints. And a European visitor to our shores, himself a representative of the people in a German District, was at once reassured that—let the decision be what it might, it was the decision of an enlightened people, of an intelligent people of voters, and that therefore the State was safe and humanity's cause would not be impeded by the result of that election. (Applause.)

Our Public Library is thus the sheet anchor of public safety, and will be so in every election, no matter what the issue may be. As long as there are readers and as long as there are public libraries, there may be left to the voters, of male or female persuasion, the decision of financial and economic problems.

The history of America is the history of the world. For this reason, our collection, with a view to inculcating patriotism, is rich in monographs and in volumes on the historical experience of other nations. Somebody might doubt whether this library is the home and the basis, the mother of true patriotism, by looking through our catalogue and finding so many books on all sorts of subjects in foreign languages. There have been those who tell us that we make a mistake; that in this country, whose official language is English, no book should he purchased at public expense except it be written in English.

There is a place where the foreign element has no standing and should be excluded; that is in politics. In public life we aught to be Americans with no qualification, no matter where our cradle stood or what the original songs may have been to which we listened when we were in the nursery. (Applause.) But in a public library like this it would be suicidal to exclude books not written in the English language; not merely because this city is polyglot; not merely because every Sunday from the pulpit religion or the gospel in taught in as many as twenty dialects; not merely because in our by-ways and in our highways almost every dialect of Europe and Asia is spoken here. That would be no justification, no legitimization of the policy adopted by our Board.

But because to know other languages and to be acquainted with other literatures and to be on terms of intimacy with the experience of other nations cannot but have the same result in the minds of our readers as has a visit to Europe. Go to Europe; admire the treasures there; see the military parks and the mighty institutions of learning; admire the Alpine scenery and listen to the warbling of European songsters; you come back to America, if you have traveled with open eyes, a more thorough American than you ever were. So an excursion to a foreign literature and the reading of a foreign language is the best means of making one feel that it is a God-given privilege and a responsibility to all mankind to be an American man or an American woman.

(Applause.)

Let us not forget that America is no longer New England. It is the new world. Even before the Declaration of Independence had been written there had come to these shores not merely Englishmen, but Frenchmen, Spaniards, Germans, Dutchmen and Scandinavians, and the best that Europe had she has sent us across the ocean. From 1840 to 1861 when Lincoln called, those who came from Europe, Ireland, Germany and France answered his appeal as readily as did those whose cradles stood at Boston or New York or Chicago. Let us not forget that in this city especially the true American is he who understands the genius of the institutions of his land, and who, though he cultivate for his private amusement a literature that is not the official language of the country, may for all that be a better American than he who is stubbornly and bigotedly devoted to but one dialect. A good son always becomes a good husband; and a good son of Germany, a good son of France, a good son of Ireland, if he remembers his old mother, will still be wedded to the stars and the stripes with a deeper love than if he had forgotten what Germany was to him, what France was to him, or what Ireland may be to him at the present day.

Not a narrow Americanism, but a worldwide Americanism, is the Americanism to which this collection of books is devoted. America is still a potentiality, The future race of men, the best and the strongest, will be molded in the laboratory of God, this Western republic, and to the possession of that future man, that future woman, the world will bring its best. This library is prepared by bringing together in their original tongues the best that other nations thought and did, promoting that grand and more inclusive Americanism which will fulfill the hopes and the destinies of all mankind.

To study art we have to go to Europe. To study the old monuments of architecture we must visit Italy or Egypt. We cannot transplant the Parthenon or the Pyramids to this our Western land, but in a portable form we can bring the fruit of all the nations' culture to the very door of the poorest citizens of Chicago.

Books are the messengers of the prophets, a refinement and a civilization, which is independent of climate, of condition or of locality. This library has done this in its cramped quarters, and will better do it now that it has found a palace worthy of its associations and typical of its duty.

We who for nine long years have watched every step in the erection of this structure, and rejoiced as it approached completion; we who tonight as a reward of our efforts and a recompense of whatever sacrifices duty has laid upon us, see this grand consummation of our fondest hopes—we have indeed a right to congratulate ourselves and to rejoice. But we know that we are merely at the beginning, at a new chapter of our history, which will be more glorious than the glorious past.

And thus even to this Public Library in this hour of its triumph, applies the word of Victor Hugo, which many of you perhaps have wondered at and misunderstood, written on yonder panel:

"A library is an act of faith to generations in darkness hid, signed in witness to the dawn."

Yet, compared with what the future will be to the Chicago Public Library, this grand hour is still in darkness shrouded, but we sign our faith in the future of Chicago and in the future of its Library, in witness that we are convinced that the dawn tomorrow will be more glorious than the richly illuminated night and the star-sown sky above us.

Chicago, mighty giant of the West, famous throughout the world for push, ambition, energy and industry, thou hast no title to distinction in thy escutcheon more illustrious than the possession of this, thine own product, the People's Library, the People's University, the hope and the confidence of Chicago, the pride of the future. (Great applause.)

THE JEWISH PREACHER:
Rabbi Emil G. Hirsch, Ph.D., LL.D.

Faithfulness

Friday October 10, 1902
Reading: Jeremiah 18

Loyalty more than liberty; enthusiasm more strong than enlightenment; poetry much more strenuous than practicability; intuition rather than instruction; divination rather than dissection, I held last night, are the requirements of our religious situation.

And I contend that if the promise of the dawn has not been redeemed but the night has once more settled upon us, it is due to the fact that in all our liberty we have lost loyalty; in our enlightenment we have dashed from our hand the flowing goblet of enthusiasm. That in our passion for analysis we have annihilated the possibility of building up, and that in our zeal for dissecting we have become blind to the divinations. We have no intuition notwithstanding the copiousness of our inspiration.

It seems to me that the old Prophet Jeremiah was also of the same opinion. Jeremiah occupies a peculiar position in the ancient Hebrew literature. The rabbis of the town would even tell us that Isaiah was a courtier who belonged to the higher class of Jerusalem, and his style betrays the man of culture. Jeremiah, on the other hand, was a villager, a man without culture, and his phraseology also reveals the fact, and yet this man from the common people is really the man of suffering rejected of men. His life is the poetry of him as written and traced in the christology of the church who has become the Savior of mankind according to the creed of the church.

Not Jesus of Nazareth, but Jeremiah was the man of suffering. No other personality in history has displayed so much courage as this man fresh from the village. Kings had to listen to him, and courtiers felt the sting of his words. They cast him into prison. What cared he? They persecuted him. What that to him? He spoke, and spoke; and what he spoke history has verified.

This man now chides his people for lack of fidelity, and in a graphic manner worthy of a master, he puts in contrast to their attitude the firmness of Lebanon. Does the snow of Lebanon ever cease from the mighty rock, and do the bubbling, quickening, rushing waters ever fail? You have failed, but the snow of Lebanon ought to shame you into repentance and reflection.

He spoke for his time, but his sentences have also value for our day. I beg of you, study with me the implications of this simile: Jordan coming out of the snow of Mount Lebanon; Lebanon standing white and chaste, high above the surrounding landscape, a monument of firmness and a memento of faithfulness. Faithfulness! That is the accent of Jewish religiosity. Not faith, but faithfulness.

Water plays a considerable part in the metaphors of the bible. And why? The streams in Palestine for the greater part dry up when the sun's heat becomes oppressive. Just at the time when water is most needed it has disappeared.

Throughout the bible, running water stands for all that is pure and good, sustaining and spiritual; and those little water courses that trickle out for a brief week or two and then are evaporated stand out as symbols of man's unsteadiness, the insecurity of human conditions, the unreliability of human measures.

The water courses in Palestine have still another peculiarity. The bed of the rivers dry this very minute and the next moment without apparent cause it is flushed; thundering come down the masses of turbid water, and after a brief turmoil they disappear, and the bed is again as dry as if it had never been kissed by wet lips.

But the waters that come from Mount Lebanon, from that eternal snow on yonder white peak, they never fail. It is true they do not foam and froth; it is true they do not carry stones and boulders in a brief spell of passion; but on the other hand they flow steadily, they never fail.

Like that is the character of the Jewish religion. It is not a matter of faith, but it is a matter of faithfulness. The gist of all things that make for life, or claim to comprise life, is after all whether they forsake us or sustain us in the hour of need and of peril.

Do you know of aught else that has this power to so great an extent as has the philosophy of Judaism? Go through the various propositions to take its place; is there one among them that is like Lebanon's water, from eternal snows, never failing and never leaving us in the time of our need?

You say, philosophy. Certainly; the water of sweet taste and invigorating freshness; but that philosophy leaves you in the saddest moments of your life. It has no key—unless it be more than philosophy, unless it be religion—to the mystery of individual trial and individual triumph. Philosophy may explain why the masses of men prosper, or why they be poor, but it can never go beyond this, it can never answer the question: Why must I suffer, or why am I selected to be basking in the sunshine of happiness. Music, perhaps, and art—another water course—perhaps they run on forever.

Indeed, they do bring refreshing beverage. But again, music and art is of a nature to satisfy only the few, and they must first have been touched to responsiveness before the muses find in the heaven a chord to vibrate in reply. And then, what can music do?

It may sooth at its best in the moments of despair and suffering; it may join the conqueror's triumph in the hours of victory; but music cannot solve the great question: Why for what purpose do I suffer? Science is a cold mistress; it has no feelings, it has no passion. The very scientific spirit, which prevails among us, has resulted in making your congregation an icehouse, a refrigerator, where life would ask for some warmth.

We are in a condition as though a spiritual coal strike had been on and we could not get any fuel. Science is cold. You cannot treat anything scientifically; your personality is not attached, and no science can advance beyond the general; it cannot say to the particular why he suffered, and why he was crowned the conqueror.

Frivolity; some have said that is the water of life. Eat, drink and be merry. But then, frivolity leaves us in the most fatal moments of life. This frivolity is indeed the river that fails. After a while our nerves do not respond; we need stronger doses until we become besotted, and instead of staying men we become indeed idiots and beasts, burned out craters.

There is no other stream that stands like the stream trickling down from the snow-capped peak of Lebanon. Lebanon was the temple; for the temple had the power to make white and pure the sins of the worshippers.

Yea, that is the effect of religion that it never fails. How so, does it not fail? Because to the individual it always speaks of one thought, it always addresses the one word, *duty*. But where is in Judaism, faith?

Alas! I know that in these peculiar days of confusion we have rabbis, homemade rabbis, with the Union label, who do constantly ask their congregations to have more faith, more faith, and again, more faith. One of them recently told his congregation that if a good man suffered he suffered because he had not prayed enough. And another one sounds an appeal that the ministers should pray together on a certain day that the strike might be settled. A presumption, to tell God what he should do. This idea of prayer is Christian, it is not Jewish; never was a Jew of good Jewish conscience ready to pray that way. But this is the new Judaism. Judaism does not know faith, but it knows faithfulness and faithfulness to what now?

The prophet tells Israel: You have forsaken me and taken other Gods. Faithfulness to the destiny of Judaism by the distinction conferred upon the Jew as the exponent of certain facts and forces. We call that faithfulness to God, but it really means faithfulness to that which history has asked us to do for the world at large.

You have forgotten God and taken other Gods. You have forgotten faithfulness to your destiny. You have violated your conscience and consciousness. Return to your historical appointment. Be faithful to the God of Israel; and as the nation must be faithful to God so the individual must be faithful to whom? To himself.

But what am I? Am I merely a beast of prey? That would be faithless to my mentality, to my spirituality. Man is more than a potter's vessel. There is content in that vessel. He has heart; he has feelings, and he has a soul.

Science has tried to explain these phenomena on materialistic basis; it has failed. But even if it hadn't failed it would not have so much effect on real thinking beings, feeling beings, in that each one of us in a lucid moment's consideration come to a vision of the something that he may do, yea, that he must do. Faithful to yourself as a higher being. Faithful, therefore, to the principles of life that you owe to others. Faithful to duty.

That is the water of Lebanon that can never fail. And therefore, Lebanon or religion becomes the well out of which all rivers flow. Man needs harmony in and with himself.

There are men that are light, as it were, without a central sun from which the rays do radiate. You don't know what they are, really; you never have the power to lay hold of them; one time they are this, and the other time they are that. Why this? Because to their life there is no central rhythm; there is no source like the source of Lebanon from which all the rivers flow.

Now, the only thing that can furnish this central concentration of all that you do into one thing that you are, is religion. Religion becomes faith—intones faithfulness—becomes character. And the Jewish religion was always for making character. Character means purpose, dominating in all things; means steadiness reappearing under all varieties of activities and ambitions.

Of course men that pursue gold have character. This one passion draws up and holds together the different phases of their being; they have character, but it is not the highest character. And men who are consumed by the passion of knowledge also may have character, but it is not the highest character.

The highest character comes through religion. Religion being faithfulness to yourself brings harmony to your being and steadiness to not so much what you have, but what you are.

Character then is the second nature, and the Jew needs character, in two senses of the word. Character is a beginning, and every Jew is charged also with the responsibility of the keepership of certain vital principles. Our religion, not being a matter of faith, cannot be made a matter of argument; you cannot argue about faithfulness, but you can about faith.

The Jew is constantly under this law of responsibility, and therefore, his life must be harmonized under this law, and must become harmonized. We are all responsible one for the other. What you do reflects on me, and what I do reflects on you. What the lowest Jew in the Ghetto does and is, is measure of what we do and of what we are. And *noblesse oblige*—the duty increases in weight as opportunity enlarges, as means become more plentiful. The richer Jew has to show much more character than the poor Jew, and the wise Jew has to show more character, Jewish character, than the untutored and illiterate Jew.

We must be mindful of the fact that as our religion stands for character, and as Judaism requires a character of its own, in order to illustrate and emphasize its teaching we as Jews should have a Jewish character. Some fool or other will now go out and say I am inconsistent; am I not instrumental in digging the grave of Judaism? Is

Reform not a departure from Judaism?

Well, indeed not; because you have misunderstood the purpose of Reform, you have come to the present pass where Jewish character is about being wiped out among you. Reform was a going into Judaism, not a going out of it.

And our Sunday movement has its sole justification on the basis that we need more Judaism, and not less of it. If you wish to have less Judaism, keep the Sabbath of the Decalogue; that is the surest method of keeping your children from knowing aught about Judaism and making them feel that Judaism is after all only a sort of an annex to an undertaking establishment.

Where are the young men that under the Sabbath of the Decalogue—or congregations—that have been turned into Jews? In this congregation certainly those that were opposed to the Sunday movement have no right to brag that their children have been better Jews than ours, or will be better Jews, stronger in their Jewish sentiments than ours have been.

The Sunday movement was merely begun to bring back to us our Judaism. Judaism is not bound up with any law, and it does not stand and fall with any day. There is no seventh day.

By this time in the Philippine Islands this seventh day is passing over into the first day of the week; and there are places on this globe where the Jews are just now getting ready to sing when we are about to go home to our Sunday dinner. So all this twaddle about the seventh day is sheer ignorance, and this ignorance plays into the hands of convenience.

It is a most convenient thing to do, to hire somebody to keep the Sabbath for you. If you are logical you can save yourselves all that trouble of hiring a man; get a phonograph, speak prayers into the cylinder and turn the crank, and you have the Sabbath of the Decalogue observed as well by the phonograph as now by the hired pulpit parrot with his eloquence and his learning thrown into the bargain.

We need a Sabbath again, not a make-belief; we want it, to get into Judaism again, not out of Judaism. But many of us did not understand the movement. We thought it was a convenient bridge out of Judaism. As long as it was new, then they were with us, and now when the thing has become old they have become indifferent; their religion is like the water that fails. The true Jewish religion has character, is like the water course from Lebanon, from the eternal snow that never fails. In order to make of our life a sweet harmonious symphony through the key of Judaism, we needed our new and live Sabbath.

Character is, however like Lebanon, a protection. Have you ever been in Palestine? I have never been there, but I have studied the map, and I have read the literature, and I can picture vividly before my eyes what Lebanon does for the big valley below. There is a desert on the one hand and sea on the other, with a narrow strip of hot territory, swampy and full of miasma. The only fertile strip in Palestine is the valley between the ramparts of Lebanon. Into that valley trickles the waters from the eternal snow, and that valley is made a garden spot, all the more beautiful because the surroundings are so desolate.

So is religion that makes for character, and everything walled within the space included is fertility. The sin of selfishness cannot cross the barrier. Miasma stays in the lowlands. Yonder ocean may rage with passion, but the waves cannot dash over the beautiful white mountain standing guard over the fields below.

Yea, character through faithfulness is rich in fruit. The rabbis in their extravagance used to say that one who takes a real bath of purification will find by the time that he leaves the water the seed he has planted before he went has begun to sprout.

Yea, when character is there, when we take a bath in the pure waters that come from Lebanon, the very seed that we planted an hour ago will sprout out in the Talmudic dialogue.

Character—religion is the best protection for all that is true and noble and humane. Consult history and you have the verification. The Church has been the inspirer of art. Greece would never have become a people of worshippers of beauty had not religion led the hand of her painters and held the chisel of her sculptors. Religion again, in Rome, made for society and for the State. Religion has kindled the lamp of the sciences. Little high school boys and those mighty philosophers that point out so much in these days, may prate about the conflict between religion and science—the truth is, it was the searching for God and for the beginning of the better appreciation of man that captured the sciences and made them conquerors in the darkest of territories.

Religion inspired even commerce and industry; and as long as religion guarded the energies, as it did in the Middle Ages, as long as religion was the power behind and underneath society, there was social peace. We have left religion out of our business, and we have social strife. The rampart has been weakened and the valley ceases to be fruitful.

Religion has also been the inspiration of our philanthropies. It was religion that made men acknowledge that rich though they were, the poorest was their brother; and it was religion that went into the hovels of misery and brought not merely the manna of heaven but the bread of life. It was religion that brought to man the new knowledge of how to be just to his fellow men, even in the charities.

And now finally another thought in conjunction with the snow of Lebanon. The waters are described as running steadily, bubbling. If you will look into your ordinary translations—and I know one of our members who will do it, he never fails to do it, to see whether I have learned my lesson correctly—if you will look into the ordinary translation you will find that the translation runs "Waters which are far-off and cold." But that is a mis-translation. The Hebrew word means waters that bubble out, waters that well forth, waters that run. If we have faithfulness in ourselves, and if that faithfulness is built on character so that we know what we are and may be found wherever we are needed, and if behind the rampart of character all there is of humanity, in the best sense of the word have ripened—then we shall have something that the laughing water has, which is steadily running on and welling out; and in the running and in the welling out it has found health and it gives health and healthfulness.

We need this above all. I grant most of you friends—this congregation as a whole—understands that we stand for faithfulness and not for faith. I know that most of you, I daresay, all of you, are men of character and women of character. I know that underneath the protection of that character great things have been planned and have sprouted forth. I know also that the intention of this congregation, the majority of this congregation, barring a few that are indifferent for one reason or another, because they are either too orthodox or too liberal to be with us—that the bulk of the congregation understands that we must do something.

But one thing we lack, and I must repeat it, we lack that spontaneity, that heartiness which the Prophet alludes to when he calls the stream from Lebanon the running, running, running, bubbling with life and joyful and healthful in its life. I don't know what it is—and this is the day to be candid. I don't know what it is. I have preached elsewhere and I have felt a warmth and a spontaneity grateful to my soul and lending wings to the best that is within me. I have talked to learned people, and I have had the privilege of addressing those without learning; I have found response all over; but when I come to you it is in an ice chest I find myself. There is no spontaneity.

Why, I don't know; and it is not simply for the purpose of saying something that I say this; God knows I have had my sleepless nights thinking seriously of vacating the pulpit; that somebody else might be found who has that which I seem to lack, the power of evoking spontaneity and heartiness.

We lack that spontaneity. We need a new temple. Smaller congregations build new temples. They are glad to do so. I recently dedicated a temple, a beautiful structure, built by a small congregation in Scranton—a mere handful, sixty men, and in Scranton where the strike has worked havoc in business circles. Yet they have built their temple, and they were joyful in building it, knowing for the character of the Jew, and for the cause they needed a new temple.

And so in many other congregations— Philadelphia they made a museum out of their temple, a beautiful structure, paintings on the walls, a tribute to art and an inspiration.

Nothing of this kind here. And these people they ask me to help them; they asked me, "Come and help us," and they believe I have the power to help them, and I have not the power to stir one here to do something except just what is selfishly our own.

I am the editor of a Jewish Encyclopedia; the editor of a biblical department, the honor of which might be coveted by greater scholars than I; yet, though I am an editor, there are not five of you members who are subscribers to the Jewish Encyclopedia.

I have tried in my private capacity to build up a mouthpiece for Judaism, our Judaism, and yet do you know there are members in my congregation, men that asked me to stay in Chicago, made personal efforts to have me stay, assured me that I was needed by them, who have subscribed for that mouthpiece, but when asked for anything else, tell me they have paid a year's subscription to the Reform Advocate.

This lack of spontaneity is the cause of why in our efforts we have been chilly. We need spontaneity, great and glorious as we are. I am open to confess that nowhere on God's footstool could we have a pulpit freer than ours is. I am open to confess that perhaps in no community could we find a welcome—outside of Judaism—that we have found here in Chicago. I also confess that one thing about this work for this congregation may be compensation for everything else and that is the fact that a man must study with you. There is something in the spirit of the congregation that places upon the preacher the duty of keeping to his studies.

It was this that brought me to you. Where I was, the people were hearty, they were spontaneous. Ask them today and they will tell you wonders about me; that no one has ever sneezed as beautifully as I did; that none ever blew his nose as daintily as I did. Ask them today, after twenty-two years, and they will tell you of sermons that I delivered.

I could have stayed there, and would have been among friends there, and they were good, dear friends, spontaneous, hearty, cordial and warm. I left them, and they felt it was a slight undeserved, and so it was. I left them because I knew from father's lips and from my brother-in-law's testimony that here was a pulpit that asked much, and therefore gave me an opportunity to grow and develop.

All this granted; now, when we have all this shall we merely have the cold snow of Mount Lebanon? Shall we stand above others in cold? Shall we not at least become spontaneous? Be not afraid; spontaneity is no reflection on intellectuality. The cynic is not spontaneous, and cynic intellectualism has passed its usefulness. Become a little more warm, more personal. You are virtually a lecture association, and not a congregation, and there is a difference between the two.

A lecture association has no personality; a congregation has personality. Work that into your hearts, then the waters that come from high Lebanon will be spontaneously bubbling, and therefore, refreshing.

The rabbis say that in the Messianic kingdom all men will have the aroma of Lebanon. That is an Eastern phrase. In the East, beauty is apprehended through the nose; the odors are the central expressions of the sense of perfection. In the East, all is perfume for that reason. And thus whenever you find in biblical literature or rabbinical translation the word smell, or odor, or savor, you have what we today would express in moral terms, sweetly scented as Lebanon. It is the symbol of modern perfection and in the Messianic Kingdom the rabbis say all men will have that sweet odor about them.

Shall we strive for that Messianic Kingdom of perfection and harmony, of faithfulness and character, of eternal things in the valley, and of spontaneity in the flow of the rivers? God grant that we shall try, and may thus then become this hour for us too a day of self-searching and a day of strong resolving, a day of harmonizing and a day of re-awakening in steadiness, in faithfulness in character.

Liberty not so much as loyalty; instruction not so much as inspiration and intuition; chilly criticism not so much as warm constructiveness, and refreshment of soul, not refrigerating processes under which the mind may take on a pale luster, but the heart and soul are blistered and bled.

Let that be remembered: Spontaneity, character, faithfulness; Lebanon's snow, symbol of a river that does not fail, simile of a temple, simile of the Jewish religion which stands for faithfulness, not for faith; for character, and not for creed; for enthusiasm, not for emancipation and enlightenment at the expense of soul at the waste of the spirit.

Amen.

THE JEWISH PREACHER:
Rabbi Emil G. Hirsch, Ph.D., LL.D.

Will Rich Men Go To Heaven

Circa 1898

The question, which I propose to discuss this morning before you, has not merely an academic interest, but it is involved in one of the vexatious problems of our day. I may safely say that there is not one—I repeat it—not one thinker on economic matters but is convinced that the accumulations of wealth in the hands of single individuals becomes dangerous to society when it goes beyond a certain limit.

Some weeks ago, I was asked by one of our dailies in this City, to act as one of the judges whose duty it was to decide which of little children's stories written for and about Christmas were of such a character as to deserve special recognition for content and conception, and thus about three or four scores of these little papers, written by children ranging between the ages of eight to eleven, were put into my hand, and with one single exception, among the sixty to eighty that I read, all of them told the story of a boy or a girl that was poor, and then all of a sudden became rich—or became rich later in life—but all of them, with one exception, had this as the life motif. It shows the ambition that burns in the hearts of these future men and women. To be rich is the sum all and the substance all of today's ambition.

I cannot blame the little folks for dreaming that the millionaire is the only happy individual on God's footstool. I cannot censure them for writing about the young newsboy who becomes a lawyer, and then as a lawyer, rakes in the heaviest fees imaginable, and in ten years from the beginning of his practice is a lord on earth. I am quoting from one of these papers. Do not misconstrue my remarks, I ask you, for God's sake. I am merely repeating what I read in one of the little children's stories.

I can indeed not even wonder that all these little folks had within them the hunger for gold, to quote a classical expression, for do they not see that everywhere today it is the rich man who is courted. We do not ask how came he by his wealth. As long as he has, we are all willing to bow down before him into the dust. The old story of the crown prince to the Roman Empire's throne, who objected to a peculiar tax that his father had placed upon certain absolute natural functions of human life, on the score that that tax might perhaps be somewhat suspicious, comes to my mind. The Emperor, at once taking a few of the golden coin into his hand, thrust them out to the boy: "There attaches no odor to gold".

And this is indeed true. Who are the courted and coveted men and women today? The 400 who represent the aristocracy of New York or of this City, among Jews and non-Jews alike—it is the man with a stout bank account. He knows that he has the right to be courted and woe betide that man who would not court him. The rich man's joke is always answered by a good round of laughter of his parasites. His opinions in public meetings get attention. He may not be able to speak any language correctly. What does that matter. Behind him stand figures with a dollar sign before them. He knows more than the wisest. This cannot be denied. The rich men feel that they have a generation that courts riches, and I do not blame them for their arrogance; but I deplore the generation that has lost interest in all else but in the one brutal success, and that success is the equation of money and bank account alone.

A little philosophical thought might show that after all, the millionaire is not the one who is to be envied, or even to be emulated. That old skeptic of ours in our own bible has said it clearly, and mind, if there be such before me as do not know this already—apparently the writer of that book was one of high rank. He had more money at his disposal than is generally under command of the young dudes and dudiness's of even our age. Tradition has it that he wore the purple robe of the crown prince. So, it is not the envious disposition that fills with gall his calamus, his pen; but he is the possessor of all that wealth can confer, and he comes to the conclusion that all is vanity.

Can rich man enter heaven? I say no. No rich

man ever went to heaven, for when we are ready to go to heaven, we are poor. What doth the rich man take along, says this old skeptic? Nothing. He is naked in the last hour of his life as he was naked in the first opening of his earthly career. What is the difference between the millionaire's corpse and that of the pauper buried in the pauper's field? The one will be enshrined in a mausoleum, and posterity will admire the architectural outlines of the pyramidal dome to which were consigned the embalmed dust of one mighty on exchange and successful in financial speculations. The other's grave will be unmarked. But let five hundred, a thousand years from now, one come—one of those New Zealanders about whom Macauley wrote, who will stand by the ruins of the London tower, on a broken span of London Bridge, and wonder why the mighty metropolis of the 19th century has been laid low—let one of these New Zealanders come and pick up a bone, or two bones—the one from the Potter's field and the other from the ruins of the Mausoleum to which were entrusted the mortal remains of one of our courted and bloated bondholders. Will he discover any difference? Perhaps the bone of the pauper will serve much better the purposes of being stored away in an anatomical museum in New Zealand for the instruction of the young New Zealanders than the half stunted bent and curved bones of one of the richest men of the world. Yes, there is absolutely no difference between the two; and if there is one, it is in the favor of the pauper.

So, finally no rich man goes to heaven. In

death we are all alike. Death cannot be bribed. Death will not be bought off. It comes and asks no question. There is weeping in our avenues as there is crying and sighing in our by-alleys. There death garners home as well as here. He is no respecter of person or of condition, and when he speaks all must follow and all are alike.

The old Jewish custom of making no distinctions in the funeral shrouds and funeral appointments was indeed a beautiful admonition, and all the greater the pity that we of this beautiful generation have departed from the simplicity of the fathers. There the white shroud clothed millionaire and the poorest; plutocrat and pauper alike had the same uniform in which they had to present themselves at the brink of the grave.

And it is not merely our own skeptic who sounds the warning. We have read this morning the sayings of that Jew who more than any other Jew has influenced the thought and the action of the world. I suppose I need not tarry to assure you that in appreciation of that Jew's genius we will not yield to anyone; and so we may listen to his words.

And what is it that he announces? That it is easier for a camel to pass through a needle's eye than for a rich man to enter the kingdom of heaven. Will you now say that Jesus was jealous? Belonged to the order of scamps who are of no purpose to this world? Ah, it is blasphemy even to connect his name with such adjectives and such criticism. He certainly is a star that will not set, and is accompanied by constellations of light and each little jewel that flames in the heavens—

does it spell the rich or does it spell the righteous? Visit the Walhallas of fame. Go to the Westminsters of the world. Stand in awe before the monuments and the testaments of mortal dust touched into immortality. How many rich men do you find buried in Westminster Abbey? How many myriad-millionaires have been admitted to the cluster of those that shall shine with the effulgence of the sun from generation to generation? The Rothschilds are numbered; they have come to be not an individual concept but rather a generalization. To those it is always the Vanderbilts, the Goulds—after a while they lose their individuality. They come to mean a general concept. So far they are sure of immortality. But now contrast even with these the most favored among those blessed with large resources those whom Clio, the genius of history, has inscribed with indelible letters on her tablets the record. There is always one. There is no other, a third one—they do not merge together in a hazy, indistinct, nebulous mass to be designated by a generic term. They stand out boldly in their individuality. If kingdom of heaven means immortality, it is true that the mere rich man, courted as he is in life for his wealth, will not enter into the kingdom of heaven. But the poorest among the poor, those that have served humanity, are inscribed with the diamond pen of fame across the galaxy of glory. Their name is not blurred, and their fame will never cease sounding through the ages. There is, of course, a certain sense in which the words of Jesus have been taken, to which we as Jews must take exception. I have no doubt that

Jesus had in mind the construction put upon his phrase by the communistic theorizers of the modern day, for to every scholar, the law is obligatory to read men by the light of their age. Even Jesus is not a star that shines alone. He is a meteor that bursts forth from central gloom into eternal glory. He is the son of his time, and he speaks the dialect of his age, and those much admired teachers of the present time who, in order to win the favor of their mixed audiences, blur this fact, that Jesus is the son of the time, the true scholar will call out a halt—whether he will find the applause of his audience in consequence, he may perhaps be doubtful, but nevertheless, he will say that those fail to appreciate Jesus and the characteristic element in his genius who would make him be of all time, and therefore deprive him of the right of every man to his own age and his own earth.

Thus, Jesus in teaching that it is easier for the camel to go through the needle's eye than for a rich man to enter heaven, had before him under the designation of Kingdom of God that social state which he expected would come on earth with his recognition as the Messiah. For him, and men like him, the present—the then prevailing social order was to pass away, and was to give place to a realm, to an order of social adjustment in which the old distinctions between rich and poor would be unknown; where communism prevailed, where all property was held in common. It is thus, if we take Jesus' words in their original sense, in his phrase—a corroboration of the wildest communistic dreams. Now, in this sense,

I and no other Jew—none who is imbued with the ethics of Judaism will allow the phrase of Jesus to have potency. We say, and Judaism has at all times said, that man shall not merely have the right to become wealthy, but shall have even the duty to honorably try—to *honorably* try to rise into affluence.

What is wealth? It is the reward of labor. It is the recompense that nature brings for the work bestowed upon her. Nature is not complete until man appears. And here lies the creative element in man. As God creates, so does man create. This is the sense of the old myth that man was made in the image of God. Let those that must, display their emptiness of all philosophical thought, cry out that an old Greek philosopher has already said, "If the lions were to make Gods, they would give them claws and manes, and shape them like lions, and that therefore God is made in the image of man, and man is not made in the image of God." Let our learned young men applaud when this shallow empty pretense at philosophy is rehashed and rehearsed within their hearing. Those that understand the language of figure and simile, and those that can think out a proposition without the crutches of actual exposition as a mathematical proposition is always intelligible to a mathematician, though the x's and the y's, and the root signs, and the equivalent signs, and the greater proportions and the minor proportions abound, so in these philosophical statements, the philosophic mind will at once read the symbols correctly, and if we read these symbols correctly, we know what the Bible intended when it said that man was created in the image of God—God creates, hence man is a creator.

Nature, for man, is the crude material. Nature is not perfect before he comes, and is never perfect, and when man puts the spade to the soil, the axe to the tree, or the pickaxe to the rock—when he changes the bed of the river, when he forces nature to give of its stored powers and to weave those stored powers into cereals to be broken again into bread, the staff of life, when he does these and a thousand other things which make nature the footstool of man, the image of God, he creates as God created when he called forth this wonderful universe, and he recognized for creation his love.

Wealth then is not unethical. Its destruction would be unethical. For it is a law of justice that labor shall be rewarded. He that works shall enjoy the fruit of his labor, or, as the Bible states it, he that plants the vine shall eat the fruit thereof.

But wealth becomes merely dangerous when the other phase of the ethical proposition is neglected. When wealth is not the fruitage of labor, then it is indeed dangerous, because it is not its own justification. And much of our wealth today is not the fruitage of honest labor. It is the reward for cunning. It is the booty brought home from an expedition to rob fellow men of the fruitage of their labor. In every creative transaction, there is no loser. Take whatever commercial transaction you please, if it be honest, and therefore full of labor in the broad sense of the word—not merely manual labor, intellectual labor, foresight, combination, conjuncture, all this being human labor, the human element added to the crude material, you will find that in any honest transaction, all parties to the transaction are gainers. I buy my garment. I exchange the tokens for labor done by me for the production of the labor of another. I receive what I want.

The other one receives what he needs. I am the gainer—he is the gainer. And not merely we two are the gainers—the profits accrue to all humanity. I am made more of a man by having the garment that I need, and he again is stimulated to new creative energy by seeing the product of his labor serve someone. And in this world humanity is profited in the meanest, in the smallest transaction where labor is involved—honest labor—and where the return for labor or wealth passes in increased proportion from hand to hand.

But, friends, who is the gainer in a transaction where there is no labor? Is there labor in puts and calls? Is there labor in merely betting that tomorrow wheat will have that price, and finding another fool, or one who is less shrewd than we are, to take that bet? Is there labor? Who is profiting in that transaction? Humanity? Is there one sheaf of wheat produced more by that transaction? Is one mouth that is hungry fed by that bet and arrangement that as the wheat goes up the one receives, and as the wheat goes down, the price of it, the other receives? Is here humanity profited? No one is profited except the one who was the shrewdest and speculated on the weakness, on the greed of his neighbor.

You say it is each man's duty to look out for

himself. If this speculator had not found "suckers" as they call them, he could not have speculated successfully. It is the fault of all the others. We are not our brother's keeper.

But, "we are our brother's keeper." As every honest transaction profits all humanity, so every dishonest transaction injures all humanity. This temptation to become rich suddenly without labor—without creating—of taking without giving—is so fatal that if such an accumulation of labor passes without question into the hands of one, many hands become idle, and many hearts become darkened. The poison enters their system. And who is here that will dare deny that here I strike the keynote to the creed of most of the rising generation? The older generation knew that labor and wealth were in a relation to one another that could not be broken, They also knew that he who lives up to the very fullest extent of the return of his labor is selfish, for it is the duty of every man to keep within the limit of his production. For he is responsible for posterity, and posterity needs his savings, or else all progress is impossible. And thus, the men of the older generation were workers. They saved. They laid aside. None will say that this man cannot enter the kingdom of heaven.

But the new generation has come and their creed is that the swiftest road to wealth shall be taken, and as they look about and see one or the other who has become rich in this way, and who is worshiped by his companions—every door flings open to him, no matter how he got his wealth—whether he ever did an honest stroke of labor in his day or merely plotted and planned to catch in his net the "suckers" that would bite. They see that his wife is received all over, though she be a perambulating jewelry establishment, blazing forth with diamonds which even a queen would not wear because they are so vulgar in their abundance—the young generation sees all that, and the common talk is: "Here was a party. Didn't they have a glorious time. Their money bought all the luxuries that are within reach, and the papers are full with the description of the dresses and how they walked in and how they walked out"—and if you look at the names, to one an honest lover of his kind, will raise the blush of shame for his race. Yet, the young generation sees this, and here is the fatal effect, that they think any road to wealth is good as long as it leads there, and the honest, slow ascent, and the narrow path of labor and economy are forsaken.

Go through our penitentiaries, and you find there a population composed, with few exceptions, of two classes. You find such there as by nature were neglected, and by society—I say it without hesitation—forced to have their hand against everybody because everybody's hand was against them. These Ishmaelites, the waifs of our slums and our back yards—the haunts of crime and criminals—these you will find in the penitentiary.

But you find also in there men over whose cradle a song of greater hope had been sung by mother—who had received at society's hand care and opportunity—yet why are they there? What brought them thither? The fatal worship of wealth, regardless of the means by which it was accumulated. Innocent pleasure was the first step on that inclined plane. Whose business is it how we spend our days of leisure? Certainly not the pulpits, not the preachers, who could not live if we did not support them. Yea, if it were merely a matter that concerned you or another, it would not be the pulpit and not the preacher's concern. Your own conscience and your own inclination should be guidance enough. But there is that blanched face looking out behind the grated windows on this Sunday, where the workshop will not drown for him the sounds within his heart—he stands against the opening in the door of his cell, sighing, for memories of home come to him—they must come to him—and perhaps the first hour looms up before him now as he has fallen—full of its fatal possibilities for the fall and the temptation—that blanched convict in our penitentiary remembers perhaps in this very hour the day when he was ushered into polite society—when he saw that certain things were respectable, and made respectable by the social indulgence and indolence of certain classes. An innocent game, a relaxation—he joined his comrades, and the passion grew—not merely the passion. He was unfortunate one day perhaps—and these things are matters of honor! They must be settled! No debt is as sacred as the debt contracted at the gaming table.

But the kind people that invited him knew that he was not rich enough to rival them. What cared they for it? They wanted their fun and their game, and they admitted the young—the mere stripling, the clerk, to their circle, and the hour draws near when he must settle his debt of honor, or be looked upon by his comrades as a man void of character. Character! Good God, character at the gaming table! Honor for gambling debts! And in that fatal moment, for he is as yet a trusted employee of his firm—one figure changes from his pen. It succeeds this time. The next week he makes good the balance—the cash in the drawer—he destroys the ticket that he has put in, and the temptation comes again.

Yet why must I picture the details of that downward course? Am I drawing upon my imagination? I have had convicts speak to me. I have visited, in my ministerial capacity, the penitentiary of our state, and they have told me, as they have told our chaplain in New York—for the ministerial Association of New York employs now a chaplain—a Jewish chaplain for the four and five hundred Jewish convicts that are confined in the State of New York in the prisons—as they have told him, that had it not been for the social game in our eminently respectable clubs, they would not be where they are. Let it go forth as the warning of ethics—the flaming law of God and humanity—that labor must lead to wealth and where labor does, it gives legitimacy to wealth; but that all wealth made at the expense of others without contributing to the store of humanity, is not legitimate.

Public opinion can do much to change the tide, and law must do still more. As long as stocks are watered and dividends are paid from capital merely in order to create false impressions, as long as within corporations there be those who try to freeze out others in order to rake in the shekels themselves, so long as we cannot wonder that there be voices to protest that all wealth is criminal, and that under a just system of society there would be no millionaires, as there would be no men to want. But when the law makes those things impossible; when every honest transaction has the sanction of the law, and every dishonest transaction quibbles of lawyers and shrewd movements of attorneys of corporations to the contrary notwithstanding, will be visited with all the power of the state, then the voices that now cry out against wealth as such, will be hushed.

If wealth has rights, it has also certain duties; and it is a matter of justice that those that have shall contribute in proportion to their having, to the maintenance of all institutions that the state and society need in order to do their work effectively. In matters of taxation, it is a moral law, not merely a law of conventionality, made operative through statute, but a moral law, that the rich man shall bear in proportion to his wealth the burdens of society. As long as it is the rich man who escapes taxation, and the poor man bears the burden, as long as our banks when taxing day comes around show a ridiculously small capital, while on other days they have almost inexhaustible resources, we cannot wonder that in the by-streets of this city and other cities, the voice of the agitator finds a ready hearer, pleading for the abolition of all wealth, and the confiscation of all landed property.

An income tax is just if it is justly carried out.

An income tax which releases labor, and taxes most heavily the returns from investments, in which we as a personal laborer are not interested, is a just tax, constitutional objections to the contrary notwithstanding and lawyers' quibbling to protect us to the contrary, again notwithstanding.

This is an ethical proposition and a matter of ethics that he that has and enjoys opportunities shall bear his proportionate share of the public burdens—not merely his relative share, but his proportionate share. An increasing income tax is just, for we are not all on a level, even all of us who like myself, by your kindness, are above the minimum laid down by law for exemption—we are not all on level—some of us work, some of us merely enjoy the fruitage of other men's work, hence those that enjoy the fruitage of other men's work shall pay a larger percentage than those who by their labor, by their energy, by their foresight, by their intellect, are still increasing the wealth of the nation and of humanity.

This brings me to another point that is argued in this question, that inheritance and the right to bequest shall be restricted by law. What prompts men mostly to work is the love for their own offspring. Men will slave—forego pleasures—bring sacrifices when the thought of their little ones looms up before them—to make the path easier for those that bear their name, and to assure them against all accidents and the vicissitudes of fortune is one of the noblest ambitions, as it is one of the best impulses of men, to labor and to work. Take away this prospect from the individual, and unless he is an exceptionally strong character, his energies will droop. The communists and others that argue for the abolition of the right to bequeath are poor hands at human psychology. They would destroy much that is helpful to humanity and by way of compensation would give us but little. For take away the right to bequeath the fortunes that would accrue to humanity and to the state, as they claim they should, would be eminently and ridiculously small.

But, on the other hand, let it not be forgotten that wealth received by bequest is ethically on a different plane from wealth the result of our own labor and foresight and economy. This wealth then, come to us by gift shall carry greater burdens, as it has greater obligations than the wealth that is the result of labor and foresight.

Perhaps you will allow me to prove to you that the right to bequeath is not a natural right, but an acquired right. For instance, when an estate is found in this State, where no heirs appear, it falls to the state, and every estate has to go through a probate court before it can be settled. If it were a mere natural right why should the court meddle with it? I can give you what little I have, to make a present to you, and no court can meddle with it; but when I am dead, what little I have to leave you has to pass through the hands of the court, and has to be approved by the court, showing that the law even makes a distinction between the right of the living and the right of him who is no more, to the control of his property. You see then, even you, if you merely think on this proposition, laymen as you are, and not lawyers, that there a distinction patent and palpable in these two cases. Thus the right to bequeath and to receive by bequest is what La Salle has called an acquired right, not a natural right.

I would not abolish that acquired right, but it is a proposition of ethics that this kind of wealth shall bear larger shares of the burden than wealth which comes to us by dint of our labor. Thus the law might do much by enforcing honesty, by putting an end to all speculative temptations, and by adjusting burdens equitably to guard against the danger of accumulation in one hand of the resources of society. And then the moral, the ethical conscience of the individual can do much. Wealth certainly has the duty and the obligation to maintain our philanthropic enterprises.

And now, to sum up, friends, true ethics teaches that he that labors shall be paid for his labor. True ethics teaches that one man has no right to use up the product of his labor to the limit, but that each one must save and economize for the future. Reward of labor and economy of labor, by ethics and law, should be protected. But only that wealth shall be protected that is legitimate, which is through the channels of labor and of economy. And when it comes by bequest, as father or someone else has labored for it, the recipients assume corresponding duties; but that wealth which is the result of robbery and thievery, of speculation on the greed and the folly and on the vices of our fellow men is illegitimate. This then is the ethical position of Judaism.

Judaism never taught that the rich man is less

moral than the poor man. But Judaism never either said poor but honest—it insisted that wealth be so constituted that the same might go without question—rich but honest.

By law not much more can be done for the limitation of wealth than a strict protection of honesty, and an enforcement of honest methods in business. By the moral conscience of men, much may be done to awaken men to the understanding of their obligation—to the comprehension of their responsibilities, and if thus law and the moral consciousness of the public, of society, cooperate, the time will come when such gigantic fortunes will no longer pass from hand to hand. When they will not be used when they have accumulated, for the destruction of the weak, but for the building up of the weak into the strength.

That time will be the time of social peace, where the independence of the individual will give way to the social interdependence of all social factors. This is Jewish ethics, and in this, as in everything else, the ethics of Judaism is the healthiest, the most humane, because it always strives after righteousness and justice, and never forgets to emphasize duty and obligation.

Can the rich man enter heaven? In death we are all poor. If by heaven is meant the power to do good to mankind, yea the rich man will enter into heaven. If honesty is his crown and righteousness his staff—if to do good to his kind he works to amass wealth and means, then indeed, in the sight of Him who is Father of all, the righteous wealthy man need not sell all he has to follow the master. He will, with all he has, follow the master, doing good to all and lifting up all to God's sunlight heights of peace, of honesty, and righteousness . So may it be with all of us, under God's blessing.

Amen.

THE JEWISH PREACHER:
Rabbi Emil G. Hirsch, Ph.D., LL.D.

One Hundredth Anniversary
Birth of Samuel Hirsch

Part 1
April 24, 1915

A mountain peak stands aloft by the centuries, a station for retrospect and prospect. Nations are invited to bethink themselves of the path they have trodden whenever one hundred years are completed, marking off prosperity from adversity. Or whenever a great man who had part in the shaping of people's destiny is wheeled back into memory by the fact that the birthday of the year, which recalls him, is the one hundredth anniversary of his birth. And so great movements ought to be studied and are best analyzed when the one hundredth anniversary comes round for the incarnation of a leader whose voice was potent in the announcements of the cause's great principles. I have ventured to invite my congregation to spend an hour or two with me in studying not the life but the teachings of one great man who had a terminating share in the unfolding of a liberal interpretation of Judaism.

Of course, he was my father and teacher. This fact alone, however, would not have induced me to invite others to take part in the memorial tribute to him. Had he been naught but this, my teacher, I might have set aside in the solitude of my study a day and gone to his works and refreshed my mind by dipping once more into the limpid stream of his instruction. But he was more than that; he was really the prophet of that understanding of our religion, which I had hoped might be the common conviction of the members of Sinai.

We have to go back in order to understand my father's position—which is virtually ours—to the chapter telling how the reform movement was prepared. The first notion you have to disabuse yourself of is that the reform was cradled in America. That is not true. It may not be to your liking just at present to hear it, nevertheless it is true, the reform was "Made in Germany." Had it not been for the German spirit, German scholarship and German philosophy, there would never have been any reform movement. You have the proof of that in the fact that in those countries where German thought is not tolerated and German philosophy is not deeply studied, there has not been a real Jewish reform movement, and what passed for reform in America before the advent of the great masters of German Jewish scholarship was really a travesty on reform. Only those congregations were lifted to the height of outlook which he who would understand liberal Judaism must stand on, who had the good fortune of being taught by men trained in Germany, men deeply filled with the method and the spirit of German research and German thinking. Now, in Germany too it is generally held that Moses

Mendelsohn must be held the father of Reform Judaism.

That is another misstatement. Moses Mendelsohn, in his thinking, was an orthodox Jew; in his practice too as a philosopher, Moses Mendelsohn belonged to the school that contended that religion is universal and religion is a natural, spontaneous expression of humanity. That principle is correct, but if Mendelsohn had accepted this principle throughout, he would not have concluded that Judaism is not a religion. He argues that Judaism was a national legislation; it was contained in the law divinely, supernaturally revealed by God to Moses. This is the position of Orthodox Judaism. For the orthodox Jew Judaism is equivalent to the divinely revealed system of legislation contained partly in the Pentateuch, partly incorporated later in traditional literature.

And Mendelsohn throughout his whole life was ever punctilious in the observance of the legal enactments, as punctilious as ever was an orthodox Jew. But what did Mendelsohn do? He taught the Jews of Germany to speak and to write again the tongue of their country, and he accomplished this through translating into German, first the Pentateuch and later the other books of the Bible—the German translation written with Hebrew characters, which Mendelsohn made of the Pentateuch, as the gate through which the Jews of Germany gained access to German culture.

Before that time, while they lived in Germany, they had not been Germans. Now they became, in thought, Germans to the core. That is the great work accomplished by Mendelsohn and his fellow writers. But the fact that he did make of the Jews in Germany—Jewish Germans—was one of the most important steps towards bringing about a reformation of the synagogue.

Mendelsohn's immediate successors were enabled, through having learned German, to go to the German Universities. There they came to be disciples of the great philosophers of Germany, the exponents of German idealism. They could not remain for a long time blind to the fact that Judaism too must have had its development, and especially those of these young students who came under the influence of Hegel, were led to see that the great forces of all ages were those that made for progress; that through development God was revealing Himself constantly to men.

That is the fundamental thought of the Hegelian system of reasoning. Having been taught to take this view, these Jewish German students, at home in the Talmud and in the Bible could not but learn to read anew both Holy writings and the books of tradition. Where their fathers had believed that there was not any element of time in the making of the law, these men soon realized that the law itself was not the production of one day nor the work of one man, but that the law itself showed traces of being a growth an evolution. Therefore, at one time the Jewish cult must have been different from what it was at a later period. That the prophets, for instance, often urged thoughts, which in the Pentateuch are not recognized. That there is opposition between prophesy and the law in many vital points.

This coming to these men with a spontaneity of revelation necessarily brought them to know that the synagogical service as having been developed in time was not of divine origin. That it must be changed where its institutions conflicted with the newer ideas and that it might be changed because what was claimed to have been original does now seem to be secondary.

And among these great men who had gone—having first learned German through the instruction of the Mendelsohnian translations—through the German universities, was Samuel Hirsch, one of the younger of the great pioneers.

He was a junior by six years of David Einhorn, by five years of Geiger. Phillipson too was older than he. Samuel Adler was also his senior. He was one of the younger of that band of rare men who rushed to the German universities in order that they might be equipped with better weapons wherewith to wage battle for God and Israel. Samuel Hirsch's studies deviated a little from the ordinary plan followed by the others. The others, for the most part, gave themselves to the study of Semitic languages and literature. Geiger, for instance, in the University of Bonn, in the main gave time and attention to the mastery of Arabic, and since Geiger's day, in Germany that has been the prevailing fashion. The rabbinical students at the university must, above all, endeavor to become experts in Semitic philology. There is a reason for this, for you cannot understand Hebrew unless you have some acquaintance with another Semitic idiom. The Bible remains a closed book to you, in many a chapter of its contents, unless you have made yourself familiar with similar story and similar institutions of which Arabic documents bring you the proof. You must be a student of Semitics would you be a master of Hebrew.

Samuel Hirsch, however, was not satisfied with becoming merely a philologist, he was one of the few Jewish rabbis or students—then he was not yet a rabbi—student that young though he was, felt that if one was to understand Judaism he must, above all else, familiarize himself with other religions. Now at that time, when my father matriculated at the University of Bonn, the science of Comparative Religion was not yet born. No one knew anything about that, and studies by the comparative method in religion no one had yet carried on. So the genius of the man, though scarce eighteen years of age, he felt that just as you must know Arabic to understand Hebrew, you should know of another religion would you comprehend full and truly Judaism.

Now at Bonn at that time, there was no chair for the study of Hindu religion, for the study of Semitic religions, but there were professors of protestant dogmatics. Samuel Hirsch became a member of the classes studying Christian dogmatics; he became a student of the New Testament. He was one of the first Jews who felt that the New Testament was a piece of Jewish literature, and he devoted time and attention at the University and later to the research work in the domain of New Testament thought and New Testament history.

And just because, at Bonn, he followed the identical courses which the protestant theological students had to pursue, he came away from his studies there all the more impressed with the truth that what Protestantism had to teach of vital importance to men had been anticipated by the doctrine of Judaism.

He continued his studies later at the University of Berlin. All along, however, as I have indicated, he was a devoted reader of the German philosophical literature, and especially the system of Hegel attracted him. Just as Protestant theology did, Hegelian philosophy confirmed in him the conviction that Judaism after all was competent to lead men aright, and that in many ways Judaism occupied a higher position than ever may Christianity or ever was assigned to it by the Hegelian philosophy.

Protestant theology up to the present day contends that Judaism is law; Christianity is grace and love. Judaism, being law, is the religion of the slave; the Jew is bound by the law and he is cursed by the law. That is the position first taken by Paul and ever since reiterated by Christianity. Again, in Hegelian philosophy, Judaism is assigned the role of a very inferior religion. For Hegel Christianity is the absolute, the most perfect religion.

Judaism, however, according to Hegel, is at its best preliminary; at its worst—-and he generally computes it at its worst—it is a meaningless system of ritual practices; it is a hopeless memory of a glory past; it is a soul wearying and a soul exhausting regret at its own incompetence.

Now here were two points where Samuel Hirsch felt it incumbent upon him to set his own teachers to rights, and his whole life was devoted just to these two duties. His great writings are dedicated to this duty, and he was a great writer. Among the great works even of deep importance to the student today is what he called *Un Yuden,* a very big volume, which he had intended to be the first of a series. In this volume Samuel Hirsch shows that by the very system of Hegel and the method that Hegel employs Judaism is entitled to the high rank; that it is in content and in outlook of much finer grade than is Christianity. That Christianity is not the absolute religion, but if there be an absolute religion—and that may be doubted and is doubted by Samuel Hirsch—that function and that distinction must be assigned to Judaism. That big volume is also remarkable for another thing or two. In the first place, over one hundred of its pages present a comparative study of all religions.

Mind you, the book was written in 1843. At that time nowhere had been chairs in universities appointed to the study of comparative religion; no one had attempted to set Judaism into the scheme of comparison with other religions. Samuel Hirsch was the pioneer in this province of investigation. And another thing that book is remarkable for—the life of Jesus is studied in detail—and Hirsch follows in the wake of the

Strauss school. He shows that in the New Testament we have not one Jesus; we have four so-called biographies of the Master. Yet, each one of these biographies presents a different Jesus and a Jesus molded by the partisan bias of the reputed biographer.

One Jesus is a Jewish nationalist; another Jesus is a universalist; the third Jesus is a compromise between these two viewpoints, and the Jesus of the fourth gospel is a philosophical reconstruction, a symbolic adaptation of the personality of Jesus. Samuel Hirsch was the first Jew to handle in a spirit of perfect candor and frankness—without any equivocation and reserve—the material contained in the New Testament bearing on the life of Jesus. As I said before, this book in the main is to my mind a successful attempt to correct Hegel's estimate of Judaism's intent and content.

There is a later book by my father—and a more popular one—whose title would be best translated from the German, as *Humanity is my Religion.* That book is a collection of lectures delivered before the Masonic Lodge of my native town, in Luxemburg. Why delivered there? Because in that small town at that time the Masonic Lodge was really the center of intellectual life. Before his own Jewish congregation in Luxemburg, at that time, he could not have ventured to give these lectures because, honest men and plain women, as most of the constituents were, they had not the intellectual culture to follow so systematic an exposition as father carried through in this, which I call his master work—a work written in 1854 and yet as modern as anything you may read today.

If you were to stumble upon it and not look at the title page, and read it, you would come to the inevitable conclusion: "Here is a man up-to-date," as you say, "who is speaking to us in up-to-date language, with an up-to-date vision." Exceedingly modern even now. That work father dedicated to the task of showing that Paul's construction of Judaism, as slavery unto law was radically false.

And he had another object in view. He wanted to show to the non-Jew—and most of his auditors were non-Jews, among them ministers of state, the chief justice of the Grand Duchy, professors in the higher schools and in the highest academies of the land that the New Testament contained no thought of vital strength, of deep appreciation of life's tender and dearer implications, but it is the property of antecedent Judaism. In his prophecy he says, "I challenge the Christian theologians to prove that any of the teachings of Christianity are strangers in the ethical content and conviction of Judaism. Judaism is the religion of humanity." Of course, this being father's conviction, he could not subscribe to the doctrine advanced by orthodox Judaism as well, that Judaism was law, and in making the point that Judaism is not law father dissented from all other reform leaders in the synagogue. His opposition is sustained throughout.

In the main, three tendencies were strong in the developing of reform philosophy. Of course, it is generally held by superficial people in this country and elsewhere that reform is intended to accommodate men and women of easy terms of mind; reform is meant to make the eating of prohibited food possible and comfortable. Now, as I said, there are three tendencies in the philosophy of Reform Judaism, because Reform Judaism is a philosophy; it is not the child of an intention to make this life easy; it is not an accommodation to the desires of the men with the big purses and the women with the big plumes on their hats; it is not a catering to the ignorant.

The true reform, of which Geiger, Einhorn, Holdheim, and my own teacher and father were the leaders and exponents, was based on a philosophical view. It was Holdheim who urged that Judaism had ceased to be nationalism, and he desired to make of Judaism a church; therefore, whatever had bearing on national history was to be eliminated, whatever had value to religious conviction was to be preserved. Hence his practical reform work in eliminating from the prayer book every allusion to national past or national future. Geiger in the main was of the same opinion, but he was more conservative practically than was Holdheim, for Geiger was by temperament a historian, and he loved to keep intact the monuments speaking of the past. Therefore, he was in favor of retaining much in the service of ancient custom and ritual. For Einhorn Judaism was of double nature—an eternal moral law and a temporal ceremonial law—both, according to Einhorn's thinking, of divine origin, the moral law, however, being obligatory for all time, the ceremonial law being subject to change, according to time and circumstance. So you see, Einhorn never got beyond the notion of law: Judaism was law, withal divinely revealed, but only this distinction did he draw—between ceremony and moral principles.

My father, anticipating with the power of genius much which later science has confirmed as fact, did not draw the distinction between ceremonial law and moral law. He declared Judaism is not law. The genius of Judaism is against law. Prophets laid down principles not precepts, and Judaism is the evolution of a fundamental principle. The ceremony, so-called rites, these are symbols. They are meant to illustrate the principle, and as long as they do this they have their value, but the moment the symbol becomes opaque, no longer competent to teach, it has lost its right to be observed, it must be changed—it may be neglected altogether. In father's system there is no break; it is consistent throughout. Judaism is principle. That principle found illustration in practice where most in our time try and seek such expression for the principle as appeals to us.

And now, to be brief today, for I shall take up the thread next Sunday, what may be that principle of Judaism? Now I daresay you are ready to say *The unity of God* and the non-philosophical interpreter of Judaism would corroborate your statement. That is what you are taught in the ordinary religious schools; that is what you will hear the moment you go to the confirmation exercises in other synagogues—except maybe one other in this city: *The unity of God.* You know that the conception of God is not primary but secondary.

What is, then, the primary conception of God-man? This is what father showed. This is the leading thought of every one of his writings, and his collected works would fill a pretty large shelf in a good-sized library. This is what he contended for throughout in the pulpit, in his contributions to very many periodicals, writing both German and French with equal ease and elegance, speaking both of these languages in his early time, later here in America continuing to contribute his writings to many periodicals, largely in German, sometimes in English—and in his collected lectures and works and sermons constantly urging this one thought: Judaism stands and falls with a conception of man as what? As God's image. What does that mean?

Father turns now to the opening chapter of Genesis, and briefly, father had his own method of reading the Bible. He has been called the modern Philo for that reason. If there be one here who is acquainted with Philo's method he need not be told that Philo allegorizes the Bible; that an event told in the Bible was not the narrative of a happening, but was, in the language of a story, the detailing of a great danger to soul or a great victory accomplished by the human soul of a duty laid on man.

Now this method father employs in his interpreting of the Bible. Adam is not a man that lived, but Adam is the man; he lives today, and the story of Paradise is not a narrative of what once happened, but is a story that illustrates how what happened to Adam happens to us every day; how temptation speaks to us, and if we listen to temptation how we fall. Therefore, going back to the story that man was created in the image of God, father asked, what does that mean? That same chapter tells of God what? Any description of God? No. A long list of attributes? By no means. What does it say God created man as the image of God. What does that mean? And man is a creator just as God is. Why does God create?

Out of love as an expression of His very being. Therefore, man must create out of love as an expression of his very being, without calculation of results, without expectation of reward, and not under the lash of fear of punishment. Therefore, man is free; free to work out himself— and the world is so created that a man who is free can work out his freedom if he only so wills. That is the principle of Judaism, and Judaism announces a principle unknown to every other religion—unknown in every other culture—a principle still imperfectly realized in our own culture.

Whatever else Judaism may teach is a deduction from this principle; it flows from it as water flows from its fountain. The regenerating of Judaism consists in this anthropology, in this doctrine of man. We need no further proof for that than human experience, and the question is not what is God, but what is man.

Hence, Judaism is the religion of humanity, the human being distinct from man the brute— man the human being—the superior of whatever is brute and brutal, earth and earthy. Man is the real law in his freedom, appointed to be on earth what God is in the universe—the creator of changed conditions and things—and men in such a way that human life in its highest sense may be possible.

From that position father drew conclusions bearing on the Sabbath question for instance; on the question of mixed marriages and other institutions; on the question of what is the mission of Judaism; what shall Judaism stand for; what shall the Jew consecrate his life to. These points I shall take up for those of you that will come next Sunday. For today let me assure you it is not merely out of filial love for a man who to me was more than any other, and my teachings are but the feebler echoes of his great instruction.

It is not merely out of filial love that I have ventured to remember father before you in this the centennial year recalling his birth, one hundred years ago; but because I feel that you, as other congregations in Israel have begun to forget the fundamental things for which Reform Judaism stand, and are largely lax in living up to the history of your own congregation. The one congregation of all others much truer than all others to the reform idea as carrying into practice the principles laid down by the great leaders—distinct among whom was he who was born on the 8th of June, 1815, in a very small village, then still under the French dominion, a week later—in consequence of the Battle of Waterloo joined to the Kingdom of Prussia—Thalfang, a little village in the mountains near Treves in the Eifel Kingdom of Prussia, German Empire.

Next Sunday, if you will come, I shall try to show you how and why the principle invoked as fundamental applies to the Sabbath problem, the problem of ritual and other problems that must be seriously studied even by us. Will you forgive me for having ventured to bring to your notice the memory and work of my father and my teacher.

Amen.

THE JEWISH PREACHER:
Rabbi Emil G. Hirsch, Ph.D., LL.D.

One Hundredth Anniversary
Birth of Samuel Hirsch

Part 2
May 2, 1915

Those of you who were here last Sunday will remember that two propositions in the main were advanced and defended by the thinker and philosopher whose name I would ask you this morning once more to remember—or, if you never heard of him, to take it with you into your busy life.

The great philosophical system then, when Samuel Hirsch was a student, the ruling presentation of thought in Germany contended that Christianity was the absolute religion, and to Judaism it assigned a very inferior rank. Applying now to the contents of Judaism the very theories advanced by Hegel, Samuel Hirsch showed that if there were any absolute religion, this distinction belongs not to Christianity but to Judaism. And again, the church had, ever since Paul, its founder, contended that Judaism was law, while Christianity was liberty.

Hirsch showed that Judaism is not law. In this he took issue with the orthodox Jews, of course, and also with many of his colleagues—leaders in the liberal camp. Einhorn, for instance, is as convinced as ever was an orthodox that Judaism is law. What distinguished him from the orthodox is this: he draws a difference between what he calls a ceremonial law and what he labels the moral, eternal law. But for all this distinction, Judaism is bound up in law. It is descended on the Jew from on high; it is imposed on the Jew. Judaism is not a development from within, but a revelation from without and from above.

This position Samuel Hirsch rejects. He is perhaps the only one of the reformers who maintains this insistence: Judaism is not law, but principle. What is the main principle upon which Judaism rests? It is this: that man is created in the image of God. In every man the godlike takes on will, and flowers forth into human personality. From this principle then is easily deduced the content of Judaism's particular doctrines.

Christianity contends that man lost this distinction of being God's image; original man may have been this, but he fell by being disobedient to God, and in that fall not merely the original sinner forfeited his divinity, but everyone born of him shared with him this degradation. Only one who ever assumed personal form, human shape, was free from this taint; that one was the son of God, sent by God Himself to His death to satisfy God's sense of justice, to redeem from the sin all who accepted his sacrificial death, for whom He died, therefore, vicariously.

Against this dogma of the church, Judaism protests. One of the principle teachings of Judaism is that man never lost his divinity; that therefore, he needs no redeemer to re-establish his relations with the Creator. Man is created in the image of God. For what is given him in the hour of his creation man must of his own choosing utilize and develop.

Here is another doctrine of Judaism flowing logically from the first position that man is created in the image of God: one who is like God must be free. Man is even freer than God is. We cannot conceive of God doing wrong, but when we analyze the content of the concept of man we must conclude that this concept only receives its full valuation if we insist that man is free to act the right and is at liberty to choose the wrong.

Man must not sin, but he may sin. Sin is an attitude of mind and a purpose of action in opposition to the divine purpose of creation. Sin is not the violation of this or that statute, is not the neglect of this or that ceremony. There is no law, which binds man and the violation of which might be called sin against God.

Sin is always action contrary to the ideal purposes of humanity. Therefore, sin is always anti-social conduct. Has sin any power? No. Man may set himself in opposition to the intentions of God, but he never can carry out his designs. He can only accomplish his own undoing. That is one of the clearest thoughts presented in crystal, crisp definiteness in the philosophy of Samuel Hirsch.

More clearly than in any other work of Jewish or Christian theology is this aspect of Jewish doctrine presented: Man may sin, but if he does he merely accomplishes his own defeat. With God man is godlike, that is to say, powerful;

against God he is impotent. He has absolutely no power to do that which he would wish.

Here Samuel Hirsch develops his notion of freedom. For most of us freedom seems to cover the privilege to do what we like and the prerogative not to do what is not to our liking. In the philosophies of the Jews freedom represents duty. You may do what you ought to do. That is your freedom—you can never succeed unless you do what you ought to do. You must make the eternal *ought* the law of your life, by your own volition—under no other compulsion than the recognition that this eternal *ought* is the very law of your human life. And that is the Jewish notion of freedom. Hence the Jewish religion is the religion of duty, and being this, is at the same time the religion of freedom.

I cannot go into details for time is too short. But I hope I have at least suggested to you the easily demonstratable proposition that since you grant that man is not a beast, is not an animal merely under the conditions of life such as prevails in the animal world, man is something higher—that nature in creating man gave to man certain powers which other beings had not, or, to put it in theological phraseology, that man is created in the image of God and since you concede this, it necessarily follows that man is under freedom and that man's freedom does not spell license but duty; and that duty means the right to do what is right and the power to do what we ought to do.

Religion is the consciousness of this freedom. It flowers forth into the consciousness of duty—duty not as a burden but duty as an expression of man's own dignity and the fulfillment of man's own destiny. In no other religious system was this note struck except in ours. That is the dominance that ever recurs in the preaching of the prophets—hence this religion is prophetic Judaism.

There can be no other Judaism but the Judaism of the prophets. Whatever passes for Judaism must square with the system of the prophets, must be ethical monotheism. What about rabbinical Judaism, for instance? How did it come that Judaism grew in the course of time to be now something at least of a religion of outward law instead of being the enthusiasm born of inward consciousness of freedom, of the joy of duty. Why did it come, for instance, that in Talmudic Judaism the highest duty is placed on the level with a duty that has no consecration whatsoever? That, for instance, not to lie is treated as of no greater obligation than not to eat a certain kind of food.

Here again Samuel Hirsch struck out a path discovered by none other among the great liberal leaders of his day. There is a way of thinking about life and of living life which is Jewish. Now it was this notion that God reveals himself in history: that in this process of self-revelation God gives to different groups of men different possibilities, therefore different duties. And that out of the full concordance of all these differences will in course of time come to flower the new humanity, enriched by all the distinctive contributions made by the different historical groups. It was owing to this thought that our great liberal leaders came to teach the doctrine so much laughed at, that the Jew, as the Jew, has a historical mission; is responsible for the guardianship of certain thoughts—for the development of these thoughts—to the whole world.

That if he neglects to develop these thoughts and to activate them in life he is faithless to his duty and is faithless, therefore, to the God who reveals Himself in history and speaks to historical groupings of men of the ultimate goal toward which the divine in man shall be brought to develop itself. And now what is the distinct path for which in history God has appointed the Jew? Of course, if you deny that God and history are in any relation—if you refuse to read the volumes of time by the cipher key of God's plan and God's purpose, the theory of mission at once falls to the ground.

But then, with God eliminated, man is only a brute. Then all is reduced to a question of power, to a question of numbers, to a question of gold and silver. Then honesty becomes necessarily a mere policy; truth merely a convenient assumption; hypocrisy is justified when it carries its purposes; rapacity has credentials which can only be questioned, since rapacity brings home the booty coveted—the booty taken away from another.

With God eliminated success is the ultimate test. Suffering then becomes practically nonsense. Man should not suffer, and if he suffers he is a fool. If there is no other gate through which he can pass out of the house of torture, a pistol, a poisonous phial—suicide is advised and is legitimate.

Then life must only be for the strong. The strong are under no obligations to the weak.

With God eliminated, despotism is natural; virtue is ridiculous, unless it leads to honor and pay; vice that pays cannot be discreditable—all is in the pay. And if you reason that twenty years of penitentiary are worth serving provided you get a million or two which you hide away successfully, why, there is no stigma to the penitentiary sentence. It is a matter of business. Then vice, crime, are merely miscalculations. Now, of course, if you deny God—and another thing you have to deny is that your own life means something, that your grouping with other men has a significance—then there can be no mission for the Jew or for anyone else. Then chance is the ultimate key to every puzzle of human experience. But you cannot read Jewish history without coming to the conclusion that there is something for which the formula of materialism and success has absolutely no word.

You say numbers tell. Well, the Jew has always been in the minority and he is still living. You say the fittest survive. You must then grant that the Jew was fittest to survive. What then does the Jewish survival point out? That fitness to survive is not dependent on what? On strength of arms and possession of land, on control of vast resources, for the Jew never was the wealthiest of the world. That is a fiction—the story about the Jew controlling wealth is as egregious a piece of willful, malicious inventing as any ever given currency through lies and falsehoods in this subliminal world of ours.

The Jew had nothing of the things that we are told should make for survival. Then fitness to survive means something more; means equipment with mentality. But that alone does not account for Jewish survival. He was equipped with that. It was the weapon with which he fought his battles. But the mere mentality would never have succeeded in keeping him among the living in the world. To his mentality came his morality—and by morality, please don't understand what you generally claim to be the sum and substance of morality—the not doing of this and the not doing of that. By Jewish morality and the morality which preserved the Jew, which therefore made him fit to survive, was the consciousness that life means something, the sense of duty which was keen, individual, and to that came the consciousness of the one Jew's responsibility for the life, character, the conduct of all Jews.

So your very materialism is brushed aside the moment you begin to study Jewish history. Now that which has preserved the Jew is just that for which the Jew is commissioned to stand out among men. Religion is not bound up in belief. I have told you that in the name of my own teacher and father. That is the keynote to his whole philosophy. Judaism is not bound up in a belief, it is involved in a life, and the cardinal precept of Judaism is that man is a creator, that quality which we assume is God's quality has come to reality in him.

Each one of us has God in him the God within and not the God without—is the fundamental contention of the Jewish religiosity. Construe your God within as you wish. If you think clearly you cannot construe that God within to be less than what you deem to be the highest. That God within you is a confirmation of higher things than what your body needs and your body feeds on and your pocketbook is filled with.

That God within you is the fore thinking of your own condition harmoniously developed into an agent, a free agent of all the things and all the thoughts that make man better, nobler, truer and more just; that bear upon the conduct of man and eliminate selfish matters to make true the mutual helpfulness in the dealings of true humanity.

And hence father's system was one of the first to recognize that religion must be socialized. One man is no man. Men are co-workers. The relation between master and servant, between owner and slave is unethical. We all work together. The changing of life into a paradise of humanity is the duty incumbent upon all men. And where you help another to be what he should be you get more than you give.

You are not entitled to thanks for giving to the other, for whatever you may give to him enables you to be truer to the law of love, the implications of your humanity. So in father's books you find over and over again the emphasis on the social responsibility, on the mission of the Jew in his life to bring to flower the contents of the social brotherhood, which ought to prevail among all men. And hence he also conceived the notion that as the Jew in his communal life was to be an exemplification of the social justice and righteousness, in his international relations the Jew was to be the protest against despotism and the prophesy of universal freedom, of peace founded on justice. All this deduced from the simple proposition that man is not an animal, that man's life is not intended to be exhausted in animalism, that man's life is meant to be a responsibility, that man is created in the image of God.

Now two or three deductions from his theories; the first bears on the Sabbath question. Father was the first, or among the first, to recognize that if Judaism is to live it must have a Sabbath. The Sabbath really is the proclamation of every principle that Judaism announces. It stands for the liberty of man. It is the denunciation of slavery. It stands for the dignity of labor. "Six days shalt thou labor." Father, quoting an old rabbinical observation, insisted that if the Sabbath is a covenant, labor is as much a part of that covenant as rest.

Father insisted that one who worked five days and rested two violated the Sabbath law and the Sabbath principle as much as any who worked seven days during the week. Labor is the expression of humanity—creative labor. Rest on the seventh day is the proclamation of man's freedom. He labors when he will out of the consciousness that labor is the highest of his life, and he ceases from labor when he wishes, to show that though labor is the highest, he as a person is even higher than that highest to which his life must be given.

And as Hirsch has said, the Jew must not be

distinct from others except insofar that he is a better man, quicker to do the right, more anxious in his corporate life to make real the social obligations, more quick to help the weaker brother to become strong than perhaps others are, because he contended that the Jew must be a part of the community, and never apart from the community.

He at once insisted that in the new day, when we have ceased to be in the ghetto, the synagogue shall again have a Sabbath and that Sabbath shall be on that day when the whole community—a part of which the Jew is and apart from which he shall not be—is abstaining from labor. Of course, very few listened to him. Most of his colleagues were too timid to take the step, though many of them theoretically agreed to it.

In 1864 he laid that proposition before the Rabbinical Conference of Breslau, in a little pamphlet. And in his catechism he has maintained that position throughout. His confirmation classes were taught this principle. Have we seen to it that our children shall feel the need of an hour to think seriously about life and about what it implies, about Judaism and what Judaism means?

The second practical question was that of what is called mixed marriages, Father believing as he did, that the historical organization of Judaism is the instrument of God's purposes. He believed that Judaism was the gift of birth. We say Judaism is not a matter of belief. We are not a church. We are not a nation, say I, a political nation, but we are a people. You are received into the people by birth. The people express the wealth of influences that come through the people's past to your own life. We are, by birth, differentiated as Jews; just as by birth we are differentiated as Germans, as Frenchmen, and even as Americans.

But there is no conflict between Americanism and Judaism, and even between German-Americanism and Judaism there is absolutely no conflict. Our mentality is so potential of wealth that one can be at the same time a bearer of the culture inherited from Germany and an exponent of the culture given to him in his Jewish descent and a bearer of the cultural development in America.

There is no conflict between the spiritual Judaism and the spiritual Americanism. You can only be a member of one political nation. You cannot be of two. We hyphenated Americans never dream of declaring ourselves members of another political nation.

Now, because Samuel Hirsch believed that we are a people he had the greatest hesitancy about barring one who was a Jew by birth out of the Jewish community. When one of Jewish birth desired to marry one of non-Jewish birth he claimed only this, that the non-Jew would give a promise, in case the union should be blessed with children, to rear them in the spirit and in intimate communion with the Jewish historic synagogue, then he would consecrate that union, for he felt not to do that would be thrusting the Jew out of the Jewish community.

Father was an idealist. He still believed that

those who asked the Rabbi to solemnize their marriage were moved by deep thought, and thus he would not refuse to speak the word where his refusal might have resulted in barring the gate before one who might have become a member of the Jewish community.

Father was not merely a theorist and a philosopher; he was also a practical man. He was one of the first who urged upon the Jewish community of Philadelphia the necessity of consolidating their philanthropic societies. He came to Philadelphia early in 1866. He was not there half a year when he began to preach the necessity of consolidating. I call it associating, or federating the Jewish charities.

Another thing father did, and that in the second year of his American stay, was to organize the first home finding society for orphans. You know I preached that doctrine here for years. More fortunate than father in many things, I have also been more, and less deservedly, fortunate in having in this congregation one or two men who were open to conviction, whose generosity, never bounded, made it possible for this community to undertake that work on a large scale. I shall not, however, forget that before even through the generosity of one man, whom to mention is not necessary, the Chicago community was enabled to undertake this great, this humane work, this work of justice.

A good woman, whose daughters are among the best of our own circle, left a certain sum to be devoted to the plan. She was influenced in doing that through my own father who had, on a visit here in Chicago, the privilege of having a personal interview with her. Now Eliza Frank was a pioneer in this work with us. We have carried it out, and the result has justified the plan both in Philadelphia and here.

When the President of the United States, Theodore Roosevelt, asked me and others to come together in Washington for a White House Conference to consider the grave problem of the dependent child; there was unanimity of opinion throughout that conference, composed of experts, of leaders in the Catholic, Protestant and Jewish circles, of leaders outside of any church connection, the greatest men and greatest social workers, there was unanimity of the opinion that the day of institutionalism has passed.

It is possible to find homes for the homeless; it is possible to save them from institutionalism and to let them live their normal lives. As a pioneer here, father has earned immortality.

You have practically been led by my father. Whatever I am I became through him. By my many shortcomings my few virtues are but the pale reflection of the glorious life, which was his. I can only look upon Sinai as his monument.

When he was with us, he knew no honor more valuable to him than that which old Sinai gave him in looking upon him as the honorary member.

That old Sinai knew of him. Julius Rosenthal, I know, had studied his works, had them in his library, read them repeatedly. When I first came to this city, the second day I was here and presented myself to Julius Rosenthal, a mere stripling, and shaking my hand he said, "The son of Samuel Hirsch can certainly grow into and grow with Sinai Congregation."

I have grown with you and occasionally—I think you will agree I am justified—the sad impression beclouds my more hopeful view that even this congregation has become colder, less eager to be loyal to that which Reform Judaism implies:

Loyalty to humanity, because it is loyalty to Judaism, and Judaism, not a form, not a belief, not a superstition, and not a mechanical sacrifice or service, but the Judaism making of every Jew a model man and of all Jews an influence for good throughout the world in every line of human activity. An international influence for making the nations more righteous and ultimately peace possible on the basis of justice, the one word which is sacramental in Jewish philosophy and in Jewish life. To have taught me this was my father's work and to him I owe what I am.

One hundred years soon will have rounded since he came, twenty-six since he left us. One hundred years full of experiences for the human race, but whatever they may have brought they have only emphasized the need of religion such as father conceived, a religion of freedom, a religion which makes of the individual Jew an example of all that humanity can be and all that humanity demands we shall be.

Thanks to God that he gave that teacher to me. Would that I had grown up to this distinction. My failings are my own. Whatever I could have done and did do I was enabled to do by him, the great philosopher, the great reformer, the pioneer in many a field of social work, of social redemption. The man whose heart glowed for freedom, political, religious, moral freedom. The man whose God was the highest symbol for humanity.

Amen.

THE JEWISH PREACHER:
Rabbi Emil G. Hirsch, Ph.D., LL.D.

Easter and Passover

Easter Sunday, April 23, 1916
Reading:Exodus 12

The few of you who last Monday night paid attention to the old custom among the Jews, rehearsing the story of their remote ancestors' liberation from Egyptian thraldom, may I daresay recall the one insistent urging during the evening's contemplations.

Everyone now living, so runs the demand placed on the lips of the ancient teachers, everyone now living should regard himself as having been one of those who were delivered from Pharaoh's slavery. If we come to analyze this profound admonition at once leaps to our understanding the deep significance of this day's festivity. We shall learn readily by studying this counsel of the ancient teachers that this day is meant to be the holiday of enthusiasm, as well as the holiday of hope. Enthusiasm, a word used, the etymology by no means is clear. They have argued that the term denotes the God within us, but I daresay strict accuracy in weighing the import of the Greek syllables will not bear out this explanation.

In the non-Latin dialects of modern times for

what we in English and in French and Italian and Spanish call enthusiasm they use a much more suggestive word meaning fullness of the spirit. Now, whether enthusiasm means what it is generally held it does, the feeling that God is within us, whose mark is upon us, whose demands we cannot refuse to obey—for whether the other implications when the spirit is upon us and seizes hold of us and controls us and brings us to a resolution of giving up all that we have, all that we are in order to be loyal to the spirit in whose grasp we feel ourselves to be, the fact is that whatever view we take of this mood, this day is an appeal unto us to lay aside all that would interfere with the work of God or spirit within us!

This day is an admonition that whatever makes life livable and that whatever be the purpose of our living can only be that which is touched by the divine and is enwrapped and enraptured by the spirit.

Now, what does the spirit mean? Here again we are confronted with a puzzle, far from me to weary you this morning with stony, barren metaphysics; that would be a waste of time; but we need not lose ourselves in the clouds of metaphysical speculation to secure an insight into the essence of that which we designate as the spirit or as the God within us. Right when we use the word *Spirit* comes to mind a distinction between it and matter. Let that distinction be before our eyes just now, as we wish to learn how so this day is a day of enthusiasm.

Do you live in and for the body alone? The things that are material have their function and their importance, but are they the ultimate things; this day protests that they are not. The very mythology of this day underscores this note of dissent from the common, convenient, comfortable conception that matter is all there is to life and that the things material constitute life's measure of triumph or of failure. In all religions, in all legends associated with this strange festival we hear the jubilant assertion that death is conquered.

A body dies, matter decays, but the spirit lives. Nature claims its own, the material, the dust; but in a higher sense nature restores its own again and in a new form and a new emphasis out of the grave comes new life, not identical with the life that was, but nobler, sweeter, newer, stronger, more radiant! That is the eternal truth in the Christology today intoned in all the Churches throughout this, alas, blood-drenched, tear-bedewed earth of ours.

That is the kernel of the verity which non Christian and non Jewish tribes tried to stammer out when they spoke of the death of Adonis, of Thomas, or of any other deity—under any other name. They wept for dead Thomas in Tyre and in Antioch they lamented for departed Adonis in the Greek Colonies in Asia Minor and in the Mediterranean Sea. And the lament and plaint, the tears and the sobs of the South were taken up by the winds of the North and in the forests of primeval Teutonic settlements, in Scandinavia, the same melody in minor notes was dirged forth God is dead, death is supreme!

That is the burden of Good Friday's announcement;

that is the framed melody by every mythology in which only the son's career furnishes basis, color and content. But this morning, Lo, Adonis rises from the dead. Balder is escaping the clutches of his enemies. The new life bursts forth—a new life, and the fields have heard the shout with joy and they answered. Where yesterday was bleakness today is verdure; where a few weeks ago the trees stood shivering, unprotected and unadorned, bending to every whim of the wind and bowing to every blast of the tempest, today they put forth a new relation of life, a new crown on their royal brows, and the brook begins to babble and the song birds begin to sing new life. Not of death but of life is today's story—a story universal.

The materialist, however, says death is conqueror and seemingly, the materialist is justified. You and I die, as did the fathers before us. What we call history you might describe as a succession of cemeteries. Where is there a family that has not paid the toll. Throughout all time, in every clime no house, no family, no tribe, no nation but when it thinks of the past is reminded of death's sway and of death's tribute.

Buddha is reported to have been moved by this consideration to lay aside the purple robe of royalty and in its stead to don the reeking rag of a beggar. They tell that at his solicitation messengers were sent out throughout the land to inquire at every door whether death had ever crossed it or whether misery and wretchedness, poverty and hunger, disease, agony had ever lodged under the roof of the hut or of the palace; and the messengers came back and everyone reported that no matter at which door he knocked, whether at the door leading to poverty's haunt or opening to the splendor of richest ease, the answer was uniform, unvaried. Death has stepped across, poverty—if not of body and food at least of soul and of fear has lodged here.

So the materialist has but one conclusion, if all is matter then all is death. Nature reproduces matter; similarity is the outcome of this succession binding father to son, mother to daughter. As it was in the beginning so it is now. Is that an answer, which satisfies this morning's appeal? No! Underscore an emphatic no!

There is a resurrection! Life triumphs over death, and in the succession of matter under death's sway is born something which is not of the dust; there is progress; there is change for the better; there is rise from the low to the high; there is stepping onward and upward.

They who were in the valley are not there forever; if they die in the valley perhaps out of them will come others that will scale the peaks guarding and shutting in the depression below. That is the message of this day, and it is a true message indeed. Love for the things that die. What is life but a great depression, but love for things that do not die, then unconcerned you can be whether life of matter is prolonged or not. You may pass away but you leave behind something, which has made the world richer, and in another and in a new form you will have your second, your immortal life.

That is not the case with them who live merely for the things that dust breeds and dust sweeps away. That is the truth, the truth with them who have lived for the divine. Now you say, "Is this pointed out by the observation of our teachers?". Everyone of us should consider himself or herself to have been actually present when the angel of death passed over the houses of the Jews and snatched his prey from the homes of the Egyptians.

The moment you approach the question of the spiritual, you are brought face to face with the working of history's forces. Otherwise what is the sense for you and me to think today of a distant time when our possible ancestors—for there are some that claim we are not related to them at all, were set free from Egyptian thralldom.

But does that matter to me or to you? Some of us I know believe that they belong to a Jewish Nation and others of us do not agree to this proposition, even they who are of the belief that we are a sort of political nation, or destined to be, or must be, have to ask themselves the question, what does it matter to us whether the imputed ancestor of ours had an interview with Pharaoh and forced Pharaoh to give the order to let us go out. What does that matter if all that is involved in our being Jews roots only in the political, social or material conditions under which we are living, conditions which may be very hard, end conditions which maybe perhaps more comfortable, if the conditions are all that are determinative or essential. What does it matter?

If they know that one time so many thousand years ago in a wind, which we would not believe it possible, some so-called ancestors of ours felt the breath of death go by their houses while its fire and wrath burned to nothing the pride and pomp of the the land of the Egyptians. What to us that an ancestor of ours was led out of Egypt.

That has no bearing, has it on your or my religion. What does it matter whether Moses, Aaron, Levi and Reuben, Simeon and whatever their names, felt the shock of that wonderful night and rushed out of Egypt. Taking good care, however, before they went, to take along a lot of silver and gold and other valuable things. Does that fact give us more surety that duty is the highest and that the God of duty is our God? The connection between the fact and the principal is certainly very plain and may well be doubted.

But perhaps there is another view to be taken, a view which both our analysts and we, who would rather be religionists than anything else may profitably analyze and lay to heart. What we call the spirit is the connection of history. We are all intoxicated with wine of dogmatic—my figure has necessarily to be somewhat mixed—with the wine of dogmatic pressure, the drink as taken from the tree of belief. Now, there is dogma of liberalism as well as there is dogma of orthodoxy, and one of the most fatal dogmas—it is merely dogma—is that which impassioned the French Revolution, a dogma that is today yet befogging many a mind among us, and making many a heartthrob with the great philosophy, the dogma of equality.

We are all equal, and by that we understand that every one of us is the exact reproduction of the other. History makes for difference. Nature begins with equality. The lower you get down in the scale of life the greater the similarities that you meet. Can you distinguish one worm from another? They look alike and they are all alike. Nature begins with similarity and equality, and it leads up to dissimilarity and difference, and history continues that process and intensifies it. In the beginning all are equal.

The savages are all equal, they are equal in mentality and equal in body, the differences are very slight. But those races that have come under historical influence gradually (but never does that process cease) gradually and uninterruptedly are making for further, wider separation and difference.

Now what we call the spirit within us is just the deposit in us of the gold that history has mined and melodized. The Jew and the Christian are not similar and are not alike; that may shock you. There is an essential difference, a difference created by history. You and I are Jews because behind us is Jewish history; there are the centuries of persecution through which the fathers passed; there are the thousands of years of expectation that justice be done and righteousness take lodgment an earth; there be millions of men and women who hoped and suffered, who put into books that we call holy; their story of life. We are distinct from the others; I don't say we are better than they, far be that thought from me; but we are distinct from the others, because our past is another than that to which they are heirs. You cannot blot out the historical past, but in you it may come, it should come to new life. The past you may consider fertile, as it is, in newer forms of life, as a grave; you are rising out of that grave to new life, but the past is yours and you are the product of that past.

The question has often been investigated, as it was put by great thinkers. What makes the distinction between the nations? Are these differences all artificial? Can they be blotted out? Christianity has said they are and they may be blotted out, but behold, how Christianity has failed, had to fail, because it violated the very principle of the life, of the spirit which is historical. History's might and history's weight makes the men that are today and casts them into different molds. Think of it, friends, if you can; I cannot without tears coming to my eyes think of it, this morning wherever cross is raised they speak of the one great divine Man who rose from the dead, and while they speak of that they are killing one another. So-called Christian nations and our own political nation among them are getting ready now to increase the toll of wretchedness, of death, exacted from whom?

From their brother Christians. Christianity has failed, has it not? It has failed because it assumes that you can wipe out the differences as with a wet sponge on a slate when these differences are rooted in the very life of the spirit, when the spirit is—what shall I say—the distilled savor or sap of the past era. Because one nation has a different historical experience, therefore its character is also different; its way of looking at life is different.

That nation that has always been free, that has never had to dread invasion—never was invaded; a nation that was left in control of earth, air and ocean naturally develops a disposition other than that of a nation that had first to grope after, its national unity, that has for years and years dreamed of becoming one, knowing that its being in one was a constant invitation to the others to rob it of what was its own, to oppress it, to exploit it; a nation that was never sure whether the territory that cradled it was safe from incursions by robbers, by plotters, naturally became a nation eager to defend with armies the national hoard.

It is unjust to say that is the wicked spirit, which works in men. And here is the saddest of all sad phenomena in the offhanded judgments, that are now passed, that none stops to consider why and that none is fair enough to remember that if there are differences they are made by history, and a nation that has waited for thousands of years for national unity will naturally be distrustful lest others, want to break it up again and will go to the last extreme to save what for centuries was for it but a dream.

Now to compare something as yet not realized with facts that have come to be factors in our own sad day, suppose Zionists should succeed in getting possession of Palestine again. They and all Israel, orthodox Israel, have dreamed of this restoration.

Suppose ten or fifteen years, or say forty-five years, after having come into their own, another power or combination of powers would rise with a possible intention to undo again what has come to pass recently and to bring back again the condition such as the people felt was their shame, their misfortune. Would not to the last man there in Palestine, and to the last woman and yea, child, resolve rather to die than yield?

But let us not be hasty in our judgments. Let us be fair enough to know that unless you are in the place and position where the other is, you have no comprehension of the other's spirit. History has made these differences, are they idle? No. Here again is very much loose talking these days.

You hear a lot about internationalism; you forget that internationalism presupposes nationalism first; blot out one nation that is a real nation, let it be small or large, from the fellowship of nations, whatever that nation will suffer all the others will suffer something too, it will be a loss to all of us.

The brothers of Joseph who sold Joseph into Egypt wore coats of one color, but Joseph who was sold was given a coat of many colors. The slaves are garbed in uniform livery—that is the livery of slavery—uniformity, monotony, similarity.

But mankind is not meant to wear one uniform; we need color lines, many of them, the more variegated the pattern be the richer life; and so you need the Jew; that is what our teacher meant when he said, let each one of us, think of himself as if he had been in Egypt; during that night. We must think that by our past; we are appointed to be a color line, not by ourselves, but in the beautiful spectrum of all humanity, and that should give us the spirit to resist the whole world if it must be.

Turn the searchlight on Jewish history from whatever angle you may and to whatever intensity you propose, you find one thing that history, which begins with that night in Egypt, is glorious in just those things that made for the nobility and the divinity of human life. Have you ever thought of it, friends? I daresay you have, why it is that the *Man of Sorrows* has come to be the symbol of the divinity of our humanity throughout the world.

It is not merely Christianity that has chosen the man of suffering and sorrows to incarnate this all—underlying, very potent truth for which none of us can take, if in his right mind, the least exception, it is the *Man of Suffering and Sorrows* who is the bringer of new life, the prophet of the new thought.

Go throughout the world. You find that as the best of our kind who have been held all over, the men who suffered, the women who bore the burden of pain; and in our love for our mothers, be they living among us or have they departed to the higher realms, the fundamental note is if we have grown to manhood and womanhood ourselves, that for us mother was a sufferer.

Why has biblical poetry looked upon the childless woman, not as now to be envied, but to be deplored, because she did not taste the glory of that mother's martyrdom, more radiant than which crown, there is none on earth, and no sign in heaven shines with greater splendor than do the royal diadems that stud the diadem of suffering, self-sacrifice, self-devoting and self-dedicating maternity.

Now if you bear that in mind have you cause to deny, are you justified in trying to blur the fact that your ancestors were in Egypt? No group has ever suffered what we did suffer. All the horrors of this war, black they are but blacker still its horror where the Jews are found in large numbers, today, yesterday, in Russia. Today in Poland. Today as in Egypt of old it is the Jew that has to eat the bread of suffering, the bitter herbs. It is the Jew that crouches in his little hut, not so sure as were his ancestors that the angel of death will pass by without exacting its terrible toll.

Sufferers we were, I repeat it, the sufferer who they have named the Savior and the suffering people are God's people. That is what our teacher had in mind when he said, you living now ought to consider yourselves having been in Egypt on that momentous night. You too were slaves in the slavery of your parents, that made you distinct, that gave you the spirit to be inspirited, by going back to the natal day of that spirit.

Friends, this holiday is yet another holiday. It is the holiday of hope. Christianity points out, leaning on the mythology of the Christ life, this eternal avenue of hope; and it is just because the Christian myth has associated this emphasis on hope that the myth itself has retained its grasp on the imagination and its hold on the belief of the people. Analyze that myth. Of course, for us it is difficult to accept it as fact; yet fact is a poor argument against myth and the Christian myth has for millions the proclamation of undying hope.

This morning they will again make of the empty grave the forevision of other graves opened, will tell the mother this morning, "Your little babe was laid to rest on mother earth's bosom, but take hope, the little babe rises—it has risen." That myth will speak to the maimed soldier in the hospitals of France and Germany this morning. The same story will be told whatever be the flag that flies over the house of misery in which those heroes are facing death in a more horrible guise than ever it appeared to them on the battle field—the foreknowledge of mutilation, the fore-sentiment of becoming burdens to others, the sturdy men who used to be the bearers of the burdens of others—to all of these this morning the chaplain will speak of hope, a hope foretold in the dying and in the rising of the King of Life.

And they say, oh, how poor are you, you Jews, who have no myth like this, come then to us and learn of its sweetness and clutch to your burning, parched hearts its comforting assurance of life. But the Jew has access to the same fountain of hope in his own history: "I am not dead but I live." So sings the psalm read to us and sung to us this morning. "I am not dead but I live" is the unbroken chant of Jewish experience throughout the ages.

Oh, they tried to kill us; they have not succeeded; they cannot succeed as long as every Jew bethinks himself of the fact that he virtually is participant in the drama of resurrection.

The conquest of death enacted of old in distant, dark Egypt under the Pharaohonic despotism.

There is new life constantly, there is hope. The Jewish hope has not been defeated and it will not be deceived. What is that hope? Not like the hope so beautifully symbolized in the Christian myth is it, involved in a life hereafter for us, but that hope is the unshaken confidence in the ultimate triumph of justice over injustice and of righteousness over wrongfulness.

Nearer and nearer are we coming to that hope? Are we? Doesn't this war seem to deny that we have approached nearer to that hope? Isn't the insanity, which, alas, is also coming upon us in this our land, an insanity of, hatred and disloyalty to all love—is that not proof sufficient that we have not advanced towards it? No, it is not. There is no one that feels the shame of this disloyalty to love. Not one of the nations engaged in this struggle believe they are in it of their own choosing, but think they are defending what to them is more precious than life, their national existence. And we who are about going into the terrible experience have we the courage to say we are in it because our speculation is that if we take a side, whatever it be, we shall be the beneficiary later?

No. We add to insanity hypocrisy. We shout we are going in it for humanity. Did we go into humanity's fight when the Russian Jews were slaughtered by the thousands? Do we remember them today? No. Do we think of humanity when we learn if it were not for the remarkable power of organization of one nation their women and children would die of starvation; they that killed one life or another. God forgive them for killing, but what about the agony of the mothers of that one country, who must see their little babes pass away crying for milk, and they cannot give them milk. The international law says that such measures cannot be taken. Didn't they take those measures forty-five years ago and force Paris to surrender? Ah, before a fortress is besieged the women and children who desire may depart from the fortress. Whither shall the women and children go from that one land? Will we send out our ships to bring them over here? Will we be allowed to do that? Humanity?

Yes, humanity for our own selves at the best, but not humanity for others. Oh, the men of those starving women have committed outrages. Haven't the others done the same thing? Speak in the darkest possible colors of Belgium. Have you heard what was done in East Prussia? Oh, that is different; the one is East Prussia and the other is not. Have you heard what was done in Galicia? Oh, that is different, that is in Galicia. Oh, that is right, that is not against humanity. Away with this hypocrisy! Let us be fair and honest. I plead for humanity, but I know my Jewish humanity embraces them all.

They have all sinned, each one of them is a shame; they have been disloyal to the higher law! We have advanced and we shall advance further, and out of this night on which the angel of death snatches its victims by the millions shall yet come a new morning, a new liberty, and a new loyalty to all that is truly divine in our humanity.

And so let us not despair. The darker the hour the more intense shall be our faith, the great

Pharaohs will be defeated, the shackles will be rent, death will not triumph! We know now what is meant by the appeal that you and I should know too that we ourselves were in Egypt when the angel of death passed over the houses in which we were preparing for the service that is ours, the service unto our God.

Oh, thou, in whose hands the times and the centuries are, speed thou the day of Peace; wean us all of our pride; let us all humbly profess that we have sinned and sinned grievously; let the Pharaohs be dethroned; let love soften the hearts of the others. Then speed, speed the day for which Israel has watched and Israel has waited and Israel has prayed and Israel has suffered, the day not of uniformity but of cooperation among all men, all coming to thy temple, as it were, the day of enthusiasm for the right and of love one for the other, which is the love of thee.

Amen.

THE JEWISH PREACHER:
Rabbi Emil G. Hirsch, Ph.D., LL.D.

The Crossing Of The Jordan
Inaugural Sermon Chicago Sinai Congregation

Sunday, Sept 5, 1880

In this hour, for me so momentous, allow me, first of all, to obey the promptings of my heart and return thanks to you for your kindness and confidence, so signally evinced in calling me to the leadership of your congregation, so deservedly renowned among the sister congregations of the land. I know the great responsibility which today I assume, and I am painfully conscious of my inability to do justice to its wide scope. But every petty fear is silenced, every hesitating doubt is hushed, if, as I do, I bear in mind what high vocation today becomes mine. To be privileged to work in your midst for the consummation of mankind's highest ideals, in the sense and according to the tenets of progressive modern Judaism, is a calling which may well lend new wings to my soul, and brace even such weak powers as are mine with a perseverance and courage, never to tire in the effort to attain the noble end, which, under the trusty guidance of my honored predecessors you have recognized as the goal of your congregational aspirations.

Indeed, to be the banner bearer in the battle for Israel's, and mankind's lofty interests may, in our age, so strangely moved by the conflict of divergent tendencies, be a difficult task, but it is surely one that cannot fail to bring in return rich reward.

We are standing at the threshold of a new year. The weirdly mingled emotions, with which we usually greet the birth of this youngest daughter of time, cannot but be intensified tonight by the reflection that not only as individuals but also as a congregation, we are now brought face to face with the uncertainties of the future. The message which this pivotal hour of years announces, comes home to us laden with double import, and more urgently than perhaps ever before are we admonished to see to it that we be *"registered unto life."* For to him who can rise above his own individual desires and apprehensions, regrets and anticipations, the quaint Talmudic legend that today the book of the dead and the book of the living lie open before the divine arbiter of human destinies must find a well nigh startling application. He must observe that the genius of the times is busy recording unto death views and conceptions of a defunct past, that he stands ready to unclasp the volume of the living, wherein to chronicle the hopes and aspirations of the nascent future! The advent of the new year to him must be symbolic of the coming of the new era, the rosy dawn of which even now colors the horizon; the lengthening shadows of the sinking sun be emblems to him of the parting salute of an old world of thought and sentiment, which is taking leave of us!

Yes, friends, a world of thought and sentiment, in which our fathers moved and lived, is taking leave of us, the children. There is no sphere of human activity, no field of human energy, but displays the portents of the revolution. No age before ours was swayed by such burning desire after knowledge, was ruled by such ardent longing after truth as is ours. Carried along and aloft irresistibly by this craving and yearning, we have explored the highest and the lowest, have traversed the immensities of celestial space, have unsealed the mouth of mother earth, have lifted the veil from off the countenance of nature, and wrenched from her many a secret of her work and working.

And though much still remains unknown, and many a question is wafted back upon the wings of laughing echo, unanswered, perhaps unanswerable, yet the inheritance bequeathed to us by our fathers has proven too narrow in its restrictions. The old temple of knowledge has lapsed into ruins, even though the new one still await its architect.

And the reflex of this movement is most clearly felt in the province of the religious. Conceptions which to those that lived before us were among the dearest; ideas which in all the vicissitudes of life were to them staff and stay; hopes which in genial sunshine or chilling rain were their trusty companions; thoughts which braced their arms for the contest and work of life, all these no longer convey to us messages of divine peace! With those who cherished them, they are recorded unto death. In the book of the living about to be unclosed, we shall have to learn to read new inscriptions with which to adorn the portals of our heart's sanctuary.

That Judaism, too, is undergoing a similar process no one can deny; no one can wonder at! As the German poet has so aptly styled it, it is the *heart of mankind!* It was, at all times, the first to respond to the impulse of contemporaneous mental life; and today, it has not lost this characteristic function. It, too, appears before us today, bearing in one hand the book of the dead, speaking of a Temple which our fathers pilgrimmed to, then majestic in its architectural completeness, now in ruins; in the other, the book of life, many of its pages still to be unraveled, but the signs of which Reform Judaism is destined to decipher! Thus, turn whither we may, one world is sinking, another arising! In this, the first hour of my ministry among you, no question, therefore, presents itself to me with greater urgency, than does this one:—"how are we, a Reform Congregation, to build up this, our new world?"

In turning to Biblical literature for guidance to find answer to this question, no crisis, therein related, impressed itself so vividly upon my mind in its similarity to our own position, as did the condition of the tribes, encamped along the banks of the Jordan, after Moses' death, under the command of Joshua, the new leader.

The order is given to proceed. The river seems a formidable obstacle to further progress; and the conquest of the land, therefore, almost an impossibility. But, nothing daunted, the leader's voice calls out to the hesitating multitude: "forward from the spot at which you are encamped. The river's rushing waters cannot impede the onward march of the Lord's host. Let the priests, bearing the ark of the divine covenant plunge in courageously, and a path will open in the very midst of the gushing waves. Take, however, twelve stones from out of the river's bed, whereon rested the feet of the priests, and on yonder shore erect with them a memorial column for your children after you!"

Such, in brief, was the marching order of the new general. Its details, I think, are also well adapted to show us the way, and teach us a method, as to how we should proceed to perform successfully the work before us!

Forward from the spot where we are resting! This the first essential. Of one fact today we are too prone to lose sight. The praises of the Reform movement have been sung so loudly; the benefits which from it have accrued to Israel have been so frequently urged, that we too easily forget that, after all, much still remains to be done before the land of the future is ours. For, if we have succeeded in throwing off the yoke of Egypt, if we have crossed the reedy sea, if even in the desert we have received the tablets of the law, and feasted on heavenly manna, we have, at best, but traversed that desert while the Jordan still remains to be bridged, the land of our promise has still to be conquered in many a hotly contested battle.

In saying this, no one can accuse me of ingratitude

toward those great leaders that during the past fifty years and more have directed the Reform movement; no one will charge me with underrating the scope or the effect of their self-sacrificing efforts.

But as Moses could only lead his people to the brink of the frontier river; as he could but from the summit of the towering mountain behold from afar the shaded hills and laughing plains of the country, for which he had so ardently yearned and to which he had consecrated every sentiment of his pure heart, so also the Moses' of our second liberation could but show us path and track in a howling desert, bring us to the very border of the land of our future habitation, but they could not marshal the triumphal march of conquest.

The mission of Reform is twofold, *critical* and *constructive*. The remark has recently, and very truly, been made that hitherto it has been the bane of liberalism to have been too exclusively critical That this observation holds good as to Jewish liberalism, no one acquainted with its history and development can gainsay. If today we hear so often the complaint and the accusation that the Reform movement has been fraught with disastrous consequences to the truly religious spirit, and if seemingly the charge is substantiated by facts, patent and incontrovertible;—those consequences adduced and those facts harped upon are, in very reality, not so much the outgrowth of the Reform movement in itself, as the necessary result of that exclusive criticism which unavoidably has hitherto swayed the liberalism of the day.

Criticism, certainly, has its legitimate function. It is the pioneer that marches in the van of slowly advancing civilization, and the pioneer's work, too, at first blush, seems destructive. His sturdy axe cuts down the mighty oak of a thousand years; his reckless daring blasts the rock, nature's original fortress. He bids the waters take new direction, and disputes the dominion of their native soil to the original owner of the forest. And in return for all he destroys, he can but hastily timber a rough cabin of logs—a temporary makeshift, giving neither promise nor pledge of stability or security. And yet, his destructive work is necessary. Without him, the constructive civilization of those that follow after him is impossible!

So with us, Criticism had first to prepare the way, and its seeming destructiveness is in earnest of the solidity of the construction, which we now may, nay must rear. And still another consideration will show us that the much deplored criticism of Reform was necessary.

Criticism is essentially aggressive, and all great and beneficent movements of human progress are aggressive in their first stage. So is the sun when he first bursts open the portals of the East; the first hour of his triumphal course along the horizon is one of conflict, waged against the sullen vassals of darkness, that would fain hold dominion for ever. The peaks of the mountain summits, indeed, eagerly accept the morning's kiss, but the valleys beneath long yet reject the conquering hero's loving salute!

So did the mission of Moses begin by aggression,

and his whole career, his constant attacks upon the heathenish propensities of his contemporaries are but typical of the aggressive, critical spirit that animated the leaders of the reform movement. They, too, found their people not only politically, but also spiritually enslaved.

The God of their fathers, Israel knew no longer; intolerable oppression had crushed out every recollection and consciousness of Israel's priestly mission. The present, so dreary, held out no promise for the future; and the past, with its ruined temple, its overthrown Davidic State, its sacerdotal and sacrificial ritual seemed the Paradise lost,—miraculously to be regained.

And more than all this! While, like that of Moses of old, the hearts of many burned with indignation because the lash of the taskmaster cut deep and dire furrows into the back of the poor enthralled, while many dared resist the emissaries of the cruel Pharaohs, many and many again, alas, swayed by ambition and the desire for political preferment, joined the ranks of Israel's tormentors, and had but scoffing words for those who expostulated with them.

Under such circumstances, from the midst of 'the burning bush of their love for their people, the Moses' of our times received the divine appointment to go and reclaim the enslaved. And the fetters were sent asunder, the people liberated, and led out of the house of bondage. But though the land of their fathers, no less than the mountain of the Lord was the goal of their journey, the generation that left Egypt could not enter Canaan. In the stony waste of the Sinaitic peninsula, the people had to undergo a purifying process.

So also in our modern exodus from mediaeval Egypt. The generation that bore the yoke of Pharaoh could not conquer the future. The fleshpots of Egypt and the golden calves had, as yet, too many charms for them. During this period of conflict with these constant hankerings after the past, Reform had, of necessity, to be aggressive, and consequently wield the sword of criticism. The claim to eternal authority on the part of Talmudical Judaism, the legitimacy of tradition had to be investigated. The rock of the past had to be struck, and lo we found the limpid waters wherewith to quench our thirst. Like the geologist, we succeeded in separating stratum from stratum, and assigning to each period its peculiar formations; we discovered traces of gradual growth unfolding everywhere, and thus indicated our right to discard withered leaves for green buds just springing into life. That conflict, however, is now decided! Criticism has performed its function: it becomes our duty to leave the desert, for those who forever would stay in that arid wilderness cannot expect to be participants of the future.

We must now begin the work of construction. The sword and the book, so relates an ancient Midrash, were given toiven together, and so in Reform Judaism criticism and construction should henceforth be firmly joined. Thus, then, we, too, are ordered Up, forward from the spot of your encampment!

Yes, friends, perhaps louder than ever before does today the genius of the time call upon us to march forward. Who is there among us that does not know, that life today, with its many problems, its many doubts, its many claims, is the river full to overflowing, that rushes and gushes with sweeping current between us and the land of the future?

Yes, life today more urgently and more piteously, than ever it did since man began to breathe and move under yon arched sky, clamors for an answer to its questioning. The solutions, offered by the civilizations before our own, have lost their value and potency. If in antiquity the mere accident of birth—a sign of divine favor or displeasure—stifled every doubt, and compelled man to accept as inexorable the decrees of fate, under which he could groan, but which he dared not question; today the spot at which our cradle stood, and the circumstances by which it was surrounded decide naught, and are often but a fresh source of burning dissatisfaction and galling unrest.

If; in the middle ages, the Church, while retaining the theory of divine grace and preferment manifested at birth, held out to the weak and lowly, the troubled and perplexed, the hope of a future compensation and retribution; today, the hidden regions beyond the grave are quick with no incentive to endurance and patience. In one word, the world has lost the compass whereby to steer life's fragile bark.

"Is life worth living?" This the harassing problem to which no response will come; and the times are charged with volcanic energy; social upheavals multiply in number, increase in horror, and the whole fabric of our boasted culture seems out of joint.

And for this very reason, it today becomes the sacred duty of modern Judaism, to construct on the eternal principles of Judaism, an all-embracing philosophy of life, to study man in his ethical relations, to listen to his doubts, and to confirm him in his hopes, to brace him for the struggle of life, and show him the palm of victory to be striven after. Mere negative criticism cannot do this. Therefore, like Joshua's host of yore: Forward! Onward!

But, friends, let us recollect here, at the very outset, one essential point. The very river of life, which it is ours to ford, will open its sweeping current only to the priests bearing the "ark of the covenant."

If we do not wish to be swept away by its swift waters, we, too, have to take with us that ark, emblem of the covenant, which makes mortal man kin to his Maker. In other words, the adamantine rock upon which we are to rear the temple of the future must today, as ever in Judaism, be and remain the living consciousness of the sublime relationship that links us to God!

Perhaps, the sciences refuse to adduce proof of this covenant. The telescope and the spectroscope are both silent on that score; and the astronomer, when computing the orbits of the stars, will not take account of this factor. And even so, the geologist, tracing the developments of the earth's incrustation, successively through all its periods, will not point out in the fossil remains of the burned epochs or in the formations of the present day evidences thereof. Nor can we hope, in the laboratory of either chemist or physiologist to succeed better.

But what of that? The covenant, which we are to cherish, is not an outward one. "Not in the heavens and not in the sea, but in thy mouth and in thy heart to do it."

The raging ocean of fire, the whirling tempest failed to bring home to the prophet of old the knowledge of his God; the soft voice of his own heart revealed to him what he could read neither in the stars above him nor in the rocks around him!

Philosophy has, indeed, demolished the so-called evidences of God's existence deduced all from the outward work and working of Nature. But the lessons, which the life of man and mankind teaches—these no philosophy can controvert or render nugatory. What if without phosphorus there be no thought—the mind which works through the instrumentality of the brain will ever remain more than a mere secretion oozing from brain matter. The heart will ever be more than a pumping apparatus, the tear more than a chemical salt,—man more than an automatic machine and the man of science, who would deny his own manhood is at best a giant Samson, blinded by his prejudices, laying hold of the pillars of the sanctuary and in their fall working his own destruction.

What makes man a man is the eternal prompting, which he alone of all creatures feels down in his heart, to rise above his finite surroundings and soar up to ideal heights, to enter into close union with the infinite.

How far so ever we may follow the footprints of man's work on earth, we find this power operative within him. True, often, very often, the flight of his aspirations took a wrong direction, but as the erratic course of erring stars confirms even in its irregularity the laws according to which the others are held in their even paths, so still in its errors the human heart reveals the eternal law of its constitution. Nor can the infinite remain for man an abstract idea; he ever feels it as a living reality.

Conscience and virtue are its ministering angels within him. And virtue is not an euphonious sound for selfishness and policy. The eye of the little child, whose mind is certainly free from all guile or utilitarian calculation of its own interests, involuntarily sparkles with holy fire of enthusiasm when it beholds the noble faces and figures of those who devoted their lives to what is good and noble; and even the criminal, steeped in the most abject mire of moral depravity, cannot stifle the plaintive voice within him: "Man, where art thou?" and escape the chiding of his conscience; he must quake under its lashes, for whom neither dungeon nor gallows had any terrors.

That virtue and conscience partake of the characteristic trait of all that is human, that from small germs, with changing standard, they, too, have shared in a progressive process of evolution, this fact does not disprove their reality and universality. For they are not merely individual, they are cosmic forces.

History is the Sinai from which, if shrouded in clouds and trembling with fiery commotion, above the peal of its thunders and by the glare of its flashing lightning, we hear the jubilant declaration "I am the Lord, Thy God!"

On the tablets of the law, there promulgated, we may read, that if virtue be a policy it is a divine policy; that nations as well as individuals only then flourish when in accord with virtue's dictates; that they perish, if they dare oppose its behests, which, notwithstanding human opposition, will be carried out to a successful issue! Yes, virtue, or better, God with conscious purpose rules the world!

And this idea, this covenant must also be the cornerstone of the system we have to construct. Otherwise it will be a child's card house, which cannot endure! Otherwise the fate that awaits us will be similar to that of those daring Titans, who raised a tower to storm the heavens, but to find their undertaking end in dire confusion.

For the thoughtful, history points out one lesson: Atheism has ever been the gravedigger, never the architect of civilization. Look at Rome, in the first century of our era; contrast her with Jerusalem! The seven-hilled city, then at the zenith of her power; Zion and Moriah, but faintly aglow with the rays of the setting sun of their decline.

Both had opened their gates to Greek thought and culture. But, though the mistress of the world gladly patterned her own songs after the strains that once filled with their sweet music the Olympian arena; though she sat an eager disciple at the feet of masters full with the lore of the Stoa and the Academy: could she touch with new life the genius of Hellas? She became its tomb, because atheistic, frivolous, she had lost all comprehension of love for the ideal.

Not so on Palestine's sacred soil! There, Greek culture was quickened into new life; the God-idea of Israel endowed it with potencies hardly conceivable; and Christianity went forth from thence, not merely to bury a world, but also to construct one.

And again, when fourteen hundred years later, Greece stepped out once more, from the ruins of Byzantium, where long she had been secluded, and in Italy and Germany found willing adepts: when the "eternal city" at the bidding of a Medici on the papal throne, saw rise in stately proportions St. Peter's majestic dome; while, in yon little Saxon town, a much less stately cathedral began to resound with the burning eloquence of an iconoclast, a monk but recently emerged from the cloister's solitude; which of these two, Rome or Wittenberg, proved the Mecca of the New World, then spreading?

The papal court, frivolous and atheistic, though fostering the new arts and sciences, could but erect sad monuments over the grave of a civilization, the last remnants of which it was, while Protestantism, the Bible as the word of God in its hands, called up to life, energies and tendencies, the beneficent rebound of which we yet feel, even today.

But why go so far? Follow me to the dying decades of the eighteenth century! A hurricane is sweeping over both hemispheres; America and France are in the throes of a new era. But where does the storm bring in its folds life, where death? Beyond the ocean they defy reason. But she can with bloody hands only tear down, not build up. Here, on this side of the Atlantic, with the God of their fathers a living presence in their heart, the sturdy champions of the Revolution, not only tear down, they build up.

Let these instances suffice! Let us, too, heed their warning: Forward! That is, indeed, the order of the day; but only when the ark of the covenant leads the way. But, on the other hand, let us not forget that this idea of the covenant which makes us kin to the Infinite must ever remain a living thought, not degenerate into a dead dogma. If Judaism protests with all the fervor that strength and truth of conviction can command, against the dogma of materialism! It does no less raise its voice against the materialism of dogmas.

Our religion was never dogmatic. Liberty of conscience, untrammeled by any restrictions of a formulated creed, was the treasure over which all ages watched with never fagging zeal. Its greatest men could never dare reduce to authoritative articles the ever-living principles of our faith, without encountering a jealous, and always successful opposition!

While the synagogue, here and there, perhaps pronounced the ban of excommunication against men bold enough to emancipate themselves from the mandates of practical custom and ceremony, it very rarely, if ever, made theoretical dissent from prevailing opinions the basis of the decree of exclusion. Some are ready to see in this a symptom of inherent weakness. "What is Judaism?" so they exclaim, "no one knows, because no one can formulate it."

They forget that Judaism is not confession but conduct; that it is a life: and life can never be formulated, being no crystal but a constant flow.

Indeed, not the tongue that glibly repeats articles of faith, not the lips that are ever ready to pronounce the name of the deity are the tests of how deeply we are conscious of our relationship to our God within us, around us, above us; but the heart aglow with love of all that is true and beautiful; a hand ever ready to do what is good and noble.

This characteristic trait of Judaism is not an element of weakness; it is its tower of strength. It alone spares it the futile and frantic efforts under the necessity of which all dogmatic religions are smarting, to reconcile with new standards of knowledge, old standards of belief. It alone steers clear of the cliffs, upon which dogmatic religion is in constant danger of foundering, the assumption of two kinds of truth—the one scientific, the other religious.

No, keeping pace with the advance of mankind, it scaled round after round of the ladder, reaching from the earth up to God, with its hopes, the ascending angels, but also its doubt, the descending angels, its steady companions.

And so today, whatever the cosmogony we accept; whatever the views we entertain as to the character and composition of our sacred literature—if our theism be a principle of action, rather than dogmatic assertion, these opinions do not conflict with our Theology. In the land of the future, the manna may cease falling from above, but the Ark of the Covenant, with the eternal tablets of the law, the ever blooming staff of life, is still with us, because it is within us.

And finally a third essential is suggested by our text "Take from the river twelve stones, erect with them a memorial column, so that when thy sons ask thee about their significance, thou mayest be able to acquaint them therewith."

In constructing our new system, we cannot break the historical nexus with the past. Whatsoever is truly human is historical. The distinction between instinct and reason, beast and man, manifests itself mainly in this, that instinct has no history, while reason has. In our day, the claims of what is historical are often overlooked. Idealism today attempts to build the shrine of the future without remembering that the future can only be a continuation of the past, through a living present, and thus in vain delusion the edifice rises upon the quick-sand of individualism.

Where the thread of history is rent asunder, the bark of idealism carries only sails, no anchor. The physical universe is held in equipoise by the conflict of two forces, the centripetal and the centrifugal; so the moral universe loses its balance, would it refuse to submit to the operation of the centrifugal, the historical force.

And pause one moment, and reflect, what history is that with which we are to retain connection! We see there before us as a people, swayed by one idea, and often martyrs to that idea: "It is the priest-people of the world, banded together for the purpose of marching in the van of true humanity."

And this claim to this privileged position is well substantiated. It is easy to show that in Israel the issues of humanity were first recognized and first solved; and that its solutions have victoriously stood the fiery test of actual life!

Nor can we afford today to give up our priestly mission. The Levitical purity-laws and dietary regulations, indeed, we may discard; but the priestly robe woven with bitter tears and dyed in the life-blood of thousands of martyrs,—this we cannot resign, for our task is not done, the victory of true humanity not yet won.

Thus, we, too, have to take the stones, and erect them into a memorial column! We will preserve our historical organization, observe our historical holidays, chant in our services the old songs of the Jordan and Euphrates, and address our petitions before the throne of grace to a certain extent, at least, even in the language which our fathers spoke.

But, I cannot forget that the memorial stones are not an end unto themselves. They are but means to acquaint the young with the great lessons and truths of our history, imbue them with the spirit of our past, instill into their hearts the love for our task in the present. Have we been able to carry out this intention heretofore? Who would say, we have? Certainly, I am the last one to detract one tittle from the historical value of the historical Sabbath. But, we live under such circumstances that it has, indeed, become a historical reminiscence, is no longer a living institution.

Certainly, I am the last to desire a schism in Judaism. But, I cannot shirk the duty of providing for such as cannot observe the historical Sabbath additional services on such a day, as it is possible for them to attend. I deny that this step is a surrender of Jewish principles. Nay, furthermore, I insist upon the introduction of these services on the general civil day of rest in the name of the priestly mission of Israel, which is sacred to us all.

The great prophet of the captivity, living in a time when, like in ours, a new heaven was spreading, and a new earth was founding, held out to his contemporaries the goal: too insignificant it is for me that thou shouldst be a servant unto me for the mere purpose of raising the tribes of Jacob and bringing back the guarded of Israel. I have given thee as a light for the nations.

Our efforts cannot confine themselves today to our own circle; the world, thirsty with the thirst of knowledge, claims our services. Our salvation is to become also its salvation. In the words of my honored predecessor: "Judaism has to express its views on all the vital questions of the day; and the forum for this is not the Sabbath trampled upon, but the civil day of rest!"

These, then, are the principles, which shall guide me in the administration of my office in our midst. A great work lies before us. Like Reuben and Gad, our congregation is commissioned and pledged to march as the advance guard of the army and bear the brunt of the battle. Let us be true to this trust! Let us all, in the New Year, rally with old enthusiasm around our flag! Then, indeed, our names will be recorded in the book of life and God's blessing be with us.

Amen.

Part Two

The Biography Of
Rabbi Dr. Emil G. Hirsch

By David Einhorn Hirsch

Introduction

Today I am an old man, eighty years old. When I write about my distinguished father I am lost in high thoughts; memories of the far off past come to my mind. I am a lad of twelve years and I am sitting with him in his spacious library—books stacked everywhere—18,000 books, written in all languages, Hebrew, German, French, Spanish, English, Russian, Greek and Latin. He was conversant with seventeen languages. The library was on the third floor of our sixteen-room, graystone home at 3612 Grand Boulevard in Chicago. Our family consisted of my mother, Mathilda Einhorn Hirsch, my sisters, Dora Hirsch, Beatrice Hirsch (Mrs. Sigmund Kirchheimer), Elsa Hirsch (Mrs. Gerson B. Levi), and my brother, Samuel E. Hirsch. We had moved to this home several years earlier.

At this time of which I write he is in his forty-eighth year. We are about to turn the century. It is the year 1899.

As I see my father, in my mind's eye, I still remember him. He is a large man-about five feet, nine inches tall—well proportioned, a massive forehead, deep brown eyes, protruding chin and a trimmed black mustache. My father is bald. He is dressed neatly in a gray suit and he wears a black tie. His shoulders are big. His hands are big and he walks very erect. His weight is about 175 pounds.

At the moment of which I am reminiscing, he is busy at his typewriter constructing a sermon to be preached before his congregation next Sunday morning, a day in the early fall of the year 1899; but the sermon will not be delivered as it was typewritten. My father did not use notes. A mere outline of his thoughts sufficed. This image of my father, as a thinker and a scholar, I shall remember even as I recall how great an orator he was. As he works, I recall his heritage. I wonder if I too would like to be a rabbi, but a rabbi like my father. Now I know that could never be. Somewhere in these first twelve years of my life it was never wished for me to follow in his footsteps. He would be the last of the great rabbis of our family. I would not carry forth that torch of learning, nor would my brother, nor would my sons, my sons' sons, my nephews, nor any blood member of my family.

My father's rabbinical education began when he was only three years old. That is when his gifted father began to teach him Hebrew.

From this beginning, his mind and tongue were honed through years of study to enable him to cry out as the spokesman of Reform Judaism for social justice, religious truth, and dignity of man.

He embodied the ideas and ideals of his learned father, Samuel Hirsch, and captured the fire and fervor of his father-in-law, David Einhorn.

Emil G. Hirsch was the teacher and preacher of Prophetic Judaism.

D. E. H.

August 8, 1967

The Beginning

My father was born in Luxemburg. He was the youngest son of Dr. Samuel Hirsch, the Chief Rabbi of Luxemburg. Samuel Hirsch, in Jewish history, is called the philosopher of the reform Jewish movement. A brief look at Samuel Hirsch's life will explain the importance of the first few years of a child's training.

Samuel Hirsch was born June 8, 1815, in a small hamlet—Thalfang—in the Eifel region, near Treves. Ten days after his birth the Battle of Waterloo was fought and Napoleon was defeated. Thus this small hamlet fell into the hands of Prussia.

Samuel's father was a horse dealer, and while not conspicuously successful in this business, he was well acquainted with the Tenakah, a knowledge of Jewish law, and his ambition was to have his son, Samuel, become a rabbi.

Hence, since Samuel was predestined to become a rabbi, before he was three he learned the Hebrew alphabet. After his Bar Mitzvah, he went to the Yeshiva in Metz where he studied for a few years. But, on his own resolve, he departed to Marentz where he mingled and studied with famous masters of Talmudic lore. From there he wandered to Bonn, always studying, always improving his mind; from Bonn to Berlin, and then he was ready to be a rabbi of a congregation.

Thus, at twenty-three, he became rabbi of a congregation at Dessau. He did not remain rabbi of this congregation long because already he had begun to evolve ideas of radical reform Judaism. However, as a student, he caught the eye of the Princess of the Dutch Royal Family. She besieged this young scholar to lecture her on philosophy. So enamored did she become with his challenging ideas that she influenced the King of the Netherlands, in 1843, to appoint Samuel Hirsch Chief Rabbi of Luxemburg, and his salary was paid by this Grand Duchy. Here, in Luxemburg, Emil G. Hirsch was born on May 22, 1851.

Emil, at the age of three, like his father before him, began the study of Hebrew. Emil's father was his teacher. From his father he learned the poetry and meaning of Hebrew Literature. Samuel taught his son that Torah is teaching; that Torah was to be lived, not lectured. Through strict discipline of training, Emil—before the age of ten—was well enough acquainted in his studies to merit college ranking. He was already equally at home in Hebrew, Greek, Latin, German or French: He was proficient in mathematics.

My father told me that his mastery of seventeen languages is what honed his mind. From his mother he learned English as well as French.

When Emil was fifteen years old, his father

received a call to immigrate to America to become the rabbi of the reform congregation, Keneseth Israel, in Philadelphia as the successor to the renowned rabbi, Dr. David Einhorn. Little did anyone know that David Einhorn would one day be Emil's father-in-law. At that time, Emil only knew that his father was taking the pulpit of a great American Rabbi—Einhorn—the friend of Lincoln who had to flee from Baltimore just before the Civil War because of his militant preaching against slavery.

Emil continued his secular studies at the Episcopal Academy of Philadelphia. Later, he graduated from the University of Pennsylvania in the year 1872. And to those people who knew about my father only because of his scholastic and oratorical abilities, they may be interested to know that he, for several years, played on the football team at the University of Pennsylvania. After graduation, my father spent four years of continued study at the Universities of Berlin and Leipzig to broaden his knowledge of Judaism. In Europe he studied under the great and profound Dr. Abraham Geiger who was the tutor of a whole new breed of philosophical thinkers.

After obtaining his Ph.D. Degree in 1876, he returned to Baltimore to his first pulpit, Har Sinai Congregation. Emil had been elected rabbi of this congregation through the influence of David Einhorn. David Einhorn had been their rabbi years previous to the Civil War. And so Emil journeyed to New York to thank David Einhorn in person. My father told me that when he rang the bell at the rabbi's residence a very pretty daughter of the minister opened the door. This tall young man, with his charming way, impressed her greatly. She asked him his name and when he replied, "I am Rabbi Emil G. Hirsch and I have returned recently from Europe," she introduced him to her father.

Emil Hirsch visited Dr. David Einhorn often during the next two years and it was not only David Einhorn, but his gay young daughter, Mathilda, that was the magnet that drew Emil to New York on many visits.

In 1878 he married the Rabbi's daughter, Mathilda Einhorn. The story is told that when Emil became engaged to Mathilda, her mother, Julie Ochs Einhorn, in the excitement following the announcement of the engagement, misplaced her glasses. They were actually on her forehead and she exclaimed, " I have lost my glasses, but I've found a son-in-law."

At the time of his marriage Emil was Rabbi of Adath Israel Congregation in Louisville, Kentucky. These two short pulpits were the prelude to a forty-three year reign, beginning in 1880, with Chicago Sinai Congregation.

Here in Chicago his life work was to begin: The translation of dynamic, liberal Reform Judaism into a way of life; into a guiding light for social justice, for education, for the nobler things of life.

In his inaugural sermon, "Crossing the Jordan," Emil G. Hirsch said to the Chicago Sinai Congregation, "Yes, friends, a world of thought and sentiment in which our fathers moved and lived is taking leave of us—the children. There is no sphere of human activity, no field of human energy, but displays the portent of the revolution. No age before ours was swayed by such burning desire after knowledge, was ruled by such ardent longing after truth, as is ours."

The Search For Truth

As my father suggested in his inaugural sermon, he continued his search for truth fervently in his new pulpit. At this point in this biography, I must pause and remember that the early years of Reform Judaism in the United States were now at an end. The scholarly and sturdy pioneers of Reform Judaism had planted its roots here.

It was now the work of the second generation of Reform Rabbis to carry on their noble efforts in the cause of spiritual growth and enlightenment.

Emil G. Hirsch became the leader of this valiant band. America had changed from an agricultural land to an industrial civilization. No longer were beautiful mansions erected like those that George Washington built at Mt. Vernon or Thomas Jefferson at Monticello. After the time of the Civil War, large manufacturing plants were built. Huge banking establishments arose. Many of the railroads appeared on the scene to transport passengers from one part of our prosperous land to distances far away.

The names of Morgan, Gould, Carnegie, Harriman, Rockefeller, and Vanderbilt became household words. And in another generation the names of Schiff, Rosenwald, Guggenheim, Strauss, and Lehman would be added to this distinguished list.

This country changed from an agricultural land to an industrial age in the pursuit of great wealth. The young preacher became conscious of glaring injustices. Child labor commenced. Giant sweatshops arose in our midst. Against these wrongs, Emil G. Hirsch thundered with all the potent power at his command. He demanded an eight-hour day be enforced and a living wage be paid to employees of mercantile establishments. In one of his sermons, entitled, "The New Social Adjustments Suggested by the Implications of My Religion," he stated: "The conception of human life must be under the inspiration of religion. So arranged that out of them comes the possible maximum of human life and human love, and in consequence, also human happiness.

"We must remember that man is more than an animal. That man cannot live by bread alone. That man must live by higher, and for, higher ends. That man has need of man. That he is not as an animal. And the other principle—that one man is dependent on all men. He owes social duties because his whole life is conditioned by social relationships. Have we not all one Father? Has not one God created us all? As soon as you apply to humanity the principles that are to be applied to dead material, you invade the sacred precincts of man's divinity and enslave him. You buy and sell in the open market what really cannot be bought and sold—humanity—human beings. When human beings are bought and sold, they are reduced and degraded to slavery, and that is the worst of our present system.

"You must remember that when we pay a man for his work, our duty to him and our responsibility towards him are not ended. A man has rights to other things than merely so much wage for so much work."

In a sermon, published in The Reform Advocate (my father's weekly publication, which he founded in 1891, to advance the cause of Reform Judaism), he states, "In days like these when the foundations of civilization seem to tremble, when distrust stalks everywhere, when man has learned to regard man as only a machine and tool, when incendiary torches are lit and dynamite bombs explode, when rulers of republics are killed by the dagger of the fanatic; and cities quiver for days in anxiety and anguish lest the firebrand be thrown into peaceful homes, and busy hives of commerce be reduced to ashes, shall we have nothing else to do but lose ourselves in metaphysics about the existence of God, and to sigh, and to pray, and to fast for our own self-satisfaction.

"The world waits once more the prophet, would once more hear the word of a nobler view of life than gain and profit and greed, and hurrying and chasing after the booty. We need once more to feel that humanity is more than a pack of wolves fighting for the carcass by the wayside. We need once more the stern sacramental words of duty and obligation, of righteousness and justice—*justice*, mark you, not charity—away with this pretender. Off from the throne with that usurper. Away with all this charity. Justice we need. Social justice everywhere."

And in another sermon, preached in 1894, Emil G. Hirsch's voice cried out, "Sweatshops are an expedient of hell. God in heaven, and Judaism, professes that he who works shall eat—and eat sufficiently and not be robbed of his manhood. Your duty is to stamp out this barbarous system. It is a blot upon the face of our civilization."

My father opposed the ideas of the Manchester school of philosophy. He was in bitter disagreement with their thoughts. According to their leading capitalist, Jay Gould, "Labor is a commodity that will, in the long run, be governed absolutely by the law of supply and demand..."

In other words, human beings are just so many numbers—so many figures in a statistical or financial report. They have no individuality and no soul. Was there ever any morality in such a society so governed?

The proper observance of the Sabbath was, a cause of chief concern for Dr. Hirsch. Dr. Kaufmann Kohler, Hirsch's scholarly brother-in-law and immediate predecessor in the pulpit of Chicago Sinai Congregation, introduced a Sunday Service there in the year 1874, along with the regular Saturday Service. But, because the merchant members of the Congregation were tending store, the Saturday Services were poorly attended. The Sunday Services drew a larger audience. My father did not feel that he desired to preach to empty pews. As he expressed it, only millionaires could attend the Sabbath Services on Saturday.

Hence, in the year 1885, Chicago Sinai Congregation inaugurated services on Sunday, exclusively.

This radical reform congregation was the first one in the United States to take this step. Their Sunday Services were most successful. Audiences of two thousand people—both Jews and Gentiles—came to hear the gifted and eloquent Rabbi on Sundays, and the synagogue was not large enough to accommodate the worshipers. In the year 1891 the sanctuary at the Southwest corner of 21st and Indiana Avenue had to be enlarged.

Dr. Emil G. Hirsch's pleas for social justice, his oratory, and his scholarship won for him a national and international reputation.

A newspaper article from Atlantic City, July 20, 1902, is worth quoting:

"Dr. Emil G. Hirsch, of the University of Chicago, addressed a great audience today on the Steeple Chase Pier in the auditorium. The Jewish Chautauqua is in session there, and as they begin work tomorrow in applied philanthropy, they had as a preparation in thought a sermon from this famous professor and lecturer. Jew and Gentile were there together, the agnostic as well as the philanthropist who bases his work on reason, not religion. Dr. Hirsch speaks to more than Jews. He is one of the eminent students of the world promoting prophecy, and he adds the reputation of oratory to that of a learned man.

"In Chicago he has the chair of semitics for his daily work, and a synagogue for his Sunday task.

"Not on Saturday, but on Sunday, for he is the head of the Jewish idea to have services on the same day of the week as the Gentiles.

"He told me that there were some old people in the church who did not approve of the innovation and for these was held a service on the day they desired to attend.

"After an especially fervid quarter of an hour, the hearer finds by relaxation that his muscles have been as tense as a strung bow.

"His talk is honeycombed with the phrases of the modern university.

"His reasoning smacks strongly of the professional chair.

"His words are those of the purist, almost the pedagogue.

"Yet, he talks directly to his audience, never in the air. Even the few who do not follow him in some moments of sheer learning are made enthusiastic by his impassioned manner of speaking.

"He hesitates not to voice certain sarcasms through the medium of every day pleasantries, and here and there, his patriotism brings every hand in the audience to applause.

"There is a terseness about what he says that catches the ear, complexities of language are too unscholarly for him to permit.

"English, as he uses it, is a study for those who roll wit and wisdom in a slipshod cover. No matter what day or night he preaches, he could command an audience, is the opinion of his friends.

"He has the rare gift of appealing to your mind, and your nerves.

"When he begins to speak, there is a rapid fear that his precise manner and artificially raised voice will detract from what he has to say. As he goes on, the hearer either gets used to the latter or the preacher modifies it. He loses the manner as he warms up. He is more natural when excited.

"He is calm only when he begins. He is never too vehement, but he speaks as one under high pressure. He has much to say, and he has to condense it into a small space. He does not use notes and either his memory or his imagination must be good, for his style is not of the extemporary speaker.

"His phrases are a wit too polished to be accidental. He does not waste words. He never leaves gaps which would be excellent places where he might stop.

"Another good quality is that he knows how to begin.

"Mr. Frank of New York, the manager of the United Hebrew Charities, presented him as a man who needs no introduction at anyone's hands, Dr. Emil G. Hirsch, student, philanthropist, theologian. He replied, by saying as he arose, that it would be a great burden to stand for such titles. Distance lends enchantment to the view and a Chicago professor looks his best from New York.

"Dr. Hirsch looks like a pale, smaller nosed Pierpont Morgan.

"The same eyes, shape of face, and general concentration of gaze when speaking. Probably there is no one he would care less to look like, for one would judge from his talk that the captains of industry do not receive an unqualified approval from this student.

"He is a large man, with iron gray hair that has ceased to grow on top of his head; a full face, somewhat nervous from mental activity; a man of fine constitution, one would judge strongly Semitic in his accent more than his features.

"Nothing could have been more out of the atmosphere than his sermon.

"He called it 'Social Unrest.' It might have been called 'The Problem of the World.'
"He dealt with the strenuous serious work of life, its diseases, the possible cure; the humanities, the wail from the hovels, the responsibility of power and brains.

"As he talked, his voice vibrated with earnestness, as the laughter of the masses flooded through the windows, as the gusts of salt air blew in. Outside, the beach was a moving, writhing, singing, dancing mass of happy human beings. From every point came the crash of human voices raised in merriment.

"The bands played continuously. Some of his most earnest sentences were given to the distant accompaniment of 'Good Morning Carrie' by braying brass instruments.

"Yet the incongruity of it all impressed one only at the beginning.

"The man and what he said held fast, while the other was only a background.

"He first claimed much for theory in answer to what the critics of university, philanthropy, and social work called academic theorizing. He applied Emerson's saying that 'the world was not built on iron and cotton, but on ideas.'

"He finished up with this clear-cut remark, however, that 'the philanthropist should remember into which atmosphere he was taking his lamp.' He often left the direct statements for bits of pure oratory like this:

"'We have put our ear to the body of creation, and listening to the heart beats of time and space, have diagnosed her condition.'

"He spoke well and vehemently on the Jewish question, and the social theory of putting the Jews from the suffocating tenement life to the plow. 'Nothing less than the committing of crime allows the Government to compel a man to do what he doesn't want to do. You can apply philanthropy to persons like ready-made garments. The same trouble results. It is hard to persuade the applicant that the coat fits like a glove.

"'He who deals with humanity must deal humanly' is a wise saying, and that Dr. Hirsch is capable for his task was told by his phrases on wrong doing.

"'Some men are good,' he said, 'because they are irresponsive to temptation. Not a nerve tingles when the serpent smiles. Other men are so high strung that the least smile from a jade of temptation sets the mind vibrating. Each applicant works in averages.'

"Dr. Hirsch made only one quotation from the Bible during his sermon. That, of course, was out of the Old Testament from Isaiah. Yet he gave his hearers a wonderful lesson in well doing.

"The very fact that he doesn't preach philanthropy as a means of personal gain was proved in one of his last remarks. 'None can call it charity to utilize the poor as a stepping stone to Heaven.'"

The Age Of Industrial Unrest

Strikes, labor disputes, and riots, were a source of great anxiety to my father. In the year 1886 the great McCormick Harvester Strike and the riot in Haymarket Square in the city of Chicago occurred. In 1893 there was a large financial panic, causing great misery and unemployment all over the United States. Following this panic, in 1894, there was the vast Pullman Strike.

These industrial disturbances caused Dr. Emil G. Hirsch to preach powerful sermons, during this unsettled era, pertaining to the nature of these disputes.

About 1896, the liberal and reform movement of the late nineteenth century was at its highest pitch.

As a result of these strikes and riots, social reforms were inaugurated.

My father and other leading liberal rabbis and Christian ministers were responsible, in large measure, that these reforms took place. To lighten the lot of the working class, slum clearance, government regulation of the hours and wages of labor, factory safety legislation, compulsory workmen's compensation and insurance laws, the protection of women in industry, the control of child labor, prison reform, improvement in public education, were the major measures considered by the State legislatures of this nation.

Even at that time, Emil G. Hirsch predicted a system of unemployment compensation would go into effect in the not-too-distant future in this land, tiding over a worker laid off from his job through no fault of his own. If a man is willing to work, and is seeking work and cannot find a job, the unemployment compensation system should take care of him. If he is not seeking work, he should be penalized.

We all know this system is in effect in the United States, today, and also in foreign lands.

My father's thinking, in these years, was influenced in large measure by the ideas of men like the noted Episcopal divine William Graham Sumner, who championed the Darwinian doctrine of the survival of the fittest and was a follower of the Manchesterian school of thought.

Emil G. Hirsch admired Sumner as a sociologist, but he was in complete disagreement with Sumner on his theories of the Manchester school of thought.

Dr. Hirsch studied Richard T. Ely's views; Thorstein Veblen; Henry George, the proponent of the single tax; novelists like Edward Bellamy who, in Looking Backward (1888), described a utopian society in which prevailed a full social, economic and political equality; and revolutionary socialists like Johann Most and David DeLeon; and moderate socialists like Eugene Debs.

In his study of history my father perceived, in the middle ages, a society founded on social function and the duty of the individual to contribute his share to the welfare of society.

The individual doctrines of Adam Smith and the Manchester school did not appeal to him. In a sermon on "New Years Reflections," preached in 1895, he stated, "History has judged of Adam Smith's theory; the theory, so brutal, has failed. We are not individuals—we are not made to be individualistic. We are human beings that live in, and with others and through others. History has spoken. What the Middle Ages had, we must have again—the sense of our belonging one to the other. If we have it, the social problem and the social contest lose much of their sharp edge."

My father was a firm believer in the individual rights of man.

In a sermon preached in 1895, entitled, "The Inalienable Duties of Man," he declared: "Can it be denied that the mere doctrine of the rights of man has played into the hands of the selfish? While it has been the lever to lift up a few, it has also, contrary to the hope and confidence of its first coiners, proved a weight to drag down the millions. The bold theory of rights has prospered the capitalist and none other. It has sponsored a new kind of selfishness of which the former ages knew nothing.

"The time is now ripe for man to consider what his responsibilities to society consist of. Human beings have rights to life, liberty and the pursuit of happiness. Such rights cannot be questioned. But men have duties to society, too, which they cannot shirk." Emil G. Hirsch indicated, in no uncertain terms, what these duties were. "If the right to life is inalienable, the duty to make the proper use, thereof, is as emphatically inalienable. The individual is always under the social relation. This is the fulcrum for his lever. Not as he lists, but as the social welfare and his power for social service suggest, must the individual shape his own career. To own the fruit of one's own labor is an inalienable right. To dispose of one's earnings by will and testament may even be included in this category, though some theorists would question the legitimacy of such latitude. Yet, property is our own only to do therewith what shall prosper the common life. The right to possess is limited by the duty to utilize one's own for the social good. Nor is property ever more sacred than humanity. Wherever the right of property clashes with a duty toward humanity, the former has no credentials that are entitled to consideration."

In 1899, at the turn of the century, Emil G. Hirsch reviewed what the years had brought to life. To be sure, suffering, injustice, and poverty, had held sway. The masses were still oppressed, and yet, my father was not discouraged. He felt progress was bound to arrive in the new years of the new century. The present gloom, he insisted, was merely "the darkness before the dawn." In a sermon preached in 1899, entitled, "The Dying Century," he emphasized, "In all Messianic legends the thought is central that the advent is announced by disorganizing and disrupting wars. I, for one, cannot concede that revived nationalism and racial bigotry—of which the Jew above all men have most to dread—portend more than that the day of battle is upon us. The Messianic agony is stirring the depths. The century to come will not belie the promise of our deeper and wider sympathies."

In 1901 Governor Richard Yates appointed Dr. Emil G. Hirsch as a member of the Illinois State Board of Charities, and he served in this capacity also under the administrations of Governors Charles S. Deneen and Frank O. Lowden.

Among many honors bestowed upon him, he was the acting President of The Congress of Liberal Religions. Dr. Hirsch was convocation orator at the commencement exercises of several American Universities. The following honary degrees were conferred upon him: L.L.D. Austin College Illinois, 1898; L.H.D. Western University of Pennsylvania 1900, D.D. Hebrew Union College 1901, D.C.L. Temple University of Philadelphia 1908.

My father was elected a member of the Board of Governors, Hebrew Union College, 1901, and at the installation of Dr. Kaufmann Kohler as President of Hebrew Union College in 1903, he delivered a most scholarly address on this occasion in Cincinnati, Ohio.

To make clear the aims of Reform Judaism of which he was the leading exponent—recognized, as such, both nationally and internationally—he founded a weekly paper, The Reform Advocate, in

1891.

Dr. Emil G. Hirsch was editor of the Bible Department, *Jewish Encyclopedia*, from 1903 to 1906.

In 1902 he was the Percy Trumbull lecturer at Johns Hopkins University in Baltimore. His subject was Jewish poetry.

In 1901 and 1902 I was a student at the well-known Weingart Institute of New York City. I attended, also, the summer school which was housed in a beautiful building, situated in the Catskill Mountains, High Mount, New York. The summer school had a large, open-air swimming pool adjoining their building. Many boys from all over the United States attended this school, including Ernest and Eugene Byfield, of Chicago, with whom I traveled. Their father, Joseph Byfield, proprietor of the Sherman Hotel, accompanied us on our trip to High Mount, New York.

My father visited me at the New York school of the Weingart Institute, in 1902, and he took me with him to Baltimore where, as I mentioned before, he was the Percy Trumbull lecturer at Johns Hopkins University.

I remember visiting the learned Dr. Benjamin Szold, the father of Henrietta Szold, with my father on his Baltimore visit. Rabbi Szold was a very old man at that time. But, nevertheless, the visit of Dr. Emil G. Hirsch gave him great joy and honor.

I remember, too, my father returning to speak from the pulpit of Har Sinai Congregation—his first pulpit charge when he became a Rabbi.

A lad of fifteen at that time, I attended the

synagogue services there. The admiration which the members of Har Sinai Temple showed for the sermon that Emil G. Hirsch preached instilled in me a feeling of great pride.

In 1904, before the Congress of Religions—held at St. Louis, Missouri, at the time of the St. Louis Worlds Fair—Emil G. Hirsch explained the aims of the Jewish Religion before a large and interested audience.

Another speaker on the program was Dr. Felix Adler, head of the Ethical Culture Society of New York. Dr. Adler was a fellow student of my father at the Hochschule fur Die Wisenschaft das Judentums (High School for the Knowledge of Judaism), in Berlin, in 1872.

He was also a son of a distinguished Reform Rabbi, Samuel Adler of Temple Emanuel, New York City. Dr. Felix Adler was ordained as a Reform Rabbi by Dr. Abraham Geiger, but he never followed the profession of a rabbi. Instead, he founded the Ethical Culture Society.

Also, among other fellow students present were Dr. Emanuel Schreiber, and Dr. Samuel Sale of St. Louis. Schreiber, Sale and Hirsch adhered to the tenets of Reform Judaism, which Felix Adler had rejected.

I accompanied my father on this trip to St. Louis, and the beautiful exhibits of technological progress, scientific advancement and literary accomplishment which were unraveled made a deep impression on my young mind. My father and I were guests of Dr. and Mrs. Samuel Sale. Dr. and Mrs. Sale and their lovely family were splendid hosts, and they saw to it that we had a very good time during the week we spent in St. Louis, Missouri.

My father and I heard Dr. Felix Adler's scholarly address at the Congress of Religions, and at the end of his discourse, the two young pupils of former years in Berlin embraced each other warmly.

I remember attending a dinner party given for my father at a famous restaurant at the St. Louis Worlds Fair. Among the guests were: Julius Rosenwald, celebrated Chicago businessman; President William Rainey Harper, of the University of Chicago; and Sigmund Zeisler, leading Chicago attorney.

I was interested, especially, in meeting Dr. Harper as a few months later I became a student of the University of Chicago. My father informed Dr. Harper that I intended to start my college years at this great hall of learning and Dr. Harper was happy to hear this news. At least, I thought so.

My Father's Public Activities

My father took a leading part in public activities from the time he became Rabbi of Chicago Sinai Congregation up to the last years of his life. During the presidential election of 1896 he was an Elector-at-Large for the State of Illinois.

He was instrumental in the founding of the Jewish Manual Training School of Chicago in 1888. He believed children should be taught the importance of the three "H's" in their education—the work of the *Head,* the *Heart,* and the *Hand.* The children of newly arrived Russian Jewish immigrants attended this school located on the West side, and their education and acquired skills were a source of great pleasure and pride to my father. Many future leading citizens in business and the professions graduated from this school.

Professor Gabriel Bamberger—a teacher of note—was the principal of this school until his death, and he was a mighty influence in shaping the characters of his pupils so that they should become future upright citizens of Chicago.

My father was a founder of the Associated Jewish Charities of Chicago—an organization dedicated to the downtrodden—to help them get jobs, to give them courage and self respect, and instill new hope into their souls.

My father was interested in the advancement of Jewish women's organizations. He assisted Mrs. Hannah G. Solomon in founding the National Council of Jewish Women at the time of the Columbian Exposition of 1893, in Chicago.

He admired Mrs. Solomon's organizing skills, her charm of manner and keen interest in cultural affairs; and the energetic, enthusiastic ladies with whom she surrounded herself. For example, Miss Sadie American, who became the first Secretary of the National Council of Jewish Women. In later years my own sister, Mrs. Gerson B. Levi, was President of the Chicago Council of the National Council of Jewish Women's organizations, and she presided over the meetings of the organization in a most exemplary manner and with much finesse.

In 1915 my father founded the Chicago Sinai Temple Sisterhood, and in its more than fifty years of existence, it has done much good work and has been an influential factor, along with other sisterhoods, in its city and nation.

The question was once asked my father if he objected to women adopting the profession of rabbi. At that time women began entering the professional ranks, such as Law, Medicine, Architecture and Engineering. He replied, "There is no objection to a woman occupying the Jewish pulpit, but if a woman adopts the career of rabbi, she must adopt the obligations of men in scholarship and earnestness. Maudlin emotionalism, and faithful imitation of clericalism, will not be accepted as a substitute for sound scholarship and a thorough familiarity with the literature and philosophy of the Jews."

Sinai Temple was the first Jewish pulpit to offer its platform to a woman. The first honor was given to Jane Addams; and the second, in 1897, to Hannah G. Solomon. A newspaper account of the appearance of Mrs. Solomon, in his pulpit, described the novel event as follows:

"Mrs. Hannah G. Solomon filled the pulpit of Sinai Temple yesterday morning. It could have happened in no Jewish Temple but Dr. Hirsch's, and the congregation predicts that the incident will put it further from orthodoxy than any other innovation which it has been its pride to make. It makes Sinai and its leader the talk of the Hebrew world. There was not a vacant seat in the gallery or elsewhere. There did not seem to be a voice from the congregation—save one of praise."

In 1887 Mayor John P. Hopkins appointed Dr. Hirsch a member of the Chicago Public Library Board, and he served nine years as a member of this board.

He was President of the Chicago Public Library Board when it was decided to build the present building on Randolph and Michigan Avenue. He was the principal speaker when the cornerstone of this edifice was laid.

When the University of Chicago was founded in 1891, President William Rainey Harper asked my father to become a member of the first faculty as Professor of Rabbinical Literature and Philosophy. Dr. Emil G. Hirsch accepted this position gladly. It gave him the opportunity to teach, and it cemented a life-long friendship with Dr. Harper, who, in addition to his other talents, was also a great Hebrew scholar.

During the years when my father was a member of the faculty of the University of Chicago, he was the convocation orator when the cornerstone of many of the new buildings were laid.

My father took a leading part in getting contributions from members of his congregation and others so that the great educational work of this school of learning should be developed most fully. He was active in the securing of contributions of $400,000—on the raising of which, John D. Rockefeller's initial subscription of $600,000 was donated.

The great merchant prince, Leon Mandel, who also was Vice President of Chicago Sinai Congregation, gave $85,000 to the University of Chicago. Leon Mandel Assembly Hall was named after him. In years to come Julius Rosenwald, a great humanitarian, who also served as a Vice President of Chicago Sinai Congregation, gave millions to the University of Chicago. Rosenwald Hall is named after him.

Both of these philanthropists acknowledged Dr. Emil G. Hirsch's influence on them in the giving of their wealth. Julius Rosenwald asserted that he gave $50,000 to the Hebrew Union College in Cincinnati, in 1908, at the suggestion of Rabbi Emil G. Hirsch.

In addition to his civic activities, during the years of the Twentieth Century, my father was an arbitrator in a national coal strike, a streetcar strike, and one of the arbitrators in the settlement that Hart, Schaffner and Marx made with their workers.

At the Columbian Exposition of 1893, held in Chicago, my father played a prominent role in the deliberations of the Congress of Religions. He was chairman of the first meeting. Eminent divines of all faiths attended these sessions. Noteworthy gatherings took place. A Jewish denominational congress was founded.

In response to the address of welcome given by C. S. Bonney, President of the World's Congress Auxiliary of the Exposition, under whose auspices all the Denominational Congresses were held, Dr. Hirsch said, "This hour, on the one hand, is a willingly accorded recognition—not that it is marvelous that in this country over which floats the emblem of religious liberty, the Jews should be given the permission to witness before the world to the faith that is within them—it is self evident under the principles upon which American society and civilization have been reared. Not this, then fills us with joy—that we may, without trammel, tell the world at large of our aspirations; of the foundation upon which rests our ideas—but that the world should now recognize us not as a nation among the nations, not as a race among the races, not as a people among the people, but as a religion among religions. It is that which wings in this hour our soul to bold flight." Dr. Hirsch concluded his remarks by saying, "We are glad of this opportunity to invite the world to the secrets of our faith and the ultimate tendency of our hopes, and we shall be glad that when men have heard us, they shall say, 'Why you Jews are not different from us; you are men as we are; your hopes are our hopes; your beliefs are our beliefs.' And why should the world not say this, 'Have we not all one Father? Has not one God created us all?'"

At the closing session of the Parliament of Religions a most dramatic incident occurred. The head of the Eastern Church, the Archbishop of Zante, came to this meeting clothed in his priestly vestments. My father introduced the venerable Archbishop to the audience. The Archbishop of Zante spoke as follows: "Most honorable ladies and gentlemen, I am not a Jew—I am a Christian—a profound believer of the truth of the Gospel. I am always bound to defend the truth, and for this reason, I present a paper here tonight."

The Archbishop requested that Professor Albion W. Small, of the University of Chicago, read his paper. Here are the contexts of Archbishop Zante's message: "In the East the belief is current among the ignorant masses of the population that the Jews use, for purposes of religious rites, the blood of Christian children, and in order to procure such blood, do not shrink from committing murder. In consequence of this belief, outbreaks against the Jews are frequent, and the innocent victims are subjected to many indignities and exposed to great danger. In view of the fact that such erroneous ideas are also current among the ignorant of other countries—and during the last decade both Germany and Austria were the scene of trials of innocent Jews under the accusation of having committed such ritual murder—I, as a Christian Minister, ask this Congress to record our convictions that Judaism forbids murder of any kind, and that none of its sacred authorities and books commands or permit murder or the use of human blood for ritual practices or religious ceremonies. The circulation of such slander, against the adherents of a Monotheistic faith, is un-Christian. The origin of calumny must be traced to the Roman conceit—that early Christians used human blood in their religious observances. It is not consonant with Christian duty to allow this horrible charge to go unrebuked, and is so in the interest of Christianity's good repute that I ask this parliament to declare that Judaism and the Jews are innocent of the imputed crime, as were the Christians of the first century."

My father wrote an editorial in The Reform Advocate concerning the Archbishop's address. "The venerable Archbishop of Zante is entitled to the thanks of all Jews and Christians alike, and none who witnessed the scene when the prelate, at the conclusion of the reading of his paper, lifted up his hands toward Heaven and broke out in the solemn words, 'Standing before God Almighty, I declare this humble charge to be sinister,' will ever forget the remarkable incident or not deem it the fortune of his life to have been present."

Dr. Emil G. Hirsch preached a sermon from the Sinai pulpit on the significance of the World

Parliament of Religion. He stated eloquently, "God's truth is like a ray of the sun, broken by the prismatic medium and spread into the glowing tints of the rainbow. Each line stands for a certain element in the one thread of light that passed through the medium. Each line, therefore, has its own beauty. This was the fundamental thought of the Parliament of Religion—not for conversion, not for controversy, but for cooperation did they meet together. The representatives of the most different creeds were invited to witness their faith and voice their message. The Parliament of Religions—unique in the history, of the world—will not pass away without lasting effects. It is, of course, too much to expect that seventeen days undo what in seventeen centuries has been produced; that overnight the seeds of prejudices and bigotry be uprooted. But the seed has been cast, and soon, here and there, a voice will be heard pleading for the higher and nobler religion of humanity; for a union of men and women, made all in the image of God, pilgrimaging up the heights toward the last peak, when God's glory will be seen as a glory unknown to the Temples erected on the lower levels.

"This was the crowning glory of the Exposition this year—that Buddhist and Mohammedan, that Hindu and Chinese met with Jew and Christian, of different beliefs themselves, and under one roof testified to the mystery of the one Father whose greatest blessing to man is the thought that all men are made in His image; and therefore are brothers. Though this session cannot have come and gone without lasting blessings, may we then—remembering the inspiring sights when the buildings shall have disappeared, and when the last vestige of beauty shall be swept away—treasure beyond and underneath the external, the materially marvelous, this eternal and internal miracle—the principle for which, and of which, this exposition was the outward monument.

"Prometheus freed, because slavery is no longer in this world. Prometheus unbound, because competition is no longer the fetish, but cooperation the sacred duty. Prometheus, God-like and God-blest, because in all climes and in all creeds, in all lands and in all liturgies, the grand anthem chanted by him is of the dignity of man, in which is proclaimed the Glory of God."

In the following year after the Parliament of Religions was founded, the first American Congress of Liberal Religious Societies was convened at Sinai Temple, in Chicago, on May 22-25, 1894. My father sent out a letter stating the purpose of the meetings:

"Believing in the great law and life of love, and desiring a nearer and more helpful fellowship in the social, educational, industrial, moral and religious thought and work of the world, the undersigned unite in calling an American Congress of Liberal Religious Societies, and such other churches and organizations of any name as may be willing to recognize a common duty and to work in the spirit of kinship herein indicated."

The Call To Temple Emanuel

On February 12, 1896 Dr. Emil G. Hirsch was one of the chief speakers, along with Senator Chauncey M. Depew of New York, at the Abraham Lincoln Banquet, held in New York City by the Republican Club of New York. On that occasion my father delivered an eloquent oration on Abraham Lincoln. He said:

"One is safe to maintain that today-four score years and seven after his advent, and more than three decades after his ascension to glory—Abraham Lincoln belongs to no one state. In the flesh the son of one nation, in the spirit he is proudly acclaimed, and his memory is treasured as a priceless inspiration by all humanity. The whole earth is a willing pedestal to his fame, and the best and noblest of all nations asks for the privilege to garland afresh, every year, his memorial in their hearts. The memory of such a man is a veritable sun, giving light and warmth to the habitation of all men on the spinning globe.

"But at the same time, nowhere is its radiancy more deeply known and prized than in the places that knew him when, in mortal clay, he went in and out among men.

"It was in Illinois where he challenged his great rival for the Senatorial toga to the tournament—the like of which no minstrel ever sung—in which the chivalry of ancient days had a resurrection in the noble deportment of the two contestants, while the sparks that flew from their steel aroused the nation from its indifference and prepared it for the inevitable conflict. It was in Illinois that the defeated aspirant for a seat in the American Areopagus was named to be the banner bearer of the young but earnest Republican host. It was from Illinois that he set out to assume the high duties of his high destiny—to guide the nation through the fiery flames of war that the Union might be preserved, to stand guard over the patrimony of Washington; and a second Moses—with the sweep of his pen to strike the shackles of slavery from millions of human beings. It was to Illinois that his consecrated dust was carried back after he had fallen. The people of Illinois feel that much distinction the ownership and trusteeship of such a memory inspires, and entails higher obligation. Peace, in a democracy, calls for as loyal soldiers of duty as did the war; deserters and bounty jumpers are out of place in the army corps gathered to defend the Flag of Freedom. Political indifference and apathy, and patriotism for revenue only, are the civil equivalence for—what the vocabulary of the camp designates as—shirkers and bounty jumpers.

"But politics is a muddy business. Political indifference of many has made it so. Lincoln, too, was a politician. In a republic every citizen must be a politician. Public business is his business. If he refuses to make it so, let him not complain if those who have no private business turn public affairs into private concerns of their own for their own gain and profit exclusively. But politics is partisan. Yet, Lincoln was both a partisan and a purist; such partisanship as was his is the highest co-efficient of patriotism. Without party antagonism and discussion, stagnation of thought will ensue. Winds must blow from different points that life be sustained on earth. The Republican Party has demonstrated its right to be, by its achievements sponsored by such men as Fremont, Lincoln, Washburn, Seward, and Chase. It has spread strong and broad the foundations of national industrial independence and national financial integrity. We believe that Republicanism is a matter of principle, first—a question of persons and places only in so far as, through persons in office, these principles are made effective."

At the conclusion of his address my father received a tumultuous ovation. The New York newspapers, morning and evening editions, carried headlines concerning the Chicago Rabbi's great speech on the life of the great commoner—the immortal Abraham Lincoln.

At this time, Temple Emanuel of New York, the largest Reform synagogue in America, was looking for a successor to their senior rabbi who was about to retire.

This great Lincoln Day speech focused nation-wide attention on my father. Immediately, the trustees of this most influential Reform Temple felt they should obtain the services of this outstanding orator and scholar as their minister. Here was a rabbi who, they maintained, by the force of his eloquence, fearlessness, independent thinking, could draw large audiences to their synagogue just as he had done at Sinai Temple, in the city of Chicago. Of course, Dr. Emil G. Hirsch's reputation as a leading Reform minister of their faith was known to them even before his Lincoln address or his recent appearance before their Temple as a speaker.

Accordingly, a committee composed, among others, of Jacob H. Schiff, Louis Marshall, and the Guggenheims, wrote a letter in behalf of Temple Emanuel, extending the call to become their Senior Rabbi. My father felt honored to have been chosen to become the leader of America's largest congregation, and he accepted the call.

His salary was to be larger than that which he received at Chicago Sinai Congregation, and his election was for a ten-year term.

When Chicago Sinai Congregation heard that their beloved Rabbi had accepted the call to become the Senior Rabbi of Temple Emanuel in New York, they were dumb-founded. Dr. Emil G. Hirsch's nineteen years of devoted service in their midst had made Chicago Sinai Congregation one of the leading Reform Congregations in the land.

His pleas for righteous living, and ethical mandates of upright conduct, had made a deep impression among them throughout these distinguished years in their presence, and they determined to make a mighty effort to have Emil G. Hirsch ask Temple Emanuel to release him from his contract with them.

The University of Chicago joined them in their appeal, and the Chicago newspapers and civic organizations also asked my father to remain in Chicago. The newspapers added that too many leading ministers of different faiths had accepted calls to continue their spiritual work in other cities. Chicago could not afford to have Hirsch leave the city.

Chicago Sinai Congregation held an important meeting. A membership drive under the direction of Leon Mandel, Vice President of Chicago Sinai Congregation, and President Albert W. Fishell, and leading members of the Board of Chicago Sinai Congregation, such as, Harry Hart, Adolph Loeb, Joseph L. Gatzert, and Leo Fox, started the campaign for an increased membership; and as a result many new members joined Chicago Sinai Congregation.

Dr. Emil G. Hirsch was elected a Rabbi for life and was asked to stay.

My father was touched deeply by these tokens of esteem; and he decided to remain.

Accordingly, most reluctantly, Temple Emanuel of New York released him from his contract with them. Years later, at a White House Conference, President Theodore Roosevelt said to my father, "You should have come to New York."

The White House Conference

In 1908 my father received the following message from President Theodore Roosevelt:

> "The White House
> Washington, D.C
> December 25, 1908

I have received a letter of which I enclose a copy together with a statement of the official positions of the persons who signed it, and a memorandum which is suggested for consideration and action if the conference which the letter suggests be held. I am confident that you will be impressed with the very great importance of the subject touched on, in this letter, and the desirability that there should be the fullest discussion of the propositions—a memorandum of which I enclose. Surely nothing ought to interest our people more than the care of the children who are destitute and neglected, but not delinquent.
Personally, I very earnestly believe that the best way in which to care for dependent children

is in the family home. In Massachusetts many orphan asylums have been discontinued and thousands of children, who have formerly gone to the orphans asylum, are now kept in private homes—either on board with payment from public or private treasurers, or in adopted homes provided by the generosity of foster parents. Many religious bodies have, within the past ten years, organized effective child-placing agencies.

I am, accordingly, inviting a number of men and women—a list of whom I will announce—to a conference to be held in Washington, January 25th and 26th. The conference will open by my receiving the members at the White House, January 25th, at 2:30 P.M.; can you attend? Will you please communicate with Mr. James E. West, 1343 Clifton Street N. W., Washington, D.C.

Sincerely yours,
Theodore Roosevelt"

My father was invited to this conference in his capacity as Rabbi of Chicago Sinai Congregation, a member of the Board of Commissioners of Charities of Illinois, and Vice President of the Jewish Home Finding Society of Chicago. The topic assigned to him was "The Home Versus the Institution by Rabbi Emil G. Hirsch, President of the National Conference of Jewish Charities." The address was delivered at a Public Session, at the New Willard Hotel, on Monday, January 25th, 1909. The Chairman introduced Rabbi Hirsch, as follows: "The subject of the next address is 'The Home Versus the Institution, by Rabbi Emil G. Hirsch.' Dr. Hirsch said, in part:

"Mr. Chairman, ladies and gentlemen.
Of different religious beliefs, of various political creeds, and perhaps members of different economic and philosophical schools, yet are we all united by the magic powers of certain convictions basic to our meeting here; to the effect that if it is worthwhile to conserve the natural resources of our country, it is a thousand times more important to conserve the children of our nation." (Applause) "The weak are the true barometer indicative of the altitude attained by the race. Not the regard had for, and respect paid the strong, but the consideration shown, and the anxiety manifested, in behalf of the weak, reflect the true glory of a nation's might and reveal the distance that separates it from barbarism. This view is not in accordance with a philosophy, at present, much in favor; according to which, this world is planned to be the home of the strong alone. The weak—this is the gist of Nietzche's reasoning—ought to take pride in the thought that they serve for pedestals to the few predestined for strength. They have not been silent, who, appealing to the misapplied catchwords of Darwinism, have deplored the sentimentality of these late-born generations, evoking to its disadvantage the under determination of—if more primitive, yet also more robust—tribes that without false pity exterminated the weak and superfluous. If we draw one lesson from this fanaticism of the prophets of the church of the strong, it is that our efforts must be directed to enlarge the chances of the weak to grow to be

strong.

"Human weakness is of many degrees and infinite variety. Our concern, today, is for that weakness which is incidental to childhood and results from circumstances in the creation of which the children certainly had no share.

"The State, too often, has taken cognizance of abandoned children only after dependency has turned into delinquency, and in the more advanced communities modern methods have been energized in dealing with the young who have come into conflict with society's will, embodied in law and statute. The States that have not risen to the understanding of the difference between juvenile delinquency and adult confirmed criminality are still very uncomfortably numerous.

"Moreover, neither the churches nor the private and public philanthropies that held out the helping hand to the neglected and orphaned children, made well divided and concerted efforts to study the problem in all of its complex bearings. Institutions represent the line of least resistance.

"But in morals the line of least resistance is never the first, but always the last that ought to be chosen. Childhood is too sacred a possession and too mighty a potentiality to be handled on the ready-made plan. The best of institutions, after all, must neglect individual differences. They cannot take account of personalities. They deal with inmates, and inmates necessarily fall into the nondescript devitalized state of a number.

"I shall not weigh, in this connection, the importance attached to institutions to the per capita. They have had dealings with public and, for that matter, with private charitable institutions, and need not be reminded of the fatal role the per capita plays in their administration. Better methods, indicated by the progress of medicine and pedagogy, are shown no toleration when their adoption is at all likely to increase the per capita.

"A low per capita is the fetish and obsession of the superintendents and legislatures, and even private institutions suffer from blind worship at the shrine of this idol. To keep the per capita at the lowest figure possible, large population is coveted and invited.

"At all events the institution segregates its inmates. But segregation of the young into a class is always beset with peril to their morality.

"How easily institutions become foci of moral, or rather immoral, contamination, educators need not be told. Of this I shall not speak at length, as elaboration is superfluous.

"But attention should be given the injury wrought the soul of a sensitive child by the consciousness, constantly vivified by institutional life and discipline, that he is other than are all the children outside the institution grounds. He is uprooted *devacine*, as the French have it, and placed in surroundings where he is not expected to strike roots anew; though in the better asylums of this land, therefore, this form has been discarded, and thus their wards are spared the humiliation which custom persists in exacting from orphans in Amsterdam, where many girls may be seen walking the streets in garments of many colors designating their wearer as one of the beneficiaries of public bounty.

"Institutional life for the young would be less objectionable if society at large were institutionalized. Asylums and orphanages, of necessity, are organized on a plan which is not that of the world, which, sooner or later, their protégés have to re-enter.

"As now constituted, the basic rock on which society rests is the home. The family is the structural cell. It seems thus a very queer proceeding first to unhome the young when later they will have to do their part in a society founded on the home and rooted in the family. This expedient may appeal to theorists alone, who have come to regard the family as the Upas Tree, abundant in the fruit of selfishness. From the days of Sparta to them, many voices have been heard in laudation of systems fatal to the family spirit and devised to neutralize it.

"If there is one certainty, it is this; that the family is the direct outcome of nature's own planning to secure the safety and growth of the child. Man stands in need of maternal care much longer than any other animal. This dependency of the child upon the mother forced, in course of the ages, man to adopt the family and to adapt himself to it. Students of the history of marriage are agreed on this. The helplessness of the child, entailing upon the mother for a long continued period duties to her offspring, and their stimulating ever anew the maternal instinct, reacted upon the father. It served to endow with permanency the relations subsisting between him and the mother.

"That the home and not the institution is the normal environment for children, they have recognized, who have made strong efforts to modify the institutional policies, with a view to approximately reproducing the conditions of home surroundings for the dependent children. The cottage plan was devised to meet the shortcoming of the preceding institutional methods; that it was a step forward is well assured. But even it is not free from the objections that lie against the institutional device. In the first place, the cottage as a rule is not a reproduction of the home. Families of over thirty children are certainly exceptional. Again, in the cottage, as a rule the sexes are segregated, and that for good reasons; and indeed the children are classified according to age, numbers of this artificial family being selected for living together on account of correspondence of age.

"The normal family does not segregate the sexes nor does it classify by the age line. In some of the institutions that I have knowledge of, this defect has been remedied. In the Asylum for Soldiers' Orphans, at Normal, Illinois, one of the charities of the State of Illinois, the families are so constituted as to comprise children of all ages. But even then, the number constituted the various cottage households is by far in excess of the normal, and dormitories with 25 to 35 beds are a poor substitute for the privacy and intimacy of the bedroom in a natural family. If the cottage plan is to be continued, this is clear; the household must be multiplied and the families reduced in number. Otherwise, the defects of institutionalism and its artificiality cannot be eradicated.

"The home plan, of course, does not work automatically. The placing of the child in the home is only the first step. Supervision through guardians and by agents of the State is the close second. In Illinois the State Board of Charities is empowered by statute to inspect and visit, through agents appointed for this purpose, the homes where children have been placed. The legislature, however, has not appropriated sufficient funds to carry on the work on an extended scale.

"Furthermore, the State Board of Charities must pass upon the character of any society organized for home finding before the charter is issued by the Secretary of State, and when a certificate is granted, it is for one year, renewal depending upon the favorable judgment of the board. In this way, exploitation of children, and the raids by selfish men and women on the community under pretense of finding homes for dependent children, are circumvented.

"The State, however, in my opinion, should be entrusted only with the general supervision of all the societies engaged in this work and with the duty of visitation of such homes where children have been placed by county authorities.

"More difficult are the cases where dependency is the result of abandonment or of parental viciousness and immorality. But, again, most cases of abandonment are due to wife desertion. Let the mother be aided to keep the family together under the same precautions as to guardians and visitations as have been outlined in the case of dependency due to the death of the parent. 'Out of the mouths of babes,' sings the old Hebrew poet, 'Thou hast established strength.' Yea, the degree of civilization which a nation may boast of, is never higher than that which is indicated by the strength established out of the mouths of babes. 'What Ye do to the least of these you have done for me.' This is true today as it was when it was uttered by the great Jewish lover of children whose love made radiant the hilltops of Palestine in days of yore.

It is my opinion that the line of least resistance has been too largely followed in this work. Institutions were created, and they represent to my mind the line of least resistance. But in morality the line of least resistance is the last one to be chosen and not the first to be followed.

"Institutions may be necessary, and when they are necessary, they are necessary for the child whose parents are still living as well as those who are dependent; but the institution should only be invoked for the dependent child in cases where even if nondependent, they would be asked to receive them. In all the other cases I think the family life is the natural life. It is the life which nature has decreed through its evolution; it is that form of life in which the human species can best develop." (Applause) "One other thing is generally forgotten. Who can look into the soul of a child? Many children are indifferent to the fact that they are set apart from the others, but there may be children who are touched and tortured to the quick by the thought that they are different from all other children. Children I saw in Amsterdam—and many of you may have seen them—children of a public orphanage, parading the streets in garments of an historic mold and make; and those children, by their uniforms, were set apart from all other children. While some of the girls seemed to enjoy the distinction, some of the eyes of those that paraded the streets in those uniforms were wet with tears and their cheeks were suffused with blushes. The delicate sentiments of the child were injured by the very fact that he had become an object of exhibition—a sort of public recipient of public benevolence.

"Is it possible to give to the dependent children, family life? It is.

"Fifty percent of the dependent children are half orphans where the mother is still spared to the child. No mother will give up her child willingly. Every mother will keep her child—every good mother, and most mothers are good—provided the economic burden is lifted from her shoulders. The mother being alive, the home is ready without any need to look elsewhere. The home is there. Of course the mother alone may not be sufficient. Then appoint for every child a guardian, and not a guardian necessarily appointed by the court or by some institution.

"We have to preserve the family as the cornerstone of society. At two ends, family life seems to be in danger at the top of what is called society, and at the bottom. At the top we have departmental life, or flat life as it is significantly called, and it is flat life leading to a shirking of the responsibilities of maternity and paternity.

"At the bottom, home life is in danger in the lower strata of society. Let a law be passed making the tenement house impossible. Give to those who have children to rear a real home, and my plan will enable you to do this. Let us give to the dependent children what we gave to our children, in all cases where it is possible—the family life. For the great lover of childhood, whose life made radiant the hilltops of Palestine, has said, 'Whatsoever you have done unto one of the least of these, you have done it unto me.'"

The Two-Hundred and Fiftieth Anniversary of Jews in America

The Jews came to the United States in the year 1655. Their first settlement was in New York City. The two-hundred and fiftieth anniversary of their coming to this country was celebrated appropriately in all the large cities of the United States.

Many leading Christians, as well as Jews, joined in these festivities.

President Theodore Roosevelt sent a letter to the New York City Meeting held at Carnegie Hall, Thanksgiving Day, November 30, 1905. It was addressed to Jacob H. Schiff, Esq., Chairman of the meeting, and in his letter President Roosevelt said, "The celebration of the two hundred and fiftieth anniversary of the settlement of the Jews of the United States properly emphasizes a series of historical facts of more than merely national significance. Even in our colonial period, the Jews participated in the upbuilding of this country, acquired citizenship, and took an active part in the development of foreign and domestic commerce. During the revolutionary period they aided the cause of liberty by serving in the Continental Army, and by substantial contributions to the empty treasury of the infant Republic. During the Civil War thousands served in the armies and mingled their blood with the soil for which they fought. I am glad to be able to say, in addressing you on this occasion, that while the Jews of the United States who now number more than a million have remained loyal to their faith and their traditions, they have become indissolubly incorporated in the great army of American Citizenship—prepared to make all sacrifices for the country, either in war or peace, and striving for the perpetuation of a good government, and for the maintenance of the principles embodied in our institution."

Former President Grover Cleveland delivered an address at this meeting. He said, "We join, today, in the celebration of the two-hundred and fiftieth anniversary of the settlement of the Jews in the United States. This event created such an important epoch in our country's development, and its relationship to our nation's evolution is so clearly seen in the light of present conditions, that every thoughtful American citizen must recognize the fitness and usefulness of its commemoration.

"What our Jewish fellow citizens have done to increase the material advancement of the United States, is apparent on every hand and must stand confessed. But the best and highest Americanism is something more than materialistic.

"On this higher plane of our nationality and in the atmosphere of ennobling sentiment we also feel the touch of Jewish relationship. If the discovery of America prophesied the coming of our nation and fixed the place of its birth, let us not forget that Columbus, on his voyage in search of a new world, was aided in a most important way by Jewish support and comradeship."

The Chicago meeting was held at Sinai Temple.

Judge Julian W. Mack delivered an address on "The Pledge of The American Jew." He said, in part: "Grateful are we that a haven of rest was found in this United States for the Jew. Grateful is the Puritan himself, persecuted as we were, that a similar haven was found for him here, and grateful is the Catholic that he too was permitted to settle on these shores when he was driven by fanaticism from countries of Europe. We Jews, settled here for two hundred and fifty years, need not bow our heads in thanks to, need not crawl before any man in America. We stand here the equal of all of them, with as much right, purchased in the same way by the blood of our ancestors in every war through which this country passed, as does the descendant of the Puritan and the Cavalier. The Jews of America are true American citizens in the full sense. Every call of their country have they answered with their treasure and their blood, and every call the country may hereafter make will they answer in exactly the same measure, to say little, as their fellow citizens."

Then my father delivered a brilliant oration.

The Concordance Of Judaism And Americanism

Where the Canadian Pacific, that mighty miracle of modern man's daring and doing, winds its ever narrowing embrace of steel arms around the giant frame and then the snow-hooded brow of the mountain sentries mounting the guard over the Rockies' midcontinental bastion, the wondering traveler wheeled along this imperial highway's upward coil in dramatic suddenness is brought face to face with one of the most striking exhibitions of Nature's curious capriciousness.

However much he may have been impressed with the defiant boldness that reckoned not the menace of the roaring canyons over which bridge and span are thrown in proud unconcern, or with the stupendous assumption of security that holds in contempt the perils of precipices along which the roadbed skirts with tenacious grit; when at the great divide he notices how the chance interval of a hairsbreadth between the peak's wrinkles determines the direction of the water rills and the leaping cascades, he is stirred to reflection as by no other observation.

Twin children of the clouds, cradled in one nursery, the raindrops are here bidden separate. One rushes on to his destiny, meeting in his descent the morning's sun, the other hastens to his goal in the van of the evening's approach. Spun on the same loom, one silvery ribbon unwinds its broadening folds until they are tangled in the Atlantic's mightier nettings; the other unbobbins its stretching lengths to festoon the slopes inclining toward the Pacific. Though he know the law which compels one of heaven's tears to seek its grave in the birth chamber of the day-star, and the other to hasten to its funeral in advance of the sinking sun, at the impressive recognition of the phenomenon in the concrete, the observant witness is involuntarily oppressed by the consciousness that similar "accidents" determine the direction of men's gropings, and enforce divergency of paths leading to different and widely separated destinies.

But this depressing obsession soon yields to the inspiring certainty that only in the seeming, whim and chance preside over the allotting of our fortune. Closer attention to the intention which underlies Nature's dividing decree soon will reveal that underneath the superficial divergence is operative concordance of duty.

Both waterdrops that at the line must part from each other, are commissioned to one and the same task. It is theirs to coax forth flowers, to fertilize field and forest. Both are messengers and ministers of life. And again when they shall have reached their respective goals, be it the sea which laps the Eastern shores or that which sings the lullaby to the Western States, the miracle of the resurrection which awaits them will wing both alike to new upward flight and on the heights their divided destinies will finally converge.

Seemingly doomed to eternal separation, snowflakes and dewdrops that part company at the divide are foreordained to identity of obligation.

Thus, when closer analysis unfolds this ethical purpose, which, cloaked or clear, is always fundamental in the Universe and which is never dissipated even when the factoring process seems to reduce the all to incoherent fragments, caprice of division is at once lifted to the potency of planned appointment.

Accident under this view takes on the consecration of vocation. Differences are blotted out in the recognition that they are means to an end, and in the prevision of this end, divergence of paths sinks out of sight, while identity of responsibility, which neutralizes all variance of direction, looms up large.

Name the watersheds which force division and divergence upon men what you will, race, religion, nationality, at the great divide the space which separates is infinitesimal. These channels through which humanity runs on to its goal are means to a common end. On all of them that along these divergent paths apparently tend apart in contrary directions, one common burden is imposed. Theirs is the equality of function under the variety and difference of equipment. Like the river systems draining into different oceans, the various and differently endowed components of humanity are appointed to fill earth with life, ever enriching and deepening and broadening. This conception reconciles diversity with unity. It sees in the polychrome spectrum only unfolding white light.

Little dower of imagination, I hold, is competent to apply the pathos and poetry of the watershed's influence upon the direction of the raindrop's ambition, to the symphonic theme of this memorial day's chorus. At first hearing, its jubilant notes seem to carry the invitation to remember differences. It is the landing of Jews that it commemorates. It seems to emphasize those distinctions that set off the Jew from his neighbor. Or, again, if stress be laid on the country's name whose hospitality these earliest immigrants of Jewish origin claimed, the intention of our synagogical celebration may be misunderstood, as planned to throw on the screen the peculiarities of American Israel, enlarged out of all proportion, and thus invigorate the American Jew's insistence upon being accorded a distinct position of his own in the common household of Israel.

But give this day's jubilee overture a second hearing! If it be true—and it is—that man is microcosmic reproduction of the Universe's macrocosmos, then it is equally beyond all doubt that in the plan of God, nations and peoples are called to be microcosmic illustrations of the plan of the macrocosmic humanity. To the American nation was assigned task and opportunity to exemplify essential unity, notwithstanding the influence of the various watersheds at which the lines of descent diverge. Almost all the races of the planet have made this land their trysting ground.

Hither they have brought the best and strongest which it was theirs to develop. Religion in this country, re-enacts the Pentacostal outpouring; the flaming tongues that token of the spirit, speak their message in varied tones and widely differing dialects. Social customs, the ripples from many distant sources, give color and mobility to home and exclusive circles. Even in press and on the platform, in our streets and villages, the confusion of languages is documented. This exceeding abundance of variety constitutes one of the secrets of this nation's nervous vitality. Apparent discordance results under the consecration of patriotism ineffective harmony.

True, this morning's festal reveille stirs to glad reflection only a little more than one of the eighty millions of God's children that call America mother or spouse. Yet, it is not in conflict with, nay, it is in confirmation of America's distinctive genius that the commemorative occasion addresses its call to one alone of its many components and contributors. *E pluribus unum* formulates a truth, radiantly visible in the vision of this day. By rejoicing as Jews we are accentuating our Americanism.

And in similar manner the pride of our Americanism which possesses our heart and is yearning for expression today, is not a protest against, it is a proclamation of our fidelity to our Judaism. Like America, Judaism has been appointed to pattern the richer diversities of polychrome human life. Its aspects are many; its vocalizations numerous. Catholic Israel wears neither the uniform of military barracks nor the livery of the penitentiary. It is Joseph's coat of many colors. This continent has augmented the prophecies and proclamations of Judaism by another variation. This new articulation again is not rigid. It is vital and therefore flexible. In this, its elasticity and vitality, American Judaism only conforms to the historic plasticity of Pan-Judaism and carries it out to fuller productivity.

It looks like an accident that we were, directed at the watershed Americanward, while millions of brothers were sent into Russia. To our lot fell American citizenship, to theirs slave service in the house of bondage more oppressive than ever was Mizraim. But that "accident" signifies duty. In emphasizing now our Americanism, we vow to be true all the more devotedly to the obligation that our Judaism imposes.

In fact, he is ignorant of the implications of Americanism and Judaism both, who would hold that between them towers a mountain range decreeing and enforcing their divergent separation. The contrast, not to say conflict, between them, I know, is commonly summarized in the statement that America names the civilization of hopeful prospect, Judaism that of regretful retrospect. The latter is a tearful memory, the former a joyful anticipation. Tradition is Judaism's store; outlook, America's strength. No more arrogant misconception was ever coined than this artfully pointed antithesis. Judaism is, if anything, the one religion of impatient prospect and ecstatic prevision of the unborn tomorrow. America has its traditions as clearly determinative as are the influences of the past that anchor Judaism to its historic moorings. The traditions of America reach back further than the discovery of the continent. Our jurisprudence is grounded on the old common law of England. And in these precolonial traditions, which have been among the most prolific stimuli of American thought, conduct, and character, Judaism has had a dominant part.

In the Mayflower, our Bible crossed the Atlantic. At Plymouth Rock in sober reality the Pentateuch was recognized as one of the inspirations of the young commonwealth. The Puritans were, indeed, more Hebraic than were the Jews who landed thirty-six years later. Narrow were they, but their narrowness was ransomed by their strength. Serious were they, but their seriousness dowered them with the fortitude without which none may hope to yoke untamed nature to his purposes. Puritan Hebrewism alone enabled the Pilgrims to exercise dominion over the wilds of their new home. This Puritan spirit was nursed at the breast of Jewish literature. It was the gift laid by old Judaism into the cradle of this new civilization. It had share in preparing the advent of the era of independence, as in the thinking of the men that later phrased our political documents undoubtedly Old Testament principles had had determinating influence.

One who can pierce through verbal husk to inner kernel can harbor no doubt on the essential concordance of Americanism and Judaism. The stronger the Jew in us, the more loyal the American in us will grow to be. What is the fundamental announcement of Judaism? You say the "unity of God. " This may and may not name the characteristic element. What if the One God were conceived of as a forbidding despot? There have been those among our enemies to misconstrue in this way the meaning of our monotheism. They have said that the Jew, in declaring his God to be One, proclaims the rulership of an autocrat whose caprice alone tempered by bribes is the final arbiter of the world's and the human race's fate. This monotheism, they proceed to explain, is therefore differentiated from polytheism only in its numerical notation. I adduce this misrepresentation for the purpose of demonstrating the advisability of qualifying our definition. Ethical is the attribute usually introduced to distinguish the monotheism of Judaism. But what does the phrase signify? A German thinker of fame tells us that all religion is anthropology. In the doctrine concerning man, flowers into view the true content of our consciousness of God's all pervading, all sustaining presence. One God is the highest expression of our conviction that as every man is created in the image of God, every man by his birthright is the equal of every other man. Every man as partaking of divinity has a value which is independent of all the accidents due to the action of the watersheds. Man having a value inherent in his humanity, has personality, and therefore has no price. Things may be purchased, persons cannot

The value of man is inexpressible in terms of the market. Men are not like the products of mine or mill equivalented in coin. Low or lofty, every man incarnates something inalienable which is not affected by circumstance. In this something roots his free sovereignty.

Is not America's political creed the practical execution and activization of these fundamental conceptions of Judaism? Judaism's philosophy spreads the basis whereon rests the political practice of America. No other justification is there for the assumption that men are born free and equal than the conception of man as the incarnation of the divine, his personality constituting his unpurchasable worth and being the exponent of the One in whose image all alike are created.

This inalienable freedom of man is the freedom to live out the law of his being. Law and freedom are not contraries; they are complementaries. Judaism, the religion of freedom, was of necessity also that of the Law. To whatever degree the Talmudic system through micrology may have mechanicalized the Law, none who understands the character of Judaism but must insist that liberty to activize the freedom which it posits as inherent in man's participation in divinity, postulates submission to the high law of moral majesty and final supremacy. The law of the moral order is imperfectly expressed in the self-given law of state and society. Law is liberty potentialized, liberty is law actualized. The American's passion for liberty vouchsafed by law and for law grounded in liberty, is foreshadowed and sanctified in the teachings of Judaism.

But the congruence of Judaism and Americanism extends further. Judaism postulates cooperation and coordination as the principle of organized society. In the chapter all the richer in truth because it echoes old mythology, which records the creation of man, the duty and destiny of this last of God's creative acts is defined as rulership over all the preceding works of God. "They," in the plural shall have dominion, is the phraseology of the account. In other words, one man is incompetent to fulfill this appointment. No man may be spared in the realization of this aim. Through cooperation and coordination of effort and purpose in ever larger scope, the divinely decreed destiny will be attained. Our political method is cooperative and establishes the coordination of the various organs. Our national Constitution is often described as a noble compromise. It had to be this as exponential of the principles under which alone freedom and law can be made effective, viz., cooperation and coordination. But not only that written charter, the very life of the nation's plan of self-government is imbued with these principles and informed by them. home autonomy and national authority are the two poles. America begins with the free individual, leads him for cooperation with other free individuals, his equals along ascending steps, to come to the town meeting, which then expands into the municipality and county, these autonomous corporations growing into the State, and the States finally constituting the Union. Above the Union the unwritten yet wonderfully effective Highest Law, the law not only of this nation but of all nations, the Law which is the outflow of the Moral Order of the Universe, the moral meaning of all humanity's strivings and struggles. If the Jewish Commonwealth was a Theocracy, our Government is also in the true sense of the term theocratic. The implications of the belief in the One God are basic to our democracy.

Often antagonism is predicted of Judaism, as of religion in general, to the buoyant, energetic spirit of America, its assertive self-conscious self-reliant realism. How far this suspicion is justified in the case of other religions, it is not for me to verify. Against Judaism the imputation cannot be maintained. I know that in some synagogues the conceit has been encouraged which would make of Judaism another scheme of salvation, a preparation for and an assurance of immortality. Under this misapprehension, indeed, Judaism would have little sympathy with the realities of this world; nor would it have any but an indistinct message for this life. But is other-worldliness the dominant in Judaism's proclamation, or the inspiration of its prophecy? Clearly not. Judaism would inform this life, this world. It would, through its spirit, transmute conditions and characters here and now. It was the first to pray " Thy Kingdom come." But this kingdom, this Olam ha-ba was not beyond the cloud. Its portals were not those of the grave. That world to be, which is the vision of Israel's hope and faith, is this world of ours reconstituted under the sanctifying, reforming sway of justice, righteousness, and love. With justice triumphant, righteousness socialized, Judaism hails the advent of the Messianic age when conditions on earth will be such. that no man is denied opportunity to realize his own divinity. Therefore, the dominion of religion according to our doctrine is coextensive with the range of life. Rail out of the plenitude of your prejudices at Talmudic ritualism. That ritualism is perhaps the caricature but still the expression of the vital truth that nothing in life is indifferent to religion. The most trivial acts are tremendous acts. There is no divide at which the secular parts company from the sacred. Religion must be in all things, or it is in nothing. That misinterpreted phrase "My Kingdom is not of this world," as understood by Catholic dictionary of Judaism.

Judaism as a religion has concern with commerce and industry. It is characteristic of Judaism's realism that on the "tables of the law," doctrine preludes duty. "Thou shalt not steal" was as solemnly thundered forth as "I am the Eternal." This construction of Judaism as ideal realism, as passion for righting things of this world, as preparation not for death but for the perfect "world to be," the perfect state and social order of the future, is not new. It is the burden of the prophet's censure and caution; it is the content of Pentateuchal legislative provision. The Rabbis express this conviction when they observe that the Torah was not given to the Angels, and describe the dramatic reception of Moses in the council chamber of God when come to claim for earth the Torah. The angels objected. But at the bidding of the Holy One, the son of Amram proves that angels need not the Law; that its commands apply to men and earth alone. How far have they strayed from genuine Judaism who would have the Jewish pulpit be silent on the injustices of earth, the maladjustment of society, and under the plea that Temple and Synagogue must be sacred to religion, would have religion shrink into a contrivance to arouse pleasurable emotions in the worshiper—ecstatic, sensuous foregleams of heaven felicities; into an apothecary's laboratory where patent drugs are concocted for the easing of heartache, or opiates are held in readiness for the dulling of grief and pain at the death of dear ones.

Religion consoles and eases, but only when it stimulates to action, when it quickens conscience and directs aright conduct. Remember, great Rabbis exposed the iniquity of negro slavery from their pulpits. Remember that our greatest Reform teacher, David Einhorn, used to say "no politics in religion but by all means religion in politics." Negro slavery has been wiped out, but alas other and worse slavery still prevails in this world of ours. Shall they who hear the clanking of the chains forego speaking through their old Jewish prayer book praises to God thrice daily, for having led His people from bondage of slavery? No, Judaism is for this world. Its genius of hopeful realism has syllabled the spiritual message which a people like that of the United States is in need of. Because its kingdom is not beyond the clouds, but a vision of justice and freedom realized in the tents of man, Judaism strikes the note that sets vibrating the heart of America similarly attuned to energetic realism, similarly tender to the sufferer from injustice, similarly hopeful of the future dawn of universal peace and liberty.

Our reform Judaism has come to understand in fullest measure this concordance of its own genius with that of the institutions and the soul of America. We feel that if anywhere on God's footstool our Messianic vision will be made real, it is in this land where a new humanity seems destined to arise. Not to Jerusalem are our eyes turned, but to God! We cannot honestly declare that we are here in exile. We cannot honestly petition that we be led back to Palestine as our country. We have a country which is ours by the right of our being identified with its destinies, our being devoted to its welfare, our sharing of its trials, our rejoicing in its triumphs.

Two-hundred and fifty years has the Jew sojourned in this country. He is not an alien here. His views of liberty and law, of man's inalienable rights and duties hallowed by the sublimities of his religion, are in creative concordance with the distinctive principles pillaring American civilization.

Not an alien, the Jewish American has the right to ask that now, when in darkest Europe, humanity is outraged, this, his land, remain hospitable to all that would escape from the hell of persecution and intolerance, and like the Pilgrim Fathers of Puritan faith and the first Jews, the vanguard of the million and two hundred thousand American Jews, would make this land their home. The Jew in America, as we have the good right to say, has been faithful to his pledges. The community at large was not burdened in consequence of its generous and just policy of the open door. Whatever may come now, we shall assume the same responsibility without haggling.

I myself, an immigrant, and you, the children of immigrants, if not immigrants yourselves, must prepare to receive new thousands of immigrants from Russia, which is a hell; from Roumania, which is an inferno. We must ransom the pledge given by those who settled two hundred and fifty years ago, that "none of ours shall be a burden on the community." In this awful calamity all American Jewry must band and stand together. It is a duty we owe to Judaism and to America; one of the many obligations in which our Judaism emphasizes what our Americanism tokens; in which our Americanism proves that it is harmoniously attuned to the most profound and solemn declarations of our Judaism. The flag shall welcome the new pilgrims, and our faith shall make them know that their tottering steps shall be supported and their trembling hands shall be upheld after the terrible afflictions laid on them in the land of their birth, the land of despotic brutality, of dehumanized barbarism. Great is the joy which may possess our heart. Our escutcheon as Americans is without stain. We have had a share in the making of this nation. In the mine and in the mill, at the lathe and at the loom, in counting room and council chamber, the Jew has been at work for two centuries and a half for his America. He has sentried his nation's camp; he has been in the mast's lookout on his nation's ships; he has gone out to battle, and he was among them that fell at the firing line. Officer, private, whatever his rank, when the nation asked for life or limb, he did not hesitate to offer the sacrifice. In institutions of learning the Jew has made his mark. In the walks of enterprise his individuality has been felt as a telling potency in the development of the greater aims of American energy. In the professions he stands high; on the bench he has often had representation by the best among the best; in the pulpits of the land, the Jew has not been in the last and lowest ranks. In Boston, I believe, these days they will commemorate Garrison's services. This offers an opportunity to dwell once more upon facts often overlooked, and therefore all the more worthy of being pointed out, that in that struggle against slavery none was more eager, none was more enthusiastic than the leader of American Reform Judaism. And in evidence how intensely wedded to liberty is Judaism, his voice found strong support in the pulpit of the most orthodox Portuguese synagogue of Philadelphia. Ready to die, if necessary, among those that spoke against slavery, at risk of life and position, were David Einhorn and Sabato Morais.

We have earned the right to call this our country. The future will place new solemn obligations upon us for the country's sake and as Judaism's consecration; we shall not shirk our duties. Happy we American Jews that have a country. America is ours. We can sing with all others,

"My country, 'tis of thee! Sweet land of liberty, Of thee I sing;

Land where my fathers died, Land of our Pilgrims' pride."

The watershed separates raindrops and snowflakes to divergent destiny. Race, religion, birth, and condition, also seem to divide. But on the heights the line of separation is thin; and in duty again all difference of direction is consecrated to unity of purpose. In our nation no divides but are instrumentalities of service. Clinging to his Judaism, the Jew will be a more strenuous, a more loyal, a more enthusiastic American.

May God bless our country; keep it in His protection. May His light shine out o'er it, and His peace abide and abound in it. This is the prayer of the Jew on this, the Jewish-American anniversary day of joy and solemn resolves. Answer it, God in heaven, in Thy mercy.

Amen, Amen!

The Jewish Chautauqua Society

In July, 1903, Dr. Emil G. Hirsch delivered three addresses before the Jewish Chautauqua Summer Assembly, held at Atlantic City, New Jersey, at the Royal Palace Hotel. The subjects were *Judaism and The Higher Criticism; The Doctrine of Evolution and Judaism;* and *Judaism and Modern Religion.*

The Jewish Chautauqua Society was founded by the beloved scholar Dr. Henry Berkowitz of Rodeph Sholem Congregation—Philadelphia.

Many scholars have addressed it, and it has sponsored valuable educational work. My father covered a great deal of ground in his lecture on the relationship of *Judaism and The Higher Criticism.*

"Were even my reputation for congenital or cultivated diffidence less well established than I have reason to believe it is, I should feel constrained, by way of introduction, to ask at your hand the indulgence due 'a stranger in a strange land.' I use the phrase advisedly. There is something in the atmosphere of the East which puts us, from the West, on our guard. I, myself, have been taught by previous experience that assertions which in my home surroundings cause not as much as the slightest ripple in the placid surface of the current of thought, have had the effect to arouse violent dissent, and were put under the ban as heterodox and revolutionary.

But let me pray you to believe in the sincerity of my profession that nothing is further from my purpose than the intention to disturb your different conviction. For me, every religious opinion honestly held is sacred. I would approach that professed by another in the spirit of the biblical injunction which bade Moses, in the presence of the burning bush, take off his shoes and be mindful of the holiness of the ground underneath his feet.

"At one point certainly our interests meet. We are each, in his way and according to his light, passionate believers in Judaism, and it is because Judaism's right still to be regarded as the proclaimer of essential truths has come to be disputed, that I make bold to propose for examination the beauty which certain modern theories have on Judaism.

"Students of the history of Judaism need not be told that never was this religion indifferent to the thought movement affecting the surrounding world.

"Judaism gave impulse to others, but also received stimulus from others. The instances corroborative of this contention are many and for the most part familiar. Philo naturalized Plato in Judaism. S'aadyah and Maimonides made Aristotle at home in the synagogue. Ibn Gabirol married Judaism and Neo-Platonic speculation while the cabbalah is the precipitate of the inter-action between Jewish Theological concepts and non-Jewish philosophical concepts.

In modern times the same phenomenon is discernible , in the writings of the leaders of the nineteenth century, synagogue.

"Hegel found Jewish exposition in the system, though antipodal of Samuel Hirsch—'The Samson Raphael Hirsch, the Ultramontane.' In Einhorn's reasoning, one has little difficulty to detect the dominancy of Schelling's position, while it is not too much to say that but for the rise of the German school of historic criticism, Zunz and Geiger and Frankel and Herzfeld and Loew, and Steinschneider and the host of others numbered among the stars of first magnitude in the galaxy of recent Judaism, would not have been known to bring from the mine of Jewish literature to the surface such ripe ore. In three departments of human knowledge, more especially, have of late years theories been formulated that must invite the thoughtful Jew to the task of investigating their relation to his own deepest conviction.

These departments are easily singled out. They with more than customary notoriety, stand in the forefront of solicitude: The researches centered in our old literature, the Bible, which are commonly designated as *Higher Criticism.* Next to these in interest are the speculations based on the discoveries made during the last fifty years in the domain of the natural sciences, technically known as *Evolutionary Philosophy.*

And, finally, yielding but little in essential importance or even popular attention to the two mentioned, is that group of painful and patient study comprised under the general term, *Comparative Religion*.

"The *Higher Criticism* has been the nightmare of many a pious soul. At its mention, visions of satanic passion have risen to affrighten with horrid prospects of infidelity and unreligiousity running amuck, the loyal hearts of unsophisticated believers. It has been denominated the bastard offspring of atheism and irreverence. When oppressed by dearth of thought, the preacher of whatever sect or set finds denunciation of this devilish fancy a ready refuge. Among Jews, this *Higher Criticism* is suspected to be a willful contrivance of Anti-Semitism desirous of hiding its true motives underneath the fig leaf of scholarly or would-be scientific method and vocabulary so that the modern rabbi, scarce ever sure of the attention of his spasmodic audience, may safely speculate on arousing some of his intermittent listeners from the slumber superinduced by his voice, sufficient to nod approval when he indulges in vehement protests against this novel, but cowardly, trick of Israel's implacable enemies.

"*Higher Criticism* stands simply for the application to the Biblical writings of the canons, which philology holds never to be lost sight of, to the understanding of any book, ancient or modern. He, alone, who holds by dint of his faith that the Bible was produced in a manner in which no other book was, may advance the claim that the canons of interpretation applicable to human literary productions are not to be invoked to conserve the contents of this collection of old Hebrew writings. But for him then the Bible is a miracle. He must plead in its behalf for the suspension of laws universally regnant under a special purpose.

"The belief in miracles opens the door to twice as many perplexities as it is hailed to allow.

"One who is acquainted with Jewish thought on the subject of miracles knows that every miracle related in holy scripture was held to be a natural sequence of a condition involved in original creation. That the Bible has by many—let us even say by most men—been regarded as of super-human origin and its contents have been declared to have been transmitted in a way opened to no other work of human pen. Yet this circumstance is inconsequential.

"The Mohammedan advances the identical claim for the exceptional composition and history of his sacred book, the Koran. So does the Buddhist for the components of his canon. The Christian does not embrace, in the ascription of super-human origin and exceptional channel of transmission, merely the Old, he extends it to the New dispensation as well.

"Bibliolatry is an achievement of the Protestant Reformation. It has made inroads into Judaism only when the synagogue has been exposed to Protestant influence.

"For the old Jew, the Bible was not the sole channel of revelation. Revelation was a continuous and unending process. The written work was not final. It was complemented by the oral law. Yea, without fear of contradiction, the statement may be urged that of the Written Book, in the Jewish Orthodox thinking, on the Pentateuch, The Torah—in the technical sense of the word—was authoritative; and of its chapters, only those of a central importance that dealt not with story and therefore had to be 'believed,' but with statute and therefore had to be 'observed.'

"We who are theists certainly regard the universe as of Divine origin. Nevertheless, we explain the course of the stars by the laws established by observation and calculation; we trace the growth of life on the planet in accordance with the processes discovered in the laboratories of the biologist.

"But whether of recent date or able to point out the pedigree among the comments of predecessors, *Higher Criticism* introduced into the question the value of the contents of the books. It merely reassigns them to periods different from those assumed by former critics and attempts to explain the processes by which the documents now extant came to be preserved in the shape and order in which they are found in the existing collection.

"This involves the methods advised by philology and as impartially applied to Homer, Schiller, Chaucer, Walter Von Der Vogelweide, Dante, The Vedanta, the Koran, Tennyson or any sacred or profound book.

"The same is the case with the stories of power gathered in Biblical writings. What matter who wrote the sections and when they were written.

They are; they speak; they exhort; they advise. Inconsequential for the message to the proposition whether one Isaiah proclaimed it or that three or even more prophets of various birthplaces and centuries, but under one consecration winged its stupendous appeal and admonition, its hopes and assurances—the message speaks as solemnly now as ever it did.

"But history? Yes, what is history's value? Does it consist of dates and names? Indeed not! Dates and names are skeletons. The essential element is the spirit.

"It. may be well, at this point of the discussion, to recall a few of the axiomatic assumptions basic to the matter that national literature never antedate the nation's existence—this is one of the principal convictions.

"Before Israel could have a national literature, it had to be a nation. Again, a shepherd people will not anticipate, in legislation, the needs of its own successors, settled as farmers in fixed habitations. The Pentateuch as a whole, therefore, can not be assumed to have been written at a period preceeding the conquest of the land. History is precluded by legend and oral story. Legend often personified events, or centers around a locality. It is at times provoked by names that have become unintelligible.

"These legends cannot throw light on many of the episodes chronicled in Genesis or Judges, or the cycles of Elijah and Elisha legend.

"Again history is written to illustrate a theory. These leanings of ancient historiography are strongly manifest in Biblical literature. They account for the difference in the various versions of one and the same event.

"The Pentatuech, in its component parts, reflects the successive stages of this process; the book of Judges compares with the book of Joshua, proving that the conquest of the land and the constitution of the nation was not a concerted movement under national law and leadership, but the slow result of a laborious conflict.

"Comparison of the doctrines of the Prophets furthermore discovers variations in their respective theological views, the unifying of the cult by centralizing it in Jerusalem appearing as a late measure of reform under Josiah; while only under Ezra—and then not without opposition—stress came to be laid on the purity of descent from the holy seed of Abraham. The racial idea underlying originally only the priesthood, thus, finally coming to be looked upon as fundamental for the congregation which then replaced the anterior ruling idol, the people or nation.

"These, in brief indication, are the main theses of the much dreaded *Higher Criticism*. Do they undermine the foundations of Judaism? Do they rob the regal diadem of our religion of a single precious gem?

"If the Bible contained truth, that truth has not been silenced. Its gift to inspire, the power to kindle light, its solemn call to obedience, its majestic emphasis on responsibility as exponential of man's distinction in the sweep of creating his lordship over all that is fashioned (Psalm VII), is proclamation of purpose and will higher than man's plans and plots to which the heavens bow and the nations must bend. The Bible's God and God idea, who is not diminished through the one great leader of Israel in the Sinaitic peninsula, will have to be credited with no more than the impulse toward the truth and other hands than his to be seen tracing the letters of the Pentateuch.

"A Protestant writer, author of a famous introduction to the theological science, Die Encyclopedia der Theologie, has put the matter in a nut shell.

"The criticism merely established the process of revelation, but cannot reach over into the field of revelation itself.

"That Israel came into the possession of truth is a fact of revelation. How it came into the possession is the story which *Higher Criticism* aims to tell. It substitutes, thus, not a new truth for an old error, but simply a new and more reasonable account of how truth came for an old error less in harmony with the operation of forces as seen at work among other people and illustrated in the biographies of other literature. Under the *Higher Criticism* this Biblical literature becomes ours—Israel's possession as under no other traditional theory of its cradle and character. It was written with Israel's own heart's blood. As the silkworm spins the cocoon from the reservoir of its own life element, so did Judaism write the Biblical documents by transfusion of its spiritual life.

"It is this *Higher Criticism* which, comparing the Hebrew literature with the noblest of other ancient writings, crowns it queen of them all.

"Homer, Virgil, Hesiod, Horace, Zendavesta, Veda, Edda or the Kings, Koran or Gospel, none of these excels—if any equals—the vision of Isaiah, wisdom of Koheleth, pathos of Job, sweetness and glow of Psalm, majesty of the law and charm of Ruth.

"Anti-Semitism, Anti-Judaism, are indeed confounded and silenced by *Higher Criticism*; the stone which the builder rejected is become the cornerstone. From *Higher Criticism* Judaism has naught to fear."

In my father's address on *The Doctrine of Evolution and Judaism,* "Evolution," he argued, "is a process running through the ages that are past, which has the power to illumine the forward, untrodden path of days still to be.

"It, alone, possesses the gift to uncurtain the cradle of language and religion. It, alone, is conversant with the alphabet in which the sequence of civilization and the succession of empires write their records.

"Charles Darwin was the chief exponent championing the cause of Evolution. The year when he published *The Origin of Species* is distinguished among the dates marking a turning point in the thoughts of the races. Two years before Darwin brought out his great work, Spencer had given the inattentive world a book entitled *Progress, Its Laws and Cause.*

"But Darwin was not the first member of his family to advance these ideas of evolution; as many decades before, his own grandfather had worked along similar lines.

"In the seventeenth century, Descartes, and perhaps Spinoza, advanced similar notions. Probably the first expounder. of evolution in ancient days was the Greek thinker, Heraclitus, who taught his disciples to view life and nature as a continuous process—an unbroken succession of waves in constant flux.

The fate of the doctrine offers another illustration of the significant truth which religious poetry has garbed in the relation established between Elijah and the Messiah.

"As the sun, about to mount the chariot of his victory, sends out torch bearers to announce the glad hour of his triumphant coming, so does truth, biding the supreme moment of its rise, command the services of outsiders that before its own history, faith in irresistible power proclaims the passing of the night.

"But the human mind is so constituted that it will not rest satisfied with detached facts.

"The quest for the 'Geistige Bund,' as Goethe puts it, is, after all, of persistent importunity, and will not be disowned."

My father goes on to explain that Darwin was a humble recorder of discoveries, painfully reached by persistent observation.

"The doctrine of evolution has not weakened the pillars upon which religion has reared her temple.

"The Rip Van Winkles are not altogether on our side of the house.

"Time was when what has rightly been denominated the materialism of beer and cheese, held forth as the last word of all philosophy and the exponent of all liberalism.

"It is strange, yet it is a fact, this species of materialism is represented largely by men who the Germans dub 'Walbbildung,' and nowhere so unconcernedly than among would-be liberal Jews.

"That force and matter explain nothing, but themselves call for explanation, is potent.

"Can one tell us what matter be or what energy is? Self-created matter is as great a riddle to the human reason as is self-creative mind.

"Characteristic in this connection is the anecdote of the man who, when asked to define his favorite term, 'matter and force,' replied, 'Matter? Never mind. Mind? No matter.'

"That the beginning of all things is not accounted for by the theory of evolution is admitted by Darwin himself when, even in the last edition of *The Origin of the Species*, did he not find himself moved to modify the statement of the first in which he intimated his belief that 'Life may have been originally breathed by the Creator into few forms or only one.'

"How, from the inorganic the organic may have sprung; how, from the unconscious the conscious may have developed; evolution has failed to reveal. But, again, evolution always presupposes involution. Nothing may be in the result which is not potently present in the impulse. One who is at home in the literature of Jewish Theology need not be told that throughout Jewish thought the effort is dominant to anthropomorphize the concept of the deity.

"Here, the care of the earlier translation of the

Bible to substitute for the human symbols in the Original Hebrew such terms as remove the picture of God beyond the lower range of human passion or experience.

"Evolution reveals that life runs on through a process of interdependence. Whatever lives, lives through another and for another. In notes clearer than ever were entoned by human tongue does the philosophy of evolution confirm the essential verity of Judaism's insistent protest and proclamation that God is one.

"This theory reads unity in all that is. Stars and stones, planets and pebbles, sun and sod, rock and river, leaf and lichen, are spun of the same thread. Thus the universe is one soul; 'One,' spelled large. They who are acquainted with the positions taken in their own peculiar way by Rabbinical interpreters of the story of creation, will remember that the pre-existence of the Torah is assumed as God's instrument of creation. That many among the medieval thinkers claimed a wide latitude in explaining the opening chapter of Genesis, is beyond doubt.

"The profound reasoners found no difficulty in harmonizing their assumption of the eternity of matter with their belief in the God of their religious consciousness. We have the good right to follow the precedent thus set. That creation is revelation of purpose over power of mind is the cardinal tenet of the Jewish faith. This, evolution has not obscured.

"Yea, in a much profounder sense than the old thought was capable of expressing, rings old from anew the proclamation that '...in the beginning was the word; that by the word of God were the heavens made, and the depths took shape at this bidding.' Let it be granted that conditioned as our minds are, we cannot arrive at a full comprehension of the Deity's being. This the Jew certainly has no cause to deny. If Jewish Theology is marked by one conviction more than by another, it is that final mind cannot grasp the contents of the Infinite. Maimonides already cautions his contemporaries against the affirming of the Deity more than existence. Negative attributes therefore are the implications he reads into the descriptions current to express the contents of the God Idea.

"Mountains of phraseology are impotent to illumine the thought which, in its very nature, transcends human analogies.

"In the words of my sainted father and teacher, 'We can express only what God is for us, never what he is in Himself.' We are unable to pierce the cloud in which the Divine is shrouded. Man is not concerned in the problem lying beyond the sphere of his own duties and responsibilities. Whether in the cosmic he be central or not, what boot to know this. Of importance, alone, it is for man to feel, that placed as he is in the world, he is charged with obligations.

"To be human, one must be moral, and the stronger one's morality the deeper one's humanity. Whatever evolution evolves must be considered as involved in the plan of life. If morality, by the insistence of the new doctrines, really appears trestled all the more strongly about religion now, religion did appear and did assert itself in the life of man. It therefore must have answered a need of his. It must correspond to an element in his composition.

"Religion is like language—a universally human phenomenon. When men have been there, altars have risen. This fact, in the light of the evolutionary doctrine, at once must silence the—at one time—so very popular assertion of the rationalists that religion was a benevolent or malevolent invention of crafty priests or well-meaning lovers of their kind.

"This does not necessitate the assumption that all religions are of interchangeable worth. Religions differ in quality and atmosphere. Some were dowered with the strength to develop; others lacked this gift.

"Evolution, in accentuating this distinction, confirms the claim of Israel to be the people of the book. We of the Reform school have found in the theory of evolution warrant for our particular contentions. Judaism itself has been an evolution. Not being a dogmatic creed, but rather in the spirit of Deuteronomy—a philosophy of practical responsibilities, a religion of the deed, a life under the consecration of the passion for Justice, Righteousness and Love. Judaism is more than Bible, Talmud, or any of the books that slow accretions; and a growing deposit of centuries monument any one of its many phases rather than contain the full content of its unexhausted possibilities. Talmudism was a development out of Biblical Judaism, and marks an advance, in many respects, beyond it.

"Our own Judaism, again, is not a return to an

anterior type, but a development out of all preceeding types; central to all Judaism is that thought that man and God are at one, and that it is Israel's task to bring to flower in life this unity of man and God.

"The past as the source of power and inspiration, the present as the field of action and the domain of influence; the future, as the age for still wider accomplishments, lay on the Reform Jew obligations which he will not shirk. Knowing that progress has been the secret of Judaism's vitality, the Reform Jew conversant with the Law regularly in all things; there, pushing on for fuller life, would neither be disloyal to his past, for that would, according to the very law of progress, cut the roots from under him. He would not be false to the living present for that would waste his energy. Nor would he be blind to his obligation to the future; for, would one carry forward the tendency of life, he must acknowledge the dominion of the conviction that his attitude and activity in the *now* effect the possibilities of those that are to come after him.

"In this manner the philosophy of evolution has come to be a potent force in the ambitions and assertions of the Reform Jew.

"Evolution is to be dreaded as little as was Platonism by Philo, Aristotelianism by Maimonides. The rhythm of Judaism's own progress beats an even measure with the thought of this theory."

In his last lecture before the Jewish Chautauqua Society in July, 1903, my father spoke on the subject of *Judaism and Modern Religion.*

Among other things, Emil G. Hirsch declares:

"The frigid days of chilly indifference are drawing to their decline.

"The human race is on the threshold of a religious renaissance.

"Although admitting the conquest of science, man recognizes his obligations, and knows he is free to explore fields which the operation of mechanical law cannot account and in the formulation of which their verdict is inconsequential.

"While it is true that the feeling of a turn in the tide of human thought is shared mostly by the elect, still, those at home with the run of the spiritual currents marked in the chart of history must become aware such actions are stirring.

"The sun, when rising, imprints his morning kiss first upon the high mountain peaks.

"They who slumber in the deeper valley must wait for many an hour before they may behold the glorious king of the day enter their habitation.

"The men of light and leading have even now beckoned us of limited vision to share their joy in the flood of the nascent light: Books certainly betray the drift of thought developing the hour of their birth. Time was when the printing presses of all civilized nations were busy sending out popular accounts of the discoveries made by astronomers and physicists, when the new chemistry and geology was then introduced to every drawing room, and took precedence of every other subject in polite conversation.

"Many a pulpit, today, feels that in order to be 'up to date' they must burden their congregations with discourses on biology and petrology. The fact is that this passion for acquaintance with popularized Darwinism speculation has long since waned.

"Sociology was the besetting appetitite for those that were preparing for the leadership of men ten and twenty years ago.

"For, in the meantime, the consciousness has dispensed that sociology is under the consecration of ethics.

"'Up to date' books are emphasizing this fact. In one word, they are concerned with the realities of religion.

"Professor Eucken, of Jena, a famous German thinker, in his book, *Der Wahrheitsgelhalt der Religion* (The Time Function of Religion), shows that 'the quest for religious truth has come to be understood as one of the pressing necessities of the modern mind.'

"The same meaning may correctly be read into the controversies growing out of the appearance of Haeckel's famous publication, *The Riddle of the Universe.*

"In his lecture on the Bible and Babel, Professor Delitsch expounded views of major importance on this subject.

" The fact then stands that Religion once more occupies a prominent position in the interest of modern man. In the struggle for existence, Nietsche's theories on the survival of the fittest glorified the emancipation of the titanic men of might, or cunning, over those of lesser abilities.

"The theory, that success vindicates whatever means employed in its attainment, had gone forth to undo humanity and reduce society to an aggregate of robber competitors of economic mind.

"The realization now came to many that 'Man was, after all, more than a bread-consuming machine, and the humanities could not be expressed by dealing in an equation of food supply.'

"Therefore, the function of religion as one of the basic constituents of complete humanity was in ever increasing degree brought to the forefront.

"The studies in comparative religion have established, beyond a shadow of a doubt, that religion is not an invention or an intrigue.

"It was not an opiate, dulling the pain of the struggle by promise of greater joy to come.

"It was not born in the desire of kings, and statesmen, to render the governing of the masses easier by invoking the will of superhuman powers and devising schemes of heavenly record wherewith to coax the recalcitrants into submitting, or, of infernal punishment wherewith to frighten the obstinate into obedience.

"Religion has no hidden hygienic prophylactic wisdom. It could not have met with acceptance by the masses unless the lawgiver had palmed it off as come to him from Divine source and cloaked with Divine authority. The twaddle of certain would-be enlightened men prevailed—in which even Ingersoll indulged—that priests, anxious to increase their revenues, speculating on the greed and the fear of the people, hypnotized the credulous into accepting, as of Divine origin, statute prescribing sacrifice, or creed demanding blind belief.

"We must abandon such ideas now. The

species of antediluvian liberalism has had no standing in the court where the science of comparative religion is called to plead.

"Religion is organic, not artificial. This universality of religion is fatal to the distinction often made between religions as natural and revealed. If one religion is revealed, all are; and if one be natural, all are.

"Revelation from without or above would, to be effective, always have to accommodate itself to the mental equipment of the men to whom it is addressed, or take into consideration the needs of the people whom it would guide.

"A revelation that transcends the intelligence of the men and minds that are intended to be influenced, thereby, would of necessity be futile.

"Lessing's conception of revelation as an historic process—a method of upward education—has been corroborated by the researches into comparative religion. Every religion corresponds to the need, and the mental outlook, of the people that profess it.

"This does not vitiate the force of the influence exercised upon the process of development by the great men—the prophets. Genesis is one of the channels through which revelation flows.

"These men of genius anticipate, often by long centuries, the slow evolution of thought among their contemporaries.

"Therefore they often have to speak to deaf ears. That has been the tragic fate of the prophets in Israel. In that sense, they were exponents of a revelation transcending the conditions of their times.

"And this brings up another important consideration. It has been argued, that if the distinction between revealed and natural religion be ignored, all religions must be declared to be equivalent. The fallacy of this conclusion is patent.

"Religion has its analogy in languages. Language speaks to people, whether in stammering dialect or the fluent speech of Demosthenes. Some people did not develop a wealthier language because a halting jargon served their needs. Other people with higher cultural attainments require the use of a higher or more refined language. But language throughout the centuries was brought forth in a universal scope. Some languages, in the course of time, die. They are the dead languages. Some languages grow and blossom forth through the ages.

"The same holds good with reference to religions. Some have died; others have retained their virility and vitality after ages.

"Generally, religions are ranged, and ranked, according to the numerical exponent of the Deity. Polytheism; monotheism, and the like, is the consequent designation rated to reveal the relative character.

"Is salvation from inherited sin, is revision of sin by which the Deity has been offended, is attainment of prosperity or felicity, is consolation through assurance of compensation in the life after death, is reward or escape from punishment, the ultimate of religious prospect and the source of religious power? Or is religion the disciplinary exercise producing further realization of the human in the individual and in society, and as such, an end unto itself and not a means to something ulterior; is worthiness—not happiness either here or hereafter—the aim of religious culture? These are the vital antitheses.

"And would you know the name of this one religion, which is not to be classed with the religions of salvation? I have no hesitancy to declare that this one religion is our Judaism—the Judaism of the prophets, of the sages—the religion for which thousands willingly gave their lives in defense of their conviction that man never fell and therefore never needed a redeemer in the sense of the atoning scheme devised by the church founded by Paul.

"Christianity is the religion in which the Christ concept is central. This Christ is the atoning sufferer—the redeemer from the curse of Adam—and, as such, master and Lord of the Law, which in his death finds its abrogation, as it was merely a Pedagogue unto Christ; the historical Jesus is certainly not this Christ.

"The premises of Christian scholars—as for example, Harnack—that the religion of Jesus transcended the highest uplook of Judaism, cannot be maintained. This premise is an outgrowth of Paulinian theology. Paulinian theology denies the historicity of the historical Jesus.

"In the Paulinian scheme, the antithesis between the Law and the Gospel is fundamental. The Christ is necessarily above all historical thesis. The Jew, therefore, is under the curse of the law. Freedom from the law is only in, and through, the Christ, who, the second Adam, by his death works the atonement and thus abrogates the law by his death, which alone is the fulfillment of the law. The whole of the Paulinian system is grounded in Semitic ideas, which to controvert was one of the services rendered by Prophetic religion.

"The Levitical code rests on quite different notions, not involved in this theological speculation, but in primitive concepts found everywhere at a certain stage of social development. And I, for one, have no hesitancy to declare that the prophets, for this reason, had but little sympathy with sacrificial piety. The institutions and provisions of the priestly code cannot, at this late date, be quoted on corroboration of the thesis that Judaism attempted to bring about the atonement and cleansing from sin by means of blood, or that the notion of the atonement by substitution was fundamental in the religion of Isaiah, Jeremiah, or even Ezra or Nehemiah.

"The English term, *Redeemer*, must be translated into the Hebrew original equivalent, *Goel*, to make its implications plain.

"The *Goel* is the blood avenger. It is he who assumes the duty to see the death of another properly requited. Then it is he who sits in the stead of another. For instance, the *Goel* is the brother who marries the widow of his deceased brother that a son might be the issue of the new conjugal union, who would perpetuate the name not of his natural father but of the imputed one, who is the deceased husband of the mother. (See *Boaz* in the book of Ruth.) It is thus plain that Paul's theology is grounded in ancient Semitic tribal society and the sin therein activized. Jewish prophecy has always been against this Semitism. A protestant Judaism and Semitism are not identical. In many vital points they are antipodal. But what now, concerning the originality of the historical Jesus? That we have in the gospels no biography of him is certain. Nor are the various critics agreed as to what pacts of the gospels' accounts shall be regarded as probably more authentic. Was Jesus conscious of a Messianic destiny? This is one of the mooted points in controversy among the various schools.

"But let us neglect all these considerations. In sober, prosy earnestness, let us accept the gospels as biographies and admit the authenticity of every word alleged, therein, to have been spoken by the Masters. What do they contain that Judaism has not claimed as its own before his advent.

"Geiger, and others, had contended years ago that in all of these utterances there is neither trace of originality nor indication of the intention to be original. Beautiful as many of the sayings of Jesus are, inspiring as for the larger world his message has been, there is none of them but has had its prototype in the sayings of the masters of the synagogue. In fact, many—if not all—of his sayings can only be understood properly if translated into the technical terminology of the theology of the synagogue of his day.

Take for instance, that concept, so often invoked, that he had come to fulfill the law. To fulfill—in this connection—is the equivalent of the Hebrew *lekayyem*, which absolutely has no possible reference to the idea of abolishing the law. On the contrary, fidelity to the law is emphasized.

"It is patent that Jesus's interests were largely ethical. His views on the Sabbath, for instance, are neither new nor revolutionary.

"In one word, Jesus, as described in the gospels, is altogether within the lines of the synagogue—nowhere beyond or above them.

His Messianic self-consciousness underlines his claim, which amounts to saying, 'Why still further speculation on the coming of the Messiah? Behold, he is in the midst of you.'

"It cannot be too often repeated that religion is life. It is not belief either in dogma or historicity of an event or personality. What has been imputed to the historical Jesus, Judaism insists is the privilege of every man. Every man is son to God. The unity between Man and God is real in every truly human life. Action, not resignation; righteousness, not despair of sin, are the keynotes of the Jewish ethical proclamation. Responsibility and service are the sacramental words of the Jewish philosophy of life.

"Judaism recognizes that righteousness is independent of race or religion. The righteousness of the nations share in felicity of kingdom come. To be saved, none needed to adopt Judaism. The Jew assumes for himself the historic post of a sentinel and soldier of righteousness and justice. It is his to bring about the sanctification of the Holy name. This is all that is involved in the oft-misunderstood phrase, 'The Mission of Israel.'

"The Jewish State, if truly Jewish, would be

founded on the precepts of the prophets, and, as such, would be the organized effort at rendering justice real in the interrelations of state and state, and man and man.

"While then willingly acknowledging the good wrought by the Ethical Culture movement under the guidance and instruction of that great man, Felix Adler, we have found no cogent reason to abandon our fellowship within the historical synagogue on the plea that the ethical ambition is within the old lines—cramped, or obscured, or limited by certain credal postulates. These postulates are involved in the very warp and woof of the ethical conception of universe and human life. That the new Church will be democratic is also a certainty which is a pleasing prospect. Judaism recognizes no distinction between the layman and the clergy.

"Einhorn's words, indeed, should be carried in mind. On a memorable occasion, he said, with that incisiveness of speech that has made him famous, 'Judaism knows only one distinction—that between the learned and the ignorant.' The rabbi is not a priest. He is not a clergyman. He has no power to bind and to loosen, in the Christian sense of the term. There is one function which custom has handed over to him, but may be as religiously performed by another. To say that a rabbi may speak by virtue of the powers vested in him as an ordained Rabbi in Israel is a gratuitous assumption for which there is no warrant, either in the history or the genius of Judaism.

"All of us, however, have one sacred obligation to meet in the very days of combat and promise withal we must provide for the fostering of Jewish literature and learning.

"It is incumbent upon us to keep alive in our pulpits the best that Judaism has produced in thought. Are you surprised to hear me—a so-called Radical—plead for a deepening of our Jewish consciousness?

"If you are, it is due to the fact that our Radical Judaism has perhaps not been presented to you true to its intentions. My radicalism—and it is that which I imbibed at the feet of my own father and teacher, and found in this instruction of my master, Geiger, both of blessed memory—the Radicalism of Einhorn and Samuel Adler intends to be more Jewish than ever was official orthodoxy. We hunger for more of Judaism, not for less of it.

"We should remember that we have not broken with our past. We spin its thread out into the future. Judaism is not an external law, but an inward principal. It is a growth, not a command. To uphold the faith of the prophets and to live in accordance, therewith, is our duty.

"If we lay little stress upon ceremony, it is because we do not regard, with Paul, Judaism to be a dead law. The Law, we believe, in accordance with the results of modern criticism, to be of non-Jewish origin. Judaism stands for ideas. To quote my father 'Judaism is Lehre, not Gesetz.' Jewish to the core, Radical Judaism would be one of the many influences to prepare the modern world for the noble life as befits them who are created in the image of God. We feel, that as spiritual descendants of the prophets, this is our historical task."

The Last Years

The last years of my father's life were hard ones, lightened only by the spontaneous celebration of his seventieth birthday by Chicago Sinai Congregation, May 22, 1921. Emil G. Hirsch, like John Haynes Holmes of New York and other great religious leaders, was a great advocate of peace and deplored the necessity that the United States must enter the conflict against Germany—the Germany of Goethe and Schiller. But once we had entered the war, there was no sturdier patriot than Emil G. Hirsch. In sending me off to the war in the summer of 1918 he bid me to serve my country well. Shortly afterward, during that same summer, he suffered a stroke. My father never knew he had suffered a stroke, and his usual robust constitution enabled him to live another five years.

At the time of the Seventieth Anniversary Services at Sinai Temple, May 22, 1921, Dr. Stephen S. Wise of the Free Synagogue, New York; Dr. Nathan Krass of the Central Synagogue, New York; and Dr. Gerson B. Levi of

Bnai Sholem Temple Israel, delivered masterful eulogies of Dr. Emil G. Hirsch, depicting his lifelong labors in behalf of Reform Judaism. The Temple was packed with worshipers. In the evening a reception and play depicting the celebrant's life from the cradle on, was given.

The Reform Advocate, unknown to my father, published a special Seventieth Anniversary Edition; and leaders both Christian and Jew, in this country and abroad, in all walks of life, rendered tributes of esteem to Emil G. Hirsch for his services to Judaism and humanity.

When my father saw these articles in *The Reform Advocate* delivered to our home, tears came to his eyes and he said in German to me: *Ick kenn mich nicht.* (I do not know myself.)

In his address at the Seventieth Celebration of Dr. Emil G. Hirsch's birth, Dr. Stephen S. Wise offered the Honorary Presidency of the Jewish Institute of Religion to my father, hoping that Sinai would release their distinguished leader for a few months of the year so he could travel to New York and give the students there enrolled for the ministry the benefits of his rare scholarship. My father—overcome by emotion—accepted the Honorary Presidency of the Jewish Institute of Religion. To teach future rabbis was one of his highest ambitions.

In the year 1922 Dr. Hirsch, several months before he died, spoke at the Free Synagogue in New York on "The Sermon On The Mount—Was It The Greatest Sermon Ever Preached?" and the address was received enthusiastically.

During the summer of 1922 he was ill at his

summer residence in the Moraine Hotel, Highland Park, Illinois, and he was unable to conduct Rosh Hashana services in September. Dr. Julian Morganstern of Cincinnati officiated at services in Sinai Temple at that time. But for a while my father's health seemed to improve, and against the advice of the family he insisted on preaching in November, 1922, a Thanksgiving Day Sermon—"Echoes of Thanksgiving." He preached in his usual splendid manner, but this effort exhausted his strength and six weeks later the world-renowned leader of Liberal Judaism breathed his last. On Sunday morning, 5:50 A. M., January 7, 1923, my father died at his residence, 4608 South Drexel Boulevard, Chicago.

A little later in the morning many friends came to our apartment to express their condolences. Among the first to arrive were Julius Rosenwald, Harry Hart, Joseph L. Gatzert, Judge Kenesaw M. Landis and S. D. Schwartz.

Upon his passing, tributes from all over the world poured into our home.

The President, Warren G. Harding, sent a telegram to my mother in which he stated:

"I have been much distressed to hear of the death of your distinguished husband. I wish to express my sincerest condolences to you together with my deep sense of the country's great loss.

"Signed: Warren G. Harding."

Julius Rosenwald, President of Sears, Roebuck and Co., said, "As one who has sat at his feet almost every Sunday morning for the last thirty-five years, I feel that a great moral force has gone. He was fearless and demanding that his congregation live up to the highest standards of morality and justice; and he never hesitated to chastise any member whom he believed had been unfair or unjust. Dr. Hirsch was equally insistent that the Jew do his full share in all matters of public concern. He was recognized as one of the greatest Jewish scholars of his time. A worthy son of a great rabbi whose loss is irreparable and whose place cannot be filled."

Others pay tribute: "Dr. Hirsch was one of the greatest Jews of his time in the whole world," said Jacob M. Loeb, former President of the Chicago Board of Education. He continued, "Dr. William R. Harper, President Judson's predecessor at the University of Chicago, once said to me that 'His brain contained more knowledge than anyone he had ever met!' The Jews of Chicago and of America and the whole world have suffered an irreparable loss in his death."

"Dr. Hirsch was a man of noble character and amazing capacity. and ability," said M. Ernest Greenebaum, Chicago banker. "We have all learned wonderful lessons from him; and his work and teachings have been of untold benefit to the Jewish religion."

Shortly after my father's death, the Chicago Board of Education named a school in his memory. It is known today as the Emil G. Hirsch High School.

The funeral of my father was held at Sinai Temple, 4622 Grand Boulevard, on Tuesday morning, January 9, 1923.

Five thousand people crowded the Temple and

adjoining Social Center. Thousands more stood on the street in front of Sinai Temple.

Prominent Chicagoans of all faiths attended the services.

My brother-in-law, Rabbi Gerson B. Levi, preached the funeral oration.

About a month after my father's death, Chicago Sinai Congregation conducted memorial services for him. Rabbi Joseph Stolz of Isaiah Temple, President of the Chicago Rabbinical Association, offered the opening prayer. Moses E. Greenebaum, President of Sinai Congregation, Hannah G. Solomon, General Abel Davis and Ernest De Witt Burton, President of the University of Chicago, delivered beautiful eulogies.

Dr. Stephen S. Wise of the Free Synagogue of New York preached a most heart felt memorial address.

Dr. Stephen S. Wise
Rabbi, The Free Synagogue,
New York City

Memorial Addresss

I speak frankly as the friend of Hirsch, as one who loved him. If I err on the side of over-appraisal, I shall not be sorry. I do not believe I will, for Hirsch was a great man. But this must be said in order that you may understand that he who speaks knew Hirsch intimately, revered him deeply, loved him truly.

In the first place, Hirsch was a great Jew. His life was given to the Jewish people; the Jewish cause was his life. It was not an aside with him. Living for, speaking for, serving Israel was not a profession to be pursued Sunday mornings but his life was utterly dedicated thereto. Hirsch was a great Jew within and without Israel. Some Jews seem great to non-Jews because they spend their lives in belittling their people and in aggrandizing themselves. Some Jews seem great to the non-Jewish world, because it does not know how insecure and insincere may be their place in Jewish life. He was a great Jew, whom non-Jews knew to be a great Jew.

Emil Hirsch was greatly Jewish; he was magnificently Jewish. Hirsch was so truly a scholar and a seer that he understood the meaning and envisaged the content of Liberal Judaism. To him Liberal Judaism was not, as alas it has become to many of his colleagues, an empty name, but the substance of a great conception. He had the uniquely good fortune to have had it at first hand from all of his great teachers, his greatest teacher being his honored father, the Melancthon of the Jewish Reformation, Samuel Hirsch.

Another great teacher was Samuel Adler, the most learned Jew who has lived in the Western world. Another of his teachers, in some senses greatest of them all, the man whom he most nearly resembled, was his second father, the father of his life-companion, David Einhorn, the most prophetic figure in Israel whom America has known. And yet another teacher was Geiger, the seer and scholar. Thus Hirsch was blessed, for he was the literal and immediate continuator of a tradition which he came to embody. He was Geiger transplanted; he was Einhorn surviving; he was Samuel Hirsch thinking on and through.

There were distinct and important services which Hirsch rendered to the Reform movement of which for a generation and certainly since the death of Isaac Wise he was the most distinguished and powerful advocate. For one thing, he uttered a new note in Liberal Judaism, a new note from the viewpoint of Liberal Judaism, but a very old and true note from the viewpoint of prophetic Judaism. His accent and stress were on social justice and perhaps in no respect was he mightier in his great ministry than in his unfailing and unanswerable emphasis upon righteousness and equity as the. bases of the order under which we live. This was Hirsch's first and most distinctive contribution to Liberal

Judaism.

Hirsch may be said to have lived in the middle period of American Jewish history. The giants had done their work, had laid the foundations and laid them well and abidingly. Then came the period of accommodation and adjustment, a period of organization under a man of high gifts and most attractive personality, Isaac M. Wise. But the organizer is always in danger of sacrificing the gains and advances made by the pioneers. And there was danger in the eighties and nineties lest some of the tremendous gains be lost, as they are often lost in the period of organization and readjustment.

Then came Hirsch, the one man who carried into the next generation the zeal and courage of the pioneer. He was not an organizer; he was not an administrator; he was not a co-operator. He was none of these things. I make that concession to his vigilant, ceaseless detractors. But I say of him that he was just as truly and mightily a pioneer as Geiger or Einhorn. The pioneering spirit was his guerdon. He did not know what fear was. It is very easy for the rest of us today to have Sunday services for example and stress them as the chief services of the week, even though they are not the Sabbath service. But Hirsch made it possible. He pioneered for every one of us. We breathe cheaply in the common air things for which he dared to agonize; and they presumed to speak in detraction of him, who were not big enough to touch the hem of his garment. This man of mighty courage and undaunted faith and unlimited power was not popular with his colleagues, for his presence evoked a complex of inferiority. He was undivinely impatient with rabbinical bores.

This one thing more Hirsch did, and to his honor remembered. Liberal Judaism in its beginnings lacked one great element. It was for the largest part, as I ventured to say to you upon that happy day which we together celebrated—namely, his seventieth birthday—a rationalistic movement. That movement I do not disparage when I say that it was hyper-intellectualized and perhaps under-ethicized, so that the Ethical Culture movement grew therefrom as an explicable and yet not inevitable sequence thereto.

The element that was lacking in the days of the founding of the Liberal Jewish movement, inevitably lacking, I frankly admit, was the prophetic element. The first hint of this and of its possibility was furnished by Hirsch's spiritual father, David Einhorn. He became through his own personality and courage and moral insight the Isaiah of the latest of the Jewish exiles. The thing at which Einhorn daringly hinted Hirsch bravely and mightily stressed. What Graham Taylor and Jane Addams did within the churches of Christendom, Hirsch did for the Synagogue of Israel. He reaffirmed its moral theses. He restressed with thunderous power its ethical imperatives. Not by chance or accident did he step into the pulpit of Sinai, for of his pulpit he made a new Sinai—with his, at his highest, majestic stress upon the changeless moral mandate of Sinai, that unwithstandable imperative of the Jewish ethical law, which he reaffirmed with such power as it has been given to few men in all the Jewish centuries to do.

Again, one peril of Liberal Judaism to which many of its devotees succumbed was that they felt themselves estranged from the Jewish masses—that they built up the Jewish Reformation into a Jewish sect or schism, almost a Jewish faction divorced from the life of the majority of the Jewish people. Hirsch was saved, and in turn saved Liberal Judaism, from this fate—for one thing, because of his deep and unshakable Jewish sympathies, because he was too great a Jew to suffer himself on any ground to be alienated from the Jewish masses—and, again and most of all, because, underlying his interpretation of Liberal Judaism was his changeless conception of the oneness of the Jewish people, of Israel as a people, which kept him very near to them even though people ofttimes knew not how near he was in sympathy and in ideals to them. They thought of him only as an uncompromising radical when in truth he was the most deeply loyal of Jews to all that was Jewish.

I dare to repeat that I believe the tragedy of Liberal Judaism for Hirsch grew out of the circumstance that it took itself away, or that somehow it was suffered to grow away, from the great mass of the Jewish people. It became a Temple of the Jewish classes rather than the synagogue of the Jewish masses. It became a middle class institution, an institution limited by the love of the few rather than a needed instrumentality of the spiritual life of the Jewish many.

Hirsch was so truly a Jew, so greatly a Jew,

that he felt his isolation from the Jewish masses. He would be one with them and he was not, and they were not one with him save as they honored his towering personality and revered the greatness of the scholar. But Liberal Judaism, or rather Reform Judaism, which is more often technically "reform" than genuinely liberal, shut him out and away from his people for whom he yearned. He sought his brothers and he found them not, and, though in spirit he was at one with them, the walls of the liberal Temple shut him away from his fellow Jews and his heart was saddened.

Let this be clearly understood by those who say that Hirsch was anti-Zionist, that he was never in agreement with the theory of Jewish racialism. Hirsch was big enough to understand that Judaism is more than a connotation of faith, that, while there is and ever will be such a thing as the Jewish faith, the religion of Israel, Hirsch was too far-seeing and clear-thinking to fail to understand the reality of the race-element in Judaism. He affirmed as a verity the Jewish people. He used the term *people* again and again thoughout the years of his teaching and preaching. He would have laughed at those who claim that Judaism is the religious persuasion of Americans who happen to be Jews. For him Judaism was not merely a particular type of faith but a very real and enduring and imperishable fellowship. Nominally he was not with us within the Zionist movement, though I believe at his heart's core he longed to be. He could not quite, because he was no longer a young man when Zionism came into the foreground of Jewish life.

He could not quite fit it into those Reform preconceptions, which had become the rigidly dogmatic and stratified prepossessions of Reform Judaism rather than the things of his own inmost soul.

And there was another contribution of Hirsch to Liberal Judaism, not completely nor uniquely his own, but he added to it and he enriched it. Other men before him, like Wise and Gottheil, had addressed themselves to Christian congregations in America, had preached in Christian pulpits, had held forth before every manner of Christian assembly. But Hirsch was the first to speak in ruggedly uncompromising fashion in assemblies of non-Jews. Sometimes his utterance was not far from brusqueness, but it was always very far from being flabby and compromising. He spoke not without appreciation of the things that are high and fine in Christianity and in Christian life, but he spoke the truth, the whole truth and nothing but the truth, touching the intellectual errors and the moral unworthiness of many of those who call themselves Christians and their faith Christianity.

So much has always been said about Dr. Hirsch's witticisms that men almost forget that witticisms were the form in which he clothed his truth-speaking. His witticisms, however delightful, are after all quite unimportant, and I would almost have them forgotten by the side of the high and fine courage which moved him to speak the truth at all times and under all circumstances. Sometimes he was brusque, sometimes he was crude, sometimes he was even unkind, but he was always true. He served the truth with his lips and with his life. As I think of Hirsch, I recall the word that Huxley wrote of himself in a letter to Darwin: "I am full of faults, but I am real and true." Hirsch was not full of faults, neither was he without faults, but, whatever he may have had, he was real and true. Some Jews in America, particularly among his colleagues, saw only his little faults, which were the idiosyncrasies of a rugged personality, and chose to forget all about his great virtues and mighty gifts.

Men say of Hirsch that sometimes he was very bitter. He was bitter, but that fact should not hide the truth that he was a man of unlimited courage. His bitterness must not obscure the fact of his heroism. He was the directest, frankest, simplest truth-speaker I ever heard within or without the pulpit. Compare his pulpit, what it was and what it stood for, that fortress of strength, towering like his own stature—compare it with all the nice, big synagogues of the nation, his own pulpit being one in which he never arose without so speaking to men that they remembered whether they willed to or not.

In Dr. Hirsch's presence and whilst he yet lived, I said of him on his seventieth birthday that the law of his life had been the rule laid down by the prophet Malachai, touching the messenger of the Lord, "The law of truth was in his mouth." I do not know of any man in our age and generation of whom that may more truly be said. Truth was the highest and holiest law of his being. He never stooped to a lie; he never debased himself by evasion or equivocation. If ever he erred, it was only so far as a man can err by speaking the truth with uncompromising and inevasive frankness. If sometimes he was brutally frank, he was no more brutal than the truth is in the ears of a generation which wills to be fed upon equivocation and sophistries and lies.

Iniquity was not found upon his lips. It is little to say of a minister of religion that iniquity is not to be found upon his lips, for that means nothing unless it means everything—unless it means exactly what it meant touching Hirsch—that no iniquity, no wrongdoing ever found justification at his lips. How tremendous must have been the temptations in his life from time to time to be silent touching wrong, to excuse iniquity in high places, to suffer minor benevolences to gloss over tremendous antisocial practices.

Hirsch was not a demagogue, no flatterer nor soothsayer. I never knew Hirsch to stoop to untruth, to the untruth of flattery or demagoguery. Often he irritated and sometimes he embittered, but one never heard him at his bitterest without respecting him, without feeling that this truth-teller was a man, and as a man you of Sinai honored him and cherished his remembrance. You were proud of him and he loved you. Had you been less than you were, had he not lifted you to the level of fine appraisement of his truth-telling genius, you could not have been equal to that understanding and sympathy which you gave him. Such was his genius for truth that throughout his days you respected the man who stood foursquare to all the winds that blew.

Hirsch was a giant, and as a giant he will be remembered in the annals of American Israel. In every estimate of Hirsch, publicly or privately spoken during the past twenty-five years, I have chosen to dwell on what Hirsch was rather than on what he was not. I measured and I measure Hirsch by his own stature. I appraise him upon the basis of his own achievements. It is very easy to prove that he did not organize the Union of American Hebrew Congregations, that he did not inspire the congregational sisterhoods and brotherhoods, all of which, severally and collectively, are supposed to be the saving of American Israel. Hirsch was not an organizer outwardly, but he was more—a liberator and an inspirer of the soul of the American Jew.

As for his relations with his colleagues, it may be that he was too great to be patient with little men, but surely they were not big enough to recognize his greatness—with the result that violent opposition met my proposal in honor of the centenary of David Einhorn, that Hirsch should be made the President of the Central Conference of American Rabbis in order by that election to reconsecrate the Conference to the principles of Liberal Judaism. The loss was not Hirsch's but the Conference's. The little men are rewarded for the service of regular attendance at the Conference, upon the basis of card index system, and the greatest, who make Jewish history, go unrecognized in their lifetime and little noted in their passing. But Hirsch will live—not a memory but an inspiration, not a name but even as the voice and soul of Israel.

Hirsch's power for service was not limited to the Congregation Sinai of Chicago. He was just as truly the leader of the Free Synagogue as he was the teacher of Sinai. True it is that he was so wholly a part of Sinai and Sinai so much a part of him that he and Sinai became interchangeable terms. No man in American Israel has so identified himself with the destiny of a great congregation, no congregation in American Israel has so wholly wrapped itself up and aground a great personality. None the less is it true that he was over and beyond all men the leader, the teacher, the inspirer of Liberal Jews wherever they dwelt.

We of the Free Synagogue are not loth to acknowledge our debt to Emil Hirsch. The Free Synagogue is largely the fruit of his inspiration. It might never have been founded if he had not gone before. Sixteen years ago, when he alone among the outstanding rabbis in American Israel was ready to lend a hand in the establishment of the Free Synagogue movement, I besought him to become its leader and to give the remaining years of his life to its leadership. I held myself ready to stand in the second place, to be as his disciple and adjutant. I felt that as no other man he could interpret and vitalize Liberal Judaism in the most populous Jewish center in history, that Liberal Judaism which, as it seemed to me, stood in those days in New York without one truly outstanding and commanding representative in the pulpit.

Hirsch had made of the pulpit of Sinai that which was not elsewhere to be found. Sinai had speedily learned that Hirsch was a free soul and that therefore its pulpit was free, and his pulpit. Heartening and inspiration had come to me for many years, before and thoughout the early years of my ministry, from the spoken and written word of Hirsch; and that written word was made possible of widest distribution by the devotion of a friend, who later became one of the stalwart founders and has since remained one of the sacrificial supporters of the Free Synagogue.

I got a new sense of Hirsch's deep and tender piety, which his occasional jests could not completely hide and of the understanding sympathy that underlay his Jewishness, on the occasion of his seventieth birthday anniversary. The Jews of Chicago were gathered to do him honor; his colleagues voiced his praise. To me it fell to offer him on behalf of the Jewish Institute of Religion the Honorary Presidency thereof; a post which he gladly, modestly withal, accepted, instantly coupling with its acceptance an appeal to the generosity of the vast company assembled. And when his turn came to make acknowledgment, that acknowledgment took the form of a word of grateful and loving reference to his parents. He besought the congregation of Sinai to journey with him in spirit to the nearby house of rest in order that he might invoke the shades of those to whom he owed most, and then, with faltering voice and tear-dimmed eyes, he recited the immemorial prayer of our people known as the Kaddish. Thus even as Moses felt the presence of God in the burning bush, withal, as the rabbis say, heard the voice of his beloved father bid him be strong and of good courage, so Hirsch at that highest moment of his life, nearing the close of a career rich and fruitful and beneficent, hearkened to the accent of his father and of his fathers. This was Hirsch the Jew. This was Hirsch utterly unafraid in uprooting the false, utterly loyal in cherishing the true.

Decades, even generations, may pass before the annalist of the Jewish people will give to Emil Hirsch his rightful place. Whatever petty and malevolent detraction may urge, as it already has, it will be overborne by the chorus of praise which will well up from the heart of a generation that will know how to do justice to him, who was at all times, in all places, and under all circumstances, the nobly firm and bravely unstooping captain of his people, who knew its lore, who shared its genius, who served its honor, who magnified its name.

Truly, in Homeric speech, one may say as one surveys American Israel, that the sun has perished out of the heavens. There is no other Hirsch. There will be none like unto him. At best, we who stood at his side can do no more than resolve that we shall be true to the spirit of truth as he was. You, his loved Sinai, know well that no other Hirsch will stand in this pulpit. For he was unique in his gifts and in his power. Living, you used him well. Now, cherish him well as an unique, solitary, giant figure. The traditions, the memory, the inspiration of Hirsch be your upliftment and your children's benediction for all generations.

Amen.

Sinai Temple Sanctuary in 1896

Dr. Emil G. Hirsch
Rabbi of Chicago Sinai Congregation
July 25, 1880—January 7, 1923